FX: Managing Global Currency Risk

The Definitive Handbook for Corporations and Financial Institutions

Gary Klopfenstein
Editor

Glenlake Publishing Company, Ltd.
Chicago • London • New Delhi

Fitzroy Dearborn Publishers
Chicago and London

GPCo
1261 West Glanlake
Chicago, Illinois 60660
glenlake@ix.netcom.com

To Laine and Joel with love

Contents

Preface

When I began to formulate the outline for this book, I realized just how much the business of trading and managing risks in foreign exchange has changed in the last few years. On the trading side, which I define as those participants that take on currency risk for profit, the entrance into the markets of large money managers and hedge funds has caused the very character of the market to change. Additionally, central banks have changed their approach to trading as part of their market operations, and have generally become more effective. This combination has resulted in a very different market environment than we had seen only five to 10 years ago. Banks are not just quoting dollar/mark and dollar/yen, but have learned to specialize in emerging markets and exotic products. People are trading faster, bigger, and smarter.

On the risk management side of the business (those market participants who are exposed to foreign-exchange risk as an ongoing part of their core business), the products and sophistication levels have grown tremendously. Given the increased use of derivative products, and the added importance of stable returns, the risk managers in corporate treasury and investment departments are under increasing pressure not only to control foreign-exchange risk, but also to benefit from favorable currency moves. Fading quickly are the days of ignoring currency risk because of the belief that, in the long run, the markets will revert to current levels.

I categorize foreign-exchange market participants into two groups: those who initially have no exposure to currency movements, and who incur an exposure for its profit potential; and those who face currency exposure as an integral part of their day-to-day core business. The former are traders and the latter are risk managers, although it can also be correctly argued that any successful trader must also be an effective risk manager.

The book is divided into three parts. The first section provides an overview of the market, and covers foreign-exchange instruments, key market participants, and major trading strategies. Part two deals with currency risk management for institutional investors. This is the realm of global investors who are exposed to fluctuations in currency prices, which affect their portfolio values. Topics include enhanced currency overlays, immunization strategies, and performance measurement. The book's final section takes the view of foreign-exchange risk management from the perspective of the corporate treasurer. It deals with key issues including the relationship of management to effective risk control, the measurement of risk, active management, and some practical examples of managing risks within the corporate treasury framework.

This book has been an interesting and challenging project, and one that takes a unique snapshot of a dynamic marketplace. I would like to thank the following people for their assistance in bringing this project together. Thank you to Paul Klopfenstein, Colin Fitzgerald, Diane Durr, John Stevens, Rick Schendel, Beata Szponder, and Ashwin Kapur for their assistance in various aspects of the project. I would also like to thank Robert Klein and Jess Lederman for their help in putting this all together. Working with them has actually made this project fun. And finally, a special thanks to Glenlake Publishing for the opportunity to create this book.

— Gary Klopfenstein

Contributors

Thomas F. Basso

Mr. Basso is president of Trendstat Capital Management, Inc., which manages over $160 million. Previously, he held positions as president of Kennedy Futures, Inc., and as president of ABS Investment Group. Mr. Basso also serves as a director of Monarch Food Color, Inc. He is a director of the Society of Asset Allocators & Fund Timers, Inc., chair of MFA/FIA Joint Committee on Standards, and a member of the Managed Futures Association. Mr. Basso holds a B.S. in chemical engineering from Clarkson University, and an M.B.A. in finance from Southern Illinois University.

Bhaskar (Bob) H. Bhave

Mr. Bhave is a senior manager in the national office of Coopers & Lybrand L.L.P. He has been monitoring the FASB's financial instruments project since 1986. Mr. Bhave has contributed to Coopers & Lybrand's monographs, *Guide to Financial Instruments, Foreign Currency Translation and Hedging*, and *FASB Proposal on Accounting for Derivatives and Hedging*. Mr. Bhave is a C.P.A. and C.M.A., and he has an M.B.A. degree.

Shmuel Hauser

Dr. Hauser is the chief economist of the Israel Securities Authority and a senior lecturer at the School of Management at BenGurion University (Israel). He has a B.A in economics and statistics and an M.S. in finance from the Hebrew University in Jerusalem and a Ph.D. in business administration from Temple University.

Robert H. Herz

Mr. Herz is Coopers & Lybrand's national director of accounting and SEC services. Mr. Herz is a member of the Financial Accounting Standards Board's Emerging Issues Task Force and Financial Instruments Task Force. He is chairman of the AICPA SEC Regulations Committee, and a member of the New York Stock Exchange's International Capital Markets Committee. Mr. Herz has authored numerous articles and publications on a variety of accounting and financial topics. He has served as engagement partner on a number of Coopers & Lybrand's major clients in the financial services, commercial and industrial, and telecommunications industries. He is both a U.S. Certified Public Accountant (having won the gold medal on the C.P.A. exam) as well as a U.K. Chartered Accountant.

Andrew Hodge

Mr. Hodge is vice president and financial strategist at Bank Brussels Lambert in New York, where his responsibilities include market strategy, with a focus on central-bank watching, and development of structured products. Previously, Mr. Hodge was a vice president at Bankers Trust Company in New York where his responsibilities included foreign exchange, risk management, and country risk. Mr. Hodge also held senior positions in foreign exchange and international economics at W. R. Grace, Chemical Bank, and the U.S. Department of Treasury. Mr. Hodge holds a B.A. in economics from the University of Michigan and an M.A. in economics from George Washington University.

Gregory P. Hopper

Dr. Hopper is an economist at the Federal Reserve Bank of Philadelphia and a lecturer at the Wharton School of the University of Pennsylvania. He has been at the Federal Reserve since 1992. He received, from the University of Virginia, a B.A. in mathematics, an M.A. in applied mathematics, and an M.A. and a Ph.D. in economics. His research concentrates on international financial economics, foreign exchange market efficiency, and derivatives.

Earl I. Johnson

Mr. Johnson serves as foreign exchange economist for Bank of Montreal in Chicago specializing in currency forecasting. He is a 27-year veteran of the Harris Bank whose foreign exchange operations were merged into Bank of Montreal in April 1995. Mr. Johnson regularly provides economic outlooks and interest rate forecasts for personnel of both institutions. His foreign exchange commentaries often appear in *The Wall Street Journal, New York Times,* and *Chicago Tribune,* while his currency forecasts have won recognition in contests conducted by *Euromoney,* Reuters, and Bloomberg News.

Gary Klopfenstein

Mr. Klopfenstein is founder and president of GK Capital Management and GK Investment Management, president of GK Risk Management and GK Software Development, and a director of GK Risk Management SDN BHD. In 1984, Mr. Klopfenstein began trading his own capital and later that year formed an advisory business where he focused on the financial markets, researching and developing systems designed to analyze market movements, and providing sophisticated risk management strategies. In 1986, he formed GK Capital Management. In 1989, GK Capital Management launched one of the first currencyonly, interbank trading programs. GK Capital Mangement, in the early 1990s, began researching the application of its proprietary, quantitative techniques into risk management in foreign exchange. The company began providing these services to corporate treasurers and international investment managers. Mr. Klopfenstein is also a director of FINEX, the financial futures exchange with trading operations in New York and Dublin. He is a frequent speaker at international conferences on risk management and, in October 1995, he addressed the World Economic Congress in Washington, D.C. Mr. Klopfenstein graduated magna cum laude from Illinois Wesleyan University with a degree in business administration. He is the author of *Trading Currency Cross Rates*, published by John Wiley & Sons.

Alex Koh

Mr. Koh is group financial controller with Hong Leong Credit, a listed financial services conglomerate and member company of the Hong Leong Group Malaysia. He joined Hong Leong in the group finance and treasury division before transferring to his current role. Previously, Mr. Koh was the head of the cash management and funding desk at UBS Limited in London. He is treasurer of the Malaysian Association of Corporate Treasurers. Mr. Koh is a graduate of the London School of Economics, and he has qualified as a chartered accountant with KPMG.

Azriel Levy

Dr. Levy is the head of research at the foreign exchange control department in the central bank of Israel, and is an adjunct professor at the School of Business at Hebrew University. Dr. Levy has a B.A in economics and an M.S. in economics and finance from the Hebrew University and a Ph.D. in business administration from the Hebrew University in Jerusalem.

Thomas J. Linsmeier

Dr. Linsmeier is an assistant professor of accounting at the University of Illinois at UrbanaChampaign. He previously held a faculty position at the University of Iowa. In addition, he has served as academic fellow in the office of the chief accountant at the U.S. Securities and Exchange Commission (SEC). His research explores the use of accounting information in securities markets, including the usefulness of fairvalue disclosures to investors, the economic effects of changes in accounting regulation, and the information content of SEC risk management and reporting disclosures, and he has published papers in a number of academic journals. Dr. Linsmeier continues to serve as a consultant to the SEC and frequently makes presentations on risk management and reporting to national conferences and organizations. He received his Ph.D. from the University of WisconsonMadison, and is a member of the American Institute of Certified Public Accountants.

Leslie K. McNew

Ms. McNew is director, financial risk management for Reynolds Metals Company where she directs and manages the development, refinement, and implementation of comprehensive programs to manage both foreign-currency exposures, resulting from the company's worldwide operations, and interest rate sensitivity of the company's debt and investments in marketable securities. Previously, Ms. McNew held positions at Morgan Stanley, Midland Montague, and FIMAT Futures (Societe Generale). She graduated with a degree in quantitative economics from the University of Michigan and with a masters in quantitative design from New York University.

Virginia Reynolds Parker

Ms. Parker is the founder and president of Parker Global Strategies. She has expertise in both traditional and alternative investment strategies and has a strong background in currency risk and returns, independent risk measurement and management techniques, and the structuring, administering, and managing of U.S. and offshore funds and managed accounts. Previously, Ms. Parker was manaaging director and director of research and risk management at Ferrell Capital Management. She has also held positions as chief investment officer for a family office and as an account executive at Johnson & Higgins, Inc. Ms. Parker graduated with an AB degree in economics and political science from Duke University. She is registered as an associated person with the National Futures Association, is a member of the New York Society of Securities Analysts, of the Association of Investment Management Research, and is a chartered financial analyst.

Neil D. Pearson

Dr. Pearson is an assistant professor of finance at the University of Illinois at UrbanaChampaign. He previously held a faculty position at the University of Rochester. In addition, he has served as academic fellow in the office of economic analysis at the U.S. Securities and Exchange Commission. His research includes work on the development, estimation, and evaluation of models for pricing and hedging various derivatives and other financial instruments. Dr. Pearson has published papers in a number of academic journals, and is an associate editor of the *Journal of Financial Economics*. He has consulted for a number of U.S. and international banks, working on termstructure models, the evaluation of derivatives pricing models, and some issues that arise in the computation of valueatrisk measures. He received his Ph.D. from the Massachusetts Institute of Technology.

Mary Rafferty

Ms. Rafferty recently joined the Bank of Montreal as director and senior foreign exchange advisor to institutional clients. She was previously with First Chicago where she worked with institutional clients and funds managers in the foreign exchange markets and in interest rate derivatives. Ms. Rafferty is a graduate of Northwestern's Kellogg School of Management and she holds a B.S. from Boston College.

Neil Record

Dr. Record graduated with an M.A. degree from Balliol College, Oxford University, and with an M.Sc. degree from University College, London University. He spent the early part of his career as an economist at the Bank of England, where he was a member of the economic forecasting team. He then spent five years working for Mars, Inc., in their U.K. subsidiary, where he was initially responsible for commodity price forecasting, and latterly in charge of their currency exposure management. He left Mars to found Record in 1983, where he has been principal shareholder and executive chairman ever since. He divides his time at Record between client contact, product development, and general management.

Brian Strange

Mr. Strange is the founder of Currency Performance Analytics, a specialist consulting firm formed to provide analytical data to assess currency overlay managers' skills. Previously, he was with A. G. Bisset & Co., Inc., where he was instrumental in structuring currency overlay management products to protect international investor returns from adverse currency effects. Mr. Strange's experience in corporate treasury positions at Baxter International, Nimslo Corporation, and Midland Ross also focused on the management of foreign exchange and interest rate risk. Mr. Strange is a graduate of the University of Chicago's Graduate School of Business. He holds an M.B.A. in international finance. He also has a Master's degree in applied economics from the University of Louvain, Belgium, and has completed undergraduate study in economics at Indiana University. He is an adjunct faculty member in international finance for the international M.B.A. program at Baldwin Wallace College in Cleveland.

Hunt Taylor

Mr. Taylor is managing director of FINEX Europe, the European trading operation of the FINEX division of the New York Cotton Exchange. Formerly the FINEX chairman, he has worked in the futures and investment industries for more than 20 years. Previously, he was managing director of Reynwood Trading Corporation, managing director of Duich Investment Company, ran his own Commodity Trading Advisor, and served as president of Taylor Brokerage Incorporated. Mr. Taylor has been active on the trading floors of the New York Cotton Exchange, the New York Mercantile Exchange, the New York Futures Exchange, and has served on various committees of these exchanges. Mr. Taylor is the author of numerous articles on the futures and managed futures businesses. He is frequently quoted about issues and trends affecting the futures markets, and he also addresses these topics at industry conferences.

Lee R. Thomas III

Dr. Thomas is executive vice president, senior international portfolio manager for Pacific Investment Management Company. He has 16 years of experience in money management. Previously, Dr. Thomas was a member of Investcorp's Management Committee, where he was responsible for global securities and foreign exchange trading. Prior to Investcorp, he was an executive director at Goldman Sachs in the fixed-income division of their London office. Dr. Thomas has published extensively in the field of international fixed-income and foreign exchange investments. He earned a bachelor's degree and Ph.D. in economics from Tulane University.

James O. West, Jr.

For the past three years, Mr. West has managed the transition of Tenneco's capital process from its domestic to its international focus. As the director of capital budgeting for Tenneco, he and his staff prepare the firm's consolidated capital expenditure budget, review all proposed initiatives involving capital expenditures, audit project results, participate in the due diligence process for major acquisitions, prepare materials for presentation to the board of directors, and issue guidance on the preparation of economic and business analysis of proposed projects. Mr. West came to Tenneco from its subsidiary, Newport News Shipbuilding. During his 10 years at Newport News, he filled a number of positions in the government contracting field including the preparation of proposals for new ship construction, contract change management, and liaison with government financial and contract audit agencies. Mr. West received a B.A. and M.B.A. from The College of William and Mary in Williamsburg, Virginia.

Uzi Yaari

Dr. Yaari is a professor of finance at Rutgers University in Camden, New Jersey. He has a B.A in economics and political science from the Hebrew University, Jerusalem, and a Ph.D. in business administration from the University of Chicago.

Ezra Zask

Mr. Zask is president and founder of Ezra Zask Associates, a Connecticut-based registered Commodities Trading Advisor, and is a principal in Law & Economics Consulting Group, a litigation support and consulting company. Previously, Mr. Zask spent 12 years in senior treasury management positions at Mellon Bank and Manufacturers Hanover Trust. Since 1990, Mr. Zask has traded in a wide range of markets including foreign currencies, interest rates, energy, and commodities. He has specifically focused on the areas of international portfolio management, currency exposure management, and risk management using derivative products. Mr. Zask has an active consulting practice with both corporations and institutional investors. He has recently been active in providing training programs in Russia and Eastern Europe. In addition, Mr. Zask has testified as an expert witness in matters involving currency options and derivatives trading, as well as conducted education and consulting programs on securities markets, investments, derivatives, and risk management. He is a member of the National Futures Association. Mr. Zask has M.A. and M. Phil. degrees in international affairs from Columbia University, and he has taught derivatives and portfolio theory at the University of Massachusetts and Carnegie-Mellon University, as well as international finance at Columbia and Fordham Universities.

PART I

Overview of the Foreign-Exchange Markets: Instruments, Participants, and Strategies

Currency Derivatives: A Guide For Practitioners[1]

Gregory P. Hopper
Economist
Federal Reserve Bank of Philadelphia

An American company wants to import new computer screens from Japan. Company executives discover that they can buy the computer screens at a price of 10,000 yen per screen. At the prevailing exchange rate of 100 yen per dollar, the screens will cost $100 each. Market research reveals that each computer screen can be sold for $105 in the United States, a profit of $5 per screen. Excited by this prospect, the company negotiates a contract to buy 1,250 computer screens, yielding a profit of $6,250. The company will take delivery of the screens in exactly one year, at which time payment will be due in full.

After one year, the company is shocked to learn that the exchange rate is no longer 100 yen per dollar, but 95 yen per dollar. Since the company must buy its yen at the exchange rate prevailing on the delivery date, each computer screen costs $105.26 (10,000 yen/screen divided by 95 yen/dollar = $105.26 per screen) at delivery. Not only did the company fail to receive its anticipated $5 per screen profit, it lost $.26 per screen. This is a common problem in international trade. Exchange rates under the floating-rate system (in effect since 1973) have been very volatile, and it is not uncommon for exchange rates to fluctuate dramatically.

How could this company have reduced the risk of losses produced by volatile exchange rates? It could have used currency derivatives, which would have reduced the currency risk faced by the corporation.

In this chapter, we will look at the three major currency derivatives: options, forwards, and futures. Although these derivatives are used to reduce the risk in international trade, they can also be used to speculate in foreign exchange—a risky proposition that has received much media attention. A common misconception is that derivatives are inherently mysterious, highly risky, and complex. On the contrary, the basic ideas underlying derivatives are not difficult to understand; indeed, futures and options can be understood as combinations of the simplest derivative, the forward

3

contract. Moreover, derivatives are not necessarily very risky and they can be used to reduce the risk inherent in other investments.

Forward Contracts

One way for the company to lock in the exchange rate in one year is to enter into a forward contract. A forward contract is an agreement to buy or sell a specific quantity of currency at a predetermined dollar price on a specific date in the future. The predetermined price is called the *forward exchange rate*. The forward exchange rate is set to a value such that no money is required up front to enter the contract.

For example, the forward exchange rate for delivery in one year might be 97 yen per dollar. Thus, the company could enter a one-year forward contract on 12.5 million yen (1,250 screens at 10,000 yen per screen). No money is transferred until delivery. At delivery the company would be certain to receive an exchange rate of 97 yen per dollar, so that each screen would cost $103.09, thereby guaranteeing a profit of $1.91 per screen.

Another method the company might use is to immediately buy the yen it needs at an exchange rate of 100 yen per dollar. However, a relationship known as *covered interest parity* guarantees that buying the yen immediately and investing them in one-year interest-paying Japanese notes is equivalent to immediately entering a one-year forward contract and investing the dollars that would have been converted to yen in one-year interest-paying U.S. notes.

To see this, suppose that $S = 100$ yen per dollar; i, the U.S. interest rate, is 10 percent; i^*, the yen interest rate is 6.7 percent; and F, the one-year forward exchange rate, is 97 yen per dollar. The company has two strategies:

Strategy 1

Take $117,150.89, convert the dollars to yen at the exchange rate of 100 and then invest the proceeds at an interest rate of 6.7 percent. At the end of the year, the company would have 12.5 million yen, the amount it needs.

Strategy 2

Take $117,150.89, invest the dollars at 10 percent for one year, and, at the same time, enter the forward market and promise to sell $128,865.98 in one year at the forward exchange rate of 97. At the end of the year, $117,150.89 will have become $128,865.98, which when converted to yen at an exchange rate of 97 yen per dollar yields 12.5 million yen.

These strategies have the same cost whenever covered interest parity holds. Covered interest parity is a relation between the domestic interest rate i; the foreign interest rate i*; the current spot exchange rate S in units of foreign exchange per dollar; and F, the forward exchange rate in foreign currency per dollar for delivery of currency over the same period covered by the interest rate. So, for example, if i and i* are the interest rates over a six-month period, then F is the six-month forward rate.

Covered interest parity determines the value of the forward exchange rate whenever i,i*, S, and F are connected by the relation

$$F = S(i+i^*)/(1+i).$$

In the example, covered interest parity holds since

$$F = 100(1+0.067)/(1+0.1) = 97.$$

Academic studies have established that covered interest parity holds in the marketplace, which is not surprising. If it did not hold, speculators could make arbitrage profits. In fact, banks use the covered interest parity relationship to set forward exchange rates. Thus, neither strategy gives the company an advantage.[2] Nonetheless, a company could check whether covered interest parity holds in its particular circumstance. If it does not, it may pay a company to prefer one strategy over another.

There are always two sides to every forward contract: the buyer of the foreign currency is *long* the forward contract, while the seller of the foreign currency is *short*. Forward contracts are usually traded over standardized intervals: 30 days, 60 days, 90 days, 180 days, or one year. For example, if an investor goes long a 30-day forward contract for 1 million yen at a forward price of 100 yen per dollar, 30 days later the investor is obligated to purchase 1 million yen for $10,000.

Forward contracts are made over the counter. Unlike an instrument traded on an exchange, an over-the-counter security is not bought or sold in any centralized location such as the New York Stock Exchange. Instead, a company that wishes to go long the yen will call up various banks to find one that will take the other side of the contract. Making contracts over the counter means it is possible to negotiate any interval for the forward contract and any amount of foreign currency to be exchanged, as long as one can find a willing counterparty.

The payoff to the forward contract can be positive or negative. Let us return to the example of a long one-year forward contract on yen with a forward price of 97 yen per dollar. Assume that the exchange rate when the contract comes due is 100 yen per dollar. In this case, the company suffers a loss, since the forward contract requires the company to buy 97 yen for $1 when it could have obtained 100 yen per dollar at the prevailing exchange rate. However, if the exchange rate in one year turns out to be 95 yen per dollar, the company would make a profit, since the forward contract would allow it to exchange currency at 97 yen per dollar instead of the prevailing exchange rate of 95 yen per dollar.

This suggests a drawback to using forward contracts. Forwards reduce the risk of loss by locking in the future exchange rate. But if the exchange rate moves in a favorable way, the company cannot receive the extra profit. For example, suppose we had the same contract described in the previous paragraph, but the exchange rate in one year turned out to be 105 yen per dollar. At 105 yen per dollar, the computer screens would cost $95.24, which involves an even larger profit for the company with respect to what it had anticipated. But the forward contract obligates the company to pay 97 yen per dollar, a cost of $103.09 per computer screen.

Another problem with forward contracts is that they involve potentially large credit risk, particularly to banks, which typically take the other side of the contract. Suppose that the company is long the yen at a forward price of 97 yen per dollar on a one-year contract, but in one year the exchange rate is 100 yen per dollar. Then the company takes a loss. If the company refuses to carry out its obligations to purchase the yen at a forward price of 97 yen per dollar—that is, it defaults on the forward contract—the bank will not receive its profit. To guard against this problem, a bank will take the other side of a forward contract only if it is allowed to reduce the company's line of credit by the amount of the forward contract. If the company has no line of credit with the bank, the bank may require the company to deposit 5 percent of the amount of the forward contract as collateral.

Futures Contracts

Another method the company might use to reduce the risk of foreign exchange volatility is to enter a futures contract. Futures contracts are similar to forward contracts in that both involve the promise to buy or sell currency at a specific price and at a specific time in the future. The difference is that profits or losses from holding a futures contract are realized and paid out at the end of each day; in contrast, profits or losses from holding a forward contract are realized and transferred only when the contract expires.

As an example, suppose the company goes long one futures-contract on 12.5 million yen at the International Money Market of the Chicago Mercantile Exchange. At the end of the day, suppose the futures price of the yen has risen. The short side then must pay the long side a profit in dollars equal to the difference between the new futures price and the old futures price times 12.5 million yen. If the futures price had fallen, the long side would have had to pay the short side the difference between the old

---

The Chicago Mercantile Exchange (also known as the Merc) was founded in 1919 as a nonprofit organization to facilitate the trading of spot and futures commodity contracts. Over time, the exchange has grown, periodically adding new commodities to trade. For example, in 1962, frozen pork bellies were added; and in 1966, live cattle contracts began trading in order to give hedging opportunities to cattle ranchers and distributors. In 1987, the International Money Market, a division of the Merc, began offering foreign currency futures for seven currencies in standardized amounts, for delivery at standardized times. The exchange requires that no trading may take place at prices between minimum price moves, called *ticks*, and the exchange may place maximum daily allowable price moves on some currencies. The exchange also sets margin requirements for brokers who are members of the exchange. The Merc is regulated by the Commodity Futures Trading Commission.

---

and new futures prices times 12.5 million yen. This process continues daily until the contract matures. Each day, the profit or loss per yen of the long party equals the current day's closing futures price minus the previous day's closing futures price.

To see the similarity between a forward and a futures contract, suppose the company had entered into a forward contract on 12.5 million yen instead. If at the end of the day the market expected the price of the yen to be higher in the future, the company would expect to make a profit on its long forward position, but this profit could be realized only if the expectation turned out to be correct on the day the forward contract matured. To receive the profit at the end of the day, the company would have to liquidate the forward contract and enter a new forward contract at a higher forward rate. The short side would then have to pay the company its profit.

This analysis suggests that futures prices are like forward prices and that futures contracts are similar to sequences of forward contracts. However, futures prices do not in general equal forward prices on the same quantity of currency for delivery on the same date. John Cox, Robert Ingersoll, and Steven Ross have shown that futures prices are the same as forward prices if interest rates aren't random, i.e., future interest rates are known with certainty. However, if interest rates are random, as we would expect in reality, futures prices must be different from forward prices, with the difference depending on whether futures prices tend to move with interest rates.

If futures prices tend to rise when interest rates are rising, a futures contract will be worth more than a forward contract, and thus the futures price must exceed the forward price. The mechanism is as follows: when futures prices are rising, interest rates are rising as well, so the profits from a long futures-contract can be invested at higher-than-average interest rates; but when futures prices are falling, interest rates are also falling, so the losses can be financed at lower-than-average interest rates. Thus, when futures prices move in the same direction as interest rates, futures prices are higher than forward prices. Similarly, if futures prices move in the opposite direction from interest rates, futures prices are lower than forward prices. In reality, of course, interest rates are random, but in practice the magnitude of the co-movement between futures prices and interest rates is small: empirically, futures prices are close to forward prices. Thus, futures contracts may approximately be thought of as sequences of forward contracts.

Since the futures contract is settled on a daily basis rather than when the contract matures, default risk is reduced. If the losing party defaults, the winning party's losses are limited to that day's profits. Default risk is also reduced because each side in the futures contract is required to post a performance bond called *margin*. When the futures contract is settled at the end of the day, the losing party must transfer the profit from its margin account to the margin account of the winning party. If the losing party's margin consequently falls below a threshold level, the losing party must restore the margin account or have the contract terminated.[3]

Futures contracts, unlike forward contracts, are traded on organized exchanges. The exchange specifies the features of the contract, such as the quantity and manner of delivery of the foreign exchange, and makes rules governing the market participants. In the United States, foreign currency futures contracts are traded at the International Money Market of the Chicago Mercantile Exchange.

How would the company in our example use a futures contract? The company can hedge its risk by buying one 12.5 million yen futures contract at the Chicago exchange on the day the contract to purchase computer screens is signed. If the dollar price of the yen goes up from the initial exchange rate of 100 yen per dollar, the company pays more in dollar terms for the computer screens. However, the company profits from the futures contract, since the futures price will also rise. If the dollar price of the yen goes down, the company will lose money on the futures contract but will make up the loss with extra profits on the computer screens. Thus the company has hedged its risk and locked in the exchange rate of 100 yen per dollar.

The hedge may not be perfect, though, because the price on the futures contract may not move one-for-one with the exchange rate.[4] Thus, if the dollar-per-yen exchange rate rises and the company loses money, the futures price needs to rise just as fast in order for the profit on the futures contract to just counterbalance the loss from the computer screens. In general, this will not happen, and some portion of the company's yen risk will not be hedged.

If the company does not know the date of settlement, a futures contract is better than a forward contract. A forward contract requires the company to know the settlement day, but a futures contract is more flexible: the company can hedge its risk until settlement, then get out of the contract.

The disadvantage of the futures contract is that risk cannot be perfectly hedged, since the futures price, in general, does not move exactly one-for-one with the exchange rate. Another difficulty with futures contracts is that the amount of foreign currency that a company might want to hedge will usually not equal the amount that can be hedged by a futures contract. For example, a company may need to hedge 20 million yen, but since it can hedge only 12.5 million yen per contract, it will have to hedge 25 million yen with two contracts. A final disadvantage that the futures contract shares with the forward contract is that it does not allow the company to benefit if the dollar price of the yen falls.

Currency Options

The final type of derivative the company might use is the currency option. A currency option gives its holder the right, but not the obligation, to take a position on a specific quantity of foreign currency at a prearranged price on or before the date the option expires.[5] The prearranged price is called the *strike price,* which is an exchange rate. For example, if the option were on yen, the strike price would be quoted in terms of dollars per yen. The date the option expires is called the expiration date. The premium is the price paid to acquire the option. An option that allows the holder to buy a currency is termed a *call,* and an option that allows the holder to sell a currency is called a *put.* The option holder is said to *exercise the option* when he or she invokes the right to buy or sell foreign currency at the strike price. Options are European or American. A *European option* can be exercised only on the expiration date, but an *American option* can be exercised on or before the expiration date. In the United States, currency options on standardized amounts of foreign currency are traded at the Philadelphia Stock Exchange.

The option will specify a quantity of foreign exchange to be bought or sold. For example, a call listed on the Philadelphia Stock Exchange would allow the holder to buy 6.25 million yen. But options need not be bought at exchanges. They can also be bought over the counter as long as the purchaser can find someone willing to sell an option.

A currency option is a kind of currency insurance: the option insures against unfavorable exchange-rate movements, so that the maximum loss one can experience is the premium paid for the option. For example, suppose the American company buys two call options on 6.25 million yen,

Options on the major foreign currencies are traded at the Philadelphia Stock Exchange, which was founded in 1790 and is the oldest securities market in the United States. Currency options are traded on standardized amounts equaling one half the amount of currency corresponding to an IMM futures contract on the same currency. The exchange has also standardized the expiration dates of the options and the strike prices. The expiration dates are set to correspond to the expiration dates of futures contracts at the International Money Market (IMM). Currency options traded at the Philadelphia Stock Exchange are guaranteed by the Options Clearing Corporation (OCC), which acts as a clearinghouse for all options traded on U.S. securities exchanges.

and the options expire in one year with a strike price of 97 yen per dollar, or $.0103/yen. If the premium is $.0001/yen, the company cannot pay any more than $.0104/yen ($.0103/yen + $.0001/yen = $.0104/yen) when settlement is due. This means that each computer screen will cost no more than $104, yielding a $1 profit per screen.[6]

In contrast to a forward contract, the company can benefit from favorable movements in the exchange rate when using options. For example, suppose the exchange rate on the settlement date turned out to be 100 yen per dollar. In that case, the company will not exercise the option but will instead buy yen at the market rate. Thus, each computer screen will cost $100 plus the option premium of $1 per screen ($.0001/yen × 10,000 yen/screen), yielding a profit of $4 per screen.

Options have three basic benefits. First, using an option allows the company to profit from favorable exchange rate movements, although the company must pay for this benefit by remitting the option premium. Second, the settlement date need not be known in advance. If the company signs a contract to purchase Japanese computer screens at some time in the future, the company can buy an American option with an expiration date after the latest date the computer screens could be bought. Since American options can be exercised on or before the expiration date, the company could exercise the option on the day that the computer screens are purchased.[7] Third, because options can be bought over the counter, a company can tailor an option to hedge exactly the amount of currency it desires.

Users of Currency Derivatives

The main users of currency derivatives are hedgers and speculators. Hedgers use currency derivatives to reduce the risk of international trade.

Speculators use derivatives to increase substantially the potential return on their investments.

But the possibility of greater returns comes only by assuming greater risk. Suppose a speculator who wanted to invest in the Japanese yen could buy 12.5 million yen at 100 yen per dollar, which involves a dollar investment of $125,000. If the exchange rate moves to 95 yen per dollar, or $.0105/yen, in 30 days, then the dollar value of this investment becomes $131,579, a monthly return of 5.3 percent. But if the exchange rate moves to 105 yen per dollar, the speculator will lose part of his or her initial investment. To gain leverage, the speculator might have bought 200 European call options that gave him or her the right to buy 1.25 billion yen for 97 yen per dollar, or $.0103/yen, in 30 days for a premium of $.0001/yen, or $125,000. If the exchange rate in 30 days turned out to be 95 yen per dollar, the speculator could buy 1.25 billion yen for $.0103/yen and could sell them for $.0105/yen, yielding a profit of $250,000. Thus, the monthly return on this investment is 100 percent. Of course, this higher return comes with much greater risk. If the exchange rate happens to be above 97 yen per dollar on the option's expiration date, the speculator will not exercise the options and will lose the entire $125,000 investment.

Valuation of Currency Options

Speculators and hedgers may need to price currency derivatives. A speculator, for example, might be interested in trading currency options, and thus will need a method to evaluate currency option prices. Hedgers may hold a complex option portfolio that must be analyzed for potential risks. In some cases, companies combine hedging and speculation when they choose a portfolio of options. In addition, currency-option market makers, regulators, and banks obviously need to know how to price options.

If the option being priced is of the European exercise type, valuation is simple: using the Black-Scholes (1973) framework as extended by Garman and Kolhagen (1983) to currency options [Black-Scholes-Garman-Kolhagen (BSGK)], we can find a *closed-form* solution for the option price for calls and puts. A closed-form solution means that the option can be priced in terms of relatively simple formulas. However, if the option is American, it cannot be evaluated so simply. The options can still be priced in the BSGK framework, but *closed-form* solutions are not known except in special cases. Thus, when valuing American options, we must in general resort to numerical methods.

In the following discussion, we will start with a prototypical European-option-pricing problem and solve it using the BSGK method. To solve an American-option-pricing problem, we will use the so-called *binomial option pricing method*. The binomial method allows us to approximate the solution to the European- and American-option-pricing problems. The binomial method is not the only technique available; however, it is simple and intuitive, allowing the computation of option prices without understanding more advanced mathematics. The binomial option pricing algorithm is commonly used in practice as well.[8]

A European Option

Consider the following option-pricing problem. We want to price a European option on the pound. The current exchange rate is $1.60; the strike price is $1.60; the U.S. continuously compounded annualized interest rate is 10 percent; and the U.K. continuously compounded annualized interest rate is 11 percent. There are 182 days to maturity. The volatility of the pound is 12 percent per year.

In this example, the option is *at the money*, meaning that if it were struck today, it would yield a cash flow of zero, since the current spot exchange rate equals the strike price. Of course, since we are considering a European option, we cannot exercise it until 182 days from today. Notice that these interest rates are continuously compounded; interest rates quoted as being compounded annually or over some other period must be converted for use in the BSGK formula. The other oddity here is that we must specify the *volatility*, which is a measure of how uncertain we are about the exchange rate's value as we look farther into the future. As we will see, the volatility is a crucial input into any option pricing problem. We will take it as a given now and discuss how to calculate it later in the chapter.

Let us use the following notation:

S   = current spot exchange rate quoted as dollars per foreign currency
X = the strike price in dollars per foreign currency
i = the continuously compounded U.S. interest rate
i* = the continuously compounded foreign interest rate
σ = the volatility per year
T = the time to maturity in years
C = the price of the European call
P = the price of the European put

Then the price of the call is

$$C = \exp(-i^*T)SN(D) - \exp(-iT)XN(D - \sigma\sqrt{T}),$$

where

$$\exp(a) = e^a,$$

and the number D is

$$D = (\ln(S/X) + (i - i^* + \sigma^2/2)T)/(\sigma\sqrt{T}).$$

$N(.)$ refers to the normal cumulative density function[9] and $\ln(.)$ denotes the natural log.

The price of the put is

$$P = \exp(-iT)XN(\sigma\sqrt{T} - D) - \exp(-i^*T)SN(-D).$$

The definition of the parameters is the same as before.

In our example, $S = \$1.60$, $X = \$1.60$, $i = 0.10$, $i^* = 0.11$, $T = 182/365$, and $\sigma = 0.12$. Substituting the values into the formula, we find the value of the call is $C = \$0.0476$.

The Binomial Method

Using the BSGK method in the case of a European option is relatively easy, since we have a closed-form solution. But suppose we want to find the value of an American version of this option for which we do not have a closed-form solution. We can discover an algorithm that will allow us to approximate the value of the American option by mimicking the logic of the BSGK method. Although not apparent from the formula, the BSGK method relies on a hedging argument. In effect, the BSGK method values a currency option by describing a portfolio of borrowed dollars and loaned pounds that can always exactly replicate the value of the currency option at any time. Since the portfolio and call have the same payoff, the dollar value of the replicating portfolio must be the same as the dollar value of the option. Thus, using the BSGK technique, we can find the price of a European- or American-currency option by finding the prices of the corresponding replicating portfolios.

To mimic this method, we will divide the time to maturity into a number of periods and set up a replicating portfolio during each period that exactly matches the value of the call. In each period, we set the price of the option equal to the price of the replicating portfolio. To find the currency option price now, we will find its price during the last period and then work backwards, determining its value during each period until we arrive at the present period. As we reduce the length of the time intervals, we will see that the solution we obtain will get closer and closer to that which would be calculated by the BSGK method. In particular, we will verify the accuracy of the binomial approximation method by using it to calculate the pound option price we previously calculated using the BSGK technique.

To see how this works, let us focus on finding the value of a replicating portfolio during a particular period for the case of a European call option. Suppose the current spot exchange rate at the beginning of this period is S dollars per unit of foreign currency. At the end of the interval, the exchange rate can take on one of two values. It can rise to S_u or fall to S_d. To get S_u, we will multiply S by a factor u (which we will learn how to calculate later). To find S_d, we will multiply S by d = 1/u. Thus, S_u = Su and S_d = Sd. Of course, this is an approximation; in reality, the exchange rate can end up at any value at the end of the period. But, as we will see, if we pick the magnitudes of the up and down movements u and d properly, this approximation should get better and better as the time interval becomes shorter.

Suppose we have a European currency option with strike price X. The U.S. interest rate over this short time-period is r, while the foreign interest rate over the interval is r*. These interest rates are not continuously compounded. The current value of the call is C dollars. At the end of the period, the option value will be C_u if the exchange rate is S_u. If the exchange rate turns out to be S_d, the option will be worth C_d. Now let us find a portfolio that replicates the values of the call over this short time-interval.

Consider a portfolio of x borrowed dollars and y dollars invested in the foreign currency. Let x dollars be borrowed at interest rate r. At the end of the period, we will have to pay back x(1+r) dollars. Suppose we take y dollars, convert them to foreign currency at the rate S, and then invest them at rate r*. At the end of the period, the portfolio will pay off $y(1+r^*)S_u/S - x(1+r)$ if the exchange rate moves up, or $y(1+r^*)S_d/S - x(1+r)$ if the exchange rate moves down. To replicate the two possible values of the option, we must equate the payoffs of our portfolio to the payoffs of the option in each state. Thus,

$$y(1+r^*)S_u/S - x(1+r) = C_u$$

$$y(1+r^*)S_d/S - x(1+r) = C_d.$$

Since we have two equations and two unknowns, we can solve for x and y in order to obtain the amounts we need to borrow and invest in order to replicate the value of the option in each state. Moreover, the net investment in the replicating portfolio must be the same as the value of the option C at the beginning of the period, since they both have the same payoff. Thus,

$$C = y - x.$$

Solving for y and x, and substituting into the formula for C, we find that

$$C = (pC_u + (1-p)C_d)/(1+r)$$

where p is

$$p = ((1+r) - (1+r^*)d)/((1+r^*)(u-d)).$$

p is termed the risk-neutral probability. A look at the option-pricing formula for C suggests that we are taking a kind of discounted average or discounted expected value. The call takes a value C_u p percent of the time and a value C_d (1-p) percent of the time. If we weight C_u and C_d by their probabilities and sum them, we obtain the average value of the call at the end of the period. To find the value of the call at the beginning of the period, we must discount its expected value at the interest rate r by dividing by 1+r. p is called the risk-neutral probability because economic theory suggests that risk-neutral investors (i.e., investors who need not be compensated for bearing risk) would independently find the same solution for the option-pricing problem. Thus, options are priced *as if* investors are risk-neutral, even though in reality investors are *risk-averse,* meaning that they must be compensated for bearing risk. It is important to realize that p is not the actual probability of the exchange rate's movement—this is because inves-tors can disagree about the actual probabilities of exchange rate movements and still agree about the price of the option.

Now that we have a method to price a currency option in the current period if we know the two values the option can take at the end of the period, we can apply this method to the European call option on the pound in our example. First, we know that this method assumes that the exchange rate moves up or down each period. So we need to decide the length of each period. To keep things simple, let us divide the time until expiration, 182/365 days, into three periods. The exchange rate starts at S = $1.60. At the end of the first period, it moves up to 1.60u or down to 1.60d. Let us define u and d to be

$$u = \exp(\sigma\sqrt{T}/\sqrt{n})$$

$$d = 1/u$$

where n is the number of periods, three in this case; σ is the volatility; and T is the time to maturity in years. We pick u and d in this way because, as shown in the paper (1979) by John Cox, Steven Ross, and Mark Rubinstein, this choice will lead to a solution that approximates the BSGK solution increasingly accurately as the length of the period shortens.

Calculating u and d, we find u = 1.050139 and d = 0.952255. Thus, in the first period, S moves from $1.60 to $1.680223 if the exchange rate moves up, or to $1.53608 if the exchange rate moves down. Now let us move to the second period. We have two possible starting exchange rates, $1.680223 and $1.523608. Let us focus on $1.680223. If the exchange rate moves up, S will move to $1.764467. If the exchange rate moves down, S will move to $1.60. We can do a similar exercise starting with an exchange rate of $1.523608. At the end of period 2, we will have three possible exchange rates. Now, if we move to period three, we will have three possible starting exchange rates, since the exchange rate can move up or down starting from one of these three. Then, we will have at the end of the period (i.e., the expiration date) four possible exchange rates. (See Figure 1.)

Notice that the possible exchange rates fan out as we move into the future. The size of the up and down movements is determined by the

Figure 1

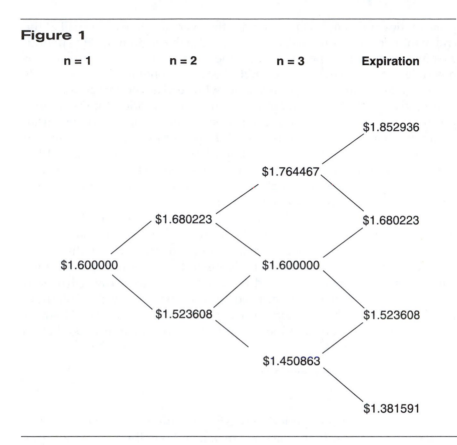

| n = 1 | n = 2 | n = 3 | Expiration |

$1.852936

$1.764467

$1.680223 $1.680223

$1.600000 $1.600000

$1.523608 $1.523608

$1.450863

$1.381591

volatility parameter σ. As σ becomes larger, the up and down movements become larger during each period, for higher volatility implies that the exchange rate fans out faster in the future. Higher volatility implies more uncertainty about the value of the exchange rate in the sense that the exchange rate is more likely to take on extremely small or large values as we look further into the future.

Notice as well that we have approximated all the possible paths the exchange rate could take during the 182-day period. The exchange rate could move straight up to $1.852936, for example. Or it could move from $1.60 to $1.523608 to $1.60 to $1.680223. We don't know which path it will take, but we do know that it will take one of these paths.

Now that we have constructed the possible exchange-rate paths, we can find the value of the option at the beginning of the period. To do so, we work backwards. We know the value of the call for each possible final exchange rate, since the European call will be exercised if it is *in the money* (i.e., makes money if exercised). If it is not in the money, it will not be exercised and will be worth nothing. Thus, at the end of the period, the option will be worth S–X or 0, whichever is bigger.

For example, suppose the exchange rate ends at S = $1.852936. Then, it will be exercised and will yield $1.852936 – $1.60 = $0.252936. In this case, the call will be worth $0.252936 if S = $1.852936. However, if the exchange rate ends at S = $1.523608, it will not be exercised and will be worth zero. We can fill in the starting values of the calls as follows:[10]

End of Period Three

S	S–X	Call Price
$1.852936	$0.252936	$0.252936
$1.680223	$0.080223	$0.080223
$1.523608	negative	0
$1.381591	negative	0

Now we move back to period two. Let us assume that the exchange rate has moved to $1.764467 in the diagram. We want the price of the call at this exchange rate. We know that if the exchange rate moves up to $1.852936, the price of the call is $C_u = \$0.252936$ whereas if the exchange rate moves down to $1.680223, the price of the call is $C_d = \$0.080223$. To use our formula, $C = (pC_u + (1-p)C_d)/(1+r)$, we need to find r, r*, and p. Note that r and r* are the per period constant interest rates. To find them, we need to first convert the continuously compounded interest rates to rates compounded annually using the following formulas:

$$i = \exp(i) - 1,$$

$$i^* = \exp(i^*) - 1.$$

Thus, 10 percent compounded annually is exp(.1) – 1 = 0.105171 and 11 percent compounded annually is exp(.11) – 1 = 0.116278. Now, we need to convert these rates to interest rates over the period using the following formulas:

$$r = (1 + i)^{T/n} - 1,$$

$$r^* = (1 + i^*)^{T/n} - 1,$$

where T is the time to maturity in years, and n is the number of periods (three in this case). Using this formula, we find that r = 0.016760 and r* = 0.018451. Now, we can use the previous formulas to calculate that p = 0.470806.

The value of the call for S = $1.76 is then

$$C = (0.470806(0.252936) + (1-0.470806)0.080223)/(1+0.016760)$$

$$C = \$0.158874.$$

Using the same procedure, we can find the value of the call for the other two possible exchange rates during this period.

Beginning of Period Three

S	Call Price
$1.764467	$0.158874
$1.60	$0.037147
$1.450863	$0

Repeating the same steps, we can find the call values at the beginning of period two:

Beginning of Period Two

S	Call Price
$1.680223	$0.092900
$1.523608	$0.017201

Now, we move back to the beginning of period 1 and find the value of the call at the exchange rate S = $1.60 and C = $0.051969.

Beginning of Period One

S	Call Price
$1.60	$0.051969

Using the BSGK method, we calculated the value of the call to be $0.0476. Employing just three periods, we managed to get close to the true value. If we divide the time to maturity into smaller intervals (i.e., let n become larger and larger), we can obtain better accuracy, as the table illustrates.[11]

Value of n	Call Price
30	C = 0.0472
60	C = 0.0474
90	C = 0.0475
120	C = 0.0475

American Option Valuation

The binomial method can easily be adapted to the American option case.[12] The analysis is essentially the same but must be modified to handle the early exercise feature of American options. Most of the calculations are the same: u, d, p, r, and r* are calculated as before. Moreover, the exchange rate tree is constructed just as it was in the European option

case. However, since the option is American, we must decide at the beginning of each period whether to carry the option to the end of the
period or immediately exercise it. If we carry the option to the end of the
period, it behaves like a European option, so we need to calculate the
European option price. But since we might decide to exercise it, we also
need to calculate the immediate exercise value. If the exercise value exceeds the European option value, we should exercise the option. Otherwise, we use the European option value as the value of the option. Thus,
at each exchange rate before expiration, the value of the call is the larger
of $(pC_u + (1-p)C_d)/(1+r)$ and $S-X$, the immediate exercise value when the
current exchange rate is S. For puts, the value is the larger of $(pP_u +
(1-p)P_d)/(1+r)$ and $X-S$, where P is the value of the put and $X-S$ is the
put's immediate exercise value when the current exchange rate is S.

To see how this works, let us consider the following option pricing
problem. Suppose we have an American put that expires in one year. The
current exchange rate and the strike price are both $1.0 per unit of foreign
currency. The continuously compounded domestic interest rate is 10 percent, while the continuously compounded foreign interest rate is 5 percent.
The volatility is 20 percent per year. We divide the year into three periods
so n = 3. Proceeding as before, we compute $r = 0.033895$, $r^* = 0.016806$, $u =
1.122401$, $d = 0.890947$, and $p = 0.543777$. Given u and d, we can construct
the exchange rate tree (see Figure 2).

Having computed the exchange rate tree, we can find the value of the
put at the expiration date. Since a put allows the owner to sell foreign
currency at a price X, the value of the put at expiration must be $X-S$ or $0,
whichever is bigger.

	End of Period Three	
S	**X–S**	**Put Price**
$1.413982	negative	$0
$1.122401	negative	$0
$0.890947	0.109053	0.109053
$0.707222	0.292778	0.292778

Now, moving back to the beginning of period three, we must compute
$P = (pP_u + (1-p)P_d)/(1+r)$ and $X-S$ for each of the three exchange rates and
choose the larger of the two as the put price.

For example, consider the exchange rate $S = \$0.793787$. The discounted
expected value of the put is

$$P = ((0.543777)(0.109053) + (1-0.543777)(0.292778))/(1+0.033895)$$

or

$$P = \$0.186549.$$

Figure 2

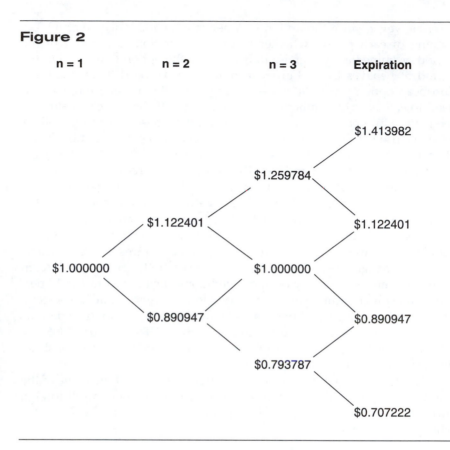

| n = 1 | n = 2 | n = 3 | Expiration |

Since the exercise value of the put is $0.206213, we use $0.206213 as the value of the put at this exchange rate.

Beginning of Period Three

S	X–S	Discounted Expected Value	Put Price
$1.259784	negative	$0	$0
$1.000000	0	$0.048121	$0.048121
$0.793787	$0.206213	$0.186549	$0.206213

Continuing with the calculations, we can fill in the values for the beginning of periods two and one.

Beginning of Period Two

S	X–S	Discounted Expected Value	Put Price
$1.122401	negative	$0.021234	$0.021234
$0.890947	$0.109053	$0.116304	$0.116304

Beginning of Period One

S	X–S	Discounted Expected Value	Put Price
$1.000000	$0	$0.062489	$0.062489

The value of the put is $0.0625. If we divide the year into 90 periods, so that n = 90, we find P = $0.0592.[13]

Riskiness of Derivatives

Measuring Option Risk

Professional users of derivatives assess the risk of currency options by examining how the option price changes with respect to small changes in underlying variables, such as the exchange rate. For example, consider a European call on the yen. Suppose the dollar price of the yen rises. The price of the call will rise as well, since it is now more likely that the exchange rate will end up higher at the expiration date, and hence it is more likely that the call will ultimately be exercised at a profit. A number known as delta measures how much the call price changes for small changes in the exchange rate. If the delta of the European call is 0.5, the call price will rise half as fast as the exchange rate rises.

Delta is crucial to understanding option risk because it allows the user to think of an option's risk as being equivalent to the risk of holding the underlying currency itself. For example, consider a call on 6 million yen, which has a delta of 0.5. The dollar value of the option will change half as fast as the dollar value of 6 million yen, for small changes in the exchange rate. But this risk is equivalent to holding 3 million yen. Therefore, for small changes in the exchange rate, we may think of the dollar risk of holding a call option on 6 million yen with a delta of 0.5 as being the same as holding 3 million yen directly.

Delta is not constant; it changes when the underlying exchange rate changes. Thus, delta is valid only for small changes in the exchange rate. To assess how delta changes, users often calculate gamma, which measures how rapidly delta changes when the exchange rate changes. Delta becomes a more realistic measurement of risk when gamma is small.

Option prices also rise when the volatility of the underlying exchange rises. As the volatility of the exchange rate rises, the exchange rate is more likely to register high and low values with respect to the average value. Higher volatility increases an option's value because options benefit from extreme changes in the exchange rate in one direction but are not penalized by extreme changes in the other direction.

To understand how increasing volatility makes options more valuable in the case of a European call option, assume the volatility of the exchange rate equals some constant value. If the exchange rate ends up above the strike price at expiration, the call will be exercised at a profit. If the exchange rate ends up below the strike price, the call will not be exercised and will be worth nothing. Now increase the volatility. The higher volatility implies that the exchange rate is more likely to have higher and lower values than it did before the volatility increased. The higher values only increase the option's potential value, since the option may ultimately be exercised when the exchange rate is substantially above the strike price. But at the same time, lower values of the exchange rate do not reduce the option's value, since the option cannot be worth less than nothing. Thus, higher volatility increases the option's upside potential without adding to its downside potential. Higher volatility, then, must increase a European call's value. Since this reasoning may be applied to European puts and American puts and calls, higher volatility of the underlying currency raises option prices in general.

Because an option's value increases when volatility rises and decreases when volatility falls, changing volatility of the underlying currency is an additional source of option risk. To assess this risk, users calculate vega, which measures the sensitivity of an option price to small changes in the volatility of the underlying exchange rate.[14]

Correlation Risk

Derivative risk may also arise from the breakdown of assumed correlations between currencies. For example, suppose a company owns Spanish pesetas but is concerned that the dollar value of the pesetas could decline if the dollar-peseta exchange rate falls. Perhaps the company would like to hedge this risk by using futures contracts, but no peseta futures contracts are available. The company decides to use deutsche mark (DM) futures, but clearly the efficacy of this strategy depends on a stable correlation between the peseta and the deutsche mark. If the peseta and the deutsche mark tended to move one for one in the past and are expected to continue to do so in the future, the company could hedge its peseta exposure by selling DM futures. If the dollar price of the peseta falls, the company will lose money on the pesetas, but that loss will be made up by gains in the DM futures. However, this expectation that the two currencies will continue to move one for one may not in fact be realized, introducing risk to this hedge. If the deutsche mark and the peseta start moving in opposite directions, the company will be unhedged and may experience more losses than it would have had it not sold DM futures.

Speculation Risk

Speculation risk arises when a company combines a hedge with speculation (i.e., conjectures about the likely future values of currencies). This problem most often arises when companies use exotic options, but may be present in any derivative investment. An exotic option is a derivative that gives a

---

Exotic Options

Cacall

A cacall is an option to purchase a call. Suppose a company enters into a contract involving foreign exchange risk. Since the company might need a call option, it might want to hedge the risk that the option will become more expensive. The company can lock in the call's price by purchasing a cacall.

Caput

A caput is an option to purchase a put.

Contingent Premium Call

A contingent premium call is like a standard call except no premium is paid up front. Rather, if the exchange rate at expiration is above the strike price, so that the call has positive value, a premium is paid at that time; but if the exchange rate finishes below the strike price, no premium is required. In our example, if the company feels that the exchange rate is unlikely to move in such a way as to destroy the profit on the computer screens, it may purchase a contingent premium option. If the company's expectations are proven correct, it does not pay any premium for an option it did not need. But if the company's expectations are proven incorrect, and it needs to exercise the option, it will have to pay a higher premium than it otherwise would have paid to purchase a standard option.

company either more or less protection against exchange rate risk with respect to the simple options mentioned in this review. The greater protection must be paid for by remitting a higher premium, but less protection requires a lower premium than would be paid for a standard option.

When a company decides to use a derivative that provides less protection against exchange rate risk, it may be implicitly speculating that certain exchange scenarios are unlikely to happen. It is thus bearing the risk that these scenarios might happen in exchange for the payment of a lower premium. This may well be a sensible calculation for the company to make, but it should understand the risks and potential for losses.

Understanding the risks may well be more difficult in the case of exotic options, since they tend to be derivatives tailor-made to a company's particular situation and thus quite complex. It is important for a company to understand how an exotic derivative's value varies with exchange rates, interest rates, volatility, and other variables, and whether very large losses are possible under some circumstances. One method a company may use to help it understand these risks is to develop the capability to value exotic derivatives in-house so that the derivative seller's claims can be verified. The company may want to *stress test* the derivatives (i.e., examine how the derivatives' value changes for plausible and not-so-plausible changes in the economic environment). The stress test may reveal the potential for substantial losses for some particular small changes in the economic environment, especially if the hedging strategy involves a portfolio of exotic derivatives.

Calculating Volatility

In the examples we considered, the volatility was used as an input to calculate the option price. How do we find this volatility estimate in practice? Unfortunately, there is no consensus on the best method of estimating volatility because many of the empirical facts and regularities surrounding exchange rates have not yet been conclusively established. In the following discussion, we will consider the common methods and attempt to form some tentative judgments about them based on work done in the academic finance literature.

The Historical Method

The simplest technique is the historical method. The BSGK methodology makes specific assumptions about the exchange rate's dynamics, which, if correct, allow us to construct an estimate of the annualized volatility of the exchange rate. Specifically, the BSGK method assumes that volatility is constant over the life of the option.

More Exotic Options

Average Rate Option

An average rate put pays off the difference between the strike price and the average exchange rate over the life of the option. Suppose a company had sales of 1 million yen daily, and each day converted the yen to dollars at the prevailing exchange rate. Then the total dollars earned will equal 1 million times the number of days times the average exchange rate. Since the average exchange rate is not known in advance, the total dollar revenues are not known either. To hedge this risk, the company might purchase an average rate put.

Barrier Option

A barrier option comes into existence or is canceled depending on whether the exchange rate crosses a predefined barrier. For example, a down-and-out call is canceled if the value of the foreign currency declines below a certain level. This type of option is useful when a company believes that if the foreign currency declines below a certain level, the currency is unlikely to rebound to a point that will cause the company losses.

At this point, we should be more precise about the meaning of the term *volatility*. To do so, let us define some notation: suppose that the daily exchange rate on day t, expressed in dollars per unit of foreign currency, is denoted by S_t. Suppose we have N days of daily data. The daily continuously compounded return on the exchange rate is then

$$\mu = \ln(S_t/S_{t-1}),$$

where ln is the natural logarithm.

The volatility is the annualized standard deviation of μ. To calculate the standard deviation of μ, we need to calculate the mean of μ, $\bar{\mu}$, which is

$$\bar{\mu} = (1/N) \, \Sigma_{t=1}^{N} \, \mu_t \, .^{[15]}$$

Then, the standard deviation of μ, σ, the daily volatility estimate, is

$$\sigma = \mathrm{sqrt} \, ((1/(N-1)) \, (\Sigma_{t=1}^{N} \, (\mu_t - \bar{\mu})^2)) \, ,$$

where sqrt refers to the square root.

Note σ can then be turned into an annualized estimate by multiplying it by the square root of the number of trading days in the year.[16] As the number of days, N, increases, the estimate of volatility becomes more accurate, but if volatility changes during the N day period, using a larger N may make the estimate less relevant.

Problems with the Historical Method

Although the BSGK and the binomial approximation methods assume that volatility is constant over the life of the option, substantial empirical evidence suggests that it is not. Figure 3 shows the daily continuously compounded dollar returns on the deutsche mark, μ_t, for the years 1986 to 1994. It is apparent to the naked eye, and confirmed by statistical tests, that volatility is not constant. Notice, for example, that the daily swings in the exchange rate seem to be larger in 1991 than in 1990, implying greater volatility in 1991 than in 1990. Technically speaking, nonconstant volatility invalidates the BSGK method and the binomial approximation technique. However, market participants often adjust their volatility estimation methods to account for time-varying volatility, but continue to use the BSGK method or binomial method as an approximate solution to the true option pricing problem.

Figure 3 Daily Percent Dollar Return on Deutsche Mark

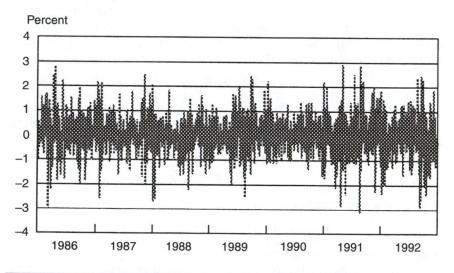

Rolling Estimators

One way to account for changing volatility is to use a rolling estimator. The analyst uses a fixed number of past days, perhaps 100, to construct the estimate. The number of past days is chosen so that it is large enough to get a relatively precise estimate of volatility, but not so large as to be misleading because volatility changed over the period in question. Every day the volatility estimate is made, the same number of past days of exchange rate data is used. Thus, if we calculate today's volatility, we use the past 100 days of data. Tomorrow, we would throw out the day's data occurring 100 days ago and add today's data. In this way, we would get a volatility estimate that changed daily. The changing volatility estimate could be annualized by multiplying it by the square root of the number of trading days in a year.

Although this daily number is easy to calculate, it is hard to use because we have no guidance about how many past days to use. Moreover, we can get strange behavior in the estimated volatility using this method; a very unusual event that produced a large swing in the exchange rate would continue to exert a big influence on the calculation until 100 days in the past, since we are weighting all 100 daily observations equally. On the 101st day, the large swing would fall out of the calculation, implying a suddenly smaller volatility. But this smaller volatility is not generated by economic fundamentals. Rather, it is an artifact of the estimation method.

Exponential Smoothing

We can avoid the strange behavior of the rolling volatility estimator by weighting the most recent μ_ts more heavily in the calculation. Assume a fixed number of past days such as 100. Then, we could construct a daily variance estimate (volatility squared) σ_t^2 as

$$\sigma_t^2 = (1 - \alpha)\, \sigma_{t-1}^2 + \alpha\mu_{t-1}^2,$$

where α is a number between 0 and 1.

This estimator computes current variance as a weighted average of yesterday's squared daily return and yesterday's variance.[17] If yesterday's daily return or variance was high, today's variance will be high as well. Thus, periods of high and low volatility will tend to cluster together, producing periods of quiet and turbulence in the foreign exchange market. This clustering of volatility can be seen in Figure 3.

Recursively substituting for σ_{t-1}^2, σ_{t-2}^2, and so forth, we can see that current variance is a weighted average of past squared daily returns, just as it was in the historical case:

$$\sigma_t^2 = \alpha\mu_{t-1}^2 + \alpha\,(1-\alpha)\,\mu_{t-2}^2 + \alpha\,(1-\alpha)^2\mu_{t-3}^2 + \ldots)$$

Notice, however, that the most recent squared daily returns have the largest weights. Thus, if we use N days of past data in the calculation (N = 100 in our previous example), we would not have the problem seen in the rolling historical method; a large event occurring 100 days ago would not abruptly fall out of the sample and significantly change the volatility estimate because 100-day-ago daily returns are not weighted heavily in the first place.

One significant advantage of the exponential smoothing estimator is that it can generate time-varying volatilities while avoiding the potential odd behavior of the rolling historical estimates. It's also easy to compute and able to reproduce the periods of turbulence and quiet seen in the foreign exchange market. Moreover, this method received a boost when it was chosen as the basic estimator in J.P. Morgan's RiskMetrics[TM] risk management system. However, picking appropriate values for α and N can be problematic. There is no powerful statistical theory to guide us, so we must, to some extent, resort to ad hoc procedures.[18]

GARCH

A more sophisticated way to model time-varying volatility which captures periods of turbulence and quiet in the foreign exchange market involves using the GARCH (generalized autoregressive conditional heteroskedasticity) method. A GARCH process is very similar to the exponential smoothing model but is more general and provides powerful methods for estimating α. For example, the GARCH(1,1) process is given by

$$\sigma_t^2 = a + b\sigma_{t-1}^2 + c\mu_{t-1}^2 .\text{[19]}$$

Thus, the exponential smoothing estimator is a special case of GARCH(1,1) in which a corresponds to 0, b corresponds to $1-\alpha$, and c corresponds to α. In the GARCH(1,1) models, however, the parameters a, b, and c can take on more general values. The parameter a contains information about the long-term forecast of volatility. In other words, as we look farther and farther into the future, our forecast for future daily volatility derived from the GARCH(1,1) approaches $\dfrac{a}{1-b-c}$.

To estimate the coefficients a, b, and c, we can use a technique called maximum likelihood. For example, using the daily percent dollar-deutschemark return over the period 1983 to 1994 (μ_t is converted to percent terms by multiplying by 100), I estimated the following GARCH(1,1) model

$$\sigma_t^2 = 0.0200 + 0.8903\sigma_{t-1}^2 + 0.0741u_{t-1}^2 ,$$

where $u_t = 100.0\mu_t$.[20] In this case, N = 2512. Notice that the problem of specifying N is solved as well: we should use as large a value of N as possible, ideally at least 8 years of daily data.[21]

To predict volatility k days in the future, we would use the following relation:

$$\sigma^2_{t+k} = 0.0200 + 0.8903\sigma^2_{t+k-1} + 0.0741\sigma^2_{t+k-1}$$

Using this equation, we would forecast volatility for each day from today's date to the expiration date of the option. We would then average the daily volatility forecasts to obtain the average daily volatility. This average volatility could then be annualized and used as the volatility estimate in the BSGK formula or the binomial approximation method.

The GARCH(1,1) estimated here is the simplest such model. In general, more complicated GARCH models would be estimated in practice.[22]

Implied Volatility

The alternative method used to estimate volatility, much used in practice, is the implied volatility method. The BSGK and binomial approximation methods allow us to calculate the value of the option, given that we input the volatility estimate. But since we can observe the option value in the marketplace, we can use the option price plus our pricing method to back out the volatility implied by the option price. This volatility is called the *implied volatility*. It is the market's estimation of the volatility of the underlying exchange rate over the life of the option.

If the assumptions underlying the BSGK model are correct, every option on a particular currency with the same strike price and time to maturity observed at the same time should have the same implied volatility. However, options that differ by strike price but are the same in other respects do not have the same implied volatility; the *volatility smile* observed by practitioners refers to the observation that volatility varies with the strike price in such a way that a graph of strike price versus implied volatility resembles a smile.

Since currency options do not give a unique value for the implied volatility, we must choose which options to use in the calculation. In practice, a set of options is selected and implied volatility is inferred as a weighted sum of the implied volatility of the options. Equal weights could be used, or the implied volatilities could be weighted by the corresponding option's vega. Another commonly used method is to infer implied volatility from the nearest at-the-money options.

In their 1989 paper, Elton Scott and Alan Tucker examined various methods of calculating implied volatility and compared them to the historical method. They found that the method used to weight the implied volatility estimates didn't affect their forecasting ability significantly; moreover, implied volatility forecasts outperformed forecasts derived from using the historical method. Thus, there is evidence that the implied volatility method is superior to the historical method.[23] Moreover, Xinzhong Xu and Steven Taylor (1995) showed that implied volatility forecasts realized volatility over a four week period better than do the historical or GARCH method.

Thus, the evidence suggests that implied volatility forecasts realized volatility well in a statistical sense for the major currencies. However, it may not forecast well in an economic sense. For example, Jaesun Noh, Robert Engle, and Alex Kane (1994) report that GARCH(1,1) volatility forecasts generated higher profits in the S&P 500 options market than did a strategy based on implied volatility estimates. If this result held true for currency options as well, then even if implied volatility outperforms GARCH statistically, it still may produce lower trading profits in the currency options market.

Obviously, the proper method to forecast volatility in the currency options market is not a settled issue. More research will need to be done by practitioners and academics on this important currency derivatives pricing question.

Stochastic Volatility Option Pricing Models

As mentioned before, the BSGK analysis is no longer valid once volatility is allowed to vary randomly over time. Practitioners often ignore this problem, preferring instead to estimate a time-varying volatility and input it into the BSGK method, which is seen as a useful approximation. This can be a reasonable procedure, since, as shown by Clifford Ball and Antonio Roma (1994), the stochastic volatility option price is approximately equal to the value given by BSGK when evaluated at the expected value of the average volatility over the life of the option. Stochastic volatility option models are much harder to solve than models that obey the BSGK assumptions. Furthermore, underlying option price parameters besides volatility must be estimated in the stochastic option pricing case. Thus, the costs of implementing the stochastic volatility model when compared to the potential benefits have slowed its adoption by practitioners. But empirical research on these models is progressing because currency option pricing methods such as BSGK have known biases (the volatility smile mentioned earlier is an example).[24]

Summary

The three major types of currency derivatives are the forward, future, and option. The future and the option can be understood in terms of the most basic derivative, the forward contract. Currency derivatives can be used to hedge risk as well as to speculate on exchange rate movements. Currency options can be evaluated using the Black-Scholes-Garman-Kohlhagen (BSGK) method in the European case. If the options are American, the binomial approximation procedure can be used. The volatility input into these procedures can be derived from implied volatility estimates, exponential weighting, or the GARCH procedure. Exotic derivatives, by allowing less exchange rate protection in exchange for a lower premium, give a company the ability to combine hedging and speculation. However, exotic derivative risk is more difficult to understand. To alleviate this problem, a company could develop the means to value derivative contracts in-house and stress test them. When evaluating derivatives' risks, derivative users should also consider correlation risk. In general, derivatives add value to the marketplace, provided they are well understood and properly used.

Endnotes

1. The views expressed in this chapter are those of the author and do not necessarily represent the views of the Federal Reserve Bank of Philadelphia or the Federal Reserve System.

2. However, if a company uses the forward market, it may have to tie up a line of credit.

3. The discussion has been simplified for expository purposes. The winning and losing parties do not directly transfer funds to each other, but rather use a clearing corporation as an intermediary. The clearing corporation also guarantees both sides of the contract against default. For more institutional detail regarding currency futures markets, see Grabbe (1991).

4. Futures rates are approximately equal to forward rates. Covered interest parity, discussed earlier, implies that the forward rate is determined by the exchange rate and the interest rates in both countries. Thus, the forward or futures rate will not in general move one-for-one with the exchange rate because interest rates in the two countries do not always move exactly together.

5. For simplicity, we focus on options on foreign currencies with prices stated in terms of the dollar.

6. For simplicity, the time value of money has been ignored in this calculation.

7. Since American options can be exercised on any day prior to and including the expiration date but the European option can be exercised only on the expiration date, an American option must be at least as valuable as a European option. Thus, American options cost at least as much as European options.

8. Other common evaluation methods include the finite difference method, in which the option price partial differential equation is solved, and the Monte Carlo method, in which the average discounted price of the option is simulated using the risk-neutral probabilities.

9. The normal cumulative density function can be looked up in standard statistical tables or approximated.

10. The calculations done for this example and the American option pricing problem that follows are performed on a pentium computer in higher numerical precision than that reported in the text.

11. These calculations were done by a program written in C by the author. It is available upon request.

12. An alternative method for calculating American option prices, which can be relatively accurate and easier to implement, is to use the approximation procedure of Barone-Adesi and Whaley (1987).

13. This estimation was done by a program written in C by the author. It is available upon request.

14. Delta, gamma, and vega can be calculated using the BSGK formula or approximated numerically using the binomial option pricing technique.

15. Because of a potentially large estimation error in the mean, it may pay to set the mean to zero instead of calculating it. See Figlewski (1994) for more discussion.

16. Since volatility has been found to be much larger on trading days than on nontrading days, nontrading days are often ignored.

17. In this model, the mean is assumed to be zero. In a more general model, this need not be the case.

18. For discussion on how to pick α and N in the context of risk management, see RiskMetrics^{TM} [J.P. Morgan] Technical Document (1995).

19. For more on the GARCH process, see Bollerslev (1986). For a textbook treatment, see Hamilton (1994). Bollerslev, Engle, and Nelson (1993) is a good survey of the academic literature.

20. This estimation was done using the IMSL fortran library. In general, GARCH estimations are difficult numerical problems.

21. However, some authors use a fixed window of past data when using the GARCH model. See the article by Noh, Engle, and Kane (1994) for an example.

22. See the estimation in Bollerslev, Engle, and Nelson (1993) for an empirical example.

23. For more empirical evidence on the forecasting ability of implied volatility in the context of currency options, see Fung, Lie, and Moreno (1990) and Edey and Elliot (1992).

24. For empirical analysis of the stochastic volatility currency option pricing model, see Melino and Turnbull (1990), Chesney and Scott (1989), Bates (1993), and Hopper (1996).

References

Ball, C. A., and A. Roma. "Stochastic Volatility Option Pricing." *Journal of Financial and Quantitative Analysis*, 29 (1994), pp. 589–607.

Barone-Adesi, G., and R. E. Whaley. "Efficient Analytic Approximation of American Option Values." *Journal of Finance,* 42 (1987), pp. 301–20.

Bates, D. S. "Jumps and Stochastic Volatility: Exchange Rate Processes Implicit in PHLX Deutschemark Options," NBER Working Paper No. 4596, (1993).

Black, F., and M. Scholes. "The Pricing of Options and Corporate Liabilities." *Journal of Political Economy,* 81 (1973), pp. 637–59.

Bollerslev, T. "Generalized Autoregressive Conditional Heteroskedasticity." *Journal of Econometrics,* 31 (1986), pp. 307–27.

Bollerslev, T.; R. F. Engle; and D. B. Nelson. "ARCH Models." CRSP W.P. 382, University of Chicago, Graduate School of Business (1993).

Chesney, M., and L. Scott. "Pricing European Currency Options: A Comparison of the Modified Black-Scholes Model and a Random Variance Model," *Journal of Financial and Quantitative Analysis,* 24 (1989), pp. 267–84.

Cox, J. C.; R. E. Ingersoll; and S. A. Ross. "The Relationship Between Forward and Futures Prices." *Journal of Financial Economics,* 9 (1981), pp. 321–46.

Cox, J. C.; S. A. Ross; and M. Rubinstein. "Option Pricing: A Simplified Approach," *Journal of Financial Economics,* 7 (1979), pp. 229–63.

Edey, M., and G. Elliot. "Some Evidence on Option Prices as Predictors of Volatility." *Oxford Bulletin of Economics and Statistics,* 54 (1992), pp. 567–78.

Figlewski, S. "Forecasting Volatility Using Historical Data." New York University Working Paper, S-94-13 (1994).

Fung, H.; C. Lie; and A. Moreno. "The Forecasting Performance of the Implied Standard Deviation in Currency Options." *Managerial Finance,* 16 (1990), pp. 24–29.

Garman, M. B., and S. W. Kohlhagen. "Foreign Currency Option Values." *Journal of International Money and Finance,* 2 (1983), pp. 231–37.

Grabbe, J. O. "The Pricing of Call and Put Options on Foreign Exchange." *Journal of International Money and Finance,* 2 (1983), pp. 239–53.

Grabbe, J. O. *International Financial Markets.* New York NY: Elsevier Science Publishing Co., Inc., 1991.

Hamilton, J. D. *Times Series Analysis,* Princeton NJ: Princeton University Press, (1994)

Hopper, G. P. "A Primer on Currency Derivatives," *Business Review,* Federal Reserve Bank of Philadelphia, 1995, pp. 3–14.

Hopper, G. P. "ARCH Filtering of Volatility in Stochastic Currency Option Pricing Models: An Empirical Analysis." Mimeo, Federal Reserve Bank of Philadelphia, (1996).

Melino, A., and S. M. Turnbull. "Pricing Foreign Currency Options with Stochastic Volatility," *Journal of Econometrics,* 45 (1990), pp. 239–65.

Merton, R. C. "Theory of Rational Option Pricing," *Bell Journal of Economics and Management Science* 4 (1973), pp. 141–83.

Noh, J.; R. F. Engle; and A. Kane. "Forecasting Volatility and Option Prices of the S&P 500." *Journal of Derivatives* (1994), pp. 17–30.

RiskMetrics^{TM}-Technical Document, Morgan Guaranty Trust Company, Global Research, New York, 1995.

Scott, E., and A. Tucker. "Predicting Currency Return Volatility." *Journal of Banking and Finance* 6 (1989), pp. 839–51.

Xu, X., and S. J. Taylor. "Conditional Volatility and the Informational Efficiency of the PHLX Currency Options Market." *Journal of Banking and Finance* 19 (1995), pp. 803–21.

CHAPTER 2

Everything You Ever Wanted to Know about Currency Futures but Were Afraid to Ask

Hunt Taylor
Managing Director
FINEX Europe

The usual reaction to one's first glimpse of an active open-outcry trading pit is bewilderment quickly followed by the firm belief that nothing comprehensible could emerge from the screaming riot below. In fact, open-outcry trading is a remarkably efficient and equitable system. It is, in essence, a massive auction, with all qualified participants having an equal chance to access the best prevailing bids and offers. Pit traders are acting as agents for clients around the world, as well as for themselves (hence, the screaming). Perhaps the best way to visualize the experience of trading in a currency pit is to picture it as a cross between high-stakes poker and professional rugby.

What follows is a brief overview of the currency futures markets, how they work, why people like them, why people do not like them, and how they are changing.

A Quick History

A futures contract is a contract calling for the delivery of a specified amount of goods at a specified place and time. I sell you a contract which says that I will deliver a set amount of sugar to a freighter in New York or of wheat to a silo in the Midwest. You, in turn, promise to pay for it. For the better part of the last century, futures existed primarily to price and hedge commodities. Most of the world's largest futures contracts did not exist 25 years ago, because volatility was not a factor in market sectors that today are quite active. Gold was $35 an ounce, crude oil was $2 a barrel, currencies were fixed under the Bretton Woods agreement, and interest rates would occasionally skyrocket from $3\frac{1}{2}$ percent to $3\frac{3}{4}$ percent.

Currency futures were developed in the early 1970s by the Chicago Mercantile Exchange (CME), which today houses the most actively traded currency futures contracts in the world. The CME was looking for new products to trade and began to explore the idea that the exchange could trade money as well as goods. The CME formed a division to trade financial products, the International Monetary Market (IMM), and a new industry was created. Currency futures were, in fact, the world's first financial futures.

How Exchange Trading Works

Exchange trading differs from interbank trading in the following important aspects.

Standardization

Unlike the interbank market, where transactions are customized to the needs of the client, exchanges trade standardized contracts. As an interbank client, one can receive prices on virtually any amount of any currency pair deliverable on whatever date he or she chooses. On an exchange, traders deal in contracts calling for set amounts of currencies deliverable according to proscribed procedures, and only deliverable on certain dates. For example, the IMM deutsche-mark contract specifies delivery of 120,000 deutsche marks four times a year. The delivery dates are typically based on the quarterly cycle that is common to almost all financial futures contracts, with delivery falling in June, September, December, and March.

One of the rationales for the quarterly cycle was that the concentration of trading around four dates would serve to improve liquidity.

Clearing and Settlement

If one single aspect of exchange trading could be identified as the critical component, it would be the clearing association. The clearing association (or clearing house) is the agency responsible for clearing and settlement of all transactions done on the exchange. Here comes the good part. With every transaction on the exchange, the clearing house stands as buyer to every seller and as seller to every buyer. In other words, no matter how many counterparties a participant might have dealt with on the floor of the exchange over the course of a trading day, there is only one counterparty to deal with at the end of the day. That counterparty is the clearing association of the exchange, who stands as buyer to every seller and as seller to every buyer. As if that were not inducement enough, clearing associations of recognized investment exchanges are treated as counterparties of the highest caliber. According to a European Community (EC) directive, European regulators treat clearinghouses of recognized investment exchanges as carrying counterparty risk equivalent to the highest rated credit institutions in Europe.

So what is a clearing association? It is an organization owned by and backed by the full net worth of its members. Its function is to ensure the timely and accurate settlement of all transactions done on a given exchange. Only clearing members have the right to carry positions on the exchange. If a generic customer wants to carry a position on the exchange, he or she must open an account with a member of the clearing association who is structured to conduct customer business. These are known as futures commission merchants (FCMs). For this service, FCMs will charge a commission on every transaction. This will compensate FCMs for

1. Taking the risk that clients will lose more money than they have posted in their accounts, and that these clients will not make good on their losses.

2. Taking the risk that some other clearing member will lose so much money that all the other members of the clearing association will have to make good on those losses.

3. Keeping track of client trading, providing clients with trade executions, sending clients statements, and generally facilitating client business.

Clearing houses create capabilities that are difficult to duplicate in the interbank market. They create the capability for small traders, or traders who have difficulty obtaining cash lines, to access the currency markets with very low margins (typically 2 percent or less). They do this by spreading the risk of systematic failure among its members and by minimizing the direct risk of counterparty failure.

Execution

Futures exchanges have traditionally used the open-outcry system to transact business, though that is rapidly changing. Under traditional open-outcry trading, the usual procedure is to assemble a large body of individual traders who will act as brokers (acting on behalf of off-floor customers) or "locals" (trading for their own accounts). The idea is to put the first line of liquidity directly on the floor in the form of locals and then to supplement it, when necessary, with arbitrage to the interbank market.

One of the more appealing aspects of exchange trading is that floor execution is conducted in a transparent trading environment. That means that all quoting and trading [with the exception of exchange for physicals (EFP) market which will be discussed later] must be done by open outcry in one of the exchange's trading pits. Any member of the exchange with appropriate pit-trading privileges has access to any quoted price at any time. Private deals cannot be arranged. All buying must occur at the lowest prevailing offer, all selling at the highest prevailing bid. In essence, market makers must compete with each other in order to win the trade. Trading is scrutinized by price reporters stationed in the pits, and all trades are disseminated publicly.

The feature of price transparency is appealing to traders who want to minimize the risk that market makers will "read" the direction in which the client wants to trade and move the quote accordingly. Clients retain their anonymity throughout the transaction. This greatly diminishes (but not eliminates) the possibility of being read by the market makers.

As we said, some modifications are being made to the standard open-outcry model. FINEX has modified the standard local pricing model in order to allow banks to quote directly onto the floor for large trades through their block-order trading system.

Regulation

Just as clearing associations add an element of safety that is hard to duplicate in the interbank markets, the exchanges themselves add another dimension. Whereas clearing associations guarantee the settlement and delivery process, the exchange guarantees the integrity of the entire trading process.

This oversight takes many forms. Exchanges guarantee that trades are executed only by members in good standing. It enforces a rigorous membership process that requires members to demonstrate sufficient industry knowledge and to maintain substantial financial backing at all times. It is responsible for oversight of the execution process, ensuring that all trading is conducted in accordance with exchange regulations. In order to comply with these responsibilities, the exchange performs rigorous surveillance and compliance functions, and monitors, through the use of sophisticated computer models, the trading activities of members.

There is a second level of regulation to exchange trading. Just as exchanges regulate the conduct of their members, exchanges are themselves regulated by government agencies that are charged with this oversight responsibility. In the United States, the regulatory agency is the Commodity Futures Trading Commission (CFTC), in England it is the Securities and Futures Association (SFA), and in France it is the Conseil des

Marchés Financiérs. In the United States, an unusual agreement between regulators means that exchange trading of currencies can be regulated by the Securities and Exchange Commission (SEC) as well. They assume oversight of the Philadelphia Stock Exchange, where options on cash currencies are traded. Any futures contracts fall under the domain of the CFTC.

The CFTC, which oversees the vast majority of currency futures trading, has responsibility for approving the specifications of any contract that an exchange wishes to trade. The CFTC also acts as watchdog for the exchanges' own compliance departments, ensuring that the departments act with appropriate vigilance in policing their membership.

In the United States, there is a third regulatory component. The National Futures Association (NFA) is the futures industry's self-regulatory agency. The NFA takes responsibility for registering floor traders on U.S. exchanges.

Exchange for Physicals

Perhaps the fastest growing area of currency trading is the exchange for physicals (EFP) market. The EFP mechanism allows a customer to take a cash currency-position and to exchange it for a futures position. EFPs, in essence, allow off-floor trading of currency futures.

EFPs have existed for years on other exchanges and were originally created to help trade-users of physical commodities to better manage their positions. In the sugar market, EFPs are referred to as AAs, which stands for *against actuals.* In the cotton market, EFPs are known as *ex-pits.* With the growth of currency futures, EFPs found new applications.

The principle appeal of currency EFPs focuses on two features. First, EFPs allow market access when an exchange is closed. It was demand from European traders, who needed access prior to the opening of the U.S. exchanges, who first discovered the convenience of EFPs. Perhaps more than any other market, currencies are traded on a 24-hour basis. EFPs became the mechanism through which futures traders managed their global exposures.

The second feature is the ability to transact the entire amount of the trade at a single price, as is the custom in the interbank market. The system of using locals to provide liquidity to FX futures contracts means that most large transactions are done at multiple prices, a feature which is not generally well-received by clients who prefer to receive a single price. The EFP mechanism allows traders to deal with an FX sales desk in the way that traders are accustomed to. They receive quotes on the full size of their transactions, which are then sent to the appropriate FCMs, and carried on the exchange.

For a bank, pricing an EFP is much the same as pricing a forward, except that the bank winds up with a futures position rather than a forward position.

EFPs do create an interesting capability for the banks who provide them. They allow the bank to separate the execution business from the clearing business. This is particularly well-suited to doing business for fund managers and commodity trading advisors (CTAs). Over the last 10 years, fund managers have become a force to be reckoned with in foreign exchange. These managers represent a desirable client-base to foreign exchange (FX) desks, in that the managers are both active traders and traders whose views on market direction are highly regarded. Dealing rooms seek their business both for the flow of business and for information.

Funds present some logistical difficulties for banks that can be overcome with EFPs. Though funds may be desirable clients, for instance, they can be very difficult to accommodate from a credit perspective. Credit committees that are used to dealing with corporations often cannot extend credit lines to funds, despite the passionate pleas of the sales desk. The same bank that may not wish to extend credit lines is often quite willing to carry the FX exposure in the form of futures contracts. Under that arrangement, the bank's FCM is paid a commission to clear the contracts, and the trading can be conducted through the dealing room as would be the case with forwards. The bank, in essence, is paid for both clearing and execution.

Banks can use EFPs to solicit business, even in situations where the bank will not clear the fund's transactions at all. Hedge funds and CTAs often have very little leeway in deciding where trading is cleared. That decision generally is made by the investor. Very often, funds will have multiple clearing relationships as various investors arrange their own clearing.

With an EFP, the bank can quote the fund manager for the total transaction, then send the fund's futures positions to the respective clearing members by way of an agreement known as a *give-up*. In that situation, a bank can capture the bid/offer spread on the transaction, though it will not ultimately carry any of the fund's positions.

Today, a growing number of banks are viewing EFPs as an important complement to the margin FX business. Through EFPs, banks are finding that they may have a large number of approved margin clients simply by looking at the accounts carried by their FCMs.

Recent Innovations

Extended Access

All exchanges grapple with the issue of providing market access once the exchange floors have closed. As risk management techniques become more sophisticated, clients need the ability to manage positions in all major time zones. EFPs are one approach, but exchanges have actively been developing others.

Several years ago, the CME introduced a screen-based trading system called Globex that allows traders access to CME products (as well as contracts traded on the MATIF, the French futures exchange) when the exchange floor is closed. The CME recently announced the formation of an internal market-making unit, whose function it would be to provide currency prices to Globex.

The Philadelphia Stock Exchange operates a night-trading session in order to provide market access for their European clients. Trading commences in Philadelphia at 4:00 A.M. (EST) and continues through to the end of the U.S. trading day.

FINEX has taken yet another approach to the question of access. In 1994, FINEX commenced operations on a second trading-floor located in Dublin, Ireland. Trading on the exchange begins in Dublin at 8:00 a.m. local time. At the start of the U.S. trading day, the Dublin floor is closed and trading shifts to the New York floor for the remainder of the session. FINEX operates a night session in New York for four hours of the Asian trading-session, though plans call for the opening of an Asian trading-floor. The FINEX approach mirrors interbank practice, where order books are passed to dealing rooms in the major time zones in order to cover global exposures.

Block Orders

Another recent innovation has been the development of block-order pricing. Traditionally, floor traders were only allowed to show the best prevailing bid or offer to clients, regardless of the amount the client wished to price. In other words, a client needing to buy 500 contracts was not allowed to receive a quote on the full amount, but rather would have to accumulate position by buying whatever smaller amounts were on offer in the pit.

In 1992, FINEX created a block-order rule whereby any client trading over 50 contracts could request and receive a quote on the entire transaction. On large transactions, the market-making is done almost entirely by banks which quote for the full amount. As many as 10 banks at a time will actively compete for the trade, when large quotes are requested.

Recently, the CME instituted a block-order capability. It is operated on a separate electronic facility and can be used by any client who is trading over 200 contracts. The CME has recently introduced an "all or none" rule which specifies that, with certain types of orders, no partial fills are allowed.

New Contracts

The CME has recently developed contracts on the currencies of Latin American countries. Early trading in the Mexican peso has been robust. They have also introduced trading in the Brazilian real. The exchange is also introducing seven mark-based currencies that will be available only on their Globex electronic system.

With the opening of the Dublin trading floor, FINEX introduced trading in a wide range of mark-based currency pairs. With the increasing acceptance of block-order pricing, FINEX has been able to introduce liquid contracts in a range of contracts that would not have been viable under the local-pricing model. By relying on interbank market-makers to provide liquidity in less-active contracts, such as mark/Swedish krona which do not produce the regular type of order flow necessary to attract and maintain a large body of floor traders, a broader range of contracts became viable.

FINEX has also introduced dollar-based currencies priced in European terms. Most of the original currency contracts developed were priced in American terms. This was due to the reality that most FCMs in the 1970s had difficulty posting margin in marks, yen, and other currencies. The easiest way to address this technical difficulty was to invert the contract and price everything in dollars. Today, technology has improved, allowing exchanges to trade contracts in European terms, as is the practice in the interbank market.

The Future of Futures

Today, the currency futures sector finds itself in a state of transition. Currency futures were the first financial futures contracts, and their use spawned an industry. Through the 1970s, currency futures represented the cutting edge in financial technology.

In the 1990s, currency futures have experienced sharp declines in volumes. The reasons include a perceived lack of liquidity on the trading floors, difficulty in convincing customers to trade in American terms, and limited access to the exchange floors.

The industry is responding with a broad set of initiatives in these areas. Liquidity concerns are being addressed, with approaches ranging from the FINEX block-order rule (which essentially turns the primary market-making function over to interbank traders) to the CME "all or none" rule (which ensures that customer orders will be completely filled at a single price).

Contracts have been developed that are more consistent with interbank pricing practices. The CME rolling-spot contracts and the FINEX dollar-based contracts are priced in European terms. Liquid contracts are now available in a wide range of currency pairs.

Exchanges have been proactive in improving international access to their products. The CME offers Globex, their electronic trading-system to cover the trading day outside the United States. FINEX operates trading floors in both the United States and Europe.

The growth of the EFP market adds an entirely new dimension to the potential growth of futures. Through EFPs, interbank market-makers can conduct the trading off-floor, and can capture the bid/offer spread and the information flow, while they still carry the positions on a regulated exchange. As banks struggle to reduce systematic settlement-risk, this becomes an increasingly appealing solution.

In short, exchanges are adapting to changes in their client base and in the underlying markets themselves. Exchanges are finding ways to make their products and their infrastructure more compatible with interbank practices. As the walls between the exchange-traded market and the OTC market continue to break down, currency futures increasingly present an interesting solution to a range of FX problems.

CHAPTER 3

Central Banks and the Currency Markets: A Practical Guide

Andrew Hodge
Vice President
Bank Brussels Lambert

Central banks buy and sell currency through intervention and therefore must be included when adding up the transactions of participants in the markets. More important, they control the entire supply of deposits of their own currency and the level of short-term interest rates. Exchange rates can be thought of as the pricing between multiple monetary systems run by the central banks. Central-bank actions are also key to the attractiveness of their country's assets. These actions either build or undermine investors' confidence, which in turn influences investors' willingness to hold assets in any given currency. We will look at all of these issues to determine when central banks can control the market by either changing fundamentals, or dominating key fundamentals such as economic growth, trade performance, investment flows, and momentum and other technical factors. We conclude that central banks often can dominate, especially if both of the central banks of a currency pair are sufficiently dedicated.

Unsterilized Intervention

The simplest way to influence exchange rates is intervention; that is, buying or selling the home currency for another currency in the open market. If the Federal Reserve, for example, buys dollars and sells deutsche marks (DM) and does nothing more, it will increase dollar demand and DM supply in the foreign exchange (FX) market. This action will also reduce the total of dollar deposits outstanding, the U.S. money supply, and increase the DM deposits outstanding. If the latter results are left to stand, the intervention is called unsterilized.

Unsterilized intervention may succeed because the favorable FX market supply/demand effects are reinforced by money-market effects. For the example above, dollar purchases would result in a contraction of the total U.S. money supply and a rise in interest rates. The higher rates and supply squeeze eventually stops excess offers of dollars. It also slows the economy and produces better trade performance—a fundamental adjustment. Announcing this as an unalterable policy may improve confidence and the committed austerity might improve financial markets. There are examples of long-term success such as the Hong Kong Currency Board and the Belgian and Dutch peg against the DM in the 1980s and early 1990s. But there are also failures, in particular the 1992-1993 European parity defences.

Sterilized Intervention

Intervention is sometimes sterilized, which requires that when the home currency is bought or sold for another currency in the FX market, the domestic money-market effects are offset, typically through open-market operations. In the U.S. example above, the FX purchase of dollars would be offset by the domestic open-market purchase of bonds for cash dollars. The U.S. money supply and interest rates would be unaffected in principal. In fact the stated U.S. policy is to always sterilize currency intervention.

Note that if a country offsets currency intervention in its domestic market, the intervention is only half sterilized. In the example above, there would still be an addition to DM liquidity. Nevertheless, if the other central bank of the exchange-rate pair is following an interest rate target in its domestic monetary management, it will offset any intervention impact on its local interest rates. This will in practice sterilize the other half. Or the other central bank could exactly offset the liquidity impact if it was aware of the intervention.

Because the supportive money-market results are lost, sterilized intervention will always tend to be less effective than unsterilized intervention. With global capital markets becoming more integrated, if dollars bought in the FX market are sterilized by dollars sold in the money markets, most of the FX impact is lost. We will also argue that central banks largely recognized this a decade ago. The huge dollar-support sterilized intervention of $165 billion in 1987 that failed throughout the year was probably the catalyst. The Japanese interventions of 1994 and early 1995 that failed until they stopped sterilizing and also targeted monetary policy to FX is a more recent example.

Nevertheless, there are examples when sterilized intervention can still succeed, partly because of the signalling effect and some remaining FX supply/demand impact. The large $2-4 billion U.S. intervention at the dollar/DM peak of 2.04 in September 1989, and the large dollar intervention—at least $1.2 billion—at the interim low of 1.46 in March 1993 were successful by most standards. They reversed a currency trend that the central banks found undesirable. The interventions were also supported by changing macroeconomic fundamentals, which will be discussed later. Most other recent sterilized intervention by major countries—Japan excepted—has been small. Recent rounds of "concerted intervention", when 10–12 central banks intervene and announce at the same time, are mainly signalling. The actual amounts have been relatively small, often less than $200 million for all of the banks together.

Sterilized intervention has therefore been less successful overall and has been diminishing in effectiveness. For the United States, there have been eight days of intervention in 1993, five days each in 1994 and 1995, and none during the first eight months of 1996, all still presumably sterilized. This compares to huge U.S. interventions, often in the billions each day, during a majority of the trading days in 1987. Several recent U.S. interventions might be counted a success. These include pushing the dollar/yen recovery in summer 1995, and the first dollar/mark support in May 1994. But these were probably small on the U.S. side and were supported by a huge shift to expansionary monetary policy in Japan in the first case and by a technical monetary ease by Germany and supportive statements in the second case. The second 1994 dollar/DM defence at DM 1.63 in August was a conspicuous failure, mainly because Germany, while also intervening, undermined the defence with tight DM liquidity and public criticism.

There does, however, remain a role for intervention, even sterilized. The United States and Japan still state that it can be effective—unlike Germany, which has publically minimized the importance of intervention and recently worked to limit their use in Europe (a topic that we will discuss later in this chapter). And certain creditor LDCs (lesser-developed countries) with controlled capital markets, such as Taiwan and some OPEC countries, have been able to permanently sterilize inflows and to add to reserves through sterilized intervention. It is generally easier for a surplus country to prevent currency appreciation than for a deficit country to prevent depreciation.

Monetary Policy

Monetary policy can directly control exchange rates even without intervention. This has become the tool of choice for the central banks of most developed countries, with the exception of the United States. By simple logic, if the supply of currency is sufficiently reduced and interest rates are raised, at some point a weakening price trend against other currencies will be stopped or even reversed. Similarly, with a monetary expansion a strengthening currency trend can be stopped.

This is not an argument for the monetary theory of exchange rates, which states that only money matters. Instead we say that monetary policy can offset other fundamentals. A central bank can be thought of as a monopoly supplier of a product. There is independant buying and selling, and the supplier accepts the prevailing price, but it can manage the price by controlling the supply. The price may fluctuate due to other fundamentals, but eventually the control over supply will dominate. Since an exchange rate is the price between two currencies, there must be control over the relative supply of both currencies.

Of course central banks have other, at times more important, goals for monetary policy, including controlling inflation, maintaining growth and employment, and stabilizing financial markets. These may conflict with exchange-rate goals, although there are techniques for reducing this conflict, which will be discussed later.

Moving from theory to practice, have central banks actually come to rely on these techniques? We believe they have. Short-term fine tuning, particularly of the overnight interest rate markets, is discussed later in this section and in the final section on daily G-7 watching. Long-term targeting, riding the business cycle, and volatility are discussed next. Official statements are analyzed not only for their confidence-building and market influence, but for their true view of the effect of monetary policy (as with intervention there is secrecy and sometimes denial). Times when control can break down, and the causes of such breakdowns, are looked at in the section on governments versus markets. Finally, the Bundesbank and the present European Mark bloc arrangements are a clear example where the Bank of France and other central banks have publically announced their commitment to maintain exchange-rate stability against the DM with interest rates, not intervention. Each of these points is discussed in the sections that follow.

Which interest rate matters? The very shortest maturities in the money markets, overnight or call money, appear most closely linked to foreign exchange.

Volumes are large and directly relate to liquid international deposits (mobile hot money). Internal Federal Reserve studies have shown this correlation to be the closest. At the longest maturities, currency movements can actually become inversely related to interest rates, as the currency trades with asset values or with a loss of confidence.

Targeting the shortest rates to FX can also reduce a conflict with domestic policy. In a currency defence, overnight liquidity can be withdrawn and the overnight rates racheted up—way up. Recently, such overnight rates as 40 percent for Belgium, 100 percent for Ireland, and 500 percent for Sweden have been seen, while longer-term rates were sometimes maintained at single-digit levels. This "twist" in the yield curve allows more lending to go on in the longer maturities than would be the case in a general credit crunch. On the other side, extreme ease in short-term money in Japan during the 1988—1991 bubble-money period was countered further out on the yield curve with quantitative controls on bank lending.

Full understanding of central-bank money-market intervention requires a knowledge of each country's unique system. Implications of reserve announcements or month end tightness, for example, require extensive understanding. But often, important direction can be gained by simply watching changes in the overnight rates for signs of easing or tightening.

Often, central banks will publicize other policies. Under Germany's complex system there is a discount facility and penalty Lombard facility, weekly repos and unpublicized influence over the very short term rates (including customer repos, open-market operations, and short-dated currency swaps). During an easing period in 1994, Germany cut the discount and Lombard rates, the latter from 6 percent to 5.5 percent. Nevertheless the changes were announced with effect *the next day*. Call money which had been trading at below 5 percent jumped to the old Lombard ceiling of 6 percent, showing extreme tightness; and the DM, which had been under pressure, appreciated that day, as it usually does on the day of a formal rate cut. The Bundesbank helps this happen by *raising* call-market rates on the day of a headline interest-rate cut. This makes the currency strengthen and builds confidence. Consequently, and against the supposed fundamentals, it can pay to be long DM on the day of a possible German headline interest-rate cut, and the Bundesbank likes it that way.

Where central banks have functioning discount windows that normally act as a floor on market rates, a drop in market rates below the discount rate can indicate extreme liquidity ease. For Germany, call money fell below the discount in August 1993, immediately after the EMS breakup. In Japan, call money has remained below the 0.5 percent discount rate through August 1996. Both cases were associated with major weakening of the countries' currencies that were intentional. For Germany, the move stopped in its tracks the huge strengthening of DM that many observers expected following the EMS breakup at the end July 1993. It permitted a return of weaker European currencies to near their old central parities.

The new techniques can be combined with intervention, giving the central banks much greater flexibility. Monetary policy can strongly support intervention or can substitute for it. For example,the new style (Figure 1) dollar defence at the beginning of 1988, a high point of cooperation, featured liquidity expansion in Japan and Germany much larger than the first three days joint intervention would have produced if unsterilized, and a continuation of that ease after the intervention ceased. It looked to the market that the tide had turned and that no more central bank dollar support was required after the first three days.

The United States, by contrast, appears to use interest rates relatively little. The narrow-band Fed-funds targeting limits flexibility. Currently, there is a strong body of opinion even among Federal Reserve governors that the dollar should be given little or no weight in setting interest rates. Looking back, however, rates may have been tightened to support the

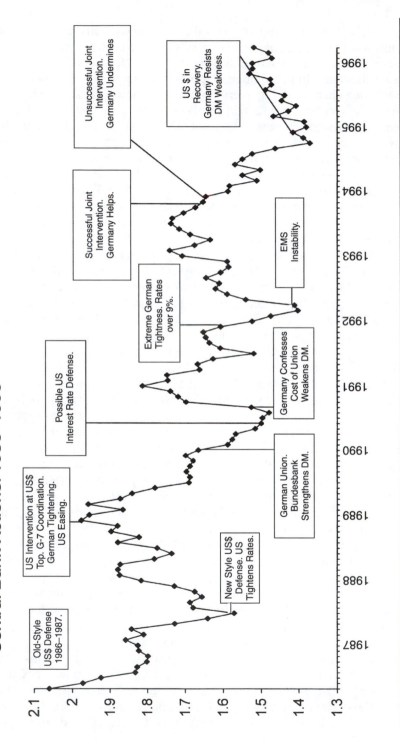

**Figure1   Historic Dollar/Mark
Central Bank Actions: 1986–1996**

dollar in 1987, and the United States was happy to ride the dollar higher on U.S. interest rate tightening in 1988-1989. The latter was part of the dollar rescue (noted earlier), which included easy money in other countries.

More recently, the dollar was weak at the end of 1990, which concerned officials. Fed funds became highly unstable for about three months, the official reason cited being new reserve procedures. The next Federal Reserve quarterly report on foreign-exchange markets cited higher average short-term rates as support for the dollar. This is at most an isolated incident. However, the New York Federal Reserve Bank has instituted an FX analysis group that closely follows the money-market influences on exchange rates of other countries.

In conclusion, the Federal Reserve probably does not apply major short-term money-market measures for FX, and it is unlikely to do so soon. The Federal Reserve does have in-house expertise and could respond if needed with major steps, for example in the event of a future dollar crisis.

Exchange Rates in the Business Cycle: Long-Term Goals

This section examines why central banks would desire *movement* in exchange rates. While sometimes deductive or even speculative—the central banks typically say they only want stability—this information is key to both the direction and the amount of future movement (volatility). Central banks might desire a rise in their currencies to fight inflation and boost confidence and asset markets; or a decline in their currencies to become more competitive and stimulate output. Or they might genuinely want relatively fixed FX rates to reduce uncertainty. When this is sincere, it may well be successful with reduced prospects for volatility, as is currently the case for Europe.

In practice, we observe that exchange rates often move with the business cycle and that this is desirable. When the economy is strong, inflation is rising, and monetary policy is tightening, it is both natural and desirable that the exchange-rate rise to aid monetary policy in cooling the economy and fighting inflation. When the economy is in a slump, interest rates fall. Inflation is less a threat, and there is more excess capacity to reduce a trade deficit. Then a falling, more competitive currency becomes desirable. This direction of exchange rates "riding the business cycle" works with the fundamentals. The fundamental trend might even be exaggerated, but it is not strongly resisted.

These big cycle trends are often profitable to invest in. And even when the central bank gives some sign of trying to limit the trend, a trader should be skeptical. For example, intervention to limit the rise of the dollar during the 1988–1989 expansion and more recently, and similiar intervention to limit the Canadian and Australian dollar during their recent rallies was largely unsuccessful. It was not supported by either monetary policy—which was contradictory—or by apparent economic self-interest. The *appearance* of central-bank resistance may be to moderate the speed of movement and save the final push until the end of the cycle, or even in a perverse way to build confidence. (This currency is so strong that even intervention cannot stop it!)

In contrast, currencies sometimes trade on what I call confidence-based fundamentals. These are often undesirable. For low-savings debtor countries, the confidence-fundamentals such as asset markets, inflation, debt, deficits, central bank credibility, and politics are usually negative. It is logical and often seen that currency defences are used to counter weakness caused by these fundamentals.

On the strong-currency-surplus-country side, there was continuing appreciation of the yen until April 1995. This resulted from flight to quality and excessively favorable confidence. As the economy was in a deepening recession, this became more and more undesirable, and was finally countered by a massive shift to easier monetary policy. It is no exaggeration to say that the large cycle of excessive yen appreciation from over 100 per dollar to 80, then back to 111 recently, was mostly driven by the Bank of Japan. The yen first strengthened, driven by a tight monetary policy that actually helped produce the recession while largely ignoring the strengthening yen. Then the Bank of Japan reacted by running a highly expansive policy that turned the yen sharply weaker and will likely continue to hold it weaker, so long as it is maintained.

Turning away now from the business cycle, the two schools of thought noted earlier—those with a strong currency bias to fight inflation and to preserve confidence and financial markets, and those with a weak currency bias to be more price competitive in foreign trade—are important. Most central banks these days favor the strong currency view, with temporary lapses in recession. They do not believe that currency depreciation alone will produce trade adjustment, particularly when internal demand is strong. Nevertheless, there are differences. For example,the Bundesbank favors the strong-currency approach while the Bank of France, even with new independence and a tougher view, still worries more about competitiveness.

Central banks may also face pressure from governments for a weaker currency. This becomes important if the central bank is not independent. The Federal Reserve faces some pressures because final dollar intervention authority is theoretically with the Treasury, even if monetary policy is independent. For the U.S. the recent Democratic administration has been less dollar-positive. But there was a major shift from Treasury Secretary Benson, who favored lower dollar/yen, to Secretary Rubin who belatedly called for a strong dollar. The Federal Reserve, while not strongly dollar-positive, is at least dollar-neutral. They also resist the calls of some academics who insist on trade-deficit adjustment through devaluation, rather than through austerity and lower consumption.

The above is intended to provide some guide to the genuine currency goals of the central bank. From a trading point of view, if the goal is clear and monetary policy supports it, this may be a favorable trade even if intervention or official statements do not support it. A more detailed view of confidence building and how to interpret official statements follows.

Managing Confidence—Central-Bank Public Relations ✂

Managing expectations about economic policy affects the attractiveness of a country's assets. Central banks play a key role here. Market participants will hold expectations about the future based on recent actions, but also based on central-bank statements about the future. The central banks' announced beliefs about, for example, the causes of inflation, the liklihood of recession, the need for quick action, the effectiveness of monetary policy, and the desirability of a strong currency, will all change expectations about future actions. Or they may simply accord or run counter to investors' opinions about good policy.

This might first appear to be an imprecise or unimportant arm of policy. But we will argue that it is a key part of success for a central bank. Just as modern governments have become adept at managing their own approval ratings, central banks have become more adept at managing financial-market and currency confidence.

How do they do this? Here is a partial list:

- Emphasizing or exaggerating the genuine austerity that has been applied over the last decade.

- Ignoring or pretending to ignore a recession/slowdown.

- Announcing decision rules that target inflation, money supply, lower bond yields, or currency stability, rather than growth or employment.

- Promoting stock and bond investors as a constituency for their own tight policies.

- Gaining or maintaining independence, or at least appearing to.

- Calling for a strong currency and rejecting calls for competitive devaluation.

- Denying that interest rates are a key currency fundamental or that rate changes have currency goals.

- Denying that they may have a temporary desire for a weaker currency with lower rates and a weaker economy.

- Coordinating all of the statements of central bank officials to project these concepts.

The first four items relate to a willingness to run policies much tighter than full employment when necessary. Financial markets favor this, particularly when fiscal or other policies require extra monetary austerity. Ten or 15 years ago, central banks appeared extremely vulnerable to criticism about recession. Now they simply brazen it through, talking about a "meaningful downturn" and "Can't fine-tune the economy to avoid recession."(Chairman Greenspan during the 1991–2 recession). Promotion of the "no long-run Phillips curve " theory (no trade-off between inflation and growth) is another example. More recently, central banks will make statements denying a downturn in the early stages and slide seamlessly to calling for early recovery.

These issues are important for currencies because 1) statements not supporting austerity will weaken the currency, 2) the central banks may deny an oncoming slowdown and rate decline where one could profitably short the currency, and 3) the central banks may make statements about the economy, interest rates, or other key variables with the intent of influencing currency.

With confidence maintained and sufficient austerity, the currencies will often trade on the business cycle. But confidence may be easily lost, particularly for the low-savings debtor countries with relatively lax central banks. Signs this has happened include a bond market that rallies on news or expectations of tighter money, and a currency that trades lower on higher-than-expected inflation reports. Increased sensitivity of currency to stock and bond movements, and debt, deficit and political news is also an unfavorable sign of lost confidence in the central bank.

In fact you should treat fundamental news completely differently based on confidence. On high-confidence, trade business-cycle fundamentals. On low confidence, trade the "confidence-based" fundamentals most.

Central banks may also make direct statements about currencies. These will not typically call for a major move except to correct past excesses—for example, the Bank of Japan calling for the yen to move back above 100/dollar. Nevertheless there are sometimes leaks or rumors about objectives or resistance points. Central banks will also call for a strong currency or a stable currency, which will build confidence if believed.

For confidence building, a brief contrast between the United States and Germany is warranted. Germany will be looked at later as a case study of successful confidence-building and as a country that issues a nearly constant stream of statements. On the economy, Germany minimizes concerns about slowdown/recession in official statements, and claims to target inflation and money supply. The United States, by contrast, shows extreme concern about the economy. The Bundesbank, in effect, sees inflation under every rock while the United States recently sees any inflation surge as a "blip" and assures that even if some shows up it will be temporary. Germany has credibly worked to make the DM the anchor and reference currency of Europe, the currency that has never devalued against any other. The United States has recently turned to calling for a strong dollar but has a long history of benign neglect, and recent active attempts to weaken the dollar against the yen. No wonder that according to some observers (including Federal Reserve officials) the dollar appears undervalued on their measures of the fundamentals.

Central Banks versus the Markets: Who Dominates?

Governments and their central banks cannot force their exchange rates wherever they wish, or demand confidence rather than earning it. The power of markets to force austerity is obvious, even when countries think they've done enough. Markets will defy government wishes if not backed by decisive action, particularly on the monetary side. Nevertheless we will contend that governments have retained a dominant position, perhaps increasing their influence, and that many of the apparent recent episodes of market dominance came because of a conflict between central banks.

The struggle for dominance has advanced remarkably over the last 20 years. Technical advances, huge multiples of trading volumes, and new derivative instruments have favored traders and markets. On the central-bank side, more austerity and market-favorable policies, better confidence-building, more cooperation, and far better technical supply-controls over currency have enabled central banks to keep pace or often dominate.

Following the breakup of Bretton Woods fixed-exchange-rates in 1971-73, exchange rates floated. There were expectations that floating rates would price markets better than governments had, and would permit more monetary autonomy and adjustment of payments. Some of these things happened, but governments did not avoid market discipline nor gain much more autonomy. The discipline took a different form.

Between 1973 and 1987, practically every advanced debtor country had a currency crisis, including Australia, Sweden, Denmark, France, and Belgium. In the 1970s, the UK and Italy had crises so severe that they had to go to the International Monetary Fund for help. And the United States had the beginnings of a crisis in 1987.

The late 1980s, and 1988 in particular, was a high watermark of coordination and reassertion of central-bank credibility. The dollar was rescued. Germany and Japan both put in place mechanisms—labelled "fine tuning" and including several types of new discount facilities—that targeted FX, allowing large additions of liquidity which temporarily drove down their currencies. The United States and other formerly weak currency countries like the UK, Canada, and Australia tightened money to where recessions were produced, also driving up their currencies. High yield became highly sought after, and the world asset-markets boomed. The old inflationary world environment was broken and old-style currency crises—such as that experienced by Mexico in the mid-1990s—have nearly dissappeared in the advanced countries. The European Monetary System entered almost five years of stability, aided by a supportively moderate German monetary policy.

More recently, markets have been less stable and coordination has sometimes broken down. Trading volumes have been rising dramatically, short-term investors and speculators have become huge factors in the market, and new instruments allow highly leveraged positions. Have the central banks lost control? Not really. Most of the new-style currency crises such as the European devaluations are better explained as a central bank conflict.

Did traders rule during those devaluations? George Soros, possibly the world's biggest and best, reportedly made $1 billion on a single trade shorting sterling before its devaluation in September 1992, with what was possibly a $9 billion leveraged position. Others joined him. Why was he successful? Huge positions and signs of weakness help. But in his recent book, *Soros on Soros*, he explains that Bundesbank monetary policy had become contradictory to currency stability, since the policy of high Ger-

---

Questioner: When did you first get an idea that a breakdown in Sterling was imminent?

George Soros: I got my first hint from Bundesbank president Slesinger. He said investors were making a mistake if they thought of the ECU as a fixed basket of currencies. . . . I asked him after the speech whether he liked the ECU as a currency, and he said he liked it as a concept but didn't like the name. He would have preferred it if it were called the mark. I got the message.

Source: *Soros on Soros*, written by George Soros with Byron Wein and Krisztina Koenen. New York: John Wiley & Sons, 1995, p. 81.

man interest rates was inappropriate to conditions in England. Further, the Bundesbank was preparing to withdraw support from the old fixed parities.

In fact, all of the devaluations appeared promoted by the Bundesbank. Its monetary actions and statements actually increased the pressure. And those devaluations are better understood as speculators taking advantage of a conflict between central banks. In this case, the traders and speculators profited by aligning themselves with the dominant central bank in its efforts to appreciate its currency, not by opposing it.

Similarly, the sharp drop in dollar/yen in early 1995 below 100 and down to 80 reflected a conflict as well as insufficient Japanese action. The United States in fact may have enjoyed placing additional pressure on Japan during trade negotiations. They reasoned that, without trade measures to reduce the Japanese surplus, a strong yen would be deserved.

The defences of dollar/mark in 1994—shown in Figure 1—also fit this view. The confidence-based drop of the dollar in spite of a strong economy was resisted by the United States. Coordinated group intervention was arranged. At the first rounds in May, the Germans joined in and helped with easier overnight money and supportive statements. The dollar recovered, temporarily.

But later the mood changed. In July 1994, the Bundesbank and German Government officials mounted outright attacks on U.S. policy, criticizing inflation risks, deficits, fiscal policy, and debt. In August, the dollar weakened again, falling to the 1.63 level. There was more coordinated intervention including Germany. But this time the Germans made unsupportive statements including restating their well-known view that intervention is ineffective. German call-money rose.

The intervention was unsuccessful. The dollar headed to an ultimate low of 1.36. German comments later in this period were mixed. There were occasionally more supportive statements and actions. These often occurred at times of maximum pressure and momentum against the dollar. They may have been designed to keep the dollar weakening from getting out of hand.

Case Study of a Successful Central Bank— The Bundesbank

The Bundesbank is not only held in high regard, and its statements accepted with the highest credibility, but the DM is now the intervention and reserve currency for Europe and is widely regarded as the anchor or reference-store of value. This is quite a remarkable achievment for a medium-sized country—largest in Europe but only by a small margin.

> **George Soros:** . . . We did not act autonomously. We followed the orders of our master, the Bundesbank. Perhaps we understood better than others who our master was and we had better ears in picking up the signals than others did. But there is no doubt in my mind who was master of the hunt. . . . We have entered another period of currency volatility. We look to the Bundesbank for our cue, because it is by far the most powerful force in the currency market.
>
> **Questioner:** This contradicts the generally accepted notion that the speculators are more powerful than the authorities.
>
> **George Soros:** In the case of the Bundesbank it does. We do the dancing but they call the tune.
>
> Source: *Soros on Soros*, written by George Soros with Byron Wein and Krisztina Koenen. New York: John Wiley & Sons, 1995, pp. 84-85.

An extremely tight counterinflationary policy is essential to this stature. And for the Bundesbank, this is backed up by statutory independance from the central government, by a statutory mission solely to fight inflation, and by the support of German popular opinion.

This is not a sufficient explanation. Bundesbank dominance could not have been achieved in our view without:

- The most highly developed techniques of money-market intervention to move currencies.

- Using these techniques on a fine-tuned basis, including frequent shifts in direction both to steer markets on a two-way basis and to reward its supporters.

- A well-organized program of coordinated public statements made very frequently. Credibility is sometimes enhanced by making the markets move in line with the statements.

- Highly capable economics and research capacities combined with cultivation of market commentators and opinion leaders. When the Bundesbank changes its view, the German economics community not only reports it, but changes its own analysis to conform.

- Skills at what might be called economic diplomacy. This has permitted their involvement and outright dominance in such areas as the common currency negotiations

- A domestic interest-rate policy maintaining an image that appears even more austere than the reality, claiming to target money supply and minimizing their concern about the economy.

Bundesbank monetary intervention is complex. There are monthly reserve requirements for banks estimated by itself, a favorable discount window with quotas, a penalty Lombard facility with borrowing rates set 1.5 to 3.0 or more percentage points higher, weekly discount auctions with either price or volume set, and overnight (call) money markets that have no publicized intervention but are often controlled. The latter is often targeted to FX.

The discount and Lombard rates define a wide band in which the call money interest rates can trade and the weekly repos are set. The prospect of stable or preannounced repos permits call money to swing even wildly without changing expectations longer term. Both *changes* in call money and *levels* relative to ceiling and floor and the current repo rate can signal ease or tightness, There will often be a domestic money market explanation reported for movements. The analyst should "read backwards" from rates to spot an FX motivation.

Sometimes this is obvious. In the 1993 EMS breakup, call rates were pushed toward the Lombard ceiling to force the final rupture in late July, then pushed even below the discount floor for three weeks in August to weaken DM and restabilize currencies around the informal Mark Bloc. Extremely tight call money was also seen in the first stages of German union with East Germany, before other EMS devaluations, and periodically on a daily basis like the discount rate cut example cited earlier.

At other times the direction is less obvious, but the Bundesbank watcher can take any noticeable movement and reason backwards. If it accords with the trader's hypothesis of Bundesbank direction, it can confirm the likelihood of a favorable trade.

More than other central banks, the Buba appears willing to provide two-way stability to the markets, both against the dollar and against other European currencies. As the dollar fell to its all-time low in 1994–5, German liquidity remained tight even though Germany was in a rate-cutting mode. But when the dollar showed signs of excessive weakness, German liquidity often eased.

More recently Germany neared the end of its recession with rates near end-of-cycle lows. The dollar started to recover and marks also showed some small depreciation against other European currencies. In this case German technical action was also to limit the trend, tightening liquidity whenever the weakening mark trend showed excess.

Official statements also show some signs of steering. During the recent dollar decline, statements were critical of U.S. policy, as noted earlier. (This was the complete opposite of the 1988–89 dollar rescue when German officials refused to a man to talk about the U.S. budget.) But sometimes Slesinger and later Tietmeyer would come to the rescue. "Strong dollar desirable" or "hopeful of favorable U.S. policies" were common formulations. And when liquidity tightened at the same time, it was a good idea to temporarily stop shorting the dollar or even go long. By these combined techniques, the Bundesbank not only achieves objectives but enhances its own credibility. Other statements can also move currency. Recently the Bundesbank issued statements on strong economy and delay in common currency to strengthen marks; and delay in recovery and common currency on time to weaken marks.

When credibility is high it aids in economic diplomacy. Germany has already achieved success in managing union with East Germany, the EMS breakup, and adoption of the Mark bloc. In the first stage of union the Bundesbank publicly denied there would be serious costs or disruption and made marks strengthen technically without tightening major interest rates. This strengthening was a bad idea economically but built confidence (Figure 1). With markets stabilized, officials then confessed weakness with statements like "Economic union a disaster" (Poehl), and "worst year since 1949" (Waigel). Marks weakened and permitted the belated tightening of monetary policy needed. It was a unique time when doing damage to excessive confidence and admitting problems was a good idea.

I also expect Germany to dominate the common currency negotiations. Germany has already become Europe's informal central bank. Other countries steer against the DM with interest rates, not intervention—the so-called Mark bloc. The DM serves as anchor and intervention currency. Germany also insisted on independence for some of Europe's other central banks. Early independence was a key German demand at Maastricht.

The German blueprint for common currency was revealed in an article published by Otmar Issing in January 1996. It goes way beyond Maastricht with detailed fiscal control, transfer payment reform, labor market reforms, central banking Bundesbank style, and a Euro that is not the ECU. These negotiations could succeed, but will be difficult. If key countries like France balk and negotiations break down even temporarily, Germany may again withdraw support for European currency stability.

We will conclude on the Bundesbank with some thoughts on domestic confidence building. Germany's tough monetary policy is also supported by even tougher rhetoric. A focus on M3 monetary targets reduces apparent concern for the economy, even though studies confirm the obvious. Germany will cut rates in a recession even if M3 is above target.

Handling rate cuts is another example. The Bundesbank finds market expectations of future rate cuts undesirable for confidence. When the economy is weak and the Bundesbank is cutting, they will find a way to portray each cut as the last. This will include, in addition to M3, such arguments as "headline inflation too high," "can't cut while the U.S. is hiking," "import prices are rising."

Then they cut headline rates, and they find it useful to surprise markets on the timing. But on the day or two after a cut they have to justify. Just briefly they note that some other M3 and inflation measure is very good (last six month M3, PPI not CPI, for example) or that "there is no sign of inflation anywhere." But within a week or two they will be back to wringing their hands about inflation.

The bad news for currency traders is the Bundesbank will often surprise you on the timing of rate moves, especially cuts. They often surprise me, anyway. The good news is you can be long marks on the day of a possible rate cut, whether they cut or not, as noted earlier. Confidence building leads them to make marks strengthen, at least temporarily.

Watching The Central Banks—Some Pointers

Currency traders and hedgers want to anticipate the actions of central banks in the markets. They need to know whether central-bank actions will be favorable or unfavorable to their positions. Other fundamentals may also move the markets, and much currency volatility is technical—that is, trend- or momentum-trading not explainable by fundamental news

Therefore if a trend is in place, the key question is: Do the central banks support it or oppose it? Central-bank support for a trend is highly desirable. If business cycle and interest-rate trends are in place, the central bank may in practice support the FX trend even if statements or intervention appear to oppose it. Government statements should also be watched for their valuation of strong currency goals like inflation fighting and asset markets, versus weak currency goals like competitiveness and employment. New governments may often change policy, or the electorate may become angry about unemployment in a recession. Some of these indications may seem obvious, but they will be important to the degree that there is official influence over the FX markets greater than other markets, as we have contended.

Similarly, if a rate is being defended, are both central banks genuinely committed? If not there may, in effect, be central-bank pressure for a large movement when the market breaks. The Bundesbank undermining the European tight money defences in 1992-93 with tight money of its own is a recent example.

More often, central banks are in the business of reducing volatility. They will want to oppose a trend at some point. They may either lean against the wind on a short-term basis, wait for a level to defend, or decisively define a long-term turning point.

If your analysis shows that the exchange rate has overshot, central-bank action can define the turning points. The central banks can often have the same point of view, viewing the markets as unstable and subject to speculation. Their own defence may answer the question: How far is too far? This approach has proved useful at the peak of the yen at 80, at interim support levels for the dollar/mark on German actions in 1994-95, and in the recent belated interest-rate defences of the Mexican peso and Canadian dollar. A sharp shift in monetary policy may show that central banks are finally serious about stabilizing and defending levels. These will often be seen without intervention.

As a trend builds up there may also be increased expectations of further movement. Option pricing and implied volatility may rise. Selling currency puts or volatility at the end of a sell-off where the central bank has just started to defend—particularly if it is a hidden interest-rate defence—can be profitable.

In conclusion, central-bank watching in the FX markets may be an art as well as a science, but it is subject to a systematic approach. Good knowlege of central-bank goals and the tools they can use is often essential even if markets are also driven by other forces. And often the central-bank action or change of policy is the key and dominant force in the market. An investment or forecast can sometimes be based largely on central-bank actions alone.

CHAPTER 4

Speculative Trading and Hedge Funds

Mary Rafferty
Director, Senior Foreign Exchange Advisor
Bank of Montreal, Chicago

The term *hedge funds* has long been a misnomer in the global marketplace, since these entities have a role that is quite distinct from corporate and other institutional participants. Unlike the corporate hedger, who seeks to manage translation and transaction exposure by reducing foreign exchange risk, institutional participants are risk-seekers looking for trading as well as investment opportunities. The main institutional players in the foreign exchange markets range from fund managers to large international banks and their proprietary desks, broker dealers, investment banks, and financial corporations.

Fund managers can be further defined as traditional investment advisors who are registered by the Securities and Exchange Commission (SEC), and who primarily represent equity and fixed-income investors such as mutual funds (retail clients), and pension funds (both public and private) and other tax-exempt entities. The majority of the foreign exchange markets' trillion-dollar-a-day transactions have become dominated by these investment flows, as individuals and institutions have increasingly delegated the management of their portfolios to professionals.

Traditional investment advisors act within macro investment guidelines set forth by regulatory bodies governing investment advisors and the regulatory requirements of their clients. On a micro level, investment advisors must also comply with client specific restrictions as outlined in mutual fund prospectuses and investment management agreements. Investment advisors' mandates may be broad enough to allow adjustments of their portfolios in anticipation of currency movements. International investments are typically measured against industry benchmark indices (e.g., MSCI EAFE index) which could range from zero to 100 percent hedged. In the foreign exchange market, positions taken by an investment advisor are restricted to the unsecured credit lines available from banks, which are usually determined by the size and stability of assets under management with that investment advisor.

International equity managers and global bond managers often look at currency risk from different perspectives. Equity managers may view currency risk as a small component of overall return in stock selection and therefore see hedging as increasing the risk of an investment. The majority of their transactions in the foreign exchange market are securities related (purchase, dividends, and sale). Global bond managers, however, view interest rates and exchange rates as highly correlated and are often active managers of currency risk. Hedging adds flexibility to portfolio management in the following ways: (1) market timing for future investments, (2) protecting an existing investment, (3) yield enhancement, and (4) trading for short-term movements.

Hedge funds are also fund managers. Hedge funds indeed use derivative instruments commonly applied to hedge risk; but instead, hedge funds assume the role of the speculator, much like in the futures market. The term *speculator* actually evolved from the futures market, where participants are considered to be hedgers if they own the underlying assets and take physical delivery, or are considered to be speculators if they look to profit from short-term movements. Hedge funds are commonly referred to as speculators and differ from investment advisors who utilize traditional hedging techniques. Many hedge fund managers are veteran investment advisors who have decided to go into business for themselves.

What Is a Hedge Fund?

Hedge funds are broadly defined as privately subscribed investment vehicles that take speculative positions based on careful market analysis of different asset classes under both rising and declining market conditions. Some hedge funds may specialize in a few market sectors but they have wide-ranging flexibility in terms of instruments and risk management techniques. The asset size of a hedge fund may range from $1 million to $10 billion, and hedge funds seek to maximize total return rather than to outperform benchmarks.

The hedge fund concept evolved from the equity markets as a method for protecting long equity-positions. The first hedge fund manager was A. W. Jones who instituted the idea of hedging against shifting market sentiment by going long some stocks and selling short other stocks in equal proportions. The hedge fund industry has since developed into more than just "hedging" and has evolved into an *alternative investment strategy*. Traditionally, the majority of hedge fund investors have been wealthy individuals. However, institutional investors have recently become more significant participants as they have come to recognize the benefits that hedge funds can offer as an alternative investment vehicle.

Hedge funds are relatively new to the foreign exchange markets and have joined the trend toward international diversification. Exchange rates were allowed to float in 1971; and in 1985, the central banks began to drive the U.S. dollar lower in order to stimulate U.S. exports. Hedge funds recognized the opportunities available and were attracted to these markets where business is conducted in the privacy of bank trading-rooms. The cash foreign exchange markets are open 24 hours with trading starting on Sundays in Australia and closing on Friday afternoons in North America.

Types of Hedge Funds

Hedge funds can be categorized by the strategy they employ within a market sector.

Global macro (also called opportunistic) hedge funds seek to profit by positioning for changes in interest rates, exchange rates, and/or equity prices in global markets. The trading horizon may be very short term and the style may be discretionary (fundamental), or systematic (technical), or a combination of both. Global macro hedge funds employ leverage in the foreign exchange markets with the majority of assets concentrated with a few large managers.

Event driven hedge funds profit by investing in special situations such as bankruptcies, reorganizations, or mergers. Hedge funds may be both long or short the securities of companies involved in these corporate transactions.

Relative value hedge funds are structured to profit from pricing mis-alignments by going long the undervalued and/or short the overvalued securities. They can specialize in equities, convertible bonds, fixed income, or some combination.

Emerging markets hedge funds seek to profit from uncovering and exploiting inefficiencies in the developing financial markets by using a variety of securities listed in Asia, Eastern Europe, and Latin America.

What Makes Hedge Funds Unique

Hedge funds differ from traditional investment advisors in several ways. First of all, hedge funds are *less regulated*. Depending on whether they are chartered as onshore or offshore, hedge funds escape the registration and reporting requirements that apply to traditional investment advisors. Also, hedge funds are not required to publicize the performance of their particular fund. They may be subject to some oversight by the Commodity Futures

Trading Commission and National Futures Association if they are involved in the U.S. futures markets or if they act as commodity trading advisors.

Onshore

Hedge funds chartered in the United States are generally structured as private limited partnerships with the manager acting as general partner along with the limited partners who invest in the fund. Onshore private funds are limited to 99 shareholders and are restricted from advertising in order to receive exemption from the Investment Company Act of 1940 and the Securities and Exchange Commission (SEC). Investors are required to be accredited, which is defined as having an annual income exceeding $200,000 or a minimum net worth of $1 million. The client lists include a growing number of institutional investors as well as the money management offices of wealthy families. Minimum investments range from $250,000 to $10 million. Fund of funds, which allocate capital among several hedge fund managers, may have a lower minimum investment while possibly obtaining additional diversification. Overseas investors in U.S. onshore hedge funds are subject to U.S. tax and securities laws that impose withholding taxes and require that earnings be distributed annually.[1]

Offshore

The main market for hedge fund investors is outside the United States as offshore wealth is attracted to fund performance, and investors are exempt from U.S. taxes. These funds are generally structured as corporations whose shares may be listed on a non-U.S. exchange, and therefore they do not limit the number of shareholders. Some U.S. investment advisors offer offshore private funds to their overseas clients.

Leverage

Another factor that distinguishes hedge funds from other traditional investment activity is leverage. Leverage is a method of increasing the potential gains of an investment using limited capital or borrowed money. In the interbank foreign exchange market, most hedge funds are fully collateralized. Banks require initial margin such as cash, Treasury bills, and in some cases, stock. Position limits are established based on available collateral, much like in the futures market. Depending on the client relationship, a typical margin would be 5 percent with a potential leverage factor of up to 20 times capital. Position risk is monitored 24 hours a day and continuously marked to market. If the margin level becomes inadequate, additional margin is required, or the positions are reduced or even liquidated. Settlement risk is not an issue because currencies are not delivered. Instead, profits or losses are converted into U.S. dollars. Few funds are offered unsecured credit lines by banks, but some may have a hybrid or "quasi" arrangement whereby collateral is posted once a threshold position is reached, or where currency settlement lines are established for delivery purposes.

Large asset-valuation changes may occur with leverage. High profit-or-loss potential exists by the same leverage factor when the change in market sentiment is largely one-sided. However, the use of leverage is not the only factor in a fund's overall risk. It is just one measure along with the liquidity of the investment, diversification of the portfolio, experience and integrity of the fund's principal, and the risk management techniques employed.

Compensation

Traditional investment advisors are usually compensated with a management fee based on the assets under management. However, the incentive for hedge funds is performance-based. The primary objective is to maximize overall returns rather than to increase assets under management. Although fee structures vary, a typical management fee is 1 percent of the assets under management and an incentive fee of about 20 percent of profits. Some funds only charge incentive fees once a benchmark return has been reached. Furthermore, when losses occur in any year, funds will not collect management fees until those losses are recovered. This is commonly referred to as the *high-water mark.*

Historically, hedge funds have strictly targeted and controlled the amount of assets under management. They recognize that at some point, an increase in assets may make it more difficult to deliver returns, and this increase can actually hinder performance over time. Some hedge funds have even returned capital. The prevailing sentiment in the hedge fund industry is that smaller can be better.

Hedge funds are perceived in the currency world as *market leaders,* and trading by some of the largest funds can serve as a signal for other institutional participants to reexamine their own unleveraged investment positions. The 1992 European Monetary System (EMS) crisis serves as a reminder that international capital markets can be prone to quick shifts in sentiment regarding the exchange rate outlook.

What Happened in September 1992

The growing perception by international investors was that member countries of the European Monetary System were on a continuous path towards European Monetary Union (EMU) which prompted investment flows into the higher-yielding European rate mechanism (ERM) currencies.[2] This was known as the *convergence play*, based on the idea that interest rate differentials would eventually narrow.

The Danish and French referendums on Maastricht in September 1992 challenged the certainty of EMU, and speculators bet successfully that the European central banks could not artificially support the British pound, Italian lira, or Swedish krona at unrealistic levels. Hedge funds reportedly sold these vulnerable currencies forward and established interest rate positions in anticipation of a short-term interest rate defense of the currency by the central banks. These funds later bought back the devalued currencies and locked in large profits at the expense of the central banks. These moves were further exaggerated by institutional investors who unwound their convergence strategies. Italy and the United Kingdom were eventually forced to pull out of the ERM.

Summary

The distinction between hedging and speculation occasionally converges when market participants become convinced that existing parities are out of line with fundamentals and that the change is likely to be in one direction. Institutional participants, and hedge fund managers in particular, play a significant role in the current market environment because of their investment flows and their ability to influence market direction.

Endnotes

1. *Institutional Investor*, January 1992.

2. International Monetary Fund, 1993 *World Financial Economic Survey*.

CHAPTER 5

Fundamental Analysis

Earl I. Johnson
Foreign Exchange Economist
Bank of Montreal, Chicago

Introduction

Fundamental analysis involves a detailed study of macroeconomic indicators that interact to determine the performance of individual economies, and a fundamentalist is generally defined as a trader or forecaster who relies primarily on the analysis and forecasts of economic fundamentals to predict exchange-rate trends. Since 1973, the global economy has functioned under a floating exchange-rate system in which currency values primarily reflect market forces resulting from external balance adjustments subject to occasional governmental intervention. Exchange-rate volatility has characterized the floating exchange-rate system and attempts to explain currency fluctuations typically involve a detailed analysis of the fundamental macroeconomic variables determining the relative performances of global economies. Over the long run, currency movements are primarily influenced by underlying economic factors such as inflation and trade flows, however, in the short run, economic fundamentals are often swamped by speculative capital flows, political events, or technical considerations.

Sophisticated versus Judgmental Models

Sophisticated econometric models can be constructed in an attempt to accurately predict changes in key macroeconomic variables that influence currency fluctuations. Unfortunately, such mathematical exercises are expensive and time-consuming; therefore, nonmathematical or judgmental approaches to fundamental analysis are more widely utilized within the dealing community. Since few foreign exchange traders are formally trained as economists, the majority of dealers would not properly be classified as fundamentalists. Nevertheless, virtually all dealers at times are forced to utilize economic fundamentals in formulating their trading strategies even though they may not always be consciously aware they are doing

so. Many experienced foreign exchange (FX) dealers become skilled practitioners of economic analysis even though they have received no professional instruction in economics. Economic knowledge acquired through
on-the-job training in a dealing room often proves to be more valuable in
trading and forecasting than formal lessons learned from a textbook.

Understanding the significance of widely publicized economic indicators and learning how to forecast trends in these economic variables is
critical to analyzing and understanding the complex global economic environment in which foreign exchange rates are determined. An exchange rate
is simply the price of a currency expressed in terms of another currency,
and these currency prices are determined by supply-and-demand forces
resulting from the interaction of domestic and international macroeconomic variables. When conducting global economic analysis, it is important to remember that international economics involves comparisons of the
relative economic performances of different countries. In 1995–1996, the
United States registered an unimpressive 2 percent real economic growth;
however, this moderate growth performance was dollar supportive since
it compared favorably with the 1 percent real growth performances of many
European economies.

Market Psychology and Expectations

When judging the importance and relevance of specific economic variables,
it is also necessary to study prevailing market psychology and existing
market expectations. At any given time, market psychology may be positive
or negative toward a country or a currency, and this prevailing sentiment
can determine how traders react to economic statistics and magnify currency fluctuations. When bullish sentiment prevails, dealers tend to down-
play or ignore bearish economic statistics while eagerly reacting to positive
economic data that confirm the bullish viewpoint. The consequence is a
market "bandwagon effect" which exaggerates swings in exchange rates,
since prevailing sentiment tends to be self-reinforcing and pushes currency
values beyond reasonable trading ranges consistent with economic fundamentals. Prevailing market expectations about pending releases of economic data can produce surprising market responses. When financial
markets hold strongly held expectations about pending economic data, the
release of actual economic statistics can elicit a perverse response if actual
data deviate significantly from market consensus. For example, a "good"
economic number, if it proves to be significantly less favorable than widely
anticipated, might trigger a market sell-off.

As mentioned earlier, judgmental evaluation of economic data is the
most common application of fundamental analysis to foreign exchange
trading. When attempting to forecast the future value of a currency, the

dealer or economic analyst may simply construct a list of positive and negative economic variables that influence future supply and demand forces for the currency. A sample grid for the Canadian dollar is shown in Table 1. Correctly determining which economic factors should be included and assigning proper weights to the various factors will determine the success of such a forecasting exercise. Forecasting exchange rates is clearly an art rather than a science, and there is no substitute for the intuitive judgment of an experienced currency forecaster.

Shifting Fundamentals

By measuring and predicting trends of important macroeconomic variables, forecasters and dealers gain insights into the fundamental forces determining future currency values. The key to successful forecasting and trading profits is to correctly identify those specific economic and financial factors that market participants are focusing their attention on. Just as in the fashion world, there are fads in the currency markets, which means that at various times FX dealers tend to be preoccupied with different economic variables and to base trading decisions on anticipated trends in those variables. Over time, dealers often shift their primary focus from one economic indicator to another. In the 1970s, merchandise trade-flows were the dominant factor influencing exchange-rate fluctuations, and the trade performances of major economies, such as Japan, were carefully scrutinized for clues to currency trends. In the 1980s, monetarist doctrines dominated economic policy decision-making in the United States and several other nations, so foreign exchange dealers carefully scrutinized weekly money-supply data in order to predict inflation, interest rates, and exchange-rate fluctuations. The German Bundesbank still sets yearly targets for annual growth of the M3 monetary aggregate and utilizes this monetary data in formulating interest rate policies. The Federal Reserve has de-emphasized

Table 1   Canadian Dollar

Positive	Negative
• 1.5 percent inflation	• BOC easing rates
• $20 billion trade surplus	• Quebec separatist tensions
• Shrinking budget deficit	
• Current-account deficit narrowing	
• 5 percent real rate of return on bonds	

the importance of the monetary aggregates in conducting monetary policy, since financial deregulation has disrupted the close linkages between the monetary aggregates and economic activity which formerly prevailed.

Due to extensive financial integration in the global economy, capital movements and the diversification of international financial assets have dominated activities in the foreign exchange market over the past 10 years. The liberalization of global capital flows and the resulting globalization of institutional investments have triggered explosive growth in the global foreign-exchange market. Given the international perspective of institutional investors, fluctuations in exchange rates today often reflect shifting investment demands for various currencies based on yield, risk, or economic fundamentals. Shifts in short- and long-term real interest-rate differentials between Germany and the United States have been strongly correlated with fluctuations in the dollar/deutsche-mark exchange rate. See Figure 1.

In the early 1980s, the United States experienced widening budget and current-account deficits, but the resulting high real interest rates attracted sizable foreign capital inflows that caused a substantial appreciation of the dollar. A detailed discussion of the critical role of interest rate differentials in exchange-rate determination is included in a separate chapter.

Figure 1 The DM/US$ Exchange Rate and the U.S./German Real Interest-Rate Differential (10-Year Bond Yields Less CPI)

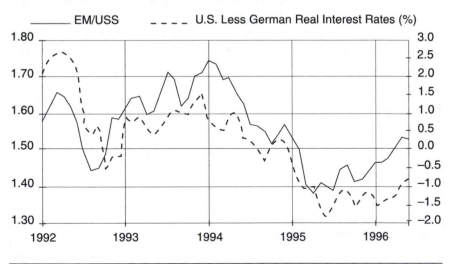

Macroeconomic Variables

Obviously, in a global economic environment, a myriad of economic variables interact to determine exchange-rate levels, so it is impossible to monitor and predict all relevant economic fundamentals when forecasting specific currencies. Fundamentalists, therefore, generally focus on the most important economic factors that traditionally have proven to have the best record in predicting exchange-rate movements. For the purpose of this brief overview, we will focus on five key explanatory variables: growth prospects, inflation, budget policies, and balance of payments, including capital flows. There is no substitute for economic forecasts prepared by an experienced economist; however, forecasts of key economic variables can be readily obtained from international organizations such as the International Monetary Fund (IMF) and the Organization for Economic Cooperation and Development (OECD), as well as from private financial institutions and governmental bodies. When utilizing governmental forecasts, it is important to recognize the inherent political bias contained in official forecasts and to make relevant adjustments in order to achieve realistic predictions.

Growth Performances

Exchange rates reflect the overall performance of individual economies, and international comparisons of economies are normally conducted on the basis of annualized real-economic-growth performances. The key statistic describing the underlying strength of an economy is gross domestic product (GDP). This is the broadest measure of aggregate economic activity encompassing all domestically produced goods and services purchased by consumers, businesses, government, and foreigners. Projections of real growth performances must be carefully interpreted, since economic growth can have an ambiguous or mixed impact on foreign exchange rates. Accelerating growth suggests a growing healthy economy with rising credit demands and higher interest rates that should support the domestic currency; however, it also suggests rising import demands and possibly a weaker trade performance. Rapid growth beyond capacity constraints could also foster inflationary pressures that might eventually yield currency depreciation. Sluggish growth performances as experienced by European economies in 1995 and 1996 yielded improved budgetary performances, declining inflation, and improved trade performances. European currencies should have benefited from these favorable benefits of weak growth; however, monetary authorities adopted accommodative monetary policies to stimulate economic growth, and the resulting lower interest rates undermined these currencies relative to the dollar, which benefited from faster growth and favorable interest-rate differentials.

Inflation—Purchasing Power Parity

Inflation, which is defined as an increase in the general level of prices, tends to erode the domestic and external purchasing power of a currency. Purchasing power parity (PPP) is one of the oldest theories of exchange-rate determination, which simply states that over time changes in exchange rates reflect the relative price performances of different countries. If inflation in the United States exceeds Japanese inflation by 3 percent, relative PPP predicts the dollar will eventually decline by 3 percent against the yen. Unfortunately, the time frame over which exchange rates shift in response to inflation differentials has proven to be of uncertain duration, so PPP is considered to be of little value in predicting short-term exchange-rate trends. Calculating PPP equilibrium levels for currencies is complicated by several conceptual problems, namely selecting the proper price indices to compare inflation performances as well as choosing an appropriate base year when currencies were near equilibrium levels.

Historical studies confirm that over longer time-periods exchange rates tend to move toward the equilibrium rates calculated by PPP theories; however, over short and medium time-horizons currency values can deviate significantly from PPP levels. The problem with PPP calculations is that they focus solely on price adjustments in order to achieve equilibrium among internationally traded goods, and they ignore the financial and capital flows which currently overwhelm global trade-flows. For traders, PPP calculations have little or no relevance in their trading strategies, but when economists prepare 5- or 10-year currency forecasts, PPP studies provide a useful guide to the longer-term trends of currency values. Empirical studies also indicate that PPP calculations can be effective when forecasting Latin American currencies in economies experiencing hyperinflationary conditions. Although few traders pay attention to PPP in a formal sense, comparative rates of consumer price inflation that are prevailing in major economies clearly are studied for clues to shifts in monetary policies and relative interest rate levels.

Fiscal Policy and Exchange Rates

Government expenditure and tax programs play an important role in global economic stabilization policies, so fiscal policy decisions obviously will influence exchange-rate movements. Fiscal policy adjustments have dominated economic policy decision-making in the 1990s as chronic budget-deficit countries, such as the United States, Canada, Australia, and Sweden, implement deficit-reduction programs while European Union members struggle to comply with strict Maastricht fiscal criteria in order to gain membership in the proposed single currency—the Euro. Economic theory provides no definitive models to explain the specific pressures which fiscal policy will exert on the external value of the domestic currency; in fact, tax and spending decisions by governments often exert positive and negative influences on exchange rates, so the overall impact of fiscal policy in determining currency values is difficult to ascertain. Since Japan was the last major nation to register a budget surplus in 1990, we will focus our attention on government budget deficits, which represent an excess of federal outlays over tax revenues. Federal budget deficits exert an initial stimulative impact on economic activity while exerting upward pressures on interest rates. Higher domestic interest rates will initially attract foreign capital that will put upward pressure on the domestic currency; however, protracted budgetary deficits that produce escalating government indebtedness will eventually push the domestic currency downward. Rising levels of government debt in chronic budget-deficit countries eventually prompt foreign investors to demand a larger risk-premium, and this financing burden may depress the domestic currency. Budgetary deficits constitute national dissavings in a macroeconomic sense, and this generates current-account deficits which historically are strongly correlated with exchange-rate fluctuations.

United States
The United States has registered continuous, yearly, federal budget-deficits since 1970. From 1982–1986, the Reagan Administration pursued an expansionary fiscal policy and the resulting high real rates of return on dollar assets attracted sizable foreign capital inflows that contributed to significant dollar appreciation. Safe haven flows and foreign investor confidence in the inflation-fighting credibility of the Federal Reserve help explain dollar strength in the early 1980s. The widening budget deficits contributed to escalating current-account deficits, which undermined the dollar during the late 1980s. United States budget deficits ballooned to $290 billion in fiscal 1992, but 1996 will be the fourth consecutive year in which the deficit has declined. See Figure 2.

Canada
For more than two decades, Canada has wrestled with persistent budget deficits, while net foreign debt as a percentage of gross domestic product (GDP) rose above 70 percent. When the Liberal government took office in 1993, reducing large budget deficits became a top priority, and impressive strides in fiscal austerity have been made. From 42 billion Canadian dollars (C$) in fiscal 1994, the federal deficit should shrink to C$29 billion in fiscal-year 1996, while the deficit to GDP ratio shrinks to 3 percent—second only to the United States in the G-7 nations. Further shrinkage in budgetary deficits means significantly reduced debt service charges, which will shrink chronic current-account deficits while lowering the risk premium on Canadian dollar bonds held by international investors. See Figure 3.

Figure 2 The U.S. Dollar and the U.S. Federal Budget Deficit

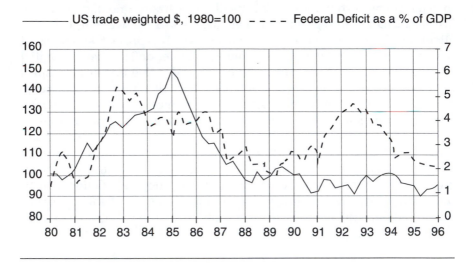

——— US trade weighted $, 1980=100 – – – – Federal Deficit as a % of GDP

Figure 3 The C/U.S.$ Exchange Rate and the Canadian Budget Deficit as a Percent of GDP

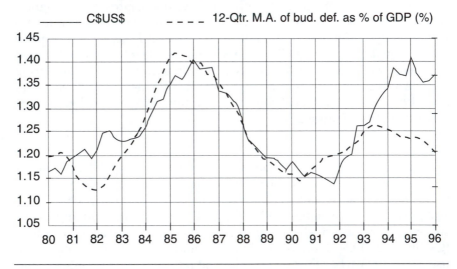

——— CUS – – – – 12-Qtr. M.A. of bud. def. as % of GDP (%)

Sweden

Severe recessionary conditions prevailed in Sweden in the early 1990s reflecting the cumulative impact of legendary welfare-state expenditures. Public indebtedness doubled in three years, while the budget deficit reached 10 percent of GDP, the highest rate prevailing within the 26 OECD nations. A Social Democratic government assumed office late in 1994 and quickly embarked on drastic cutbacks in government spending, which have paid dividends for the economy and the krona. From December 1994 to June 1996, the Swedish krona appreciated more than 11 percent versus the dollar, while the deutsche mark and other European currencies held steady versus the dollar.

Balance-of-Payments Analysis

Exchange-rate determination has historically focused on the international activities and external balances of global economies, which seems especially relevant today since postwar trade liberalization has fostered a dramatic explosion of global trade and investment. Balance-of-payment analysis has traditionally played an important role in attempting to explain the behavior of exchange rates. Balance-of-payments accounts document a country's commercial relationships with all other nations and, therefore, summarize the supply-and-demand forces that determine currency values. Balance-of-payments transactions are classified or divided into two basic categories: the current account and the capital account. The current account is the broadest balance-of-payments classification, which encompasses receipts and payments involving merchandise goods, services, investment income, and transfer payments. The capital account measures international transactions involving financial assets and is considered to be the mirror image of the current account, since it documents how goods and services transactions are financed. A current-account deficit must be financed by foreign capital inflows—asset sales or foreign borrowings—as residents pay for their excessive purchases from foreigners. A current-account surplus generally puts upward pressure on the domestic currency, since earnings from export sales exceed payments for import purchases.

The current account measures the international competitiveness of an economy and obviously is a critical determinant of exchange-rate pressures, since all the commercial relationships generate foreign exchange transactions. The merchandise trade balance, comprising the difference between exports and imports of physical goods, typically is the major component of the current account, so forecasting trade flows is the key to projecting trends in the current account. The merchandise trade balance in a fundamental macroeconomic sense is determined by domestic savings and investment flows. In practical terms, however, attempts to forecast the future trade performance of a nation typically focus on the price competitiveness of export products, import demands, and the level of domestic demand prevailing in major export markets. One of the major problems involved in forecasting trade flows is the lengthy time lags with which trade patterns respond to exchange-rate changes—often in excess of 12 months.

The export performances of resource-rich countries, such as Canada and Australia, are critically dependent on the strength of global commodity prices. A projected synchronized expansion of the global economy in 1997 should benefit the Canadian and Australian dollars. Conversely, the trade performance of Japan, which imports 99 percent of its petroleum needs, can be greatly influenced by oil prices. During 1995–1996, the United States ranked as one of the world's most competitive nations, so its export products were competitively priced in world markets. Nevertheless, relatively weak demand prevailed in major export markets, such as Canada, Japan, and Mexico, so the annual U.S. merchandise trade deficit hovered near $170 billion.

U.S. Current Account

The United States has registered continuous current-account deficits since 1982, and the excess supply of dollars resulting from these deficits is considered to be a major cause of dollar weakness over the past decade. These current-account deficits indicate that U.S. residents have been spending more on goods and services than they produce, and that they are borrowing from foreigners to finance this excessive consumption. National income accounting reveals current-account deficits constitute insufficient domestic savings relative to domestic investment. Since U.S. federal budget deficits constitute national dissavings, chronic U.S. budget and current-account deficits are inextricably linked, so most economists believe effective U.S. budget deficit reduction is an essential precondition for shrinking U.S. current-account deficits. See Figure 4.

Canadian Current Account

Since 1983, Canada has registered continuous, yearly, current-account deficits which reached 4 percent of GDP in the early 1990s. Canada traditionally has recorded merchandise trade surpluses; however, chronic current-account deficits are attributable to dividend repatriation to U.S. parent companies plus interest rate payments to foreign bondholders. Fortunately, fiscal austerity in Canada over the past four years has dramatically bolstered domestic savings relative to domestic investment, which has translated into a dramatic improvement in Canada's current-account position. A record $4.1 billion merchandise trade surplus in May 1996 suggests that in the second quarter, Canada's current account shifted into surplus for the first time since 1984. This structural shift in the domestic savings/invest-

Figure 4 The U.S. Dollar's Trade-Weighted Index and the U.S. Current-Account Balance

——— FRB trade-wgt. US$ index, 1985=100 _ _ _ _Current Account (US$ bn.)

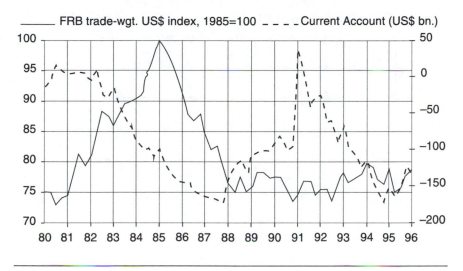

ment balance and in Canada's external accounts will pay valuable dividends in the form of reduced reliance on foreign borrowing, reduced debt service payments, and a significantly stronger Canadian dollar. PPP studies generally indicate an equilibrium value for the Canadian dollar below 1.20. See Figure 5.

Economic Theory

Economic theory naturally includes abundant literature analyzing the theoretical role which trade, money, and financial assets play in determining exchange rates. Unfortunately, this body of theory has proven to have little practical application in formulating currency forecasts. Theoretical discussions of exchange-rate determination focus on the concept of a fundamental equilibrium exchange-rate and postulate cyclical and structural forces causing currency values to gravitate toward equilibrium levels over time. Equilibrium exchange-rates are defined as currency values that enable a country to achieve full employment domestically while simultaneously balancing its external accounts. Unfortunately, fluctuations in currency values during the past 23 years of floating exchange-rates have greatly exceeded projected equilibrium rates produced by theoretical models. Equilibrium exchange-rates are strictly a theoretical concept, but analyzing disequilibrium conditions in domestic economies, global capital markets,

Figure 5 The Canadian Dollar's Trade-Weighted Index and Canada's Current-Account Balance

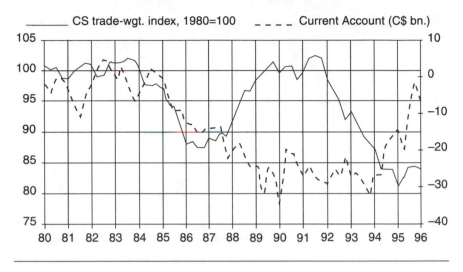

and global payment flows provides good insight into the fundamental forces influencing exchange rate fluctuations.

In the 1960s and 1970s, attempts to explain exchange-rate fluctuations and the adjustment of international payments imbalances focused attention on two types of asset equilibrium models: the monetary approach and the portfolio balance model. Monetary models of exchange-rate determination view balance-of-payments disequilibria to be strictly a monetary concept involving shifts in the supply and demand for money. Balance-of-payments deficits reflect an excessive supply of money, while excessive demand for money yields payments surpluses. Such simplistic models have proven to be of limited value in explaining exchange-rate fluctuations, but they do focus attention on the implications of monetary policy adjustments, which obviously have inflationary implications and do influence global investors' preferences for various currencies. For example, the traditional strength of the deutsche mark can primarily be attributed to monetary policy decisions of the Bundesbank, which has achieved an enviable reputation as an inflation fighter and defender of deutsche mark stability. The success of the Federal Reserve in stabilizing consumer prices near 3 percent over the past four years also provided a sound basis for dollar appreciation in 1995–1996. More sophisticated portfolio balance models focus on factors influencing the demand and supply for various financial assets, emphasizing investor preferences for either domestic or foreign securities. Initial results on the benefits of financial asset research in predicting exchange rates is discouraging. Nevertheless, since these asset models perceive individual currencies as investment vehicles, further financial research should yield insights into the construction of diversified global investment portfolios.

Capital Flows and Exchange Rates

Trade flows and current-account balances traditionally dominated balance-of-payments analysis; however, in the 1980s and 1990s capital flows overwhelmed trade flows in global markets, so capital-account transactions have assumed primary importance in exchange-rate determination. The integration of global financial markets combined with financial deregulation and technological advances in communication have significantly increased the international mobility of capital. The liberalization of cross-border financial flows and the explosive growth of securities markets throughout the globe has fostered unprecedented growth in international portfolio investments. Banks, corporations, exchanges, and investment houses have traditionally constituted the major participants in the foreign exchange market. In the past decade, however, a new dominant player has entered the market—global institutional investors (mutual funds, pension funds, insurance companies, and hedge funds). Global pension fund managers have become key players in the foreign exchange market and their portfolio-diversification decisions generate massive capital flows that are often the primary short-run determinants of exchange-rate fluctuations.

Since institutional and private investors can readily shift huge sums of investment capital from currency to currency, these changing investment demands can play a decisive role in determining exchange-rate movements. The resulting portfolio capital flows at times appear to contradict basic financial tenets. International economics textbooks normally state that higher short-term interest rates bolster a currency by attracting interest arbitrage inflows; however, rising money market rates may actually *undermine* a currency if these rates trigger a stock and bond market sell-off that discourages portfolio investment. Mid-year 1996, speculation about the Federal Reserve's probable money-supply tightening, coupled with disappointing corporate earnings, triggered a Dow Jones sell-off that contributed to a dramatic 3 percent drop in the dollar/mark in one day during mid-July. Increased capital mobility clearly complicates the task of predicting exchange-rate fluctuations. Attempting to forecast global capital movements is hampered by the lack of current data on capital transactions, as well as uncertainty regarding the decision-making strategies of global portfolio managers regarding exchange-rate expectations and risk preferences.

Fundamentalism—Practical Applications

In order to understand fundamentalist forecasting methodology, it might be beneficial to summarize foreign-exchange market conditions prevailing in late 1995 and early 1996 in order to illustrate how economic variables interacted to explain exchange-rate dynamics. Despite disappointment over the lack of a credible U.S. budget agreement, the dollar entered 1996 with a firm undertone bolstered by European interest-rate reductions and expectations of 2 percent U.S. real economic growth, which contrasted favorably with stagnant growth in Germany, France, and Switzerland. Interest rate differentials supported the dollar as strong February employment data triggered speculation about the Federal Reserve tightening monetary policy, while monetary authorities in Japan and Europe pursued accommodative monetary postures to stimulate growth.

Accelerating Japanese economic growth and rising import demands, which narrowed monthly trade surpluses, contributed to yen slippage against the dollar from 103 to 107 before speculation in the spring about firmer Japanese interest rates prompted a yen surge back to 104. The yen subsequently slumped to the 111 level before retracing back to 107 in response to expectations for rising Japanese interest rates coupled with signs that shrinkage in monthly trade surpluses was slowing. The U.S. dollar rose from deutsche mark (DM) 1.43 at year-end to a spring peak of DM 1.5490, but in mid-July the dollar reversed direction, plunging more than 3 percent in one day, due to a U.S. equity sell-off and widespread speculation that European interest rates had bottomed out. Delays in Bundesbank repo rate cuts and speculation about European monetary union (EMU) delays supported the mark near DM 1.47. At the end of 1995, the Canadian dollar closed near 1.3640, benefiting from political stability in the wake of the October rejection of Quebec independence. During the first seven months of 1996, Canadian dollar fluctuations were largely confined within a narrow 1.3550 to 1.3750 range. An accommodative Bank of Canada monetary policy curbed Canadian dollar appreciation, but the currency was supported by solid economic fundamentals including 1.5 percent inflation, narrowing current-account deficits, and fiscal austerity at the Federal and Provincial levels.

Global Implications of the U.S. Economy

Global traders and currency forecasters attempting to predict trends in major currencies must devote considerable time to understanding the intricacies of the U.S. economy, since U.S. economic variables play a critical role in determining trends within the global economy. Although the United States no longer enjoys the pre-eminent position it enjoyed in the early postwar period, it remains the world's largest economy, accounting for about 25 percent of global economic activity. Despite periodic warnings concerning an inevitable decline of the dollar's role as the world's major reserve currency, the dollar remains the currency of choice for about 66 percent of global trade and investment transactions, while dollar-holdings account for a similar percentage of global reserves. For the foreseeable future, the U.S. dollar will remain the single most important reserve currency—certainly until the proposed single currency of Europe gains credibility and respectability in the next decade.

The U.S. economy clearly exerts a disproportionately large influence on world trade and finance and is often perceived to be the "locomotive" of global economic growth. During 1995 and 1996, foreign exchange dealers and currency forecasters devoted considerable attention to U.S. employment data contained in monthly nonfarm payroll figures in order to ascertain the underlying strength of the U.S. economy. Erratic payroll data appeared to reflect seasonal adjustment problems; nevertheless, they exerted a significant impact on bond yields and the dollar. Dealers also carefully scrutinized the monthly manufacturing index published by the National Association of Purchasing Managers, which measures the health of the U.S. manufacturing sector.

Fluctuating U.S. financial assets and interest rates essentially dictated financial conditions in European capital markets during 1995 and 1996 despite widely disparate economic conditions prevailing in the United States and Europe. Shifting U.S.-interest-rate expectations periodically caused disruptions and parallel financial fluctuations in European financial markets, even though economists predicted that European financial assets should have decoupled from U.S. financial developments given the weak growth conditions in Europe. Obviously, in the integrated world economy of the 1990s, U.S. economic and financial developments are quickly transmitted globally, impacting various national economic policies with important repercussions for global interest rates and exchange rates.

Conclusion

Managing exchange-rate risks and formulating effective currency investment strategies are difficult tasks, since a multitude of economic and financial factors interact through a variety of transmission channels to influence exchange-rate movements. Since economic fundamentals are strongly correlated with exchange-rate trends over long time-periods, there is no substitute for sound fundamental analysis in currency forecasting; however, over short- and medium-term time periods, exchange rates often diverge significantly from trends suggested by key explanatory economic variables. In order to bridge the gap between long-term fundamental currency trends and unanticipated exchange-rate movements deviating from such equilibrium paths, forecasters and dealers have turned to technical analysis for assistance in predicting short-term currency fluctuations. Forecasts of key economic fundamentals constitute the foundation of exchange-rate analysis, but since currency forecasting is not a precise science, economic analysis must be supplemented by technical considerations along with an evaluation of political, speculative, and psychological forces in order to encompass the broad spectrum of factors influencing exchange-rate fluctuations.

CHAPTER 6

Technical Analysis

Thomas F. Basso
President
Trendstat Capital Management, Inc.

The Basics of Market Movements

What drives the markets movements? Why are there up days or down days? These are questions that each trader must answer if he or she is to have a basis for building a trading strategy. Some might say the foreign exchange (FX) markets move based on fundamental information such as interest rates, economies, and political policies. This information motivates many traders, but the bottom line behind price movement is far more basic. If there is more buying pressure than selling pressure, prices move up. If there is more selling pressure than buying pressure, prices move down.

This basic supply-and-demand theory of order flow drives the typical technician's work. All we have to do is to measure which direction the market's supply/demand forces are moving and go with the flow of that supply/demand. We are not talking about predictions here. All we know is the market is trending higher, and we should be long the market. We do not know if it is because of central bank intervention, interest-rate differentials, or breakouts on somebody's charts. However, we know that buying pressure has been stronger than selling pressure in the recent past, and we assume it is more likely to continue up than to reverse and go down.

Technical Trading Makes Sense

Over the past 20 years, I have traded almost everything that moves including foreign exchange, futures, commodities, stocks, bonds, mutual funds, and options. The same supply/demand pressures exist in all of these markets. Reducing trading to simple, easy-to-execute principles has helped us to read the supply/demand pressures and to react to them.

The foreign exchange markets lend themselves to technical trading. When we get a buy signal (i.e., observe a change in the direction of the market from down to up), we assume that the buying pressure is starting to win the supply/demand battle, and we should buy. Since we are talking about the currencies of major world economies, we are trading some of the most trending, stable trading vehicles that exist today. Factors affecting the fundamentals of the foreign exchange market might include interest rates, political decisions, economic condition, or trade flows, all of which change very slowly.

The most difficult thing for foreign exchange traders is to have the discipline to stay with a strategy. With all the news in the financial markets, literally all of it could affect foreign exchange supply/demand. In world commerce, currencies are the basis for most of the transfers of goods and services between buyer and seller. Potentially, everthing that happens in world commerce could affect the value of one country's currency versus another's. Simply put, technical traders let the smart guys figure out how changes in the these factors will affect the market, they observe the effect of these individuals' trading, and then technical traders go with the flow.

Long-Term versus Short-Term

Trendstat is a long-term position trader. I prefer the longer-term time-frames for a couple of reasons. First, transaction costs exist in every market. In foreign exchange, the executions costs are very low compared to many other markets, but the costs are still there. The longer period of time that you own a trade, the less impact transaction costs will have on your portfolio. Second, the advantage to the longer time-frame is the long-term effects of interest rates, economies, and central bank policies on your position. The more emotional swings in the short run will often produce noise in the long-term trend of a currency market.

However, there are some downsides to long-term strategies. The requirement for patience is the first one that comes to mind. In this information age, the senses are bombarded with world news in only seconds after it happens. It is difficult for people to strategically think ahead. For individuals observing traders who are on a major long-term trend, making money one day and losing it the next requires a kind of patience that is nearly impossible for most people. The tendency is to cut it loose, to try to trade the sideways range, or to lock in a profit. My attitude toward the long-term is that if the trend is still in my direction let it do its thing, and find something else to do. Worrying about the trade or fiddling with it just makes you less patient. It is easiest to find other, more important things to do, essentially distracting yourself from worrying about the trade. This provides the psychological room for trades to mature into very profitable positions.

Another negative of longer-term strategies is the need to be vigilant concerning risk in the portfolio. Setting stop-losses that give a trade enough room to move while protecting run-away losses is difficult. Long-term trading usually will carry with it more potential for drawdowns in extended sideways markets. Long-term traders must watch their risk and manage it well.

Short-term trading strategies have a different set of advantages and disadvantages. The more frequently you trade, the more your trading costs there are to overcome. Every announcement can be an excuse to make a trade. Stress levels will be at their highest when there are larger volumes of executions. However, short-term traders gets to compound their profits more frequently than do long-term traders. Usually, short-term traders can carry less risk on their books for the same return potential. Just because Trendstat is a long-term trader doesn't mean that I'm suggesting that long-term trading is for everyone. If you are so inclined, the foreign exchange markets can provide plenty of short-term trading opportunities. Before you start, you must know the advantages and disadvantages you face with your strategy.

Automation in Technical Trading

Efficient use of computers can be very liberating. There is no reason why people should be inputting data or performing repetitious trading decisions, when a computer can do these functions faster and with a lot less errors. This frees people to perform in areas that they are uniquely capable of performing, such as designing computer programs, working at personal relationships, or writing chapters like this one.

Automation in technical trading is a subset of my philosophies. Because any trading has the potential for generating a lot of data processing and repetitious steps, automation is logical. For example, if one moving average crosses another yielding a buy signal, a trader could call that in to a trading desk or a computer could send a fax to that same desk. I would rather have the computer call it in because this makes the process more efficient, and frees traders to do more valuable work.

Automation of your technical trading strategy has some additional advantages. Some individuals, lacking discipline, might find it easier to program the computer to do the trades. This is because these individuals realize that they are more likely to follow their strategy if they are not hands-on each day with the trades. In addition, automated trading strategies can follow many more markets that a trader can. It would be simple to run a program against 60 or 100 markets with a computer. That many markets would swamp a trader.

Another item to consider is the automation of money management and risk-control strategies. Many software systems will concentrate on the buy/sell decision, and leave the trader to figure out how many contracts or millions of a market to buy or sell. Computerizing this part of the portfolio is very productive, since it makes risk management disciplined and routine. This should provide stabler approaches to the markets and trading than a manual approach could. Trendstat is automated from data incoming by satellite to the outgoing orders telecommunicated to the desks.

Dealing with Slippage in the Foreign Exchange Market

As is the case in all markets that I have traded, the foreign exchange markets do have slippage. Slippage is the cost of trade execution. There are three major forms of trading cost in the FX markets that we have identified. The easiest is the trade slippage. Here, you are getting a worse fill than you would have seen in your theoretical models. For example, if your strategy tells you to buy British pounds at 1.5000, and you pay 1.5002, then your slippage is 0.0002. The more trade slippage that exists in a market, the more difficult the technical trading is, since slippage is rarely positive.

A second form of slippage is forward pricing slippage. After a trade is done in the spot markets for two-day settlement, the trader can ask the foreign exchange desk to mark it forward to some future date. As a general rule of thumb the premium or discount used to markup or markdown the spot price to the forward price is based on the interest rate differential between the two countries' respective interest rates. However, we have found that some desks are better than others at being fair with the forward pricing. We take the best forward pricing, and assume that any forward pricing worst than that is forward slippage. If the trader is only looking at trade slippage, and ignoring forward pricing slippage, the desk may be likely to fill the trade better and build more cost into the forward pricing.

The last form of trading costs is various commissions or charges. Most foreign exchange traders pay for the cost of execution in the bid/ask spread. However, a correspondent desk at one of the major futures commission merchants, will typically try to get you the best fill at their cost, then they will tack on a commission. In addition, some desks will charge for rolling the forwards to another future date. They consider a roll to be one more transaction, and therefore, they charge for that service. There may be additional miscellaneous once-per-month charges on the account; these could be for accounting, sales fees, or other services that the foreign exchange firm has performed for the trader.

Add it all up and you have the total cost of trading for a foreign exchange trader. For estimate purposes, we find that the cost of trading a million U.S. dollars of a typical G-7 currency is around $200–300.

Thoughts on Portfolio Risk

People's reaction to my telling them that I am a currency trader is, "Oh, isn't that risky?" My response is "That depends on your strategy in the foreign exchange markets." Currency and futures are like dynamite in unskilled hands. Although dynamite is very useful, it would not be prudent to allow just anyone to use it.

Foreign exchange trading is similar to this analogy. The amount of leverage you put into the portfolio will determine how fast and dangerous your equity will swing, both up and down. The face value of currencies do not move very fast at all. In fact, typical currency moves are a lot slower than the stock market, and few would believe the stock market to be excessively dangerous.

So why do so many hold the view that the foreign exchange markets are risky? It stems from the leverage that many traders elect to build into their strategies. For example, if you buy one million dollars worth of Japanese yen for one million U.S. dollars, and it goes up 10 percent, then you will make 10 percent on your investment. However, if you put up only $100,000 to buy the million dollars of Japanese Yen, then you will make 100 percent on your investment. The first example is much more conservative than the second example. Because the currency markets have been a good trading vehicle over time, many traders have elected to leverage their portfolios more than might be prudent. The more leverage that traders have used, the more they have put themselves and their clients in harm's way. A sharp move like the British pound plunge in the autumn of 1992 or the recent Peso devaluation would have hit their portfolio hard. A few examples of big drawdowns are enough to cause some individuals to label currencies as risky instruments, which require careful handling or avoidance altogether.

An easy way to deal with risk levels in a portfolio is to set each position's risk at a comfortable percentage of the total equity. Risk, to me, is the part of my equity I would lose if the position turned against me and took out my stop loss. I calculate this risk each day, based on the difference from where the position is now to where my stops are according to my strategy. The equity is the value of my portfolio today. Dividing the risk of the position by the equity gives the trader the percentage of the portfolio that is at risk with that single position. I would encourage most traders to stay under 1 percent with an initial position, and under 3 percent in an existing, profitable position. The more you go above these levels of risk, the more exciting the ride will be.

Any trader can dial in the risk level at his or her own level of tolerance. If 1 percent of equity in a position is too fast, try 0.8 percent. If 0.8 percent is too fast, try 0.6 percent. If you want more speed, dial it up to a higher risk-level. I would recommend starting at the low side and dialing it up as you become more comfortable with the foreign exchange markets. If you follow this approach, you will find yourself trading at a comfortable leverage level.

In addition, the technical trader should consider the total portfolio risk. If you want to start slow, I would recommend keeping total portfolio risk below 10 percent of the equity. For example, you could have five positions each at a 2 percent risk of equity, or 10 positions each at a 1 percent risk of equity. In my opinion, over 10 percent of equity risk in the total portfolio would be moving pretty fast for most traders or clients.

Selecting Your Portfolio

Since countries have currencies and need to exchange curriences with other countries, there are an overwhelming number of currency pairs from which to select trading vehicles. Several factors should influence your selection of what to trade as a technical foreign exchange trader. Generally, technical strategies have an easier time in larger, liquid markets where slippage is reasonable. What you do not want is to be long a currency and have it devalued by 50 percent overnight. The G-7 countries, and a few others, are good trading candidates due to their liquidity and volume traded.

Another consideration is how much two currencies are tied to each other. For example, there is a tremendous correlation between deutsche marks and Swiss francs. The countries are geographically next to each other, and the trade between the two countries is significant. Both countries' banks have conservative leanings. The two currencies move together much of the time. If you decide to put both currencies in your portfolio, it is almost like doubling up on the German deutche mark.

From a technical trader's viewpoint, the last thing to consider might be how smooth a market is. If the market looks like it jumps around a lot, it may be more difficult on a technical trading strategy. Jumpy markets will be candidates for more undesirable whipsaw trades that can cost the trader over time.

Historical Simulations

Historical simulations are a good idea, before you start trading; but I have to caution everyone that most historical simulations are done for the wrong reason. Most traders look at historical simulations to see how much reward, risk, and so forth, that the strategy would have produced. I concentrate on how the strategy is dealing with various market conditions and scenarios.

For example, when doing research three years ago on the foreign exchange markets, a trader might have concluded that the foreign exchange markets were easy to trade and so he or she might have created shorter-term, more leveraged trading strategies. Rather than do that, I looked at how profits and losses were created over many different currencies and decided if these currencies were ever to move together, and in the wrong direction, the result would be tough on our clients. The scenario I created was in my head, not in the historical simulation. If you obtained 100 years of data, you still might not be able to observe that scenario. What would happen if a major bank defaulted? How would the foreign exchange portfolio react if most major stock markets went up by 10 percent over a 24-hour period? In other words, look at the details that the historical simulation is providing for you, rather than looking at the bottom line 5-year return and maximum drawdown. The better you understand what your strategy is doing, the better chance you have of being successful.

Another important point is to not overoptimize the strategy. Some research software has the ability to increment some variable or variables and to optimize the best result historically. The trader then gets an inflated view of what a realistic return and risk structure will be in future trading. I prefer to pick some very different cases and to understand how a variable affects the strategy. I am not optimizing as much as trying to understand how increasing or decreasing the variable affects return and risk. Then it is possible to create new and interesting scenarios and to assess how the strategy should handle them.

Good data for historical simulations in the FX markets are not easy to obtain. There are a few major quote-vendors that have kept the data on major markets for the last five to 10 years, but good luck if you want some obscure country's currency. Intraday data are rarer. I have been able to buy some daily data, but the 24-hour data are on a different day than Trendstat's models or operations. I recommend looking at the data for flaws and then cleaning up the data. Some obvious things I have seen in the past include opens and closes outside the high and low range, and highs and lows that are more than 25 percent changed from a previous day. Remember that the simulation is only as good as the data that go into it.

The Psychology Necessary for Successful Systems Trading

Say you have gotten this far and have selected your foreign exchange markets, finished your technical trading strategy, decided on your risk management strategies, and are ready to proceed. There is one last area to consider. How are you, the foreign exchange trader, going to react to the way your profits and losses come and go? In a discretionary strategy, traders are presumably in control and can modify their position as they desire. The systems trader has outlined a strategy that essentially tells the trader what to do. Second-guessing the system may seem appropriate, but often can leave the trader in a quandary.

For example, say your model tells you to be long British pounds, and you decide that you are nervous about being in British pounds because of an upcoming election. Your model is saying you should be in and you are saying that you should be out. Well, if you go with your decision and sell out or ignore a buy signal, how do you ever get back in sync with your model. Say the election is now over and your worries are gone, but the market has rallied 5 percent. Do you go in late? Does the market have more risk then than it did when you should have bought?

Discipline in technical trading is essential. In the summer of 1979, my parents were visiting me and I got behind in updating my charts and technical indicators. I had been perfect that year in executing every trade and was very slightly ahead on the year's trading. Two days after my parents left, I discovered that a silver trade had given a buy signal a week earlier. I had missed the signal, so I decided that since I had not executed it properly, I should not chase the signal and go in late.

Months later, that signal matured into the Hunts' attempt at cornering silver, and the transaction was worth in the hundreds-of-percent return on my small account in those days. Sloppy discipline had cost me dearly. It was not the blame of the technical indicators. They had done their job as asked. It was the guy running the indicators that was the problem. I vowed to never miss a trade again, and I haven't.

I like to keep it simple, because simple things work the best. The time for discretion is when you are designing the strategy or when you do not have a position. If you have done your homework, your strategy should be able, in general, to deal with various scenarios. It does not mean that you will always make a profit. It may be normal for a strategy to lose money during a certain market condition that only happens once every five years. You can live with minor losses during that period. The point is, your discretionary decisions during design will probably be better than your discretionary decisions on a single trade. Let the strategy do what it is supposed to do. Find something else to distract yourself and to keep you busy. In trading, as in life, patience is a virtue. In trading, patience can also be very profitable.

CHAPTER 7

Option Strategies*

Neil Record
Chairman
Record Treasury Management Ltd

Options are instruments which give the option holder rights but no obligations. Conversely options confer on the writer (seller) obligations but no rights. Options will trade at prices (premia) which reflect this asymmetry. Currency options give, at their simplest, the holder the right to acquire one currency with another at a fixed exchange rate (up to or) on a fixed date in the future. All currency-risk hedging strategies using options ultimately rely on the relationship between this asymmetry and option premia actually paid or received.

This chapter reviews the use of currency options in the management of currency risk in international investments, and similar strategies utilizing option replication techniques. The early sections give a general overview of the theoretical underpinning of the option market, and review the instruments available. Later sections look at strategies for using these instruments, and an assessment of the opportunities, pitfalls, and myths.

Options: Theory and Development

For practical purposes, modern option theory can be dated from a seminal paper by Black and Scholes in 1973.[1] In that paper, the authors demonstrated for the first time the theoretical possibility of risklessly hedging written options using only the underlying security, and that this process produced *costs* exactly equal to the *fair* premium of the option. The process they described was one of continuous adjustment of the underlying holding of the security; a process we now call *delta hedging*. We will come back to the real practical significance of this finding later.

*The author wishes to acknowledge particularly help and constructive criticism from Mike Jubb, who made a significant contribution in the more technical aspects of options and their pricing. The author is also grateful to Les Halpin for his comments.

A nonmathematician entering the world of option theory will be immediately confronted with the Black–Scholes model function; an experience that will probably irritate and confuse in equal measure. To counter this effect, in the remainder of this chapter I will avoid all unnecessary equations, formulas, and functions.

Option History

Options are not new instruments, although currency options are. Equity options have been traded more or less formally for much of the nineteenth and twentieth centuries, and commodity options for a great deal longer. Indeed, many commentators have noted that quite innocent financial and commodity transactions contain hidden options.

For example, a firm quotation for the supply of a commodity or other good is an option in the hands of the customer. If the price of the commodity goes down before the quotation expires, the rational customer will decline the quotation and ask for a new one. Conversely, if the price of the commodity goes up before the quotation expires, the customer could accept the quotation and immediately sell the commodity on the open market for a profit. Full rationality would demand that the supplier demands a fee to give a firm quote to cover his or her option risk. In reality, of course, most of the time these type of risks are written off by the seller as part of sales and marketing costs.

This example is designed to show the wide application of option theory to everyday events. Indeed it has been said that all financial theory is subsumable under option theory. Without going on to debate this proposition, I will turn to pricing theory of straightforward (often called *plain vanilla)* currency options.

Option Pricing

Figures 1 and 2 show the standard payoff graphs that most readers will be familiar with for a yen put and call respectively, strike rate 100, versus the U.S. dollar.

They are deliberately drawn with the same left-hand scale, expressed as a percentage of the dollar amount. One glance at the two graphs will show that an exchange rate movement of 40 yen from 100 to 60 will generate significantly more payoff for the call (both in percentage terms and cash) than a 40 yen movement from 100 to 140 will generate for the put. This feature arises from the nature of the arithmetic of option payoffs (call option payoffs are unlimited; put payoffs are limited to the strike price) combined with the way exchange rates are expressed in these figures (linearly rather than on a log scale). I will discuss these effects later.

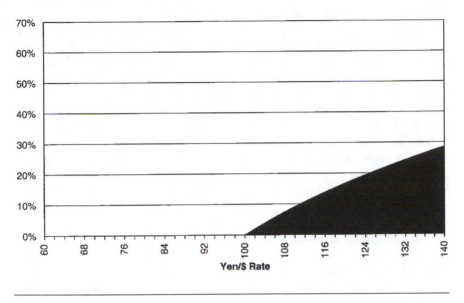

**Figure 1 Payoff % at Maturity of Yen/\$ Option
Yen Put; Strike = 100**

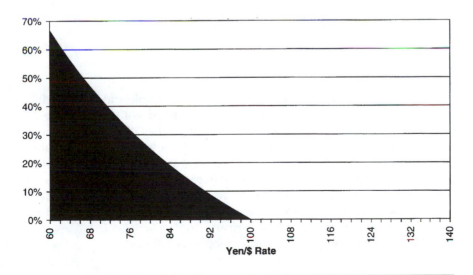

**Figure 2 Payoff % at Maturity of Yen/\$ Option
Yen Call; Strike = 100**

With some knowledge about the future behavior of the relevant market price, it is possible to calculate the expected average payoff value of an option. *Fair value* is the option premium that equates to that expected payoff. Let us take a simple example: coin tossing.

Suppose that we score 1 point for heads and –1 point for tails whenever we toss a coin. The coin is true, and it is tossed once a period. The *market price* is the sum of the points scored. We can devise and calculate the fair value for a one-period call at zero strike-price and at one dollar per point. For simplicity, assume interest rates are zero. The answer is 50 cents. Why? Because there is 50 percent chance that the score is minus 1, (when the option payoff is zero), and a 50 percent chance that the score is plus one (when the option payoff is $1): (50% × $0) + (50% × $1) = 50 cents.

What about a two-period option? Again the fair value is 50 cents: 25 percent chance of two heads (payoff = $2); 50 percent chance of one head/one tail (payoff = nil) and 25 percent chance of two tails (payoff = nil). What about a 3-period option? The answer turns out to be 75 cents, which the reader might like to verify him- or herself.

This simple model has a number of attractive features. First, the model is intuitively plausible—that is we believe it accurately describes a known physical process. Second, the underlying distribution (i.e., heads/tails) is known with confidence. Third, the model makes few assumptions, and those that it does can be tested with some rigor and verified.

This forms the ideal backdrop to a reliable valuation model; a backdrop that is regrettably diminished or absent when we move from manufactured distributions to those actually observed in the financial markets. Of course option theorists do not necessarily regret the difficulties of modeling the real financial world—if the models worked most of them would be out of a job!

Lognormality

Financial markets are not physical processes with stable and defined characteristics. Academics have consequently struggled with a model to describe the closest approximation to the outcomes they observe, and generally this has been an assumption of *lognormality.* A lognormal distribution is one where changes in the logarithm of a price at any horizon in the future lie on a normal distribution. This can be expressed either by Figure 3 or 4. Figure 3 shows the price on a linear scale (and the normal distribution looking skewed), and Figure 4 shows the price on a log scale (and the normal distribution looking symmetrical).

The logic of the lognormal assumption is as follows:

Figure 3 Lognormal Distribution on Linear Scale, SD = 12%

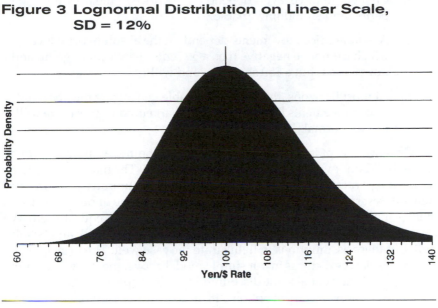

Figure 4 Lognormal Distribution on Log Scale, SD = 12 %

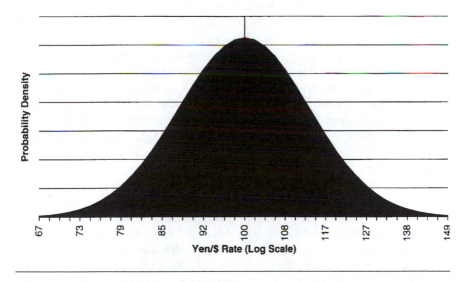

1.   Changes in price levels depend on the price in the previous period and a random variable.

2.   Absolute price movements depend on the absolute price level, which cannot be negative (i.e., a 50 cents share cannot go up and down by $1, but a $50 share can and will).

3.   At most horizons, the random variable generating the observed price movements in most financial markets conforms quite well to a lognormal distribution.

Once we accept lognormality, we need a few other assumptions to be able to build our own simple option-pricing model. The main assumptions we need (apart from lognormal random walk in continuous time) are constant interest rates; constant volatility; zero return on the underlying instrument (satisfied by forward contracts); and price-drift term equal to zero. We can build valuation models with other assumptions (as Black and Scholes did), but these assumptions will illustrate the case well. The principle of a pricing model is exactly as in our simple model above: the fair value for the option premium is equal to the discounted expected option payoff.

Figure 5 shows a yen put option with a strike at 100 (see Figure 2), with a lognormal distribution (with 12 percent standard deviation) superimposed. It also has a strip highlighted [yen/$ between 100 and 102 (actually 102.02)]. On the stated assumptions, the area under the normal curve between 100 and 102 is 6.23 percent. The mean payoff between these two points is approximately 1.01 yen for a strike at 100, or 1.00 percent. The expected payoff for this strip is $6.23\% \times 1.00\% = 0.06\%$. This process can be repeated for all the strips on the right-hand side of yen/$100, and the sum of all these expected payoffs can be used as a approximation to the fair value. Table 1 shows this calculation. Mathematicians will see that the strip width can be reduced and reduced, its width tending to zero, and that the expected probabilities can thereby be made increasingly accurate. This process, known as *integration*, is mathematically straightforward to compute, and the resulting formula is effectively the Black–Scholes equation. At the bottom of Table 1, the calculated price is compared to the formula price—illustrating the closeness of the discrete approximation.

This simple example illustrates one class of model that is based loosely around normal distributions.

There is one other major class of models based on numerical analysis. The principal representatives of this class are Monte Carlo models. These take a very different approach to pricing which can crudely be characterized as "Let's try it and see." (Incidentally, they are called Monte Carlo because the principality is a major gaming centre; the epitome of testing distributions by repeated sampling!) Generally used by banks to price more intractable or complex option instruments, Monte Carlo models take an

Figure 5 Lognormal Distribution on Log Scale
SD = 12 %

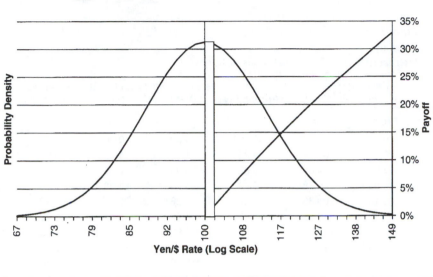

externally determined price distribution (e.g., lognormal, lognormal + jump, or binomial), and calculate one outcome of the option (i.e., whether it matures in- or out-of-the-money, and if it is in-the-money how big the payoff is) on the basis of a randomly generated price series. This process is then repeated (several thousands or tens of thousands of times) to generate a wide range of possible outcomes. The average of these outcomes (appropriately discounted if necessary) is then the *fair value* of the premium.

Monte Carlo techniques are appealing where there are nonstandard price distribution assumptions; where the option instrument is path-dependent or has other complexities; and where the model user wishes to *stress test* the option instrument and examine the range and variety of outcomes. The disadvantage of Monte Carlo techniques is that they are a sampling process whose accuracy increases asymptotically with the number of simulations run. This can be a very heavy computing requirement for on-line pricing. Indeed some banks use Monte Carlo in regular batch runs, and then create "look-up" tables with the results in order to get instant on-line quotes.

Assumptions

The meat of option pricing is not the mathematics by which prices are arrived at, but the assumptions underpinning the application of each theory. The late Professor Fischer Black[2] himself wrote, "I sometimes

Table 1   Option Valuation

Option type	Put
Strike Rate	100
Volatility	12%
Interest Rates	0% (for simplicity)

Exchange Rate (Lognormal Scale)		Probability	Mean Payoff (Yen)	Mean Payoff (%)	Expected Payoff (%)
From	To				
0	100.00	50.00%	0.00	0.00%	0.00%
100.	102.02	6.23	1.01	1.00	0.06
102.02	104.08	6.08	3.05	2.96	0.18
104.08	106.18	5.79	5.13	4.88	0.28
106.18	108.33	5.38	7.26	6.77	0.36
108.33	110.52	4.88	9.42	8.61	0.42
110.52	112.75	4.31	11.63	10.42	0.45
112.75	115.03	3.72	13.89	12.19	0.45
115.03	117.35	3.13	16.19	13.93	0.44
117.35	119.72	2.57	18.54	15.64	0.40
119.72	122.14	2.06	20.93	17.31	0.36
122.14	124.61	1.61	23.37	18.95	0.31
124.61	127.12	1.23	25.87	20.55	0.25
127.12	129.69	0.92	28.41	22.12	0.20
129.69	132.31	0.67	31.00	23.67	0.16
132.31	134.99	0.47	33.65	25.18	0.12
134.99	137.71	0.33	36.35	26.66	0.09
137.71	140.49	0.22	39.10	28.11	0.06
140.49	143.33	0.15	41.91	29.53	0.04
143.33	146.23	0.09	44.78	30.93	0.03
146.23	149.18	0.06	47.71	32.30	0.02
149.18	upwards	0.09	51.00	33.77	0.03
Expected Payoff (sum of expected payoffs by step)					4.72%
Black-Scholes Model Price (for comparison)					4.80%

wonder why people still use the Black–Scholes formula, since it is based on such simple assumptions—unrealistically simple assumptions."

Professor Black should probably not have been so surprised—or rather his surprise might have been redirected. More of this later. The Black–Scholes model has become so popular—indeed the market standard—because it is elegant and logical; is easily calculable (particularly with modern computers); and because it validates and stands together with delta hedging, and so it is practically useable. Everyone one who buys, trades, or prices options knows (or should know) that many of the model assumptions are violated in real markets, but everyone feels more able to cope with these violations from the safe haven of the model. Abandon the model, they argue, and they are once again adrift with no reference points.

But what would the world look like if the Black–Scholes assumptions were not violated? The most important thing to say is that all users of options bought and sold at Black–Scholes model prices would make zero net return in the long run. Any deviation from zero would be the result of chance. There would be no expertise that could be applied to alter that fact. However, professional sellers of options would be not be content to offer options at model prices because this would give them no opportunity for profit. But they would be content to offer infinite quantities of options at marginally higher than model prices because they could create them at model prices by the riskless arbitrage of delta hedging.

However, even if options under this environment have zero net expected return, they have risk transfer characteristics that are not net zero. Taking an insurance analogy, there are plenty of economic agents whose utility curves are such that they can improve their overall utility by buying insurance (even at premia higher than expected long-term claims), but there are few or no natural sellers of insurance, unless there is an expected net profit from the sale. Similarly with options, one would expect that commercial companies with natural foreign exchange risk, and investors with international assets, would pay (marginally) higher than model prices (and suffer an expected net negative return) in return for perceived risk reduction. This implies that any option buyer, however expert, would be condemned to suffer negative net returns in the long run if he or she were obliged to buy options from professional option sellers (and who else is there to buy them from?).

Astute option buyers, however, would observe that banks were making riskless profits by selling options, and would seek to replicate the delta-hedging process that the banks were using in order to reduce option premia to model prices. We shall return to this in the final section of the chapter.

Violation

But Black–Scholes assumptions are violated. To summarize their key assumptions (all of which apply to the underlying market, not the option market):

1.   The market is perfectly liquid and trades in continuous time.

2. Transaction costs are zero.

3. Market prices exhibit lognormal random walk in continuous time.

4. Volatility (the standard deviation of price changes at an arbitrary horizon) is constant.

5. Interest rates are constant.

Assumption 1 is possibly the most critical violation. The irony of this violation is that the major contribution that Black and Scholes made—their discovery—was that option premia and payoffs could be exactly replicated by holding a continuously adjusted portfolio of the underlying security. But their math only works in continuous time; it is simply inapplicable in discrete time. So the moment we relax this first assumption, the heart of the Black–Scholes model is ripped out. Dynamically adjusting underlying securities is no longer riskless. If it is no longer riskless, then writers of options should demand not only a small dealing-profit, but a risk premium as well. And since options writers no longer have an accurate or reliable model to calculate the risk (which arises because of their model's failure), risk premia should be generously priced. Further problems follow from other violations. Transaction costs in the underlying security are not zero, and most commentators would agree that markets exhibit short-term jumps with a frequency and of a size inconsistent with a lognormal distribution. These effects serve to increase the costs and volatility respectively of replicating option payoffs.

This brings us back to Fischer Black's expression of surprise at the success of his model. What is surprising is not that the model is seen as a landmark in option theory, but that its popular appeal was predicated on its practical applicability—a characteristic that was never really present nor even intended to be present by its authors. They were financial mathematicians who solved an important mathematical problem; not practitioners who wanted to solve the practical problem of hedging the writing of options.

Option Market Development

The Black–Scholes model was written with equity options in mind. These securities did not in 1973 have forward or futures markets, which made holding and transacting the underlying portfolio relatively expensive. It also introduced the problem of dividends which were not contractually certain. Uncertain future dividends introduced a complexity in pricing which was not particularly helpful in reaching a generalized option-pricing solution. Currency markets, by contrast, had by the mid-1970s a well-de-

Pricing American Options

The holder of an American option has a choice

1. to exercise the option, receiving the (current) payoff of the option and the subsequent yield on that payoff, or

2. to hold on to the option and exercise it at some later date.

The value of the option if it is exercised can be calculated in a straightforward manner. The value of the option if it is not exercised is much less clear and is influenced by the future behavior of the holder. In order to establish the value of the option, it is necessary to know how the option holder will behave (i.e., under what circumstances he or she will exercise the option). Option holders who behave *optimally* will aim to maximise the value of the option that they hold. Thus, they will exercise the option if the value of exercise in (1) is greater than the value of the option in (2). This illustrates the complexity of the pricing of American options: the value of the option depends on the behavior of the holder which depends on the value of the option.

Note that the value of an American option which is held by a holder who acts optimally is greater than or equal to the value of an option held by a holder who may act suboptimally.

Pricing formulae which use the BlackScholes assumptions have been developed which provide approximate prices for American options. In general, prices (of the underlying) for which exercise is optimal are calculated across the remaining time spectrum and used as the basis for calculating the value of the optional element outstanding.

veloped bank-mediated forward market which, ironically, satisfied the Black–Scholes assumptions (high liquidity, low transaction costs) much better than equity markets. It is perhaps a comment of the perspective of the authors that they saw the extension of their model from equity markets as being primarily into bond markets. Currencies were not mentioned.

Currency options did not exist outside entirely private bilateral deals until November 1982, when the Philadelphia Stock Exchange introduced the first currency option contract. This introduction heralded a rapid development of the currency option market, with banks, and their OTC (over-the-counter) products, being the driving force. By 1985, the majority of the major money-center banks in London and New York were offering a range of option products, and the major Chicago exchanges [Chicago Mercantile

Exchange (CME) and the Chicago Board of Trade (CBOT)] had introduced their own products. The London exchange, Liffe, followed soon after.

An interesting twist to exchange-traded options was that the majority of the early currency options were American style. American options are exercisable by the option purchaser at any time prior to expiry. Contrast this with European-style options which are exercisable only at expiry (actually between two times on the expiry day). Again, like uncertain dividends, American options introduced pricing complexities which are not particularly useful in the generality.

It also introduced some absurdities: a call option on a very high-interest-rate currency with expiry at, say, one year, would have the lower boundary of the at-the-money forward option premium determined by the percentage discount that the call currency stood at in the market versus the put currency. If there was a 5 percent annual interest rate differential, the option premium could not be less than 5 percent, whatever the volatility. This is because an option holder always had the option to exercise [i.e., buy the call currency at the strike rate (a 5 percent discount)], and sell it in the market at the spot rate. This just obscured the option element of the pricing, while giving nothing of value to either the buyer or the seller. OTC options, by contrast, were generally European style; or rather they were flexible and the (corporate and institutional) customer chose European. This largely unremarked characteristic may have been a contributory factor in the rise of the OTC currency option market at the expense of the exchange-traded market.

The Black–Scholes methodology tightened its grip on the market by the development of the concept of implied volatility. *Implied volatilities* are the annualized standard deviation that, if applied to an largely unmodified Black–Scholes model, would produce the option premia actually seen in the market. This is a neat, if rather inconsistent, approach to the assumption violation problem. The model does not work because several critical assumptions are violated; so the market has kept the model and "reverse engineered" an input (volatility) to take the strain of the model breakdown. This has led to observations like the *volatility smile*—where implied volatilities are higher for out- and in-the-money options than they are for equivalent at-the-money options, and term structures of implied volatilities where implied volatilities differ at different maturities.

Perhaps the most interesting observation is that implied volatilities embedded in options offered by banks have not been materially or systematically higher than actual volatilities experienced during the lives of these options. This in turn implies that banks are not building-in significant risk premia and profit into their pricing, and consequently they are not experiencing attractive profits from plain vanilla option writing. There have certainly been at least two well-documented periods where several major money-center banks in the London and New York foreign exchange markets have made significant losses in their option writing/delta hedging books. These periods (1985 and 1992) were characterized by very sharp rises in actual underlying market volatilities, along with market discontinuities and other "nonnormal" events.

Exotic Options

The moment that the plain vanilla option market began to attract customer interest, customers began to complain that option premia were too high. This expression was not a comment on the banks net expected profitability—which was not known and was probably not high—but instead was a "gut feeling" that since forward contracts were "free" and options were not, then options must be expensive.

This customer-led demand for lower premia, and the bank-led demand for less transparent products (which could command a premium price) spawned a vast array of exotic instruments more or less based on options. The box below gives a brief description of some of the most important exotic instruments. We shall return to these in the active strategies section.

Investors' Currency Risk

While currency risk has been a common problem for international companies for many years, it is only comparatively recently that cross-border institutional investment has grown to the point where attention has been focused on the effect of currencies on returns.

U.S. investment analysis is dominated by what is known as *modern portfolio theory*. This quantitative approach to investing was initiated by an article by Harry Markowitz in 1952.[3] Under this approach, a fund's investment program is *efficient* if it cannot improve its expected return without increasing its expected risk, or volatility, of return. An *efficient frontier* is the curve joining efficient points at varying degrees of risk. Under this theory, different investors will maintain different portfolios only to the extent that their utility functions are different—that is to the extent that they are prepared to embrace risk in the search for higher returns.

U.S. pension fund consultants and advisors have argued in the past 10 years that international diversification can (at worst) reduce risk without reducing expected returns, and at best reduce risk and increase returns. This case has been accepted in many major U.S. pension funds, and as a result international allocations have risen from around 3 percent of total assets in 1985 to around 9 percent in 1996. Given the rapid growth of U.S. pension

---

Exotic Options

An exotic option has a more complicated payout than a plain vanilla option. There are many different types of exotic options and new designs appear frequently. I describe a few of the general forms of exotic options below. These are often used as the building blocks for more complicated structures.

A *binary option* is an option which pays out a fixed amount if certain conditions are met, and nothing otherwise. For example, an option which pays £1 if the $/£ exchange rate is over 1.5000 on a specified date is a binary option. Almost all options that I am currently aware of can be structured as (sometimes complex) combinations of simple binary options.

The payout of a *path dependent option* is, as the name implies, dependent on the path that the underlying rate has taken over the period of the option. For example, a *barrier option* is activated or terminated if a specified rate reaches a specified trigger level between inception and expiry. The payoff of an *average rate option* depends on the average rate of the underlying during the period of the option.

A *multifactor option* has a payout related to the performance of more than one rate or asset. For example, an *outperformance option* is an option on the best performing asset from a basket of assets. A *quanto option* is an option on an underlying market where the payoff is converted into different currency at a fixed rate.

There are a number of options which have strikes which can change during the life of the option. Often these offer the opportunity to lock-in gains. A *lookback option* gives the holder the right to exercise the option at the most favorable rate seen over the period of the option. A *shout option* allows holders to "shout" when they wish to lock-in gains, profits can then not fall below the level locked in. This option is peculiar because holders can influence the value of the option by their behavior.

---

assets in the past 10 years, this has been a very sharp absolute growth from around $50 billion in 1985 to around $400 billion today.

The next, and obvious step, was to see whether efficiency could be further enhanced by removing the currency risk from international portfolios by hedging the currency risk. The conclusions are far from clear; but the issues are.

Passive Currency Hedging and Benchmarks

Most of the studies on the impact of currency hedging have concentrated on passive hedging strategies using rolling forward contracts. The way that these studies have been used, however, is almost universally to define, determine, or discuss the *benchmark* hedge ratio.

Benchmarking is fundamental to the investment process for most, (particularly U.S.) pension funds. In conventional asset class analysis, benchmark percentages for different asset classes (domestic equities, foreign equities, domestic bonds, foreign bonds, and so forth) are chosen by what might be described as a "constrained optimisation" process. However, once asset allocations are determined, asset managers are usually measured by their performance against the "natural" benchmark (i.e., if managers are given a Japanese equity mandate, then a recognized Japanese index will usually be their benchmark). In currency overlay, there is no natural benchmark. This means that overlay managers can be measured against benchmarks so different that they are virtually mirror-image. All parties (consultants, pension funds, and overlay managers) agree that this state of affairs is unsatisfactory, and therefore considerable attention and effort is being directed to finding a satisfactory benchmark that can become widely or universally accepted.

Most of the work has also been written from a U.S. perspective, which is important since the characteristics of currency overlay are domicile-dependent. A U.S. investor who hedged a Japanese portfolio during the decade 1985–1995 would have seen strongly negative returns from hedging, while a Japanese investor who similarly hedged a U.S. portfolio over the same period would have seen strongly positive returns.

Different commentators have drawn different conclusions. Summarizing the range of opinions; Perold and Schulman[4] have concluded that passive currency hedging offers a "free lunch" in reducing the volatility of returns, even though the expected long-term return from currency hedging is nil or marginally negative. The marginal negative return is explained by the (generally low) transaction costs associated with hedging using forward contracts. Following on from this conclusion, Perold and Schulman recommend a 100-percent-hedged benchmark for nondomestic equities.

Taking the middle ground, a number of commentators have sought to define optimal hedge-ratio benchmarks at values between 0 percent and 100 percent. One approach has been to define an efficient (in mean/variance terms) hedge ratio. Black[5] proposes a fixed ratio (a universal hedge ratio at less than 100 percent); Nesbitt[6], Jorion[7], and Braccia[8] link hedge ratios to whole-portfolio risk, not just international exposure. All conclude that hedging is justified under certain combinations of international allocation and hedging transaction cost, and at hedge ratios of less than 100 percent. By contrast Gardner and Wuilloud[9] approach the problem from the point of view of minimizing "regret." This approach favors a 50-percent hedge ratio, which, not surprising, turns out to minimize regret. Halpin[10] takes a novel approach in which he examines a benchmark with no regret—the "Hedge Perfection Index." Strictly speaking this is not a benchmark because it is not investable. However, it does account not just for fixed hedge ratios, but also for option-like currency overlay payoffs. Since we will see later in the chapter that option buying, option-replication, and dynamic hedging styles account for the largest general class of overlay managers, this is a relevant consideration.

Some writers, although the minority, have concluded that currency hedging is suboptimal at observed transaction costs, and therefore to be avoided.

All researchers in this area agree, however, that empirical evidence is in general inconclusive in determining final or firm answers. Correlations between currency movements and other asset classes are highly unstable over time, exhibiting alternatively positive, insignificant, and negative correlations. While currencies appear to exhibit strong trends (i.e., positive serial correlation of changes), some researchers in this area have concluded that there is insufficient evidence to reject the hypothesis that currency movements are a lognormal random walk. It is against this background that I turn to strategies for using options in the management of currency risk in international investments.

Passive Option Buying

In the section on assumptions earlier in the chapter, I argued that the expected return from buying options under conditions where the Black-Scholes assumptions are not violated was at best zero, and in practice probably negative. This is not dissimilar to the expected return from undertaking passive hedging using forward contracts, and the same arguments about portfolio risk reduction then apply. Interestingly, there is virtually no academic literature on passive option buying to parallel the now extensive literature on the use of passive forward contracts. Halpin[10] gets closest to this approach, but without a detailed analysis on the historic performance of option buying. The standard approach to portfolio efficiency (i.e., mean/variance analysis) is in any case inadequate to cope effectively with strategies of this type. This is because the key feature of option buying is that it creates a risk asymmetry—for a fixed fee, the currency downside is limited or eliminated. Mean/variance analysis weights upward movements in a portfolio equally with downward movements in calculating volatility or risk. Where a portfolio is constructed of asymmetric instruments, this can seriously over- or underestimate the "real" risk. I can illustrate this assertion with a stylized example.

Suppose that there are three funds with three different portfolios. In one, the portfolio is a standard mix of equities and bonds. In the next, the assets are 100 percent cash; while all the income (and perhaps more) is spent on option premia for call options on the underlying market. In the final one, the assets are 100 percent cash; while the income is enhanced by selling put options on the underlying market. This puts all three portfolios long of the underlying markets. Suppose all the option premia are fairly priced (i.e., at Black–Scholes model prices). On some consistent assumptions across portfolios, the long-term average returns are the same in all three portfolios. But both of the cash-plus-options portfolios turn out to have lower volatility than the standard portfolio, and would therefore look superior on conventional mean/variance analyses (see Table 2). But the option-buying and the option-writing portfolios both turn out to have similar volatilities. This flies in the face of common sense; few funds would contemplate systematically writing put options on equities and bonds because they would perceive it as too risky. In contrast, buying call options to get underlying market exposure may well be seen to be a risk-averse strategy. The mean/variance model cannot distinguish between them.

If we cannot use the mean/variance model to analyse or justify a passive option purchasing strategy, then what can take its place? The most common justification is 'risk control'. The argument, which is not usually explicitly spelt out by either overlay managers or their fund clients, runs like this. A fund invests outside its domestic marketplace because it wishes to maximise its return at constant risk, or reduce its risk for constant return.

Diversification

Diversification is a recognized risk reduction technique which is most commonly used in equity portfolio management. The principle is that the variance of the return of a portfolio of assets may be reduced by choosing assets which have lowly correlated returns. The assets are combined in an additive manner. The same diversification theory cannot be applied when considering the impact of exchange rates on an international investment. Here the net asset return is based on a multiplicative relationship between the asset and the exchange rate and will only have a lower variance than the hedged return when the correlation between the asset and the exchange rate is sufficiently negative.

Table 2   Mean/Variance Analysis

Mean Return % p.a.	12.82%				11.99%		12.86%
SD	15.14%				10.18%		7.16%
Sharpe Ratio	0.847				1.178		1.797

	Underlying Stocks		Buying Call Options		Selling Put Options	
Quarter	1	2	3	4	5	6
0	100.00		100.00		100.00	
1	108.26	8.26%	106.19	6.19%	104.97	4.97%
2	103.25	−4.63%	104.17	−1.90%	105.08	0.11%
3	122.04	18.21%	120.79	15.96%	110.30	4.97%
4	132.10	8.24%	128.26	6.18%	115.78	4.97%
5	134.86	2.08%	128.44	0.14%	121.54	4.97%
6	138.16	2.45%	129.08	0.50%	127.57	4.97%
7	141.14	2.16%	129.36	0.21%	133.91	4.97%
8	147.54	4.53%	132.65	2.54%	140.56	4.97%
9	154.61	4.80%	136.36	2.80%	147.54	4.97%
10	171.86	11.15%	148.68	9.03%	154.87	4.97%
11	170.98	−0.51%	145.85	−1.90%	161.74	4.44%
12	187.22	9.49%	156.66	7.41%	169.78	4.97%
13	199.45	6.53%	163.72	4.50%	178.21	4.97%
14	190.07	−4.70%	160.60	−1.90%	178.27	0.03%
15	170.75	−10.16%	157.54	−1.90%	168.10	−5.70%
16	155.52	−8.92%	154.54	−1.90%	160.72	−4.39%

This shows a lognormal random stock portfolio valuation series in column1, with percentage returns in column 2. Column 3 shows a portfolio of call options on the same portfolio; column 5 shows the value of a sold portfolio of put options, also on the same portfolio. The illustrated results are a typical sample of random returns; the portfolios all have similar returns, but the options' portfolios both have consistently lower volatility.

Currency risk, which is involuntarily taken on when investments are made abroad, has zero expected return and, the argument runs, adds volatility to international investment returns (see box entitled Diversification).

In particular, currency risk introduces the possibility of losses unrelated to the underlying investment strategy; losses which are avoidable. A passive option-purchasing strategy (regular rolling buying of put options on the foreign currency) addresses this problem very successfully—the fund is buying "insurance" against currency losses, and it is not materially reducing its long-term returns by buying such insurance (assuming option premia are not materially higher than fair value). The real underpinning of

Figure 6 Asymmetric Utility Curve of Fund

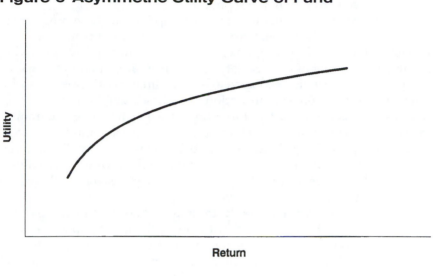

this argument, however, is that the fund has a *utility* curve shaped as is shown in Figure 6.

To say this is to say that the fund is more "unhappy" to lose x percent of return than it is "happy" to make x percent of return—particularly if the losses and gains are large and unexpected. It is, of course, nonsense to say that a fund has a utility function—but the fund is controlled by its board and its professional staff—and they certainly have utility functions. This risk asymmetry lies at the heart of the arguments in favor of the passive buying of currency options. Without it, passive option buying, passive option selling, and a 50 percent passive fixed hedge would all look equally attractive to the customer.

Typical Passive Option Structure

A designer of a passive option hedge will want to ensure that the portfolio of options is not unduly dependent on arbitrary currency or volatility events. This means, in practice, that option purchases will be spread over time, and maturities, and will roll over (i.e., the purchase of replacement options for maturing options) will likewise be spread in time. The designer has to choose original durations for the options, which for consistency will probably all be the same. He or she also has to choose whether the options are bought at-the-money or out-of-the-money. For European options (exercisable only at maturity), at-the-money means options with strike rates equal to the forward rate, not the spot rate.

The choice of option maturity in rolling option-purchase programs is one of the manager's discretionary variables. If option pricing conforms to Black–Scholes model pricing, then premia for at-the-money options are a simple square root of time. So (at zero interest rates) a one-year maturity option will be twice as expensive as a three-month option, and a rolling program of one-month options purchases will be root 12 (3.46) times as expensive (at least in premium terms) as a rolling program of one-year-maturity purchases. However, under the assumptions stated, the expected payoffs equal the premia, so the net return of all these strategies will be zero. Different maturity structures will, however, have different risk reduction characteristics, and the overlay designer will wish to take these into account.

The same considerations apply to other variables at managers' disposal. Managers can choose whether to buy at-the-money options or out-of-the-money options, and if so how far out of the money. In theory, managers could also choose in-the-money options, but in practice will probably cover the risk characteristics implied by mixing option purchases with a passive fixed hedge. Again, under perfect-market assumptions, the net returns of all these strategies are identical at zero.

Passive Option Buying under Black–Scholes Assumptions Violation

It is a rare overlay manager who offers his or her services without a claim of expertise, technique, or knowledge that will help a fund to achieve positive returns from overlay. In a passive option-buying context, this usually means that the manager will exercise discretion, or follow the recommendations of a model, in varying the timing of purchases, the maturity of options, their out-of-the-moneyness, and other variables. If the manager relies on market feel, on intuition, charts or tips, then there is little more that can be said. If the manager buys options when volatility is low, or market-times option purchases to successfully capture exchange rate market movements, then he or she will be successful. The converse also applies. All the results will be subject to options-market transactions costs, which will make random purchasing a negative contribution to returns over the long run.

Whether or not a manager explicitly recognizes it, adopting this approach means taking on board the violation of the Black–Scholes assumptions. It is likely that the most successful managers in this category will recognize this, and indeed have developed their models to exploit the assumptions violations that they observe. The assumptions most relevant in this context, and examples of the kinds of expertise that managers can bring to bear are as follows.

Volatility

The Black–Scholes formulation assumes constant volatility. If this assumption is relaxed, as it plainly is in real markets, then there is a premium placed on successful prediction of volatility. Varying volatility also eliminates possibility of risk-free hedging of an option sale using underlying market positions (delta hedging), and creates a whole new set of uncertainties. Does a large market movement mean volatility has changed? Or is this just an outlier in the original population? If volatility has changed, when did it change and what is its new value? How many small market changes are needed for volatility to be said to have reduced? How frequent is sampling of these data? Are volatility changes themselves random?

All these questions raise possibilities for profitable use of options if the manager successfully identifies a volatility model which is effective at capturing something of the underlying mechanics of the market–not just fitting the historical data. There are certainly a number of overlay managers who claim that at least part of their expertise is modeling volatility. This is explored in a little more detail in the section on volatility forecasting.

Lognormal Random Walk

The key assumption that many managers challenge is the randomness of the random walk. There has been much attention on this area, most of it centering on the idea that currencies exhibit trends [i.e., that instead of (daily) changes being unrelated in both direction and magnitude to the previous day's move, there is a weak positive correlation]. This is known as *positive serial correlation of changes.* This effect can be tested for in standard statistical tests, but, as is so often the case in currency market analysis, the results are time-period dependent, and not always consistent. Generally, however, for long periods (10 years plus) serial correlation is observed to be positive but not sufficiently positive to reject the null hypothesis that changes are not serially correlated.

However, a manager does not necessarily need to have statistical significance to add value. If the market prices options on historic volatility, any consistent positive serial correlation may show up as an *underestimate* of the out-turn payoff in relation to the historic daily volatility. This happens because volatilities are universally measured in the market using daily data, the standard deviations of which changes are annualized by multiplying by root 262, this being the number of working days in a year. However, the math of payoff values in the Black–Scholes model requires the input of the volatility of price changes over the life of the option. We can demonstrate this phenomenon using currency data. In the 16 years since 1980, many exchange rates have exhibited apparent serial correlation of changes. Taking deutsche marks/U.S. dollars (DM/$) as an example, 1980–1995, the annualized historic volatility using daily changes in the spot rate was 11.65 percent. The historic volatility of annual changes (forward-to-spot), however, was 15.39 percent. Therefore, consistent buyers of options priced off daily volatility would have experienced added value by holding the options to maturity and accepting the payoff values generated by the higher annual volatility. This characteristic of the currency markets has not been lost on overlay managers.

Active Option Trading

A natural progression for an overlay or currency risk manager who has accepted that Black–Scholes assumptions are in practice violated is to release the restriction that he or she only buys options. If options are mispriced under the manager's definition, then it is as likely that they will be overpriced as underpriced. Managers who are only able to buy options will limit themselves to exploiting only half of the opportunities available. However, in practice, approaches to active option trading fall into two categories.

Premium Reduction

It is an abiding characteristic of companies or institutions with currency exposure (in this case, investment funds with international assets) that they regard option premia as high. This assertion is generally made not with reference to any particular pricing model or expected future payoff value, but as an emotional expression of discomfort at having to lay out real cash for cover which they perceive they can also get for "free" using forward contracts. OTC option providers, generally the main money-center banks, have long since recognized the existence of this mood, and have, not surprisingly, tailored products which in one way or another reduce the option premium payable upfront by the buyer.

A competent financial engineer will be able to unravel any of the (sometimes very complex) custom-made products on offer to the market, and will discover that their universal characteristic is that the net present value of the product to the bank is much higher than for conventional foreign exchange and option products. This can sometimes be taken to extremes—prompting the much publicized disasters like Procter and Gamble and Gibson Greetings. The author has in the past been retained as an expert witness in a disaster case which had reached court, and he put a midmarket valuation on a complex option product sold to a customer at plus $62 million for the bank (i.e., minus $62 million for the customer) compared to a transaction price for the product (i.e., option premium) of $9 million paid to the customer—making the customer $53 million out-of-pocket on day one!

Overlay managers, like their banking colleagues, have recognized the desire of customers to reduce option premia, and instead of tailoring complex products, have tailored strategies to achieve the same effect.

The most common approach is for a manager to buy options providing "full" cover, and then to sell options selectively, often out-of-the-money, so as to reduce the windfall gains made when the "cover" options go out of the money. This strategy could be enhanced by a volatility forecasting model, which could be used to determine purchase and sale timing. The whole process is continuous and rolling over time. Strategies such as this can succeed in reducing option premia by reducing the "optionality" in the cover. However, they will only succeed in adding value, in common with any hedging strategy, if the manager has successfully identified stable nonrandom characteristics of the markets which he or she systematically exploits. The sale of options to reduce premia alone is irrelevant to the question of adding value—it is relevant only in as far as it allows a manager to exploit periods when the market's assessment of volatility is higher than the manager's.

Volatility Forecasting

Volatility, more specifically implied volatility, has become a recognized market in the world of option trading. Option traders, when asked what they do, will often reply that they "trade volatility." Indeed several banks offer OTC products which allow their customers to buy and sell volatility directly. There are several issues that surround volatility trading. The first is that what is traded is implied volatility, not historical volatility. In a sense, this makes the market peculiarly circular. Implied volatility is, in effect, a forecast of future volatility. Any manager wishing to successfully trade volatility is being required to forecast future changes in the forecasts of volatility. Actual volatility may not come into the equation at all.

The second point is that volatility is an artificial construct, predicated on (almost certainly violated) assumptions. Volatility is traded because the Black–Scholes formulation assumes lognormal random walk for the underlying markets, and volatility is the annualized standard deviation of these changes. However, as we have seen above, violation of the Black–Scholes assumptions (in particular uncorrelated random changes), can radically effect even the straightforward calculation of volatility.

Turning to implied volatility forecasting, there is very little academic literature on this area, particularly in foreign exchange. There have been no systematic studies of the success or forecasting reliability of implied volatility, and the vast majority of the (mainly bank-sponsored) research in this area has concentrated on the relationship between historic volatility and implied volatility. But for forecasting purposes, this is of marginal use, since even a reliable implied-volatility model based on historic volatility simply shifts the burden of forecasting to another variable—historic volatility.

Historic volatility (a misnomer since the history may be only a few seconds old) is an average of indeterminate length of the magnitude of changes in the underlying market. Historic volatility can be calculated as the observed standard deviation of a sample of changes in recent history, and this is in practice applied with the assumption that the true (underlying) standard deviation has been constant throughout the sampling period. With increasing length of history, this would be fine if volatility were indeed constant (in line with Black–Scholes assumptions), but it is not fine if population volatility is either nonnormal, randomly variable over time, or predictably variable based on other inputs. Over the past few years, modelers have recognized that the underlying variance/volatility is not constant and have contrived to use more sophisticated models to deal with this. GARCH (generalized autoregressive conditional heteroscedasticity) models forecast underlying variance as a (complex) function of its past values. This is a more realistic standpoint but unfortunately leads to an exponential growth in the number of parameters which need to be estimated (are they variable too, when do we stop?), and to further sources of model errors.

Other Active Option Strategies

Putting aside volatility forecasting, what else can an active manager do to enhance returns? Banks will trade options profitably by making prices, not taking them. A currency manager, without a customer-oriented dealing room, client base, brand and market position, and capital, cannot do this.

A manager may use options as a downside-controlled way to take currency market bets in either direction, but this is not using option expertise so much as general market expertise to add value. This brings into focus the success (or lack of it) experienced by currency forecasters over the years. Fundamental currency forecasting, that is using economic inputs, such as inflation, interest rates, money supply, GDP, trade data, and so on, to attempt to model the underlying causes of exchange rate movements. The key here is *causes*. Most econometric modelers with any macroeconomic experience can create an economic model of historic exchange rates which appears to be a statistically significant fit. The question is whether good historical fit means that a model has good predictive ability. If it is modeling not causation, but correlation, then it will not have good predictive ability; and the evidence is that this is the case for most or all of the publicly

Figure 7 Dollar/Sterling Exchange Rate

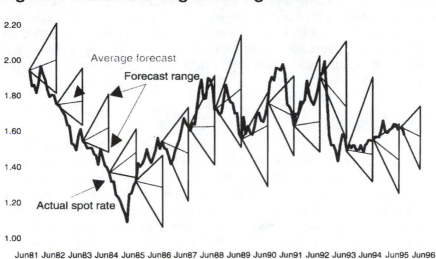

acknowledged models. Figure 7 shows a 13-year history of contemporary forecasts for $/£ exchange rates (reported in each June issue of *Euromoney*) and the subsequent spot rate movements. Even the consensus (median) direction was right less than half of the time.

Readers with a philosophical bent may reflect that if a model is devised that does accurately capture causative factors, then it may engender suffi-cient confidence in its makers that they trade large enough volumes of foreign exchange to affect exchange rates. This introduces an element of circularity that is itself likely to undermine the model. This is not as far fetched as it sounds. Hedge funds, which are geared vehicles for flexible and often aggressive position-taking, have found that, even in the very large and liquid currency-markets, their actions can affect the markets, and this can undermine their intended strategy. Occasionally, hedge funds choose to use their market-moving leverage to attempt to force price changes—this can be successful in the short term, but the history of market manipulation is one of ultimate losses borne by the manipulators.

Option Replication

Very early in the history of currency risk management, in the early 1980s, before currency options became available, currency managers recognized that option-like payoffs were an attractive goal. We have seen in the earlier sections on option models that Black–Scholes' 1973 paper asserted that it was possible to exactly replicate an option position with a dynamically adjusted portfolio of the underlying securities (or forward contracts in this case). Various assumptions violations mean that this assertion is not, in practice, true. Nevertheless, some sort of approximation is possible, and this section explores the various approaches managers have taken to this approximation.

Delta Hedging

As the OTC option market in currency options started in the second half of 1984, so the money-center banks who were offering them began to more or less crudely hedge the resulting exposure using delta-hedging techniques. The concept of *delta hedging* is, broadly speaking, to hold a position in the underlying market whose change in mark-to-market valuation per 1 percent movement in the underlying market is equal and opposite to the change in mark-to-market valuation of the option sold. A bank that sells a large portfolio of options can combine these to create a portfolio-delta, which is the elasticity of the whole portfolio of options with respect to a 1 percent movement in the underlying market. As an example, an outstanding option sold to a third party, say a $1 million call against a third currency, could have a mark-to-market valuation which varies by $3,500 for a 1 percent movement in the exchange rate. Since a one million-dollar position in the underlying market would have a $10,000 change in mark-to-market valuation per 1 percent move, this would be called a delta of 0.35 or 35 percent. Deltas will range between zero and one for vanilla options, but can vary widely and wildly for exotic options. There is a common further measure of the shape of the Delta curve with respect to the exchange rate which measures its instantaneous curvature, and this is called the *gamma*. There are a lot more Greek letters denoting the elasticities of the option valuation with respect to time, volatility, and so forth, but they are of interest more to bank risk managers than to the general reader.

The argument for currency overlay managers offering a dynamic hedging style of currency risk management runs like this. Buying currency options to protect against adverse currency movements in the fund context is attractive for two reasons: It reduces volatility if correctly targeted and benchmarked, and it satisfies the asymmetric risk-aversion utility curve that mean/variance analysis is poor at coping with. But a manager has to buy currency options from banks. This is true whether or not the options are OTC or exchange-traded since the market-makers on the major exchanges are the major money-center banks.

Banks sell currency options with the prospect of securing a profit on the combination of the premium received for the sale and for the cost of covering their risk. Banks can cover their risk in one of two ways: to buy options from third parties or to run a delta hedge in the underlying market. Since there are no natural writers of currency options who write them without a delta hedge (in contrast to equity options where institutional holders may well write covered options), banks generally are the ultimate writers of currency options. One way or another, therefore, options written to customers will be matched by a delta hedge run by a bank with the prospect of profit to the bank. Delta-hedging currency managers (or *dynamic hedgers*) offer, at the least, a delta hedge run on behalf of the investor to reduce the cost of the option premium by the amount of the prospective bank profit. These currency managers may also offer other advantages: flexibility in tailoring specific option specifications, high liquidity of the forward market compared to the option market, cash-flow improvement (no upfront option premia), and less sensitivity to market volatility in mark-to-market valuation.

In a perfect Black–Scholes world, these advantages would be unsullied by any disadvantages. The Black–Scholes model tells us that any option can be exactly and risklessly replicated by a portfolio of the underlying security (foreign currency or forward contracts in this case). As we have seen earlier in this chapter, however, Black–Scholes markets do not exist, and one of the effects of this is that option replication is not a riskless exercise.

What is the effect of this in practice? To simplify the discussion, I propose to discuss the replication of one vanilla option with the following specification:

Put currency	Japanese yen
Call currency	US dollar
Put amount	1 billion yen
Strike rate	100 yen/$
Initiation date	1 Jan 1996
Expiry date	1 Jul 1996 (date for exercise)
Maturity date	3 Jul 1996 (date for payoff cash-flows)
European style (i.e., exercisable only at expiry)	
Premium (% dollar amount)	3.02% (=$302,000)
Premium payment date	3 Jan 1996

Suppose that an investment fund wishes to "buy" this option on 1 January 1996. If it wishes to buy it by replication and not in the OTC market, what will a typical dynamic hedging currency overlay manager do? At the moment when the option is established, the overlay manager will use a Black–Scholes model variant (a variant to cope with forward contracts with no yield and no cash requirement), input the option specification and current market data, particularly the six months forward yen/$ rate, and a volatility value. The volatility value may be current implied volatilities, historical volatilities, or some model value from the manager's volatility forecasting model. The model will provide a series of outputs, the most important of which is the sensitivity of the mark-to-market valuation (in effect the option premium) to changes in the yen/$ exchange rate—the hedge ratio or delta. If this comes out at, say, 45.6 percent on the first data entry, then the overlay manager will sell 45.6% × yen 1 billion = yen 456 million against dollars in the forward market. The manager may choose to sell at any forward date, but the obvious default value would be to sell for a maturity of 3 July 1996. What happens next is very much manager specific, but Black–Scholes theory requires that the manager then conducts *continuous* monitoring of the exchange rate, and continually adjusts the hedge ratio to stay in line with model output, which will vary as the exchange rate and volatility change and time passes. Black–Scholes require that this process is literally continuous, so that thousands of deals could in theory be conducted in the space of a second, or indeed in a nano-second. This requirement is clearly impractical, so the manager must embark on a series of approximations to get as close to this as is possible. First, a manager must decide on monitoring frequency and procedures. Does monitoring take place at fixed frequency, once a second, a minute, an hour, a day, or a week? If monitoring is fixed frequency, what about 24-hour dealing? What about illiquid times of day, when perhaps only a thin Middle Eastern market is available? What about weekends and bank holidays? If monitoring is not planned to be a fixed frequency, how is it conducted? If it is triggered by a certain level of exchange rate movement, how is this movement monitored, continuously? If monitoring is high frequency, does this always trigger adjustments in the hedge position, even if these are small? Are there buffer exchange-rate zones or buffer dealing-sizes that keep dealing frequency under control? How is volatility monitored? Do market implied volatilities drive the hedge ratio, or historical or model-output volatilities? The variety of answers to these and other questions provide ample material for manager differentiation and for giving fund customers a headache.

But there is a straightforward test that a customer can apply. Has the option replicator succeeded in replicating the payoff value of the option being replicated, and at what cost? The arithmetic of this is simple. Take the two possible states that an option can expire in: in-the-money and out-of-the-money. If the option expires out-of-the-money, then the payoff value is zero. In this case, the cost of the dynamic hedge is the closed sum of the dollar values of all the forward contracts relating to the option. If the option expires in-the-money, then the payoff value will be positive. If the close-out spot rate on 1 July 1996 is 108, then the payoff is $740,740.74 (=(1billion/100)–(1billion/108)). The cost of the dynamic hedge is then the difference between the closed sum of all the associated forward deals, and $740,740.74. As an example, if the delta hedge yields $550,000, then the cost of replication was $190,740.74 (=$740,740.74–$550,000) or 1.91 percent of the dollar principal.

The key question that arises from the process described is whether it consistently reduces that cost below buying the equivalent options in the market, and how wide is the variability of the cost given that in practice Black–Scholes assumptions are violated. The evidence is difficult to find, in particular since option replication either by banks or by overlay managers is a commercial undertaking not open to public scrutiny. Under some fairly rigid assumptions about the monitoring process, however, it is possible to simulate the results of delta hedging using actual option premia and underlying market rate histories. It appears from this slim evidence that delta hedging under these rigid assumptions is not materially lower cost than typical option premium offer prices, but nor does it have materially higher cost variance. Any cost savings experienced by dynamic overlay customers are likely to be the result of the manager's proprietary refinements.

Dynamic hedging can also be operated entirely outside the Black–Scholes model environment, and a subclass of dynamic overlay managers do this. Under their processes, there is no assumption of lognormality, of continuous markets, or even of volatility levels. Their payoff outcomes are identical to delta hedgers, but the composition of their costs is different. Their costs will be higher or lower than a delta hedger's, depending on whether their models more or less effectively exploit market nonrandomness. (Note that with pure lognormal random-walk markets, all strategies are ultimately identical at zero net return less transaction costs.)

Dynamic currency overlay managers (or option replicators) represent (in 1996) the largest style class of all currency overlay managers—significantly larger than both the class of currency-forecasting managers and a sector not covered in this chapter—technical- or momentum-model managers.

Conclusion

Options and their analogues offer currency risk managers an attractive and flexible tool for currency risk management where asymmetric returns are desired. On their own, options are instruments which offer neither expected positive nor negative returns, but which are capable of being used in expert hands to exploit effectively any systematic nonrandom underlying market behavior.

References

1. F. Black and M. Scholes, "The Pricing of Options and Other Corporate Liabilities," *Journal of Political Economy*, No. 81, May–June 1973, pp. 637–59.

2. F. Black, "Living Up to the Model," *Risk Magazine*, March 1990.

3. H. M. Markowitz, "Portfolio Selection," *Journal of Finance* 7, pp. 77–91, March 1952.

4. A. F. Perold and E. C. Schulman, "The Free Lunch in Currency Hedging: Implications for Investment Policy and Performance Standards," *Financial Analysts Journal*, May–June 1988.

5. F. Black, "Universal Hedging," *Financial Analysts Journal*, July–August 1989.

6. S. L. Nesbitt, "Currency Hedging Rules for Plan Sponsors," *Financial Analysts Journal*, March–April 1991.

7. P. Jorion, "Mean/Variance Analysis of Currency Overlays," *Financial Analysts Journal Portfolio Management*, May–June 1994.

8. J. A. Braccia, "An Analysis of Currency Overlays for US Pension Plans," *The Journal of the Institute of Portfolio Managers*, 1995.

9. G. W. Gardner and T. Wuilloud, "The Regret Syndrome in Currency Risk Management: A Closer Look," *Russell Research Commentaries*, August 1994.

10. L. T. Halpin, "Overlay Perfection—A Measure of Success?" *Derivatives Use, Trading & Regulation*, Vol. 1, No. 2, January 1995.

PART II

Currency Risk Management for Institutional Investors

Maximizing Diversification in International Investing: New Opportunities to Improve Risk-Adjusted Returns through Enhanced Currency Overlay

Virginia Reynolds Parker
President
Parker Global Strategies, LLC

The single most significant investment development during the last two decades of the twentieth century is the growth in international investing. U.S. pensions have been increasing their exposure to international markets at a rate of 32 percent per annum for the past five years. Today, the average U.S. tax-exempt institution has 9 percent of its assets committed abroad. Industry experts project that the average allocation may grow to 15 percent by the turn of the century. During 1995, U.S. investors purchased $51.2 billion of international equities and $46.8 billion of international bonds.[1] International investing is a growth industry by all standards (see Figure 1).

Modern portfolio theory has provided the impetus for investors to move allocations to offshore markets. Diversification is the key driver that provides an opportunity for higher returns at reduced levels of volatility for the aggregate portfolio. What many investors have failed to realize is that a significant portion of the return and diversification benefit of international investing is the exposure to foreign currencies. From January 1986 through June 1996, over 53 percent of the return from the Morgan Stanley Capital International EAFE (Europe, Australia, Far East) Index, the traditional benchmark for U.S. investors in international equities, is from the currency component. For the same period, over 55 percent of the return from the Salomon non–U.S.-dollar World Government Bond Index (WGBI) is from the currency component. Hedging the currency exposure reduces

Figure 1 Growth of International Investments— U.S. Net Purchases of Fixed Income & Equity Securities (1973 through 1995)

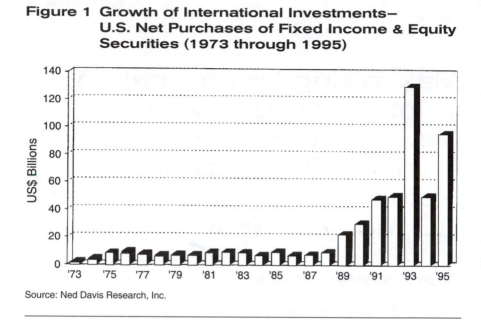

Source: Ned Davis Research, Inc.

the cumulative returns for EAFE from 54.3 percent to 46.2 percent[2] and for WGBI from 254.7 percent to 128.0 percent. Table I illustrates the depreciation of the U.S. dollar against world currencies over the period. Figures 2 and 3 show the currency impact on EAFE and WGBI over the same period.

The following equation summarizes the source of risk and return from international investing:

$$R\rho = R_l + R_{fx}$$

where

      $R\rho$ = Total Return
      R_l = Local Return
      R_{fx} = Return from change in exchange rate.

All international investors face the variables of the above equation. The Morgan Stanley Capital International (MSCI) World Equity Index performance varies according to the investor's base currency. Examining the difference in returns illustrates the influence that annual currency movements have on a global equity portfolio from the perspective of the U.S.-dollar-based investor, the deutsche-mark investor, and the Swiss franc investor. Figure 4 and Table 2 demonstrate this dramatic impact. The degree of impact depends upon direction of the investor's base currency.

Table 1 Performance of the U.S. Dollar against the Major World Currencies (January 1986 through June 1996)

	DEM	JYS	GBP	CHF	FRS	ILS	BFS	SKS	FMS	DKS	SPS	PZE	CDS	AUD	NZD
1986	-21.39%	-20.95%	-2.53%	-21.65%	-15.15%		-19.98%	-11.10%	-11.01%	-18.44%	-14.01%		-1.25%	-2.36%	
1987	-18.34	-23.40	-21.39	-21.22	-16.36		-17.85	-14.03	-15.86	-16.84	-17.80		-5.85	8.68	
1988	12.90	3.13	4.24	18.13	13.74	-13.46%	13.16	5.80	3.69	13.16	5.18		-8.26	18.41	
1989	-4.74	14.99	12.31	2.60	-4.72	11.87	-4.35	1.23	-2.82	-3.89	-4.75	1.90%	-2.92	-7.77	-5.78%
1990	-11.39	-5.60	-16.58	-17.13	-11.67	-2.98	-13.11	-9.23	-17.93	-12.32	-12.27	-11.21	0.22	-2.22	-1.33
1991	1.54	-7.99	3.33	6.62	1.86	-10.95	1.13	-1.39	24.76	2.47	1.04	1.05	-0.40	-1.21	-8.05
1992	6.66	-0.03	23.85	7.79	6.89	0.88	6.33	27.81	27.11	6.38	18.90	9.38	9.91	-9.54	-4.63
1993	7.25	-10.42	2.23	1.43	6.63	29.56	8.93	17.76	10.35	7.83	24.41	20.56	4.34	-1.48	8.48
1994	-10.88	-10.97	-5.57	-12.09	-9.86	16.38	-12.18	-11.20	-18.44	-10.46	-8.11	-10.28	5.77	14.13	14.28
1995	-7.21	3.95	0.97	-11.79	-8.02	-5.67	-7.23	-11.40	-7.93	-8.48	-7.53	-5.72	-2.67	-4.19	2.35
1996	6.00	5.96	-0.56	8.33	4.98	-2.10	6.13	1.04	6.76	5.44	5.33	4.49	-0.08	6.04	4.65
	-37.72%	-45.23%	-7.28%	-39.30%	-31.39%	17.50%	-37.39%	-12.26%	-13.80%	-34.31%	-16.89%	6.55%	-2.51%	15.69%	8.26%

Figure 2 Currency Impact on EAFE Returns
(January 1986 through June 1996)

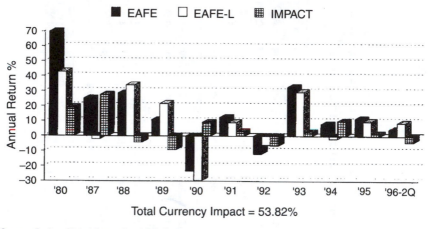

Total Currency Impact = 53.82%

Figure 3 Currency Impact on WGBI Returns
(January 1986 through June 1996)

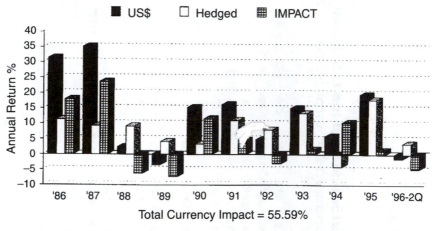

Total Currency Impact = 55.59%

Figure 4 MSCI World Index Performance
(January 1986 through June 1996)

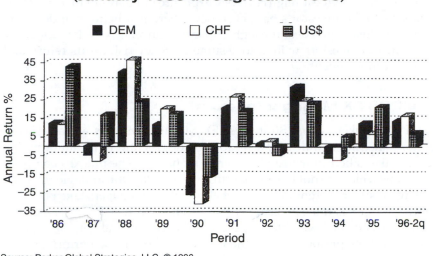

Source: Parker Global Strategies, LLC, © 1996

Table 2 Performance of MSCI Indexes
January 1986 through June 1996

	Compounded Annual Return	Cumulative Return	Standard Deviation	Maximum Drawdown	Sharpe Ratio
World (US$)	13.8%	331.2%	14.9	24.0	.58
World (DEM)	8.8	231.5	17.1	35.1	.28
World (CHF)	8.5	236.3	17.8	37.5	.26
EAFE-US$*	7.2	54.3	17.7	30.6	.20
EAFE-Hedged*	4.9	46.2	15.4	40.5	.07

*Data from January 1988 through June 1996
Source: Parker Global Strategies, LLC., © 1996

Academics and institutional investors have struggled for years to answer the currency challenge—whether to hedge always, never, dynamically, or sometimes. Those investors and fiduciaries who believe currency managers can add value hire specialists. The traditional *active* overlay manager decides when portfolio exposures should be protected against adverse exchange rate movements. Under most circumstances, overlay managers may hedge foreign currency exposure but may not increase short exposure to the investor's base currency. There is a better solution than current industry practice, through enhanced currency overlay, for those international investors willing to assume currency risk for its return and diversification benefit.

The PGS FX Manager Indexes

The PGS (Parker Global Strategies) FX Manager Indexes are a series of performance-based indexes meant to provide risk and return information from a diversified universe of currency managers. The indexes comprise programs which are not traditional currency overlay but strategic currency management, or currency as an asset class, where managers take positions that are long *or short* the investor's base currency. Each PGS index is equally weighted. A capital-weighted index would allow several very large managers to tilt the performance of the indexes, although the performance of those large managers may not be indicative of the performance of the manager universe. The PGS FX Manager Index is the broadest, including 51 currency programs representing 43 managers. The index tracks approximately $5 billion in equity capital, or $15 billion in currency positions. Results are calculated monthly since January 1986.

The PGS FX Manager Index is composed of three subindexes: the PGS Systematic Index, the PGS Discretionary Index, and the PGS Casualty Index. The first two subindexes are style-driven. The PGS Systematic Index is composed of those managers/programs whose decision process is rule based. The PGS Discretionary Index is composed of those managers/programs whose decision process is judgmental. The PGS Casualty Index is composed of those managers/programs that are no longer active. Survivorship bias is a legitimate criticism of manager universe analysis. In constructing the Indexes, the author has applied best efforts to find and include all managers overseeing at least U.S. $10 million in equity capital, approximately $30 million in currency exposures, on behalf of outside clients, at any time since January 1986. Unlike many of the commercially available manager databases, the PGS FX Indexes retain the performance of inactive managers/programs.

Figure 5 summarizes annually since 1986 the number of participants in each of the indexes. The figure at the top of each bar is the total number of programs included during the calendar year. The top segment of each bar shows the number of systematic programs; the next segment shows the number of discretionary programs. The bottom segment is the number of program casualties, the first of which occurred in 1992.

Figure 5 PGS FX Manager Index—Annual Programs Tracked (1986 through 1996)

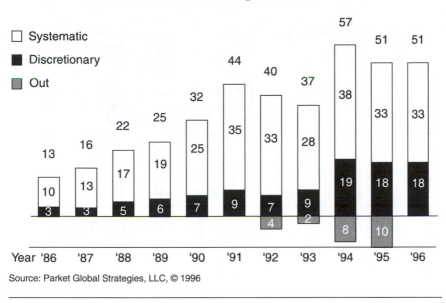

Source: Parket Global Strategies, LLC, © 1996

In analyzing the performance of these indexes from January 1986 through June 1996, one discovers some important distinctions for each. First, the PGS FX Manager Index has a compounded return of 25.1 percent, a standard deviation of 17.9 percent, a maximum peak-to-trough loss of 13.5 percent, a Sharpe ratio of 1 percent, and an implied daily VAR (value at risk) of 1.8 percent, (given a 90 percent confidence interval). The index performance tends to be stronger than that of a universe median, because of the diversification effect in measuring mean performance. As shown in Figure 5, systematic programs more heavily weight the PGS FX Manager Index than discretionary programs. The correlation of the PGS FX Manager Index is .96 to the PGS Systematic Index and .53 to the PGS Discretionary Index.

The PGS Systematic Index

In examining the two major subindexes, the PGS Systematic Index has the highest compounded returns over the period. Figures 6 and 7 display the range of annual returns for the sub-index universe of the PGS Systematic Index and the PGS Discretionary Index, respectively. On a risk-adjusted basis the systematic managers are not as strong. On average, the maximum

Figure 6 PGS Systematic Manager Universe–Annualized Total Return

P=PGSFXINDEX   *=PGS–SYS

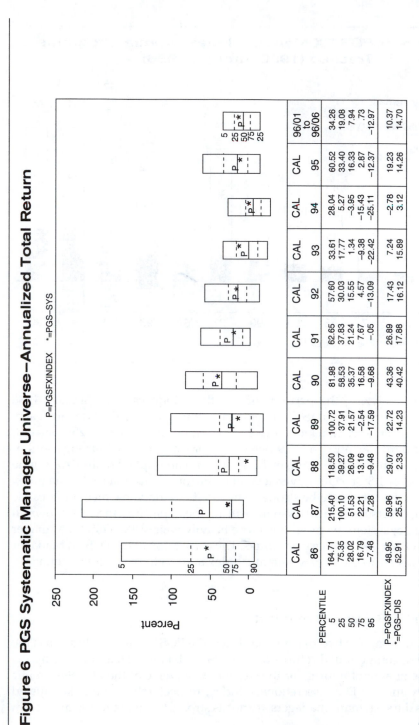

	CAL 86	CAL 87	CAL 88	CAL 89	CAL 90	CAL 91	CAL 92	CAL 93	CAL 94	CAL 95	96/01 to 96/06
PERCENTILE											
5	164.71	215.40	118.50	100.72	81.98	62.65	57.60	33.61	28.04	60.52	34.26
25	75.35	100.10	39.27	37.91	58.53	37.83	30.03	17.77	5.27	33.40	19.08
50	28.02	51.53	26.09	21.57	35.37	21.24	15.55	1.34	-3.95	16.33	7.94
75	16.79	22.21	13.16	-2.54	16.58	7.67	4.57	-9.38	-15.43	2.87	.73
95	-7.48	7.28	-9.48	-17.59	-9.68	-.05	-13.09	-22.42	-25.11	-12.37	-12.97
P=PGSFXINDEX	48.95	59.96	29.07	22.72	43.36	26.89	17.43	7.24	-2.78	19.23	10.37
*=PGS–DIS	52.91	25.51	2.33	14.23	40.42	17.88	16.12	15.89	3.12	14.26	14.70

Source: Parker Global Strategies, LLC, © 1996

Figure 7 PGS Discretionary Manager Universe–Annualized Total Return

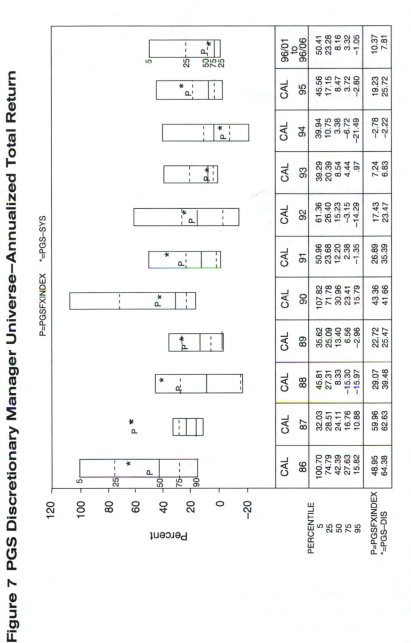

peak-to-trough loss is 24.6 percent and the Sharpe ratio is .88. For the group, the implied daily VAR is 2.5 percent given a 90 percent confidence interval. The correlations among the systematic managers are quite high. The majority of the managers in the PGS Systematic Index are technical trend-followers. These managers make most of their profits through extended directional moves in the currency markets. Historically, the currency markets have had strong directional moves two to three times a year. Most systematic managers generate their profits during those periods. Because these managers are rule based, their challenge is to minimize losses during congested markets and sharp reversals. The return patterns of individual managers can be erratic. Nevertheless, over time many are more profitable than their discretionary counterparts.

The PGS Discretionary Index

The discretionary currency managers tend to have much steadier performance. Many target earning consistent monthly returns. The PGS Discretionary Index has performed much better from a risk-adjusted perspective. Although the compounded return is only 19.2 percent, the index's maximum peak-to-trough loss is much lower at 12.9 percent and the Sharpe ratio considerably higher at 1.2 with an implied daily VAR of 1.1 percent, given a 90 percent confidence interval. The correlations among the discretionary managers are considerably lower than among the systematic managers.

Figure 8 shows the distribution of monthly returns for the PGS FX Manager Index, the PGS Systematic Index, and the PGS Discretionary Index. One can see the difference in the shapes of distributions between the systematic and discretionary managers. One can also see the strong diversification benefit indicated by the PGS FX Manager Index, composed of the Systematic, Discretionary, and Casualty Indexes. The downside tail is truncated. The different characteristics of the return distribution for the systematic managers and the discretionary managers suggest an opportunity to build a diversified multimanager currency strategy with considerably better performance than the PGS FX Manager Index which is heavily weighted with highly correlated technical trend-followers.

The PGS FX Casualty Index is composed primarily of technical trend-followers. The PGS Casualty Index's return is higher than that of the discretionary managers but lower than that of the systematic managers. It is important to note that the PGS Casualty Index has the lowest Sharpe ratio at .74. The PGS Bias Index is composed of the PGS Systematic Index and the PGS Discretionary Index, but not the PGS Casualty Index. Consequently, the PGS Bias Index represents an index with clear survivorship bias. As one would surmise, the returns are higher than the PGS FX Manager Index. Figure 9 shows the comparitive growth of $US1000 from

Figure 8 PGS FX Index—Monthly Returns Distribution (January 1986 through June 1996)

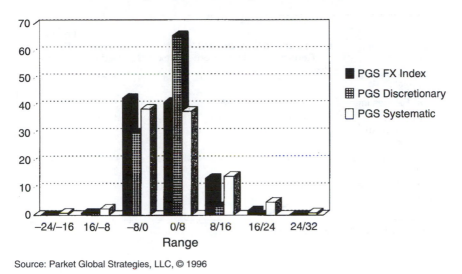

Source: Parket Global Strategies, LLC, © 1996

Figure 9 Performance of PGS FX Indexes (January 1986 through June 1996

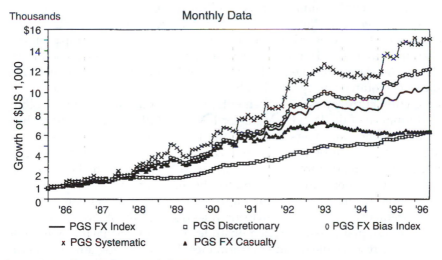

Source: Parker Global Strategies, LLC, ©1996

Table 3   PGS FX Indexes Performance Comparisons
January 1986 through June 1996

	Compounded Return	Standard Deviation	Max. DD	Sharpe Ratio	Implied Daily VAR
PGS FX Manager Index	25.1%	17.9%	13.5%	1.00	1.8%
PGS FX Bias Index	26.9	18.1	17.1	1.10	1.9
PGS FX Discretionary Index	19.2	10.5	12.9	1.20	1.1
PGS FX Systematic Index	29.5	24.6	23.7	.88	2.5
PGS FX Casualty Index	20.6	20.2	16.2	.74	2.1

Source: Parker Global Strategies, LLC., © 1996

January 1986 through June 1996 for each of the indexes. Table 3 compares the risk and return statistics for each index.

To date, the period from August 1993 through December 1994 was one of the most difficult for many of the currency managers, both for those who manage currency as an asset class and for those who manage traditional currency overlay. Continuous congestion, sudden spikes in volatility, and sharp reversals characterized the major currency markets. The top performers during that period tended to be those managers situated on bank trading floors and those managers who had bank trading-floor experience. The markets required agility and the ability to discard most traditional rules in predicting currency price movements. Figure 10 tracks 12-month rolling performance of the PGS FX Manager Index and illustrates the difficulties many currency managers had over the 18-month period. In Figure 1 the significant fall out of currency managers begins during this challenging period and extends through 1995. January 1995 marked the beginning of another strong performance period for the managers. Many of the systematic managers made important improvements to their models and risk measurement and management techniques during 1994. A large percentage of these systematic managers demonstrated during 1995 that they were able to achieve respectable upside performance despite having a more conservative risk posture.

Figure 10 PGS FX Manager Index—Rolling 12-Month Returns (January 1987 through June 1996)

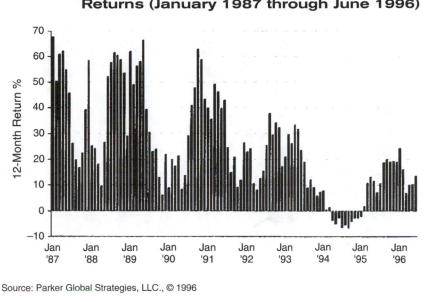

Source: Parker Global Strategies, LLC., © 1996

Putting the Pieces Together

The challenge international investors face is that over 50 percent of their returns since 1986 have resulted from the currency exposure. The EAFE Index is composed of 20 countries. From the U.S.-dollar-based investor's perspective, the performance of the U.S. dollar against the Japanese yen and the deutsche mark has accounted for 90 percent of the performance of the currency component of EAFE since January 1986. An international equity portfolio composed of 20 local equity markets and two currencies is not an optimal portfolio. Dissecting the performance of the MSCI World Equity Index from the perspective of other base currencies, one discovers again that over 70 percent of the returns are from foreign currency exposure and much of the currency return relates to the U.S. dollar, Japanese yen, and deutsche mark.

Enhanced Currency Overlay

A better solution for achieving a more optimal international portfolio is to hire currency specialists to take positions, long *or short* the investor's base currency, in the broad spectrum of global currency markets. Replacing

Figure 11 Correlation Matrix (January 1986 through June 1996)

	PGS*FX	PGS*SYS	PGS*DIS	MSCI*$	MSCI*DEM	MSC*CHF	MSCI EAFE
PGS * FX	1.0						
PGS * SYS	.96	1.0					
PGS * DIS	.53	.40	1.0				
MSCI * $	.03	.02	.09	1.0			
MSCI * DEM	(.10)	(.14)	(.07)	.73	1.0		
MSCI * CHF	(.15)	(.18)	(.11)	.71	97	1.0	
MSCI EAFE	.06	.06	.14	.94	.59	.56	1.0

Source: Parker Global Strategies, LLC, © 1996

passive currency exposure in international investing with active currency management provides investors with the opportunity to significantly improve risk-adjusted returns. The PGS FX Manager Index is a proxy for the performance of these currency managers. The PGS FX Manager Index has a low to negative correlation with the MSCI World Equity Index and the EAFE Index as shown in the correlation matrix below (see Figure 11).

The method most appropriate for determining portfolio exposure to enhanced currency overlay is an allocation based on the expected volatility of the active currency exposure. For example, if the volatility of the currency component of EAFE or the MSCI is 10 percent, and the investor wants to replace passive for active currency exposure at the same level of expected volatility (EV), an allocation of 56 percent exposure to the PGS FX Manager Index is applied, (10%/18% = 56%).[3] If an investor prefers a 50 percent hedged benchmark and targets a 5 percent expected volatility from active currency management, then a 28 percent allocation is made (5%/18% = 28%). This technique provides a more optimal approach to currency overlay through significantly broadening the investment universe. Figure 12 illustrates the considerable increased performance by adding a two-sided (long *or short* the investor's base currency) enhanced overlay approach. The compounded return for the U.S.-dollar-based investor increases from 13.7 percent to 21.2 percent for 5 percent EV and to 30.8 percent for 10 percent EV. There is a similar improvement in performance for the deutsche-mark investor and the Swiss-franc investor.

Figure 12 Risk versus Return—Adding Active
Currency Managgement to Global Portfolios*
(January 1986 through June 1996)

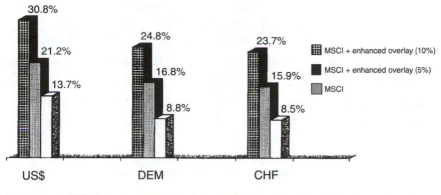

*Weighting the PGS FX Index for 10% and 5% volatility from enhanced overlay.
Source: Parker Global Strategies, LLC, © 1996

Performance Analysis for 10 Percent Expected Volatility

The standard deviation of returns increases significantly for the U.S.-dollar-based investor, from 14.9 percent to 24.6 percent, when a 10 percent expected volatility (EV) is selected. Most of this volatility is upside as demonstrated in the large decrease in maximum drawdown from 24.0 percent for the MSCI World Equity Index to 16.8 percent for the MSCI World Equity Index with the 10 percent EV allocation. The Sharpe ratio increases from .6 to 1.2. For nondollar investors, the increase in standard deviation with the 10 percent EV is much smaller. The volatility increases from 17.1 percent to 19.0 percent for the deutsche-mark investor and from 17.8 percent to 19.1 percent from the Swiss-franc investor. There is an important decrease in the maximum drawdown from 35.1 percent to 20.3 percent and from 37.5 percent to 23.7 percent, respectively, for the deutsche-mark investor and the Swiss-franc investor.

Performance Analysis for 5 Percent Expected Volatility

At the 5 percent EV allocation for all base currencies, the standard deviation remains almost in line the MSCI World Equity Index. Compounded returns increase by 7.4 percent for the U.S.-dollar-based investor, 8 percent

Figure 13 Risk versus return—Adding Active Currency Management to Global Portfolios (January 1986 through June 1996)

	US$			DEM			CHF		
	(1)	(2)	(3)	(1)	(2)	(3)	(1)	(2)	(3)
Compounded Return (%)	13.7	30.8	21.20	8.80	24.80	16.80	8.50	23.70	15.90
Standard Deviation (%)	14.9	24.6	15.90	17.10	19.00	17.30	17.80	19.10	17.80
Sharpe Ratio	.6	1.2	.91	.28	.92	.66	.26	.87	.61
Maximum Drawdown (%)	24.0	16.8	17.90	35.10	20.30	26.00	37.50	23.70	31.10
Correlation to MSCI	—	.75	.90	—	.85	.95	—	.86	.96

(1) MSCI
(2) MSCI + Enhanced Overlay (10%)
(3) MSCI + Enhanced Overlay (5%)

Source: Parker Global Strategies, LLC., c 1996

for the deutsche-mark investor, and 7.4 percent for the Swiss-franc investor. The Sharpe ratio is .91, .66, and .61, respectively. The maximum drawdown is smaller in each case than that for the MSCI Index, but higher in all cases than for the 10 percent EV. Performance results are summarized in Figure 13.

Conclusion

Enhanced currency overlay provides international investors with an important opportunity to improve both diversification and returns through expanding the investment universe. Figure 14 shows the comparitive growth of $1000 of the MSCI world Equity Index and the MSCI World Equity Index plus a 10% EV allocation to enhanced currency overlay from the perspective of the U.S. dollar, deutche mark, and Swiss franc-based investor. Managers may take advantage of currency cross-rate trends that would miss the purview of the traditional overlay mandate. Investors and their fiduciaries can determine the appropriate allocation to this active currency strategy through careful consideration of the return objectives and risk profile for the international portfolio. The PGS FX Manager Index represents a very broad range of currency managers and strategies. A carefully selected, well-diversified team of four to six currency managers should outperform the PGS FX Manager Index by at least several hundred basis points per annum, which would make the risk-adjusted returns through such a strategy even more impressive.

Figure 14 Performance of MSCI Indexes
(January 1986 through June 1996)

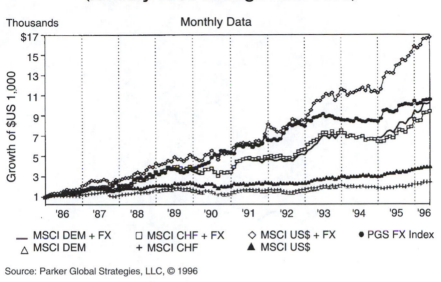

Source: Parker Global Strategies, LLC, © 1996

Endnotes

1. Source: Securities Industry Association.

2. Data for EAFE are from January 1988 through June 1996.

3. The expected annualized volatility of the PGS FX Manager Index is approximately 18 percent based on historical performance.

CHAPTER 9

Immunization Strategy for Multinational Fixed-Income Investments

Shmuel Hauser
Chief Economist, Israel Securities Authority
Senior Lecturer, Ben-Gurion University

Azriel Levy
Head of Foreign Exchange Research, Bank of Israel
Adjunct Professor, Hebrew University

Uzi Yaari
Professor of Finance
School of Business, Rutgers University-Camden

Introduction

Fixed-income asset and liability portfolios held in various currencies by multinational corporations and financial institutions are subject to the combination of foreign currency risk and interest rate risk. Redington (1952) and Bierwag, Kaufman and Toevs (1983) show how to immunize interest rate risk in a fixed-income portfolio invested in a single currency. Their approach is extended here to the immunization problem in the multinational arena, in which interest rate risk and currency risk must be managed simultaneously. The most obvious treatment of this problem is by matching the duration of assets and liabilities separately in each country. Unfortunately, this solution is likely to be prohibitively costly. In this chapter, we explore the conditions under which the multinational firm can dramatically lower hedging costs. Under these conditions, the firm is able to hedge against foreign and domestic interest rate risks through immunization by matching the *overall* duration of the asset and liability portfolios rather than the duration of asset and liability portfolios in any single market. In that setting, the optimal management of the risks of interest rates and foreign currency may be done separately rather than jointly. This chapter extends the results of Gadkari and Spindel (1989), Hauser and Levy (1991), and Leibowitz, Bader and Kogelman (1993), who show that hedging currency risk converts some or all of the foreign-held claims to synthetic domestic claims.

In the second section of the chapter, we derive the necessary and sufficient conditions under which currency and interest rate risks can be managed separately. In the third section, we present an empirical test of the assumptions underlying those conditions. The final section concludes this chapter.

Hedging Interest-Rate and Currency Risks

For the sake of exposition, the general case of two portfolios consisting of assets and liabilities denominated in multiple currencies is explored below via the simpler but essentially similar case of two-currency portfolios. The analysis takes the view of an American investor for whom both portfolios represent a mix of dollars and yens, assuming for simplicity that the yield curves in the United States and Japan are flat and subject to parallel shifts. The latter assumption has been extensively discussed in the literature and deserves explanation. The definition of Macaulay's duration assumes that the term structure of interest rates is flat; its interpretation as price/interest-rate elasticity assumes further that the magnitude of interest rate changes is infinitesimal. Given the complex stochastic nature of interest rates and the variety of yield-curve shapes and their frequent changes, the use of Macaulay's (1938) duration often fails to achieve a successful hedge through immunization.[1] For example, the presence of nonparallel shifts under immunization designed to control the risk of parallel shifts will cause the value of assets to fall short of the value of liabilities. A great number of contributions in recent years explore risk-reduction methods based on alternative duration defenitions and risk-producing stochastic processes— some recognizing the effect of transaction costs. However imperfect, immunization in numerous versions has become a popular technique for hedging interest rate risk in recent years. Its practical value for risk control may be attributed to its simplicity and flexibility in imposing relatively few constraints on the structure of assets and liabilities managed.

The immunization strategy derived in this chapter follows this tradition. We view the choice of a duration measure and underlying interest rate process as a tradeoff among imperfect immunization methods, all of which generate errors, and opt for the traditional simple Macaulay's duration. This choice makes tractable and accessible our derivation of an optimal immunization strategy, but should not be considered an oversimplification of the problem. In view of the alternatives, there is no clear sacrifice in our choice: Studies cited above reveal parallel imperfections in alternative immunization methods, and specific results of Hegde and Kenneth (1988) show that immunization errors caused by the assumptions of Macaulay's duration are economically insignificant.

An Immunization Strategy for International Fixed-Income Portfolios

Let

S = dollar/yen spot exchange rate
F = one-period dollar/yen forward exchange rate
r_d = dollar interest rate
r_y = yen interest rate
A_d, A_y = dollar and yen assets, respectively, denominated in domestic currency
L_d, L_y = dollar and yen liabilities, respectively, denominated in domestic currency
A, L = total assets and liabilities

Let the value of the assets and liabilities involved be

$$(1) \quad A_d = \Sigma_i A_{id}(1+r_d)^{-i}$$
$$(2) \quad L_d = \Sigma_i L_{id}(1+r_d)^{-i}$$
$$(3) \quad A_y = \Sigma_i A_{iy}(1+r_y)^{-i}$$
$$(4) \quad L_y = \Sigma_i L_{iy}(1+r_y)^{-i}$$

where A_{id}, L_{id}, A_{iy}, and L_{iy} are the receipts and payments in period ($i=1,2,...,n$), denominated in dollars and yens, respectively, so that

$$A = A_d + SA_y$$
$$L = L_d + SL_y.$$

Without loss of generality, it is conveniently assumed that the investor's net worth, N, is initially zero, namely $N=A-L=0$.

Based on Macaulay's (1938) definition, let D_{Ad}, D_{Ld}, D_{Ay}, and D_{Ly} denote the duration of the dollar and yen assets and liabilities, respectively, where

$$(5) \quad D_{Ad} = [\,\Sigma_i A_{id}(1+r_d)^{-i}]/A_d$$
$$(6) \quad D_{Ld} = [\,\Sigma_i L_{id}(1+r_d)^{-i}]/L_d$$
$$(7) \quad D_{Ay} = [\,\Sigma_i A_{iy}(1+r_y)^{-i}]/A_y$$
$$(8) \quad D_{Ly} = [\Sigma_i L_{iy}(1+r_y)^{-i}]/L_y.$$

Finally, let D_A and D_L denote the weighted-average dollar/yen duration calculated separately for the assets and liabilities, respectively (recall the assumption $A=L$):

(9) $D_A = (A_d/A)D_{Ad} + (SA_y/A)D_{Ay}$
(10) $D_L = (L_d/A)D_{Ld} + (SL_y/A)D_{Ly}$.

The sufficient and necessary conditions for immunizing an international portfolio are derived as follows.

First-Order Conditions

Theorem:

(a) The portfolio is immunized against interest rate risk if $D_A = D_L$, meaning that the average duration of the assets equals that of the liabilities;

(b) The portfolio is immunized against currency risk if (i) $A_y = L_y$, namely the value of the yen assets equals that of the yen liabilities; and (ii) $D_{Ay} = D_{Ly}$, namely the duration of the yen assets equals that of the yen liabilities.[2]

Proof: Let the investor's net worth be defined by

(11) $N = A - L = A_d + SA_y - (L_d + SL_y)$,

and expand (11) as a Taylor series up to the first order for variables S, r_d, and r_y. Using the definitions in (1)–(4), this expansion yields

(12) $dN = dS[A_y - L_y]$
$+ dr_d[-\Sigma_i A_{id}(1+r_d)^{-i-1}i + \Sigma_i L_{id}(1+r_d)^{-i-1}i]$
$+ Sdr_y[-\Sigma_i A_{iy}(1+r_y)^{-i-1}i + \Sigma_i L_{iy}(1+r_y)^{-i-1}i]$.

The definitions of duration given in (5)–(8) are next substituted in (12)

(13) $dN = (1+r_d)^{-1}dr_d[-A_dD_{Ad} + L_dD_{Ld}]$
$+ S(1+r_y)^{-1}dr_y\,[-A_yD_{Ay} + L_yD_{Ly}]$
$+ dS\,[A_y - L_y]$.

Given the assumption $A=L$, (13) is equivalent to

(14) $dN = (1+r_d)^{-1}dr_dA[-(A_d/A)D_{Ad} + (L_d/A)D_{Ld}]$
$+ S(1+r_y)^{-1}dr_yA[-(A_y/A)D_{Ay} + (L_y/A)D_{Ly}]$
$+ dS[A_y - L_y]$.

Given a covered interest rate parity[3] the following relationship between the forward and spot exchange rates must hold

(15) $S(1+r_d) = F(1+r_y)$

or equivalently

(15′) $S(1+r_y)^{-1} = F(1+r_d)^{-1}$.

The first-order Taylor approximation of (15) is

(16) $dS(1+r_d) + Sdr_d = dF(1+r_y) + Fdr_y$.

From (15′) and (16), we get

(17) $dr_y S(1+r_y)^{-1} = dr_y F(1+r_d)^{-1}$
$= [Sdr_d + dS(1+r_d) - dF(1+r_y)](1+r_d)^{-1}$

which is substituted in (14) to obtain

(18) $dN = (1+r_d)^{-1}dr_d A\{-[(A_d/A)D_{Ad} + (SA_y/A)D_{Ay}]$
$+ [(L_d/A)D_{Ld} + (SL_y/A)D_{Ly}]\}$
$+ [dS(1+r_d) - dF(1+r_y)](1+r_d)^{-1}A[-(A_y/A)D_{Ay} + (L_y/A)D_{Ly}]$
$+ dS[A_y - L_y]$.

Equation (18) can be simplified by substituting the definitions of the duration of assets and liabilities given by (9)–(10):

(19) $dN = (1+r_d)^{-1}dr_d A\{-D_A + D_L\}$
$+ [dS(1+r_d) - dF(1+r_y)](1+r_d)^{-1}A[-(A_y/A)D_{Ay} + (L_y/A)D_{Ly}]$
$+ dS[A_y - L_y]$

thereby completing the proof of this theorem.[4] According to the first line on the right-hand side of (19), if $D_A = D_L$, the portfolio is immunized against interest rate risk. According to the second and third lines, if $A_y = L_y$ and $D_{Ay} = D_{Ly}$, then dS and dF do not effect the net worth of the portfolio, implying that the portfolio is immunized against currency risk. The hedging of currency risk requires that the duration of assets and liabilities be matched in each currency.

As shown below, when currency risk is considerably greater than interest rate risk, it is possible to assume

(20) $dS(1+r_d) - dF(1+r_y) \approx 0$.

With this assumption, the following corollary provides a simpler first-order condition for a successful immunization.[5]

Corollary: *Given the approximation in (20), the portfolio is immunized against both interest rate and currency risks if the following two conditions hold:*

(a) $D_A = D_L$
(b) $A_y = L_y$.

Proof: Substitute equation (20) in equation (19).

According to this corollary, there may be a complete separation of interest rate risk and currency risk in the immunization process. If (20) holds, the immunization strategy of the multinational firm should be similar to that of a domestic one, requiring only the equality of duration of total assets and liabilities in the two markets combined—without the more stringent condition that the duration of assets and liabilities be matched in each market. The validity of this simplified immunization strategy is further examined against the second-order conditions.

Second-Order Conditions

We expand dN as a Taylor series up to the second order:

$$
(20) \quad dN = dSN_s + dr_dNr_d + dr_yNr_y
$$
$$
+ \tfrac{1}{2}dS^2N_{s^2} + \tfrac{1}{2}dr_d^2Nr_d^2 + \tfrac{1}{2}dr_d^2dr_y^2
$$
$$
+ \tfrac{1}{2}dSdr_dNr_{dS} + \tfrac{1}{2}dSdr_yNr_{yS} + \tfrac{1}{2}dr_ddr_yNdr_dr_y
$$

where

$$
N_s = A_y - L_y = \Sigma A_{iy}(1+r_y)^{-i} - \Sigma L_{iy}(1+r_y)^{-i}
$$
$$
Nr_d = -\Sigma A_{id}(1+r_d)^{-i}i + \Sigma L_{id}(1+r_d)^{-i}i
$$
$$
Nr_y = S[-\Sigma A_{iy}(1+r_y)^{-i-1}i + \Sigma L_{iy}(1+r_y)^{-i-1}i]
$$
$$
N_{s^2} = 0
$$
$$
Nr_d^2 = \Sigma A_{id}(1+r_d)^{-i-2}(1+i)i - \Sigma L_{id}(1+r_d)^{-i-2}(1+i)i
$$
$$
Nr_y^2 = S[\Sigma A_{iy}(1+r_y)^{-i-2}(1+i)i - \Sigma L_{iy}(1+r_y)^{-i-2}(1+i)i]
$$
$$
Nr_{dS} = 0
$$
$$
Nr_{yS} = -\Sigma A_{iy}(1+r_y)^{-i-1}i + \Sigma L_{iy}(1+r_y)^{-i-1}i
$$
$$
Nr_dr_y = 0
$$

The second-order condition is therefore,

$$
(21) \quad \tfrac{1}{2}dr_d^2[\Sigma A_{id}(1+r_d)^{-i-2}(1+i)i - \Sigma L_{id}(1+r_d)^{-i-2}(1+i)i]
$$
$$
+ \tfrac{1}{2}dr_y^2S[\Sigma A_{iy}(1+r_y)^{-i-2}(1+i)i - \Sigma L_{iy}(1+r_y)^{-i-2}(1+i)i]
$$
$$
+ \tfrac{1}{2}dSdr_y[-\Sigma A_{iy}(1+r_y)^{-i-1}i + \Sigma L_{iy}(1+r_y)^{-i-1}i] > 0.
$$

This inequality would be satisfied if, as a sufficient condition, the convexity of both the dollar and yen assets (first and second terms) is greater than that of their corresponding liabilities, and the duration of yen assets is equal to that of yen liabilities (third term). Like the domestic immunization problem, the second-order condition is met if the convexity of total assets is greater than that of total liabilities. But, unlike the domestic immunization problem, the second-order condition also requires that the third term of this inequality—if negative—is smaller in absolute value than the first two terms, or greater than or equal to zero. The third term is a function of the sign of dSdr and the duration of liabilities relative to that of assets. Although the presence of this term theoretically restricts the ability to manage separatly interest rate risk and currency risk, we confirm below that, practically, the duration of assets and liabilities may not have to be matched in each market. Going back to inequality (21), we further note that if the durations of assets and liabilities are equal: (1) the only requirement set by the second-order condition is that the convexity of the multinational firm's total assets be greater than that of its total liabilities; and (2) according to the first-order condition, both the interest rate risk and currency risk are immunized.

Practical Considerations

In this section, we conduct two tests designed to examine the empircal viability of the first- and second-order conditions allowing the multinational firm to manage separately the interest rate risk and currency risk. In the first test, we examine the relevant assumption based on the first-order condition in (20) that $dS(1+r_d)-dF(1+r_y)$ is insignificantly different from zero. In the second test, we examine for various currencies the relevant assumption based on the second-order condition that dSdr is insignificantly different from zero.

The empirical analysis takes the viewpoint of an investor who has access to Euromarkets, using end-of-month spot rates and Euro interest rates for 1, 3, 6, 12, and 120 months. These rates are used to derive forward rates assuming the covered interest-rate parity expressed by

$$(22) \qquad f_{0,n} = S_0(1+r_d)/(1+r_y)$$

where n denotes the forward contract's time to expiration measured in months, and r_d and r_y the respective domestic and foreign interest rates of the same expiration period. The sample includes monthly observations for the period January 1990 through November 1995. The results displayed in Table 1 indicate that in most cases examined here both assumptions are reasonable as both $dS(1+r_d)- dF(1+r_y)$ and $dSdr_y$ are insignificantly different from zero at the 5 percent level. The exception is the $/yen exchange rate for which the assumption does not hold for some maturities. These preliminary results indicate that currency and interest rate risks can sometimes be gainfully managed separately.

Conclusion

This chapter is concerned with fixed-income asset/liability management of the multinational entity, an environment in which foreign currency risk and interest rate risk are generally presumed to require simultaneous treatment.

Table 1 Monthly Changes of Spot and Forward Rates (January 1990–November 1995)*

Currency	Length of Forward Contract	$dF(1+r_d)$ $-dS(1+r_d)$ $(\times 1{,}000)$	t-value	$dSdr$ $(\times 1{,}000{,}000)$	t-value
$/Year	1	0.00057	1.870	−0.00777	−0.889
	3	−0.00067	−3.403	−0.00662	−0.779
	6	−0.00624	−2.849	−0.00647	−0.739
	12	−0.00509	−1.323	−0.00868	−0.850
	120	0.08890	1.331	−0.00868	−0.849
$/FF	1	0.38131	0.533	0.05684	1.672
	3	1.02409	1.399	0.03106	1.261
	6	1.00676	1.365	0.02026	1.156
	12	0.98220	1.321	0.01088	0.908
	120	−0.87698	0.465	0.01188	0.907
$/DM	1	1.57421	0.609	−0.00967	−1.226
	3	1.02039	0.386	−0.01013	−1.366
	6	1.09363	0.401	−0.01270	−1.554
	12	1.17745	0.408	−0.01229	−1.123
	120	1.51627	0.144	−0.01228	−1.124
$/SF	1	3.01459	0.931	−0.01461	−1.536
	3	2.35885	0.706	−0.01460	−1.471
	6	2.45581	0.722	−0.01157	−1.138
	12	2.65194	0.750	−0.00525	−0.433
	120	11.74661	1.303	−0.00520	−0.430

* $dF = (f_{0,n} - f_{0,n-1})$ is the monthly change of the forward rate where $f_{0,n}$ is the forward rate contracted to-day to expire n months from now. $dS = (S_1 - S_0)$ is the monthly change of the spot rate where S_0 and S_1 are the current spot rate and the spot rate a month later, respectively. The t-value is for rejecting the hy-pothesis that the average is different from zero at the 5 percent level of significance.

We explore the conditions under which the cost of risk managment may be reduced by managing those risks separately. The strategy developed here subject to fairly nonrestrictive assumptions reveals the conditions under which asset and liability duration can be matched separately in each coun-try. Our preliminary empirical investigation shows that those conditions may be frequently met and therefore be worth searching for.

Endnotes

1. See for example, Fisher and Weil (1971); Yawitz and Marshall (1981); Fong and Vasicek (1983, 1984); Fong and Fabozzi (1985); Maloney and Yawitz (1986); Bierwag (1987); Bierwag, Kaufman, and Latta (1987); Prisman and Shores (1988); Maloney and Logue (1989); Reitano (1992); Fooladi and Roberts (1992); Bierwag, Fooladi, and Roberts (1993).

2. If $D_{Ay}=D_{Ly}$ and $D_A=D_L$ then also $D_{Ad}=D_{Ld}$. The average duration of the dollar assets is also equal to that of the dollar liabilities.

3. A covered interest rate parity must hold in the absence of arbitrage opportunities when there are no transaction costs. This condition is replaced by two inequalities in the presence of transaction costs.

4. In the absence of foreign currency and foreign interest rate risks, equation (19) is reduced to Redington's (1952) first-order condition.

5. The assumption that $dS(1 + r_d) - dF(1 + r_y) \approx 0$ is tested in the text that follows. It is shown that this term is insignificantly different from zero for most currencies and maturities studied.

References

Bierwag, G. O.; G. G. Kaufman; and A. Toevs. "Immunization Strategies for Funding Multiple Liabilities." *Journal of Financial and Quantitative Analysis* 18, 1983, pp. 113–124.

Bierwag, G. O. "Bond Returns, Discrete Stochastic Processes and Duration." *Journal of Financial Research* 10, 1987, pp. 191–210.

Bierwag, G. O.; G. G. Kaufman; and C. Latta. "Bond Portfolio Immunization: Tests of Maturity, One and Two Factor Duration Matching Strategies." *Financial Review* 22, 1987, pp. 203–219.

Bierwag, G. O.; I. Fooladi; and S. Roberts. "Designing an Immunized Portfolio: Is M-Squared the Key?" *Journal of Banking and Finance* 17, 1993, pp. 1147–1170.

Fisher, L., and R. L. Weil. "Coping with the Risk of Interest Rate Fluctuations: Returns to Bondholders from Naive and Optimal Strategies." *Journal of Business* 44, 1971.

Fong, H. G., and F. J. Fabozzi. *Fixed Income Portfolio Management* Homewood, IL: Dow–Jones Irwin, 1985.

Fong, H. G., and G. A. Vasicek. "Return Maximization for Immunized Portfolio," in *Innovations in Bond Portfolio Management*, G. O. Bierwag, G. Kaufman, and A. Toevs, eds. Greenwich, CN: JAI Press, 1983, pp. 227–238.

Fong, H. G., and G. A. Vasicek. "A Risk Minimizing Strategy for Portfolio Immunization." *Journal of Finance* 39, 1984, pp. 1541–1546.

Fooladi, I., and G. S. Roberts. "Bond Portfolio Immunization: Canadian Tests." *Journal of Economics and Business* 44, 1992, pp. 3–17.

Gadkari, V., and M. Spindel. *The Currency Hedging and International Diversification: Implications of a World Reserve Currency Effect.* New York: Salomon Brothers Inc, November 1989.

Hauser, S., and A. Levy. "The Effect of Exchange Rate and Interest Rate Risk on International Currency and Fixed Income Security Allocation." *Journal of Business and Economics* 43, 1991, pp. 375–388.

Hegde, S. P., and K. P. Nunn. "Non-Infinitesimal Rate Changes and Macaulay Duration." *Journal of Portfolio Management* 14, 1988, pp. 69–73.

Leibowitz, M. L.; L. N. Bader; and S. Kogelman. "Global Fixed-Income Investing: The Impact of the Currency Hedge." *Journal of Fixed Income* 3, June 1993, pp. 7–18.

Macaulay, F. R. *Some Theoretical Problems Suggested by the Movements of Interest Rates, Bond Yields, and Stock Prices in the U.S. Since 1856.* New York: National Bureau of Economic Research, 1938.

Maloney, K. J., and J. B. Yawitz. "Interest Rate Risk, Immunization, and Duration." *Journal of Portfolio Management* 12, Spring 1986, pp. 41–48.

Maloney, K. J., and D. E. Logue. "Neglected Complexities in Structured Bond Portfolios." *Journal of Portfolio Management* 15, Winter 1989, pp. 59–68.

Prisman, E. Z., and M. R. Shores. "Duration Measure for Specific Term Structure Estimates and Applications to Bond Portfolio Immunization." *Journal of Finance* 43, 1988, pp. 493–504.

Redington, F. M. "Review of the Principle of Life Office Valuations." *Journal of the Institute of Actuaries* 18, 1952, pp. 286–340.

Reitano, R. R. "Non-Parallel Yield Curve Shifts and Immunization." *Journal of Portfolio Management* 18, Spring 1992, pp. 36–43.

Yawitz, J. B., and W. J. Marshall. "The Shortcomings of Duration as a Risk Measure for Bonds." *Journal of Financial Research* 4, Summer 1981, pp. 91–102.

Currency-Hedging Foreign Investments: Why Bonds and Equities Are Different

Lee R. Thomas III
Executive Vice President and
Senior International Portfolio Manager
Pacific Investment Management Company

Introduction

The literature on currency hedging superficially seems to support the hypothesis that if you laid all the world's economists end to end, they still would not reach a conclusion. It has been argued that the base case should be always to hedge [Perold and Schulman (1988); Thomas (1988, 1989)], never to hedge [Froot (1993)], or to hedge partially [Black (1989, 1990)]. What is a practicing international portfolio manager to do?

One thing you should do is to realize that it matters very much what sort of foreign assets you own. Not all foreign securities are equal, at least when it comes to their foreign exchange exposures. Part of the explanation for the disagreements prominent in the academic literature is that some researchers are talking primarily about foreign bond holdings, while others are largely concerned with hedging foreign equities. The major purpose of this chapter is to explain why these two cases, foreign stocks and foreign bonds, are different.

The chapter is organized as follows. The second section derives the optimal hedge ratio formally, for any foreign security. It is shown that the key variable is the correlation between the foreign currency price of the foreign security and the exchange rate. In the third section, we demonstrate why that correlation is likely to be quite different for foreign equity and fixed-income investments, using a highly simplified example to make our case. We further and more realistically consider the correlation between exchange rates and asset prices in the fourth section. The last section is a brief summary of the major conclusions.

Deriving the Optimal Hedge Ratio

A portfolio manager should consider both risk and return when choosing how much of his or her foreign currency exposures to hedge. However, we wish to concentrate on the risk reduction arguments for currency hedging rather than on any possible return-seeking motives for managing currency exposures. Accordingly, for our purposes the *optimal currency hedge* is the currency position which, when added to the underlying asset portfolio, minimizes the portfolio's total variance. You should observe that neglecting the speculative motive for buying and selling currencies is equivalent to assuming that the investor believes forward foreign exchange rates to be unbiased predictors of future spot rates. When this condition obtains the expected return associated with currency exposures is zero,[1] so an investor need only consider reducing risk.

The optimal hedge does not always equal the size of your foreign security position. That is, if you own $10 million of foreign securities, the variance minimizing quantity of foreign currency to sell forward may not be exactly $10 million. Thus, we distinguish between *accounting exposure*—in this example, $10 million—and *economic exposure* to currency fluctuations. It is economic exposure that, when hedged, minimizes risk. We will define the *optimal hedge ratio* to be the optimal currency hedge divided by the accounting exposure. For example, if the risk-minimizing hedge for a security position valued at $10 million is to sell forward $8 million worth of foreign currency, then the optimal hedge ratio equals 80 percent.

To simplify the discussion we will consider the case when a portfolio manager holds only one foreign security. Accordingly, we will seek the optimal hedge ratio for a single asset held in isolation. However, this security may be broadly interpreted to be a portfolio of foreign securities, as long as the securities are all drawn from the same market. An index of German equities, such as the Dax, thus qualifies as a security within our definition, as does the German components of the Salomon World Government Bond Index.

By simplifying in this way we avoid some potentially interesting complications involving intercorrelations among asset and currency markets.[2] In particular, you should bear in mind that the hedge ratio that minimizes the variance of a single security (or index) will generally not be the optimal hedge ratio when that same security or index is held as a portion of a broader portfolio. As a result, if a manager individually calculates the optimal hedge ratio for each foreign asset in a well-diversified portfolio, using the formula derived below, and then aggregates all the currency hedges across the entire portfolio, then that aggregate hedge generally will not be optimal. However, in practice, the differences in risk probably would be small. Moreover, it is easy to generalize the arguments we will make to apply to complex foreign security portfolios. We chose to concentrate on optimally hedging a single foreign-security holding in order to clarify the underlying principals.

Our final simplifying assumption is that the base currency is dollars. We will call the foreign currency marks. We assume the investor is concerned solely with his or her return and risk measured in dollars.

If we denote the foreign security's local currency return by R_L and the expected appreciation or depreciation of the exchange rate by R_e, then the unhedged dollar return to the foreign security, R_D^U, is[3]

$$R_D^U = R_L + R_e . \tag{1}$$

The dollar measured variance is given by

$$S_D^2 = S_L^2 + S_e^2 + 2r\, S_L\, S_e , \tag{2}$$

where r is the correlation between exchange rate changes and the foreign currency return to the foreign security.

Now suppose that we add a foreign currency hedge to the portfolio. If the hedge ratio is 100 percent—the accounting, or dollar-for-dollar approach to hedging—then in order to calculate the hedged security's return we must modify equation (1) in two ways. First, we must subtract R_e, the change in the exchange rate. Second, we must add the forward foreign-exchange discount or premium, since the hedge is affected by selling marks (buying dollars) for forward delivery. The effect of the hedge, therefore, is to add a term $-(R_e - f)$ to the unhedged return.[4] In effect, in equation (1) we replace the appreciation or depreciation of the exchange rate, R_e, by the forward discount or premium, f, giving a hedged return in dollars, R_D^H, of

$$R_D^H = R_L + f . \tag{3}$$

More generally, suppose the hedge ratio need not be 1. If we denote the hedge ratio by h, then the adjustment to the unhedged return is $-h(R_e - f)$, and the hedged return becomes

$$R_D^H = R_L + R_e - h(R_e - f) . \tag{3*}$$

Notice that (3*) reduces to (3) when $h = 1$, and it reduces to (1) when $h = 0$. It is convenient to rearrange the terms of (3*) as follows:

$$R_D^H = R_L + (1 - h)R_e + hf . \tag{4}$$

Equation (4) says the dollar return to a foreign security equals the deutsche-mark return, plus the change in the exchange rate multiplied by the fraction of the position that was unhedged, plus the forward exchange discount or premium multiplied by the fraction of the exposure that was hedged.

Using (4), and the fact that the term hf is nonstochastic, the variance of the dollar return to the hedged foreign security is given by

$$S_D^2 = S_L^2 + (1-h)^2 S_e^2 + 2(1-h)rS_L S_e . \qquad (5)$$

Now it is straightforward to select the optimal hedge ratio. Minimizing (5) with respect to h produces

$$h* = \frac{rS_L S_e}{S_e^2} + 1 . \qquad (6)$$

We have placed a superscript star on $h*$ to indicate (6) represents one particular value of the hedge ratio—the optimal ratio. Notice that we have made no assumptions regarding the kind of foreign security we are currency hedging. Equation (6) describes the optimal hedge ratio if the underlying security is either an equity or a fixed-income investment. Notice also that the volatility of the exchange rate, S_e, is the same in either case. This seems to suggest that optimal hedging policies will be similar for equity and bond investments that have similar volatilities (S_L), so long as foreign stock and bond investments share a similar value for r. Accordingly, correlation is the key. Equation (6) tells us that if hedging policies differ between foreign stocks and foreign bonds, it must be because r—the correlation between foreign currency measured returns and exchange rate changes—is different for stock and bond investments. There are good economic reasons to suspect that will be the case

Why Stocks and Bonds Are Different

Bonds are nominal assets. By this we mean that a foreign bond is a claim to nominal amounts of foreign cash, just as a domestic bond is a claim to nominal amounts of domestic cash.[5] In contrast, equities are claims to real assets, such as factories, machinery, inventories, commodities, or real property. Of course, the investor's interest is in the cash that those real assets throw off. But the amount of cash produced by a real asset is not fixed in nominal terms. Instead, it is likely to rise or fall with the domestic price level. So equities have a degree of built-in inflation protection that bonds do not have. To see how important this may be for the likely correlation between equity returns and exchange rate changes, we will consider a simple (but extreme) example based on two hypothetical German securities, one a bond and one an equity.

Suppose we own a rather unusual German equity investment: we own the only shares in a German company that has no liabilities and owns only one asset, a bar of gold bullion weighing one ounce. As this is written, the price of gold is approximately $400 per ounce, and the deutsche-mark/dollar exchange rate is approximately $0.67 per mark. Accordingly, our equity investment is worth deutsche mark (DM) 600. Suppose also that we own a German bond, which is a pure discount issue maturing tomorrow, with a market value of DM600. The dollar value of the bond, at the current exchange rate, is $400.

According to accounting convention, our exposure to deutsche-mark exchange rate changes is the same in either case: DM600. Accordingly, we will receive hedge accounting treatment if we choose to sell DM600 forward against either investment. However, that does not mean that our economic exposure to changes in the deutsche-mark/dollar exchange rate is the same in either case. In fact, our actual exposure differs considerably. To see this, suppose that the deutsche-mark/dollar exchange rate changes from $0.67 to $0.50 overnight—a substantial depreciation of the German mark. Let us calculate our loss, measured in dollars, in each case.

In the case of the bond—a nominal asset—the investor still has a claim to a fixed number of deutsche marks, specifically DM600. Unfortunately, each of these marks is now worth fewer dollars. Our DM600 German bond used to be worth $400, but now it is only worth $300. We have suffered a 25 percent loss of principal, measured in dollars.

Notice that the value of the bond, measured in deutsche marks, was independent of the change in the exchange rate. At the old exchange rate, the bond was worth DM600. At the new exchange rate, it was also worth DM600. In other words, in terms of the expression for the optimal hedge ratio, equation (6), $r=0$. Using (6), this means the optimal hedge ratio was 100 percent. We should have sold DM600 forward in order to currency hedge the position. If we did, then the gain on our forward sale of marks would have exactly offset the exchange-rate translation loss on the bond.

Now let us consider our German equity investment. The equity represents a claim to a real asset—in our contrived example, an ounce of gold. Suppose that the dollar price of gold is set in world markets, and that the price is quite independent of any changes in the dollar/mark exchange rate. The price of gold is $400. At the old exchange rate, our German equity was worth DM600—$400 ÷ $0.67. But at the new exchange rate of $0.50, the same equity will be worth DM800. This is simply the world price of gold—$400, before and after the deutsche mark depreciates—multiplied by the exchange rate. Accordingly, when the value of the German equity holding is translated into dollars after the exchange rate changes from $0.67 to $0.50, the value is still $400. There is no loss, despite the sizable depreciation of the deutsche mark.

In this case, the German equity investment had no economic exposure to the deutsche-mark/dollar exchange rate, even though the accounting exposure was DM600. This simple insight surprises investors who are familiar with an accounting-oriented framework for evaluating exchange rate exposures, but it should come as no surprise if an investor thinks carefully about the nature of the equity position. The equity was not a claim to deutsche marks, it was a claim to real assets—in this case, an ounce of gold. Accordingly, it was not directly exposed to the mark/dollar exchange rate. Of course, it might be indirectly exchange rate exposed if the dollar price of gold is related to the mark/dollar exchange rate. This is discussed in the following section.

To see how easy it is to be misled by the conventional accounting framework, let us extend this example one step further. Before the exchange rate changed, the equity was worth DM600. At the new exchange rate, the equity was worth DM800. How easy it would be to observe the deutsche-mark-measured price change and to conclude that this was a shrewd equity investment—after all, it appreciated from DM600 to DM800 overnight—only to be tripped up by an adverse exchange-rate change. In the conventional accounting framework, the equity investment gain was offset by an exchange rate loss. Next time, investors vow that they will currency hedge. However, looked at from an economically defensible perspective, there never was an exposure to the dollar/deutsche mark. It was correct not to hedge. Moreover, there never really was a gain on the equity position, and therefore the gain was not lost due to an unfavorable exchange rate change. In dollar terms, the equity never changed its price, because the dollar price of gold (our real asset in this example) did not change. If the investor had (incorrectly) currency hedged by selling deutsche marks forward, a sizable profit would have been booked. But the profit, properly attributed, would have been the result of a successful currency *speculation*. The investor would have been short German marks (as a result of an unnecessary currency hedge) and would have gained as a result of the deutsche-mark's depreciation.

What rich ironies can be created by faulty performance attribution. The portfolio manager who foolishly currency hedged an exposure that he did not have—in effect, a manager who engaged unknowingly in currency speculation—will be praised by superiors for his shrewd equity-selection skills and prudence in employing a currency hedge. A portfolio manager who properly failed to hedge an exposure that she did not really have will be praised for choosing a shrewd German equity investment—which, as we can see, is a gross misconception—but she will be criticized for recklessly speculating on currencies because she did not use a foreign exchange hedge. Of course, she was quite correct not to hedge exposure that she do not have. But of these two managers, whom do you think will get the larger bonus?

Now let us apply the insights from this example to our expression for the optimal hedge ratio, equation (6). Recall that this formula works for either the equity or the fixed-income investment. For the fixed-income investment, $r = 0$. Accordingly, using (6) the optimal hedge ratio is $h^* = 1$. For the German equity investment, the deutsche-mark price of the equity changes in lockstep with changes in the exchange rate. Their correlation easily can be calculated: it is $r = -S_e/S_L$. According to (6), the optimal hedge ratio for the equity investment is $h^* = 0$.

This section has demonstrated that the algebra of calculating an optimal hedge ratio is the same for stocks and bonds, but the algebra must be interpreted with great care. It is true that the formula describing the optimal hedge ratio is the same in either case. However, that does not mean that optimal hedge ratios are likely to be the same, or even similar, when we compare foreign bond and equity investments. As we have seen, the key parameter is the correlation between the return to the foreign security, measured in its home currency, and changes in the exchange rate. Accordingly, to see what the optimal hedge ratio is likely to be in situations more realistic than the example above, we must examine the correlation between security prices and exchange rates in more detail.

A Closer Look at Correlation

The previous section showed that the optimal hedge ratio depends critically on the correlation between exchange rate changes and security returns. In the simple example developed therein, we assumed that the deutsche-mark price of a German bond was uncorrelated with changes in the mark/dollar exchange rate ($r = 0$). This resulted in an optimal hedge ratio of 100 percent. However, if interest rate changes are positively or negatively correlated with exchange rate changes—a plausible hypothesis—then the optimal hedge ratio for a foreign bond will not be 100 percent. Similarly, in the example we assumed that the dollar price of the real assets underlying an equity security evolved independently of exchange rates ($r = -S_e/S_L$). This resulted in an optimal equity hedge ratio of 0 percent. However, there are good reasons to suspect that exchange rate changes often are related to changes in real asset valuations, and hence to changes in equity prices. If so, the optimal hedge ratio for foreign equity holdings may differ from zero. In this section, we will discuss some of the reasons why foreign equity and bond prices may be correlated with exchange-rate changes.

Bonds

In the simple example presented in the last section, the German bond was a short-maturity discount issue. The choice was deliberate, and was designed to make the bond's market value (in deutsche marks) independent of a change in the exchange rate. However, more realistically, we expect a major change in an important deutsche-mark exchange rate to affect German interest rates and bond prices. The linkages between interest rates and exchange rates are strongest for small, open economics. However, most practicing international portfolio managers believe that exchange rates are significant even in large economies, in which foreign trade represents only a small share of gross domestic product (GDP), such as the United States.

There are a number of potential transmission mechanisms linking interest rates and exchange rates. The inflation rate is the most obvious. Starting at an initial position of macroeconomic equilibrium, suppose the expected inflation rate rises as a consequence of a depreciation of the exchange rate. We expect bond yields to rise (bond prices to fall) since fixed-interest investors must be compensated for expected future inflation. Indeed, bond yields may rise by more than the initial change in inflationary expectations, if higher expected inflation also makes the bonds seem riskier. In other words, a weaker currency may be associated with higher expected future inflation and with more inflation uncertainty, both of which will tend to cause investors to demand higher yields.

Exchange rates and bond yields are also correlated because both are related to monetary policy. Again let us suppose we start from an initial position of equilibrium. Suppose the monetary authorities tighten and succeed in raising real short-term interest rates. Economic theory—the conventional portfolio balance model of exchange-rate determination—implies that the domestic currency will then appreciate. Higher short-term rates are also likely to affect bond yields. In a very austere macroeconomic model, bond yields will fall because inflationary expectations will fall. Casual observation suggests that more often bond yields rise, at least in the short run, when monetary policy is tightened. In any case, few portfolio managers would expect tighter monetary policy to have no effect at all on bond yields.

This is only a small sample of the many linkages that may exist between interest rates and exchange rates. Such linkages are common to Kenysian, monetarist, and rational expectations macroeconomic models, and are also implied by many models of exchange rate determination.[6] As we have seen, one consequence of a correlation between exchange rates and bond prices [$r \neq 0$ in equation (6)] is that the optimal hedge ratio will not equal 100 percent. For example, to the extent a depreciating domestic currency is associated with higher interest rates and lower bond prices—that is, $r>0$ in equation (6)—the optimal hedge ratio will exceed 100 percent. In other words, in this case, it would be advisable to overhedge your foreign bond holdings. It is more difficult to argue that a stronger domestic currency is associated with higher domestic bond yields, at least in the long run. However, it is certainly not impossible to imagine circumstances in which higher domestic interest rates are associated with a strengthening currency in the short run. Under these circumstances, the optimal policy would be to underhedge foreign-bond holdings, as can easily be verified by substituting a negative value for r into equation (6).

Equities

Equities are claims to real assets, but that does not mean that equity prices are insensitive to changes in exchange rates. Equities represent claims to particular assets located in particular countries, and the profitability of those assets (and hence their market values) will often be sensitive to exchange rate changes.

One reason equity prices are related to exchange rates is that the real assets underlying equity shares are not costlessly movable from country to country. As the deutsche mark appreciates against the dollar, Daimler-Benz may find it optimal to produce more cars in the United States, and less cars in Germany. Daimler can open new fabrication facilities in South Carolina, and can close existing fabrication facilities in Germany. Both of these responses take time—implying that Daimler's production will be inefficiently distributed in the interim—and both are costly. Daimler-Benz cannot respond to exchange-rate changes by moving existing fabrication facilities back and forth between the two countries. Nor can it move its trained work force. As a result an appreciation of the deutsche mark may reduce Daimler-Benz's profitability. That, in turn, will reduce Daimler-Benz's profits and its share price. However, a depreciation of the mark may hand Daimler a windfall gain. The result: Daimler-Benz's share price may tend to rise when the mark falls, and fall when the mark rises. In this case, it would be optimal to underhedge shares in Daimler-Benz, if you are a U.S. investor.

In other words, equity is a claim to real assets, but real assets located in specific places and specialized in the production of specific products. Exchange rate changes induce windfall corporate gains and losses because they change the optimal pattern of production, trade, and distribution—sometimes to a particular shareholder's advantage, and sometimes to his or her disadvantage. In either case, it would be surprising to find that a change in the dollar/deutsche-mark exchange rates had no effect on the dollar price of German equity shares, as was proposed in the simple example in the last section. As long as such a relationship exists, it is not optimal hedging policy to treat foreign equities as if they are unexposed to exchange rates.

Summary and Concluding Observations

The formula describing the optimal foreign currency hedge for a foreign security position is the same if the underlying asset is an equity or a bond. However, that does not imply the optimal hedge is likely to be the same in either case. Why? Because a key determinant of the optimal hedge ratio is the correlation between the foreign currency measured return of the foreign security and changes in exchange rates. That correlation is likely to be considerably different for foreign stock and foreign bond investments.

When an appreciating or depreciating foreign currency is unrelated to the local currency return to a foreign investment, then the optimal hedge ratio is 100 percent. The size of the foreign currency hedge should equal the size of the foreign investment.[7] However, if an appreciating foreign currency is usually associated with an appreciating foreign investment—measured in local (i.e., foreign) currency terms—then it is optimal to overhedge the position. In other words, if German share prices generally rise in deutsche-mark terms when the German mark is appreciating, then it is best to overhedge. When German share prices tend to fall in a strong deutsche-mark environment, then it is best to underhedge.

One key point that is often missed is that it is the correlation between exchange rates and the particular shares an investor owns that matters, not the correlation between an index of foreign share prices and exchange rates. Common sense suggests that this correlation might be quite different for different companies, depending for example on (1) whether they produce easily tradable goods or nontradables such as services; (2) whether they depend on imported raw materials, or if instead most of their value added is associated with locally produced intermediate goods and labor; (3) whether they sell their products locally or export them; and (4) whether they have the flexibility to move their production facilities abroad in response to exchange rate changes.

This chapter has considered the financial determinants of optimal hedging policies, but we would be remiss if we suggested that only financial considerations matter in practice. Accounting and regulatory issues also matter. A funds manager cannot always use the optimal hedging policy, particularly if that implies overhedging positions, for fear of being accused of currency speculation. Sadly, the potential penalties for managing global currency exposures in a conservative and sophisticated way may be severe until the accounting and regulatory authorities recognize that a 100 percent hedge ratio is not always optimal.

References

Black, F. "Universal Hedging: Optimizing Currency Risk and Reward in International Portfolios, *Financial Analysts Journal* (July/August 1989) pp. 16-22.

Black, F. "Equilibrium Exchange Rate Hedging", *Journal of Finance*, July 1990, pp. 899-908.

Clark, R., and M. Kritzman. "Currency Management: Concepts and Practices," Research Foundation of the Institute of Chartered Financial Analysts, 1996.

Froot, K. "Currency Hedging over Long Horizons," National Bureau of Economic Research, Working Paper No. 4355, May 1993.

Kritzman, M. "Optimal Currency Hedging Policy with Biased Forward Rates," *Journal of Portfolio Management* (Summer 1993), pp. 94-100.

Perold, A., and E. Schulman. "The Free Lunch in Currency Hedging: Implications for Investment Policy and Performance Standards," *Financial Analysts Journal*, May 1988, pp. 45-50.

Thomas, L. "Currency Risks in International Equity Portfolios," *Financial Analysts Journal* 44, No. 2, March/April 1988.

Thomas, L. "The Performance of Currency Hedged Foreign Bonds," *Financial Analysts Journal*, May/June 1989, pp. 25-31.

Endnotes

1. Because of Siegel's paradox, this is not strictly accurate. In fact, because of Siegal's paradox the expected future spot exchange rate is not even well defined, since the mathematical expectation of the future dollar per deutsche-mark rate does not equal the inverse of the mathematical expectation of the deutsche mark per dollar rate. However, this is not important in practice, and it can be avoided in modeling by using continuously compounded rates of return. For the case where forward rates are biased, see Kritzman (1993).

2. Clark & Kritzman (1996) deal with multiple foreign assets.

3. We take all returns to be continuously compounded, thus avoiding cross product terms. If R_D^U, R_L, and R_e are not continuously compounded, then equation (1) holds only as an approximation.

4. To be consistent with our use of continuously compounded returns, f is the natural logarithm of the ratio of the spot exchange rate to the forward exchange rate. In other words, f is the continuously compounded forward foreign-exchange premium.

5. Notice that we are treating conventional bonds, not inflation index-linked issues. Index linked bonds have been issued in the United Kingdom and Canada, and will soon be issued by the United States. Real (i.e., inflation protected) bonds have important equity–like qualities.

6. For example, in a Kenysian flow equilibrium models exchange rates and interest rates are linked by changes in aggregate demand. In a monetary model, interest rates and exchange rates both respond to changes in money supply or demand.

7. More precisely, the present value of the foreign currency sold forward should equal the market price of the foreign security, including any accrued interest if the security is a bond.

Measuring the Performance of Currency Managers

Brian Strange
Principal
Currency Performance Analytics

Goals of Performance Measurement

Performance measurement should give an investor insight into an investment manager's abilities, both relative to the passive returns of the market and relative to advisors who are following a similar investment philosophy. The first comparison is done to a benchmark appropriate to the manager's investment style; one that is in sync with the investor's investment goals. The second is accomplished by comparing results to an investment-peer universe.

Quantifying and comparing manager ability lowers the risk of selecting the wrong manager. A close examination of manager returns helps the investor to avoid surprises and to choose the manager who will best meet the investor's goals. Whether the goals are risk reduction, achievement of market returns, or outperforming the markets, closer scrutiny of past performance (and comparison with appropriate benchmarks and competing firms) will aid in the hiring decision. After the manager has been hired, such scrutiny will be important to monitor whether the manager is delivering the investment methodology and results that were advertised.

The criteria of performance measurement should not be any different for reviewing currency managers, although this review can be more complicated and difficult. Investing in conventional asset classes usually entails providing money to the manager to buy securities; the manager will subsequently sell the securities for a profit, and the proceeds will be returned to the investor. The amount of the profit divided by the original investment gives a simple absolute return. Taking the time period into account annualizes the return.

Not all forms of currency management are as simple as this scenario. Currency managers have different goals. Some invest in currency instruments with the goal of profiting from currency movements, no matter which direction the currency moves. Other managers hedge currency risk which arises from a portfolio of securities denominated in foreign currencies.

Currency investment or hedging strategies are most often carried out in the derivatives markets. The forward contract can be thought of as the original derivative instrument, since it derives its value from the underlying spot exchange market. Frequently, no capital is required, only a credit line.

In such a situation, it is important to consider whether the gain should be

- An infinite return.

- Measured against the total credit line made available to the manager.

- Calculated against any margin requirements that had to be provided in order to secure the credit line.

- Based on the beginning or average value of the foreign security portfolio.

- Included in the rise in value of the foreign portfolio resulting from the translation at higher exchange rates, or if the gain focus only on the returns of the hedges.

- Evaluated against a benchmark and how this benchmark should be chosen.

It is also necessary to determine if the mission and investment constraints were identical for all managers whose results are being compared.

It is easy to see that many issues can arise. Therefore, let us begin by first analyzing the issues based on the investment goal of the currency manager. For the most part, investors hire currency managers for one of two reasons:

- To invest in currencies and to make money whether exchange rates rise or fall, and to choose currencies that will rise or fall the most. The manager's goal is to *manage currency as an asset class.*

- To hedge against changes in the liquidation value of the investors' foreign portfolios due to changes in currency values. The manager's goal is to *protect the home currency value of the portfolio* by hedging the currency risk in an overlay assignment.

We will examine the tasks each type of manager sets for him- or herself and the consequent implications for measuring how well each manager performs the task.

Assessing Performance of Currency Managers in Unconstrained Assignments

Investing in currencies as an asset class involves many choices. The manager will choose when to hold currencies and when not to. He or she will select which currencies to hold (those which will appreciate the most). This is not unlike the mission of an international short-term fixed-income manager. However, the currency manager has more degrees of freedom. Unlike the fixed-income manager, the currency manager can make money when currencies are falling in value by selling them in the forward or options markets. The manager can also choose combinations that do not involve the investor's home currency—by cross-trading currency pairs. The objective is to be on the right side of the market in whichever currency pair (or pairs) of exchange rates are moving the most.

Taking Different Levels of Leverage into Account

It should be a simple task, then, to compare performance. Whoever returns the most money, relative to the amount given at the start, wins. Right? Well, yes and no. Yes, because, if managers have no constraints placed on them, the manager who uses this freedom to achieve the greatest results will be much sought after. However, two factors define success.

Which manager is better? The one whose directional signal yielded a 10 percent return, but who employed it on 50 percent of the available risk, or the one whose directional bet afforded a 5 percent return but whose confidence allowed her to apply it to 100 percent of the available risk? Each achieve a 5 percent return on the total capital or credit line. You could argue that the one with the better timing is the one to employ, because the confidence level could always be adjusted by the investor. The decisions could be applied to greater or lesser amounts of money.

This gets at the heart of adjusting manager returns for differences in leverage. A 20 percent return achieved by leveraging capital five times is no better than a 4 percent return earned with no leverage. So, while it might seem easy to say that the currency manager with the most chips wins, it could be more meaningful to adjust competing returns for the average leverage, as we did earlier. This focuses the comparison on the managers' timing and allocation decisions; although without more information, we cannot determine which is more significant. Wouldn't you rather hire a manager who makes better decisions, and adjust leverage to suit your desired level of risk?

Assessing Performance on a Nominal-Position-at-Risk Basis

In essence, adjusting returns so that they are comparable on a nominal-position-at-risk basis is the only way to equate the success of bets on direction and allocation. Nominal-position-at-risk can be thought of as the notional value of positions that a manager takes in a market. If the daily weighted-average of the positions amounts to a foreign currency equivalent of $100 million, then the returns should be expressed as a percent of that amount. If one financial institution required a 10 percent margin and another required only 5 percent, it is misleading to report the returns based on the amount of margin needed. In this case, returns with the more highly leveraged arrangement could be seen to be twice as high when using the margin as a base for calculation. Yet the average positions outstanding would be identical, as would be the returns that those positions allowed. It is incorrect to conclude that demonstrated skill in either account exceeds the other.

Risk-Adjusted Returns

The consistency of each manager's returns might be considerably different, and it is worth investigating the risk-adjusted returns of each. If two managers deliver the same average quarterly return, but the first provides less variability, then the first will have a higher risk-adjusted return. You can look at the total average return divided by the standard deviation of the returns to derive a simple risk/return ratio. This defines the expected return for each unit of risk. The higher the ratio, the higher the risk-adjusted return.

Another approach might be to determine the lowest standard deviation of returns among a sample of managers to be compared. This risk number can then be divided by each manager's standard deviation measure and the result can be multiplied by each manager's average return. Each manager could be ranked according to that score.

For example, consider the returns shown in Table 1.

Regardless of which approach might be used, the rank ordering is the same when taking the risk of the returns into account: Manager A, then B, then C, which is the opposite of the ranking arrived at when examining raw returns. Manager A is the more consistent, low-risk manager.

Assessing Performance of Currency Managers in Constrained Assignments

Nature of Currency-Overlay Management

In contrast with unconstrained bets on currency movements, currency overlay assignments are generally limited to protecting the home currency value of an investor's international portfolio. Currency exposures result

Table 1   Option Valuation

	Manager A	Manager B	Manager C
Average Return	8%	9%	10%
Standard Deviation	3%	5%	7%
Return/Risk Ratio	2.66	1.8	1.43
Ratio to Lowest Risk	1	.6	.43
Risk-Adjusted Return	8%	5.4%	4.3%

from the choice of securities an investor makes. As currencies rise or fall, the value of the portfolio will change depending on the currency denomination of the securities. Protecting the portfolio from adverse currency movements is usually the work of the currency overlay manager, and her performance can be affected greatly by the following factors:

- Rules of the assignment (the mandate)

- Exposures of the underlying investments

- Benchmark hedge ratio

- Reference or home currency

We will discuss their effects in turn.

Mandates

When appointing a currency overlay manager, restrictions will be placed on the activities in which that currency manager can engage, in order to enforce the investment management mission. These instructions commonly make up the investment mandate. Mandates can vary a great deal but some of the more common ones are described in the discussion that follows.

Defensive   The typical, conservative investor is concerned with currency risk simply because it comes packaged with the international securities in which he invested. If it is a positive force, he loves the boost to his returns. When it is negative, he wishes it would have been taken away. He wants the currency manager to be prescient in deciding when to hedge and when not to hedge the individual currencies in his portfolio—when to turn the currency risk on or off. He may allow the manager complete discretion to vary the hedge ratio between zero percent and 100 percent, hoping that he will be unhedged at just the right moment when currencies begin to rise, and to hedge them fully just when they begin to fall. He wants the manager to deal only with the currency pairs in his underlying portfolio, and only to the extent and amount that they are represented in the portfolio. Ten million deutsche marks of securities could never have more than ten million deutsche marks of hedges against them. These hedges would have to be forward sales of the deutsche mark back to the home currency, or put options for ten million deutsche marks. See Table 2.

Cross-Hedging A portfolio manager often structures the allocation of an international securities portfolio based on which countries offer the greatest opportunities for appreciation. While this country allocation decision might be optimal with regard to the potential value of the underlying investments, it is not always the best with regard to the potential value of the currencies involved. While the yen might be falling against the dollar, the deutsche mark might be rising. Wouldn't it be better to have more deutsche marks and less yen in the portfolio? But the equity or bond manager might believe that the Japanese market offers more potential than the German market, which suggests larger positions in yen and smaller ones in deutsche marks. In this case, why shouldn't the currency manager re-denominate the currency risk of the portfolio? She can easily sell the yen against the deutsche mark, shifting the weighting of undesirable yen to desirable deutsche marks. This technique of cross-hedging simply shifts the currency risk around without increasing the overall currency risk beyond that initially acquired with the investment portfolio. See Table 3.

Table 2　Defensive Mandate

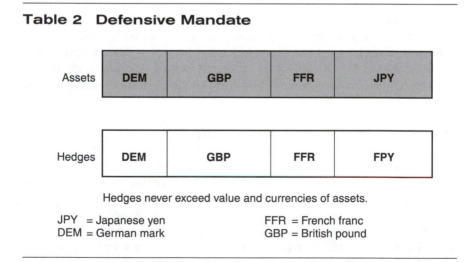

Hedges never exceed value and currencies of assets.

JPY　= Japanese yen　　　　FFR = French franc
DEM = German mark　　　　GBP = British pound

Proxy Hedging The use of a proxy to hedge currency risk is a variant of cross-hedging, but with a completely different purpose. Many equity managers strive to match or exceed the performance of Morgan Stanley Capital International's Europe, Australia, Far East index (EAFE). This index is derived based on market capitalizations of securities in each individual country. Consequently, investments may be made in many smaller countries, in small proportions. It may be inefficient to hedge in so many currencies in such small amounts, particularly if the currencies in these countries behave similarly against the investor's home currency. The best examples are the many currencies of the European Monetary System (EMS). The Belgian franc, Dutch guilder, French franc, deutsche mark, and several other currencies typically float in unison against the dollar. The argument can therefore be made that it is more efficient to use the deutsche mark to cover the risk of these currencies than it is to deal in the individual currencies directly, particularly since there is a more liquid market for the deutsche mark. Larger amounts could be traded at tighter spreads, saving costs and boosting returns.

Another reason to use a proxy arises in forward-market pricing. Forwards are driven by interest rate differentials, which can vary a great deal among the EMS partners. If the most productive currency is chosen as the proxy for others, savings can arise in the size of the forward discount/premium. Thus, the deutsche mark might be used to hedge the risk of all members of the EMS.

Table 3 Cross-Hedging Mandate

Assets	DEM	GBP	FFR	JPY

Hedges	GBP	JPY

Hedges can be in any currency up to value of assets.

JPY = Japanese yen   FFR = French franc
DEM = German mark   GBP = British pound

This strategy is much less ambitious than cross-hedging. Cost control is the main issue. Of course, the investor assumes the risk that highly correlated currencies may diverge in the future. The currency market movements of September 1992 drove that lesson home. See Table 4.

Exposure Creation   An investor may believe that a currency manager cannot add value when currencies are rising if the manager is restricted to a defensive mandate. The best the manager can do is to match the market by being completely unhedged. Should she be paid management fees just for matching the market or should she earn them by adding value during these periods as well? The only way to add value during these periods is to buy currencies that are rising against the home currency. These currencies may not even be represented by the security selections in the portfolio. The currencies could be wholly unrelated, or they could be additions to existing currency positions. In this case, the portfolio becomes leveraged.

Exposure creation can enhance returns, but it raises risk as well, and if manager decisions are wrong it can lead to greater losses than would originally have been the case. In essence, the manager takes positions in currencies that the investor doesn't have in his portfolio. This is often seen as speculation in currencies rather than control of currency risk in the portfolio. See Table 5.

Leverage   Leverage is created when positions in the overlay assignment exceed the total of the underlying investments. This can happen in two

---

Table 4   Proxy-Hedging Mandate

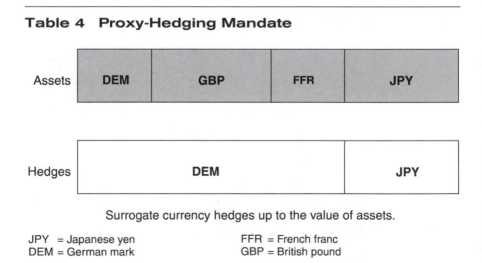

Assets	DEM	GBP	FFR	JPY

Hedges	DEM	JPY

Surrogate currency hedges up to the value of assets.

JPY = Japanese yen   FFR = French franc
DEM = German mark   GBP = British pound

Table 5　Exposure Creation Mandate

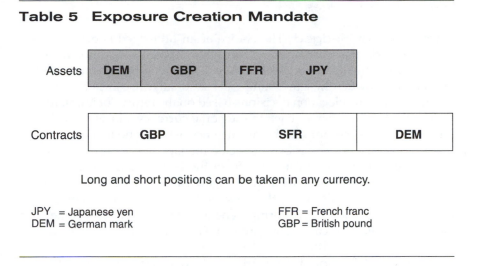

Long and short positions can be taken in any currency.

JPY　= Japanese yen　　　　　　　　　　FFR = French franc
DEM = German mark　　　　　　　　　　GBP = British pound

ways. Long positions can be taken which result in the currency composition of the combined portfolio exceeding the amount of the investment securities. Alternatively, hedges can be placed which exceed the value of the portfolio currency risk, producing a net short position. Both situations amount to leverage. Nominal positions exceed the value of the assets that they are supposed to protect.

Exposures of Underlying Investments

Assume that manager A showed a return of 6 percent compared with manager B's 4 percent. You might think that manager A's abilities were better. But suppose you look closer and discover that manager A's portfolio consisted entirely of Japanese stocks, and manager B's comprised only UK stocks. You would then want to know how much the yen had moved against your home currency and how much sterling had moved. Let us assume that, for the period, the total move in yen was +12 percent, and that for sterling it was +5 percent. Manager A captured only half of the move in yen (6 percent out of 12 percent), detracting from the move with hedging losses amounting to 6 percent. Manager B allowed 80 percent (4 percent out of 5 percent) of the move in sterling to flow through. His hedging losses of only 1 percent lowered the unhedged return of 5 percent.

In a real portfolio, the picture is much more complicated and the returns are almost impossible to compare. Exposures may vary greatly from one portfolio to the next. Unless exposures are identical for two portfolios, it is almost meaningless to make an attempt to compare results.

Benchmark Choices

Zero Percent Hedged   The choice of an unhedged benchmark is a policy decision that currencies will provide a positive additional return over the investment horizon. It is usually the position that an international investor takes when first investing internationally. It comes as a consequence of making allocation decisions based on the returns of international assets which are converted back to the home currency. Simply translating the local returns back into the home currency assumes no hedging.

Benchmarks often purposely shackle managers to a narrow range of hedge ratios, none of which is far from the benchmark. The manager's business risk rises because the investor's investment risk is heightened by straying too drastically from the benchmark. Consequently, comparing results of managers with differing benchmarks also becomes somewhat meaningless. Each has a differing investment objective.

100 Percent Hedged   The fully hedged benchmark arises from a belief that, in the long term, currencies provide negative or no additional returns and a great deal of portfolio volatility. If you cannot get paid for carrying the risk, why not get rid of it. The result is more peace of mind at no cost.

50 Percent Hedged   Benchmarks at the poles of hedge-ratio possibilities tend to produce either little hedging when it is really needed or little unhedging when it is desirable. If the maximum deviation a manager will make from the benchmark hedge ratio is 30 percent, then hedging will never be more than 30 percent when the benchmark strategy calls for remaining unhedged. Hedging will never be less than 70 percent if the benchmark strategy is to remain fully hedged.

Many pension plan sponsors who have chosen to switch to a 50 percent hedged benchmark have done so in the interest of obtaining more hedging flexibility from managers. The same 30 percent departure from the benchmark hedge ratio would produce a range of hedging from 20 percent to 80 percent, producing a greater ability to take advantage of swings in exchange rates for the same business or strategic risk. This is more in line with an active management philosophy—participate in strong markets and hedge in weak ones. As an investment policy, this implies that currencies have a 50 percent chance of rising as well as falling, and produce no long-term return. It is a flip of the coin, more appropriate in the currency markets than in the equity or bond markets where dividend and interest discount models make the assumption of continued price appreciation logical.

Option Benchmark   The argument can be made that, since all active managers are charged to be in the market when it is rising and out of it when it is falling, they should be measured against a standard that is certain to produce precisely that result. The only sure way an investor can enjoy the benefits of currency volatility and avoid the downside risk is to purchase a put option. Obviously, the question is begged as to whether the long-term cost of the premiums is worth it. Is the cure worse than the disease?

Many active management strategies believe that it is. Each manager believes that the same payoff pattern can be achieved synthetically, whether it is through a more predictable options-replication program (dynamic hedging) or achieved through momentum models or through the consideration of economic fundamentals. The results of each approach will vary greatly. It makes sense to measure a manager's performance against this standard. Option replicators then have to prove that they can manufacture options less expensively in their own workshops than they can buy them on the market. Other styles would have to prove that their approach would produce the same results at a lower cost (higher performance).

Rule-Based Benchmarks Passive benchmarks are usually the rule. However, semiactive ones, based on consistently applied trading rules, can also be used. For instance, if an investor believes that a trend-following manager is the best to employ for currency overlay, perhaps he should set a simplistic trend-following rule as a benchmark. A three-month moving-average crossover rule would be simple. Applied on a monthly basis, if the spot rate is below the three-month trailing average (calculated from the three prior month-end spot rates), then the benchmark hedge calculations place a hedge for the month. If it is above the average rate, then no hedge is taken into account for the month. If fees are paid to a manager with a sophisticated approach to capturing changes in trends, then it is hoped that she will do better than a simple approach which the investor could apply himself.

Another simple decision rule could be to hedge only when currencies are trading at a premium in the forward market and never hedge when they are trading at a discount. Empirical research has shown that although forward rates are *unbiased* predictors of future spot rates, they are not very *good* predictors. If that is the case, then why ever walk away from a premium when it is offered and why ever suffer a discount when hedging? The true test is whether the forward currency surprise[1] is biased toward being positive or negative.

Reference or Home Currency

Finally, it is almost axiomatic that comparing hedging returns for protecting the U.S. dollar value of yen securities with the hedging returns for protecting the yen value of U.S. dollar securities would lead to great confusion. Successful hedging for each investor would entail hedging at opposite points, and the calculation of the returns for each investor under identical market conditions would not produce the same results. For example, suppose that the U.S. dollar fell from 110 yen to 85 yen, and the currency manager protecting the yen-based portfolio hedged the move completely. His hedging returns would amount to 25 yen on a base of 110, or 22.73 percent. However, the underlying portfolio of U.S. dollar securities would now be translated at a lower rate. The translation losses of 22.73 percent are made up for by hedging returns of 22.73 percent. The net currency return is zero percent. The currency manager did a perfect job.

Now suppose that another manager had a U.S.-dollar-based account which invested in yen securities. This manager also did a perfect job and in this case did no hedging, as the yen was rising relative to the U.S. dollar. Hedging returns were zero percent and translation gains amounted to 29.4 percent, calculated as follows: the value of one yen rose from $.009091 (1/110) to $.011765 (1/85), producing a gain of $.002674 on a base of $.009091, or 29.4 percent. The translation gains for the U.S. investor are of a different magnitude than the translation losses for the Japanese investor.

In each case the currency manager took the perfect hedging action. Hedging returns were +22.73 percent and zero percent, respectively, and total currency returns were zero percent and +29.4 percent respectively. Which manager did better? Obviously, each could not have done better. It is only the numbers that are puzzling, demonstrating that a great deal of confusion can arise from comparing currency returns for different home currencies.

Portfolios based in two nondollar currencies cannot be expected at all times to move similarly against all other currencies.

Difficulties in Comparison

As we discussed in many of the previous examples, there can be substantial differences in the main underlying factors which affect the performance of currency managers when they are given an overlay assignment. It is a rare occurrence when more than two managers have all four key aspects in common, and it therefore becomes valid to compare their real returns to one another. It becomes even more difficult when an investor wants data going back for any length of time. The currency overlay industry is relatively new and real track records are not that long. Conventional thinking might then declare that it is an impossible task. But just like Alexander the Great who eschewed conventional thinking and didn't even try to untie the Gordian knot, favoring his sword instead to sever the knot (unconventional thinking), international investors must find a more imaginative approach to solving the knotty problem of comparing the performances of currency overlay managers. Table 6 summarizes why currency manager returns are not easy to compare.

Normalizing Portfolio Results for Comparison

Results for Individual Currencies

A common thread runs through most currency overlay assignments. The majority of currency managers make decisions on when and when not to hedge a single foreign currency back into the investor's home currency. While each may use a different discipline to arrive at the decision, it must still be made. Can investors easily compare all managers' decisions to hedge foreign currencies back into their home currencies?

Equal Weighting

If we take each manager's hedging returns for the major individual currencies we can readily compare them. This may be confusing, however. Manager A might be terrific in hedging the yen but somewhat poorer in hedging the deutsche mark. Manager B's returns might be in the opposite direction and of a different magnitude. Perhaps we could get more information if we attempt to simplify and express hedging performance in terms of overall portfolio returns.

One solution would be to take a popular portfolio, to which all investors can relate, and weight the individual currency hedging returns by the allocations of those currencies that comprise the portfolio. See Figure 1.

One of the most immediately recognized international portfolios is the EAFE index. The currency weights in the index change hour to hour and minute to minute as the relative values of the local stock markets change. These could be calculated at almost any point in time, but such a level of detail is not necessary. Quarterly or monthly weightings provide a suffi-

---

Table 6   Difficulties in Comparing Currency Manager Returns

Overlay Manager A		Overlay Manager B
Portfolio Exposures	≠	Portfolio Exposures
Hedging Mandate	≠	Hedging Mandate
Benchmark Hedge Ratio	≠	Benchmark Hedge Ratio
Reference Currency	≠	Reference Currency

**Figure 1 Weighting Currency Returns by
                Portfolio Allocation**

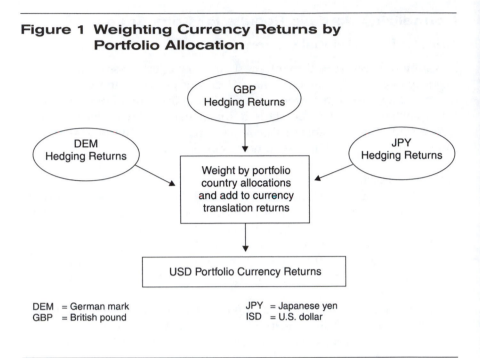

DEM = German mark   JPY = Japanese yen
GBP = British pound   ISD = U.S. dollar

cient amount of detail to approximate the currency effect of overlay hedging of an indexed portfolio. Many overlay assignments are given where the
exposures are provided to the manager monthly or quarterly, so this
frequency of changing weights replicates real life. The calculations are
simple, and might look like Table 7.

Using such a scheme does away with differences resulting from varying managers' differences in underlying portfolio exposures, which is one
of the prime obstacles to performance comparison.

Standardize Mandates by Examining Only the Returns
from Hedging Back to the Home Currency

The second most significant factor affecting hedging returns is the mandate,
many variations of which were discussed earlier in this chapter. If we insist
on including only the returns managers create from hedging back into the
home currency, and exclude all gains and losses from cross-hedging or from
creating currency exposure by taking long positions against the home
currency, then by definition we hold each manager to the same basic
defensive mandate. Managers are allowed to create currency returns only
by hedging—that is, by transferring currency risk to someone else by selling

Table 7   Calculation of Weighted Returns

Hedging Returns %

CHF	DEM	GBP	FRF	JPY
5.6	−4.0	1.3	−3.6	5.8

Country Weights %

CHF	DEM	GBP	FRF	JPY
3.6	10	15.3	13.8	48.3

Weighted Return %

CHF	DEM	GBP	FRF	JPY	% Total
.2	−.4	.2	−.5	2.8	2.3

the currency of the investments against the home currency, and by varying the hedge ratio between zero percent and 100 percent.

Benchmarks

Benchmarks can also have an impact, although it doesn't seem to concern every manager. If managers always make a buy or a sell decision on a currency pair, the implication is to be either zero percent hedged or 100 percent hedged with each call. They believe that a currency will rise or fall against the home currency, and usually follow through all the way, provided that they are confident of their decisions.

However, some managers have times when they are neutral, when they do not have an opinion about the direction of the market. Other managers employing a dynamic hedging strategy must have a starting point from which to vary the hedge ratio as markets rise and fall. Still others may set confidence levels on their market judgments and may vary the strength of their hedging with those confidence levels. These managers are benchmark-dependent and their returns will vary accordingly.

If a manager has a neutral position (no opinion positive or negative on the market) the logical thing to do is to strictly follow the client's policy on hedging. Thus, a manager will not hedge against an unhedged benchmark, will hedge half the risk if against a 50-percent-hedged benchmark, or hedge fully when 100-percent hedged is the policy position.

A dynamic hedger's starting position will usually be the benchmark position and, as the currency markets rise and fall, the hedge ratio will be adjusted from the starting position. As the market moves a certain percentage up or down, the hedge ratio is adjusted by a given percentage up or down. It is understandable that hedging returns will vary with the benchmark chosen by the investor. Starting from an unhedged position versus a 50-percent-hedged position will produce distinctly different average hedge ratios for each assignment, which produces similarly distinct sets of returns.

Managers using options may vary how far in or out of the money they purchase puts, dependent on the benchmark. The zero-percent-hedged benchmark may call for using puts which are farther out of the money than those used when the benchmark is a partially or fully hedged one.

Finally, the confidence level may be a means of adjusting the hedge ratio. See Table 8.

Active management is a series of bets which cause a manager to diverge from the benchmark. If she is 100 percent confident that her market call is correct, she will follow it completely, regardless of the benchmark. Thus a 100 percent certainty that currencies will rise produces zero percent hedging for all benchmarks. Conversely, 100 percent confidence that currencies will fall produces complete hedging for all benchmarks. However, suppose that the manager is only 70 percent sure that currencies will rise; 70 percent unhedged (30 percent hedged) is the logical place to be if either the fully hedged or fully unhedged benchmark is used. However, if the 50-percent-hedged benchmark is used, the manager feels confident in walking away from the benchmark by only 70 percent with her long call—that is, 5 percent of the hedge ratio for each 10 percent of confidence level. In the 50-percent-hedged benchmark case, that would result in a 15 percent hedge ratio (50 percent less 7 times 5; i.e., 30 percent hedged multiplied by the 50 percent benchmark). If the confidence level were 30 percent for the short call, then hedges would rise to 65 percent when the benchmark calls for being 50 percent hedged (50 percent plus 3 times 5).

It only makes sense to examine and compare returns reported for a common benchmark, because this is the only way that managers are striving for a common goal.

Home Currency

Finally, for reasons explained earlier, care should be taken that currency overlay returns are compared for common or similarly-behaving base currencies. Because of their close correlation, the results for deutsche mark and Dutch guilder-based portfolios would be comparable, provided that adjustments are made for the items detailed above.

Table 8 Relationship between Confidence Level, Benchmark Strategy, and Hedge Ratio

Market Opinion	Confidence Level	Logical Hedge Ratio Given the Following Benchmark			
		0% Hedged	40% Hedged	50% Hedged	100% Hedged
Long	100%	0%	0%	0%	0%
Long	70%	30%	12%	15%	30%
Long	30%	70%	28%	35%	70%
Short	100%	100%	100%	100%	100%
Short	70%	70%	82%	85%	70%
Short	30%	30%	58%	65%	30%

Decomposing and Adjusting Real Returns

If a manager has been protecting a portfolio, his total portfolio currency return is the result of an entire basket of currency hedges translated back into the home currency. Each of these currencies can be identified and the hedging returns reported for the individual currencies. This will enable equal weighting for more intelligent portfolio analysis.

However, if a manager places a hedge in a currency because the weight of the currency is so large in the portfolio, and not because he believes that the currency is falling, some special analysis might be in order. One could argue that if he had no opinion on the market, but merely hedged because of prudence, then this is a benchmark issue. If the benchmark is unhedged, the manager would very likely not hedge. If the benchmark is fully hedged, then a partial hedge represents a walk away from the benchmark and is clearly a manager's timing decision. In most cases it is properly included as a hedging decision based on a market view.

Substituting Model Returns to Expand the Comparison Universe

It is unlikely that more than a few managers will have all four of the following factors in common:

- Exposures
- Mandates

- Benchmarks

- Home currency.

The practice of using currency overlay programs to protect international portfolios is relatively new, and only a few managers might have all aspects in common, even for just a short period of time. Does that mean that it is pointless to compare performances? Yes, if you insist that the only returns worth examining are real returns. However, backtests or simulations might afford some insight if you believe that well-documented, quantitative approaches can produce comparable returns in actual practice. After all, the managers themselves have been comforted by similar results in deriving their investment disciplines. You run the risk, though, that the manager will not strictly follow the proposed approach when given an actual assignment.

Substituting Model Returns to Compare Real Returns to Model Returns in Benchmarking

This raises another potential use of model-based-return benchmarking. It affords a mechanism to compare actual returns to the same manager's model returns. This helps monitor how closely a manager follows her discipline and how skillfully she executes trades dictated by the model. Many believe a model should never be overridden, while many more take greater comfort when there is human intervention. A comparison of results for all managers is an excellent way to determine how effective intervention is. Thus, a pension plan with managers in place might like to compare their actual results to the theoretical model results.

What to Measure

What is the real measure of a currency manager's worth? Is it simply the value of losses saved through hedging? Or should you include the returns to the investor from letting currency exposures work for them? Should managers be measured against the goal set for them—the benchmark? Good arguments exist on both sides, but plenty of confusion can arise (as explained in the section on home currency) unless care is taken to make absolutely certain that the same measures are being applied to each manager.

Total Currency Returns

Translation Gains/Losses
When a currency overlay manager is appointed, she takes on the responsibility for all currency decisions. The underlying equity or bond managers

usually relinquish all actions on currency and are measured against the local return. If that is the case, then the currency manager's decision to be unhedged should be accounted for when calculating currency returns. Should currencies rise and the value of investments increase, it should go to the credit of the currency manager. While it may seem paradoxical that a decision to sit back and do nothing should be applauded, there are certainly times when this is the case.

Hedging Gains/Losses

Alternatively, one could argue that the only currency returns with which a manager should be credited are those the manager creates. Since hedging is his only job, only the hedging returns should be examined. However, these may be negative at times as a manager hedges in an uncertain market and then lifts them as currencies begin once again to rise. In fact, in rising currency periods, most managers will likely show some losses due to cautious hedging. Negative hedging returns do not necessarily mean a poor job. Again, it depends on the benchmark given to the manager. Negative hedging results with a partially or fully hedged benchmark are to be expected in rising currency markets.

Risk Reduction

Currency overlay managers are often brought in and given the mandate to reduce the risk of the portfolio that is due to currency movements. It doesn't seem right, then, that the entire focus of manager assessment ought be be on returns. If the job is to reduce risk, then risk should be measured. The most common measure of risk is standard deviation of returns. If a manager has done his work, the variability of total currency returns will have fallen. It is important to measure total currency returns in this case (translation gains/losses plus hedging gains/losses), since the total currency risk of the portfolio is the investor's concern.

Variance from Benchmarks

The true measure of managers is how well they meet the performance goals set out for them. The investment goals are laid out in the benchmark. The variance from the benchmark currency returns will define whether a manager overperforms or underperforms. But once again, care must be taken that the measure is consistent. Either total currency returns or hedging returns should be compared for both the manager and the benchmark.

Comparing against an unhedged benchmark is simple. If the manager lost money hedging, he underperformed, on a return basis. He may have outperformed on a risk basis because hedging invariably reduces risk. If the manager loses less or gains more from hedging than the hedging gains/losses resulting from the passive, partially or fully hedged benchmark strategy, then he has outperformed. And vice versa. A similar measure would be made for rule-based benchmarks. Compare the results (either total currency return or hedging returns only) against the same calculations for the benchmark.

Consistency is another desirable trait in managers and we will address it in the section on Risk.

It is also important to note that most overlay managers are measured against a benchmark which is customized for the currency exposures of the underlying portfolio. Periodically, the makeup and amounts of the currencies of the underlying investments are reported to the overlay manager. This same set of data should also drive the benchmark calculation. If exposures are reported quarterly, then the benchmark exposures should be changed only every quarter. This is particularly important if the currency manager has been instructed to pursue a defensive mandate, where no additional exposure to currencies is desired other than those comprising the underlying investments.

However, some investors have chosen to provide managers with a fixed exposure benchmark. If the currency effect of the EAFE index is the measure a manager is to beat, then reporting of the underlying investment currencies is obviated. In a simple mandate, the manager would pursue hedging against the currencies and amounts comprising the EAFE index. She would be compared to the currency returns of the index, whether it be unhedged, partially, or fully hedged. If the equity manager changed country allocations away from the index, it would not matter to the currency manager. It is arguable, though, whether the equity manager should be measured only on the local equity return of those variances, or also be charged with the currency return of the variance from benchmark allocation weightings.

It can get more complicated, however. Suppose that the equity manager makes a departure from the EAFE index by underweighting Japan. If the investor wants the currency return of the EAFE index, then he must allow the currency or equity manager to take long positions in yen to buy the exposure back to the weight in the index. In this case, total currency returns must be taken into account as opposed to focusing on the manager's hedging returns only. The purchase of currencies in the forward market to bring currency weights back to benchmark weights is not a hedge, and it would be very confusing to count it as such.

Quarterly Returns

Many currency investors insist on obtaining frequent performance reports. Monthly, weekly, and sometimes daily numbers are requested. This can be appropriate for highly leveraged situations where small daily movements can be magnified considerably, putting portfolio values at great risk.

Currency overlay management, though, is rarely leveraged and daily currency movements have exceeded 2 to 3 percent in only a few circumstances. Most institutional investors maintain a long-term perspective and review their investment managers on a quarterly basis. Consistency would argue for similar assessment of currency overlay managers.

Performance in Down Quarters versus Up Quarters

Currency overlay managers are usually hired to control the currency risk of an investment portfolio. A common concept of risk is that of *downside risk*. Investors love currency risk when it is a positive force on returns. They hate it when it detracts from investment returns or makes investment losses even worse. They want currency managers to be hedging the risk away in falling currency markets, and they hope that there will be little if any hedging during periods when currency values are rising. It is useful, then, to see just how well a manager meets these goals.

An investment manager's defensive characteristics are frequently analyzed by segregating performance into bull markets and bear markets. A bull market is a quarter where the index or benchmark showed positive returns and the bear market was a quarter where negative returns resulted. Managers often lag the index in bull markets, but good defensive characteristics permit them to outperform in bear markets. It is, of course, a question of how many bull-market quarters there are and how much the manager lags, and how many bear-market quarters occur and the amount of the excess returns. Managers with good defensive characteristics, and enough quarters in which to exhibit them, do better than the index over the long haul.

The analysis of defensive characteristics ought to be similar for currency overlay managers. Performance can be separated into up- and down-currency quarters, and the over/under performance versus the benchmark can be calculated. It is also true in the currency markets that managers tend to lag unhedged benchmarks in up-currency quarters. Some cautious hedging subtracts from translation gains. To succeed versus the benchmark over time, a manager must demonstrate sufficient prowess in down-currency periods to overcome the lag in up periods; and there must be enough down-currency periods. A ratio of overperformance in down quarters to underperformance in up quarters is a useful statistic.

Analyzing the effectiveness of using options to hedge uses the same framework. Options allow participation in positive markets, but they do so at a cost. The premium must be paid. This premium amounts to a guaranteed underperformance in up markets, very comparable to an active manager's underperformance in up markets, with the exception that the cost is known up front. Over time, options will outperform the benchmark, only if the underperformance (premiums) in up markets amounts to less than the outperformance (protection provided) during down-currency periods. Once again, this is highly dependent on having some weakness in the currency markets (i.e., strong home-currency periods).

Percentage of Market Moves or Maximum Protection Captured

Investment managers sometime complain that they are judged against a standard of 20/20 hindsight. Clients expect them to be in the market riding the bulls and in cash just before the bears arrive. Some pension plans have even proposed that currency overlay managers beat the better of a hedged or an unhedged benchmark. Managers cannot achieve this in the short run, naturally, but it may provide some insight to measure their performance against just such a yardstick in order to see on average what can be achieved and what is reasonable to expect.

Such a benchmark could be calculated by using the forward market and notionally applying hedges at the beginning of each quarter or year. If hedging was the wrong thing to do and lost money, then the losses are not taken into account in the benchmark. If hedging was the right thing to do, then the gains are figured in. In essence, this becomes a costless, look-back option. Over the long term, as the cumulative benchmark is calculated every quarter or year, it becomes nearly impossible to surpass, particularly for shorter hedging periods. If currencies are reasonably volatile within the hedging periods, however, adroit hedging can provide better returns.

The point of this exercise is not to expect that a manager will achieve it, but rather to gain some insight and ranking among managers as to what percent of perfect hedging can be expected. Results for active currency managers who are doing their job should fall between those for the full-cost option hedging and zero-cost option hedging, though only a comprehensive universe of returns can give us an idea of what percent of perfect can be achieved by the average manager.

Risk

As mentioned earlier, consistency and predictability of producing returns is highly desirable in a manager, whether the mandate is to invest in assets or to protect their value through a currency overlay assignment. Measures of variability are just as appropriate in assessing currency overlay as they are in other investment management endeavors.

Standard Deviation

The most common and popular measure of variability is the standard deviation of quarterly returns. Here, we have three choices of returns:

- Translation returns plus hedging returns (total currency returns).

- Hedging returns only.

- Value-added versus the benchmark (regardless of which of the above two returns are considered).

The low-risk manager is the one with the most consistent approach at producing returns, whichever return is focused on—the manager with the lowest standard deviation.

Beta

How do investors judge a manager's volatility relative to the market? Beta, the covariance with the marketplace, is the answer. The market in the currency-management sense can be thought of as the translation gains/losses from the unhedged currencies in which the investments come packaged. A manager who hugs the unhedged benchmark and does little hedging will have a beta close to one. The more active manager given a defensive mandate, should have a beta different from one, though whether it is greater or less than one depends on the movement of currencies during the measurement period. During currency down-markets, effective hedging will cause the beta to exceed one, while slight losses due to cautious hedging in up-currency periods will cause beta to be less than one. Where the balance falls depends on the ratio of up and down markets. Unlike the equity manager who can produce above-market returns by buying riskier stocks than the market index, the currency manager in a defensive mandate cannot buy riskier currencies than the index. He has to accept the currencies of the underlying investments and can only reject them through hedging when he feels currencies may fall.

Sharpe Ratio

Is the extra return worth the extra risk or uncertainty of the returns? If more incremental risk is taken on than incremental return is produced, one might think not. This gets at the heart of risk-adjusted return, and can be viewed through the Sharpe ratio. This ratio divides the incremental return in excess of the risk-free rate by the incremental risk taken on in pursuit of higher returns. In the currency markets, the risk-free return is the 100-percent-hedged return. This can be negative or positive depending on whether the forward market structure is at discount or premium against the home currency; and it is not truly risk-free because the changes in interest rate differentials which drive forward currency-market pricing cause the standard deviation of hedged returns to be positive. However, because interest rate differentials move like a tortoise compared with the spot market hare, the risk levels are low.

The Sharpe ratio is calculated for any manager or benchmark strategy by dividing the difference in returns—be they averages of all trailing quarters, years, or multiyear periods—by the difference in the risk between the manager/benchmark strategy and the 100-percent-hedged benchmark. Values exceeding one indicate more incremental return than incremental risk; values less than one imply the opposite. The strategy with the higher Sharpe ratio will always have the higher risk-adjusted return, though not necessarily the higher absolute return.

Assembling a Team of Managers

Investors deciding on using a currency overlay strategy should behave no differently than they would when considering other asset classes. They rarely employ a single manager for each asset class; investors generally have chosen multiple managers in each asset class in pursuit of diversification.

Yet, in currency overlay management, few investors have employed more than one manager. Illogically, they have not diversified their approach in this asset class as they have done in other asset classes. Greater diversification can be achieved through a multimanager arrangement for currency overlay. Not all managers and their management styles can be expected to produce identical results in all markets.

Choosing Basic Style

The core currency-manager style should be chosen based on the comfort the investor has in the basic hedging discipline and in the people who execute it. That comfort can arise because of success the manager has shown in other related areas such as international fixed-income, or due to a basic belief in the manager's process (i.e., what factors she bases her decisions on). It should also be buttressed by a thorough quantitative review of the comparative performance statistics which we have explored.

The investment policy should be decided. Should the manager focus on risk control or return enhancement, and does the potential core manager exhibit that focus in historic or simulated returns? Can they be compared with the mandate and currency exposures about to be given her?

Complementary Style

Once the core currency overlay manager is selected, a complementary style can be chosen for a second and, possibly, third manager. Currency overlay managers generally come in several varieties; they either make judgments about where exchange rates are headed or they do not; they either use their intuition and contextual market analysis to determine the relevant forces moving markets or they use rigourous quantitative models to guide them.

Table 9 provides an easy style reference. Table 9 is by no means exhaustive and all-inclusive, but provides a general guide. Many managers mix elements of each style. The most common is the combination of fundamental and technical disciplines. You could also correctly assert that many managers using options also forecast markets; they have an opinion on volatility and its impact on the cost of options, and thus on the potential for hedging returns. Others may alternate between using a rigorous, model-driven approach and overriding the model when they feel that market conditions are sufficiently different from those to which the model is fit.

As in all recipes, the proof of the pudding is in the tasting. That is why it is so important to make an attempt to quantify and compare the results of each manager and approach, not only against benchmarks, but against each other. Measuring against a benchmark provides information, but comparing against a universe of competitors evaluates effectiveness.

Correlation of Hedging Returns As a Guide to Diversification

The most useful quantitative tool to assist investors in assembling a group of diversified managers is the coefficient of correlation. Since a throrough review of performance has been done, the quarterly returns of each manager can be examined to determine how closely they correlate with the quarterly returns of each other manager and with each benchmark reviewed. Once the core manager has been selected and a diversifying style settled on, the manager in that group with the lowest correlation statistic should be closely considered. This calculation could also focus only on the

---

Table 9   Overlay Manager Styles

Judgmental				Nonjudgmental	
Fundamental		Technical		Options-based or options replication	
Hedging decisions based on analysis of market, political or economic factors, or hedging costs		Hedging decisions based on analysis of price movements or trend identification. Usually independent of hedging costs.		Hedges are placed with options to provide downside protection and preserve upside potential. Cost of option is controlled through trading or replication.	
Arbitrary	Quantitative	Arbitrary	Quantitative	Arbitrary	Quantitative

down-currency periods to provide a team which will maximize the protection against unfavorable market moves.

Summary

The goals of performance measurement are no different for currency managers than for other asset classes. Performance measurement is an aid to minimize the risk of selecting the wrong manager, and it is a tool for evaluating performance relative to both investment policies and available managers.

Performance evaluation of currency managers in unconstrained assignments (currency as an asset class) should account for differences in leverage. Performance evaluation of currency managers in constrained assignments (currency overlay management) should take differences in mandates, exposures, benchmarks, and home currencies into account.

When real returns cannot be compared for a sufficiently long period due to differences in characteristics of currency overlay assignments, model-based/simulated returns offer the only avenue to normalize comparisons and gain insight into manager effectiveness. The components of currency manager performance should be consistently measured and compared, among managers and benchmarks. Risk is also an important measure.

Diversification is just as achievable in the currency management field as in other asset classes, and quantitative data should complement investor's qualitative assessments.

Endnote

1. The difference between the percent change in the spot rate over the period and the forward premium/discount at the beginning of the period.

PART III

Currency Risk Management for Corporations

CHAPTER 12

The Relationship of Management to Effective Risk Control

Alex Koh
Group Financial Controller
Hong Leong Credit Berhad

Introduction

Between the late 1980s and mid-1990s, there have been many cases where the use of derivatives have caused losses and embarrassment to corporations. The ball started rolling in the United States, spread across into Europe and more recently into East Asia. These cases were well-publicized and many pages in the financial press have been dedicated to these losses.

The reason often given by the persons responsible for the use of derivatives was to control risk. As a result, the term risk management, or risk control, has to some extent been unfairly associated with the use and misuse of derivatives.

Another popular reason for the use of derivatives was that they were necessary in order to achieve the treasury department's contribution to the bottom line. Simplistically, this amounted to taking a gamble on the markets, with the intention of making windfall profits. Derivatives have proved popular in this respect because of their:

- Ability to segregate the timing of the cash-flow impact from the exposure taken, hence reducing the upfront cost of taking a position.

- Accounting treatment as an off-balance-sheet product, which effectively minimized the visibility of the positions taken.

The articles in the financial press have focused on senior managements' knowledge and understanding of the products used by their treasurers. The general opinions were that senior managements' understanding of the products and the manner of the products' use varied from between nothing at all to less than adequate. Much was also said about the lack of monitoring by senior management once the responsibility for managing the risk exposure had been delegated.

While derivatives have grabbed the limelight because of the large financial numbers involved, other examples of mismanagement of risk exposure have had as much impact on the bottom line. For example, leaving foreign exchange exposures open, or hedging all forecasted exposures on sight, have created opportunity losses when currencies moved adversely.

However, such opportunity losses are not quantified separately in the financial statements nor do they feature in the annual report apart from possibly a minimal mention, in the chairman's statement, that is likely to sound like "Profits have not improved by as much as expected due to the volatility of currencies experienced during the year." This seemingly innocuous statement has a great profit and loss impact for a U.S.-based company with Japanese yen payables for the 1995 calendar year when dollar/yen touched a low of 79.70 on April 1995 and a high of 104.70 in September 1995.

The approach taken to this chapter is to address two basic questions, and from the answers to build up the concept of risk control and management responsibility. The management perception of risk is explained together with the misconceptions that may arise due to a lack of understanding. Important issues to consider in implementing a risk control program are also discussed.

The viewpoint taken for this chapter is from a corporation's perspective and not that of a financial institution, although some reference to financial institutions may be made to highlight similarities or differences that arise.

The Basic Questions of Risk Control and Responsibility

The two basic questions are (1) What is the role of management in risk control? and (2) How can management ensure that it discharges this role effectively?

The Role of Management

The first question aims to define the scope covered by the term risk and management's responsibility in controlling or managing the risk exposure of a corporation. The second question then analyzes the various ways in which this responsibility can be discharged while taking into account real-world situations.

To effectively answer the first question, three elements must be defined:

- What is meant by risk?
- What is risk control?

- What is the role of management?

Definition of Risk

The different types of risk are well-defined in all textbooks on the subject. The risks faced by most multinational corporations are foreign exchange risk and interest rate risk. The other types of risk such as equity price risk and commodity risk tend to be industry specific and will not be explored in detail.

A fifth risk element quoted in some textbooks is liquidity risk. However, liquidity risk can be taken as a subset of the types of risk mentioned earlier. For example, the lack of liquidity in a currency will invariably impact both its exchange rate and interest rates. The exchange rate mechanism (ERM) crisis of 1993 provides a good example of the extremes caused by the lack of liquidity in the markets when overnight Danish kroner interest rates reached 200 percent, Italian lira 150 percent, and French francs 100 percent.

From this point forward, the primary focus of this chapter will be on foreign exchange risk, although the issues to be discussed will also apply to the other types of risk.

From the small expanding third-world exporter to established G7 multinationals, movements in foreign exchange rates give rise to:

- Translation exposure—caused by converting foreign-currency-de-nominated earnings and assets into a corporation's base currency. There is little economic cost arising from this exposure, apart from an "optical" accounting effect on financial consolidation. However, the impact on reported earnings and earnings per share may influence investor perception of the corporation's share value. There is no actual cash-flow impact. Translation exposure can also termed accounting exposure.

- Transaction exposure—arises from everyday trading activity and has a cash-flow impact which affects the amount of base-currency receivables and payables. Transaction exposures are physically converted into cash flows in the base currency of the corporation. As a result, there is a direct impact on the base-currency profit and loss account—unlike translation exposure, which only impacts the consolidated financial statements. Translation exposure, therefore, is also termed operating exposure.

Having identified the major types of currency exposures, what is the purpose of managing currency exposure? Which types of exposures should management focus on? The exposures need to be managed, because the volatility impacts the most critical of performance measures—the profit figure or bottom line—for which management is held accountable. The next impact is on the share price and shareholder wealth, of which the earnings figure is a major influence. Investor perception also plays a major part, and operating management, which consistently provides the foreign-exchange-volatility excuse for fluctuating earnings, is likely to face an investor-confidence crisis and slumping share price.

Therefore, managing risk becomes part and parcel of the whole business process and is not an isolated element or task that can be addressed after all the other business decisions on sales, production, and distribution have been made. The financial market evolution and globalization of trade over the past 10 years have ensured that all corporations are made aware of the risk of foreign exchange volatility, and, as a result, corporations are managing volatility in varying degrees of sophistication.

The Transaction-Risk and Translation-Risk Debate

The management of translation risk has been a subject of heated debate over the years. The basic issue is whether the use of hedging techniques, which incur a real cash cost in order to protect an accounting figure, is a waste of time and money. Viewpoints on this issue differ widely depending on the circumstances of the corporation and the nature of its investors.

The management of translation risk is essentially unique to the circumstances of the corporation. For example, a corporation which is viewed as a U.S. stock but with 90 percent of its profits and 80 percent of its assets arising from outside the United States and funded mainly by U.S. currency borrowings will vigorously defend translation hedging. This is because any adverse currency movements will impact both its balance sheet and earnings.

We can contrast this with another corporation which is well-diversified globally, has foreign assets matched by foreign liabilities and characterized by significant currency earnings and expenses. Such a corporation may not want to carry out any translation hedging at all on the basis that the assets and liabilities are approximately matched, and the wide spread of currency flows will even out any balance-sheet and earnings translation gains and losses over time. The costs of hedging may also be prohibitive in view of the significant foreign-currency asset base and currency spread of cash flows.

The decision to hedge translation risk or not depends on whether management performance is judged or focused on the managing of cash flow or earnings per share. A focus on earnings implies that translation risk management is likely to be practiced. However, the treasury departments of major multinationals have in the past five to ten years have focused on managing cash flows and away from translation hedging.

The need to manage transaction risk or operating exposure is undisputed because of the direct cash-flow impact which is critical for day-to-day operations. It is the sort of risk exposure that even the most uninitiated management in an undeveloped country will recognize because of the cash-flow implications. It is also transaction risk management that forms the bulk of risk products offered by banks to corporations. Translation-risk-management instruments are usually offered on a request basis and not marketed as vigorously.

Translation risk is normally only addressed once a year on the production of financial statements and that again is dependent on management perception of its relevance. There may also be instances where professional fund managers run their own overlay currency hedging strategies designed to minimize the effect of currency movements on their equity portfolio. Hedging of translation risk exposure by corporations may work against this overlay strategy. Therefore, the decision for translation risk hedging must be carefully considered with all the facts at hand as there is no hard and fast rule on this issue.

The primary focus of this chapter is on risk exposures that have an operational impact. This will primarily be transaction risk, although the issues of competitive risk exposures will also be discussed.

Risk Control

During the 1970s and 1980s, when the global economy and markets were not well-developed and currency volatility was fairly range-bound, corporations tended not to focus too closely on foreign exchange risk because the impact on the profit and loss account was immaterial. With expanding export and import markets, the emergence of overseas production facilities, and increased currency volatility, profits can now turn into losses due to either neglect or ignorance of the issues involved when the financial markets move.

The matter cannot be pushed aside as immaterial, in the overall context, because of the sizable potential impact. Corporations with a more aggressive attitude have in fact run their treasuries as profit centers in order to exploit market movements and to generate extra revenue in addition to their normal business activities. This is no longer risk control; it is a trading operation. As we discuss later, this activity brings about further complexities in responsibilities and the monitoring process.

The issue of risk control is mainly one of perception. Management perception is the key issue to risk control, because the actions taken by the corporation to manage risk will depend on the view of its management. Management may declare that it is the business policy not to take on any risk in the foreign exchange market, and, as a result, there is no need to manage that risk.

This statement, by implication, indicates that actions have been taken in order to eliminate any risk which may arise, or it implies that business decisions are made in such a way that the risks do not arise. That, in itself, amounts to management of risk; albeit questions arise as to whether *risk* has been identified accurately, if risk can be totally eliminated, or if it can be altogether avoided.

In the past, when management have stated that they "do not take risk" in their businesses, they have generally referred to foreign exchange risk. While interest rate risk is actively managed in the more-developed countries, such as the United States and in Europe, the emerging markets of East Asia are only just introducing or planning to introduce exchange-traded, interest-rate-risk-management instruments into their financial markets.

The aim of "not taking any foreign exchange risk" in the conduct of business, while being an admirable objective, is not an objective that can be entirely mitigated by management action. Carrying on any form of business activity for the purpose of profit involves the risk of being in that business, of which foreign exchange plays a significant part when there are foreign competitors or customers in the market. The company with no foreign exchange risk is a company that has a worldwide monopoly of a product, since all of its customers must accept the company's prices. The effect of foreign exchange on input materials or on selling price is not relevant, since selling price can be adjusted with no loss of sales volume, because there are no substitutes.

What then is the action likely to be taken by management who prescribe to the "no foreign exchange risk" philosophy? The actions are (1) do nothing on the basis that management will not incur risk, or (2) hedge all exposure when it is seen or when it is forecasted.

Both courses of action have their advantages and disadvantages. Users of the first "do nothing" approach claim that they do not take risk, and therefore need not take any action to manage that risk. However, the only constant about risk exposure is that it is dynamic and changes over time. Sophisticated management recognizes this and even though procedures are designed to minimize the creation of exposure, managers will maintain constant monitoring and reporting in order to ensure that management is in control.

Management using the "hedge all exposure when seen" approach, tends to preselect instruments, usually FX forwards, and to hedge everything on sight or when forecasted. The underlying assumptions are that the forecasting models are accurate and that procedures are in place to capture exposures when they arise. There will also be the remedial actions which need to be taken if the hedged payables or receivables do not materialize. While the reversing of the extra hedge position can result in a gain or loss, luck is usually not on the corporation's side and a loss is realized.

The danger for less-sophisticated managers is that they may take the "head in the sand" approach (i.e., they have instructed their operations not to incur foreign exchange risk, and, therefore, management decides that no identification or monitoring program is required). This approach makes the assumptions that (1) all risk to the business has been accurately identified and quantified, and (2) the operating management knows the course of action necessary in order to avoid or mitigate the risks identified.

However, the assumptions may push the operating management into an area that is not within its level of knowledge. Unless there is proper monitoring, and the availability of relevant expertise, such an approach will not be sufficient for effective risk control.

In addition, management which executes the "we don't have a view" philosophy to managing foreign exchange exposure by leaving all exposure open is exposing the corporation to the mercy of the financial markets. The corporation may survive one or two currency crises, but its long-term future is not secure and it is unlikely to find quality investors.

In summary, the fluidity of the risk exposures and the impact on the corporation, in terms of financial performance, places a large responsibility on management to effectively control risk. The role of management, in this context, needs to be defined so that responsibilities are clear and appropriate performance measures are determined. With a defined responsibility for risk control, management is then able to derive a plan of action and, accordingly, discharge that obligation.

The Role of Management

The responsibility for managing risk will differ according to whom the question is being addressed. To the shareholder, the management (i.e., the board of directors) is responsible for all aspects of running the company, and therefore holds ultimate responsibility. The board of directors may think that, in appointing a finance director and a corporate treasurer, they have accordingly discharged that responsibility. However, the issue of monitoring and reporting on the activities of the treasury department may not have been addressed.

This status quo may carry on undisturbed until the unexpected occurrence of market correction or volatility. At this point, losses may occur due to either unhedged open exposures or financial products purchased for the purpose of managing risk. The resulting witch-hunt for a scapegoat will result in various claims and counterclaims about inadequate reporting and supervision, unauthorized trades, misrepresentations to the board, and so on.

The derivatives disasters of the late 1980s and mid-1990s in the United States and United Kingdom have provided examples where corporate treasurers have taken on risks without the board, or even themselves, being aware of the situation. Bearing in mind the above issues, the definition of the role of management is therefore critical and must be clearly defined in order to avoid any ambiguities that may arise.

A clinical description of the role of management is that management must ensure that (1) an approved risk-management policy and strategy is in place, and (2) a properly controlled and monitored risk-management program is implemented. The corporate treasurers' terms of reference must incorporate these two objectives in order to ensure that their roles are properly defined and that appropriate performance measures are in the risk management program.

To assist in defining the role of management, we must first establish the corporation's "state of awareness" of its risk exposure. The different states of awareness (together with the risk exposure recognized under that state, and the risk management instruments used) are detailed in Table 1.

The difference between "Advanced" and "International" is debatable. For the purpose of Table 1, the "International" corporation takes into account the cross-border cash management issues, and it is not rigidly controlled by the regulatory environment in its operations (e.g., by foreign exchange controls). The "Advanced" corporation represents an informed-user operating within a fairly rigid domestic framework but with a reasonable availability of products.

The tabular characterization is fairly simplistic and cannot cater for all possible permutations. However, bearing in mind the overlaps between the categories, most corporations can be classified into one of the four types.

Most developed-country corporations will be classified under either "Advanced" or "International" categories while the developing nations' corporations will fall into the "Basic" or "Advanced" categories. Within third-world countries, "Blissfully Ignorant" corporations may exist, but they will either graduate to "Basic" awareness or they will go out of business.

The corporate treasury's terms of reference and its policy and procedures manual must be drafted in line with the corporation's "State of Awareness." To implement terms of reference for an "International" corporation to one that is operating within a tight regulatory environment, such as that of a "Basic" corporation, is a waste of time and indicates a lack of appreciation of the existing circumstances.

Table 1   FX Risk Exposure Awareness and Products Used

State of Awareness	FX Exposure Recognized	Instruments Used
Blissful Ignorance	• Trade receivables and payables—spot to one-month forward • Drawdowns and repayment of currency loans—spot to one-month forward	• FX spot trades • Forward trades up to one month
Basic	• Trade receivables and payables—usually based on forecasts of up to six-months or one-year forward • Drawdowns and repayment of foreign currency loans up to three-months forward	• FX spot and forwards • Simple cross-currency swaps (e.g. to convert a steady monthly stream of cash flows of up to one year's duration)
Advanced	• As for Basic • Drawdowns and repayment of foreign currency loans up to one-year forward or more • May identify and hedge competitive risks	• FX spot and forwards • Cross-currency swaps • FX swaps • Foreign exchange agreements (FXA) • FX options—usually buy but will write occasionally • Structured products
International	• As for Advanced • Additional processes to identify the timing and location of fund flows and to analyze the regulatory environment where the flows arise	• As for Advanced • Cash management products and services (e.g., intercompany currency netting and pooling, electronic cash collection and transmission techniques
Trading	• As for Advanced or International in terms of hedging activities • Will maintain a team of traders with profit-driven dealing objectives	• As for International • FX options—buy and write • Position-taking on currency and interest rate markets via direct positioning or derivative products

To an extent, it can be dangerous to apply a pro forma set of terms of reference and policy and procedures manual on the basis that, if it can be used elsewhere, it is suitable for everyone. This takes away the consideration that all corporations have different circumstances and that organizational structures operate within different regulatory environments and hold different views on the management of foreign-exchange-risk exposure.

Discharging the Risk-Control Role Effectively

Having explained the role of management within the terms of reference and having related that with the "State of Risk Awareness" of a corporation, we now examine the ways in which management can discharge this role, and we discuss some of the issues that arise in implementing a risk management program.

For management to discharge its role and responsibility for managing risk, management must implement an effective risk management program. The proper execution of the program depends on the main driver of the whole process (i.e., the issue of management perception noted earlier). Since the perception of management drives its actions, we will examine the issues which arise on the implementation of a risk management program and how management actions vary with the different perceptions held.

Management perception will affect implementation, since the program may impact many aspects of the corporation's status quo, which include the organizational structure and responsibilities, and operating procedures and systems. Changes are not limited to the corporate treasury department but spread across the corporation's operation in all countries.

Any inertia to change will slow down the implementation, but the objections raised must be carefully considered in order to differentiate objections that have valid justification from those which are knee-jerk reactions to change. This is because, where treasury processes cross international boundaries, due care and attention must be paid to the local regulatory environment, regulations, and practices. It also follows that organizational change may affect certain corporate comfort zones, thereby provoking an adverse reaction.

The desire to change must not develop into an urge to change everything in the pursuit of the perfect risk-management setup. The implementation of the ideal setup, where no procedure existed before, is the best possible scenario. Otherwise, where some form of procedure is in place, the process is one of change management, which must take place in a dynamic financial market situation. As a result, a highly focused approach, involving careful study, and a project team, with the necessary expertise and budget, is required for the effective implementation of the program.

We now address the issues which management needs to address in order to discharge its responsibility for risk control.

Policy and Procedures

As an initial step, the corporate policy must be clearly set out. The policy will be influenced by the corporation's state of risk awareness and should cover the scope of the risk program, the responsibilities, and accountability. Risks of a direct operating nature, such as foreign-exchange and interest-rate risk, will be covered within the scope of the policy, but the inclusion of translation and competitive risk will depend on management's perception of the relevance of these risks.

The policy may also define the philosophy on the use of derivative instruments, bearing in mind that disasters have occurred. As a general rule, a corporation should not purchase a product if the corporation does not have the ability to price the instrument. In practice, however, adhering to this rule may be more difficult. To a large extent among emerging markets and some Western corporations, the ability to value open positions still does not exist.

It is simple enough to price or mark-to-market open FX forward contracts, but anything more complex (i.e., a cross-currency swap) may pose valuation difficulties, depending on the level of sophistication. While it is possible to get another bank to value positions which were taken, the issue of confidentiality arises, particularly where mark-to-market losses have occurred on complex derivative instruments. Any adverse publicity may trigger market rumors and panic the corporation's investors and bankers.

Once the policy is set, the treasurer's terms of reference can be drawn up. The terms of reference will be driven by the policy statement and the appropriate (and previously defined) accountability, responsibility, and authority.

The policy statement should define the procedures manual as the absolute authority for guiding the operation of the program and should also determine the contents. The procedures manual will control the operation of the treasury function and may also define the responsibilities of the finance personnel at the operating subsidiaries where the risk exposure is first incurred. Therefore, the responsibility for capturing and reporting exposures to the corporate treasury can be allocated to the management of the operating subsidiaries. This documented allocation of individual responsibility is necessary in order to avoid ambiguity.

Organizational Structure

Just as the corporation's current state of risk awareness dictates its policy and procedures, the existing organizational structure forms the framework from which any action plan starts. The likely situation in a modern corporation is that a small team, or department, and some form of risk management procedure already exist. However, the department may not have formal terms of reference and the department's objectives may extend no further than to "manage the foreign currency flows" of the company.

For most emerging markets, and for some Western corporations, the current risk-department setup and functions have evolved in response to discrete needs, which were identified at different points in time and not by the implementation of a structured risk management program.

This reactive approach was taken with the aim of resolving the problem at hand as soon as possible and of minimizing the impact on the corporation in terms of process disruption and use of resources. However, this may only be a temporary solution and the long-term resolution of the problem will require consideration of the effects of wider control and procedural issues. These follow-up actions may have been overlooked, due to other issues arising, or delayed as a result of resources and cost constraints.

Since the quick-fix solutions were designed to handle mutually exclusive problems when they arise, the procedures or system fixes may not be complementary or efficient in their operation. Therefore, at some stage, a total review needs to be done with the aim of consolidating systems and procedures, and streamlining work flows.

Once the existing framework has been identified, the end structure, both in terms of corporate organization and systems solutions, can be defined. From this vision of the end result, the action plans necessary to implement the program can be identified and scheduled.

Organizational structure remains one of the major issues to consider in effective implementation. With a large corporation, the operating managers are a group of powerful individuals who have significant influence on senior management. These operating managers may not have an appreciation of the circumstances of the foreign exchange market and will blame the treasurer for currency movements which adversely affect operating results, but will happily accept the credit for any favorable currency movements.

Operating management's argument to support this view is that the treasurer's role is to manage risk, and, therefore, the treasurer should be able to predict currency movements at any point in time with 90 to 100 percent accuracy. Furthermore, operating management may pressure the treasurer to accept their views on a currency, for pricing or budget purposes. However, operating management may disclaim all responsibility for any forecasting error on the basis that the treasurer is the expert on the matter and should have advised accordingly. If, however, operating management's guess turns out to be correct, they will claim all credit and crucify the treasurer for advocating any caution. This raises the requirement for an objective performance measure in order to resolve these issues, and this will be discussed later.

Finally, we note that the corporation may have to restructure itself and to redefine the relevant responsibilities and authority for risk management. While we acknowledge that management knows its business well, there may exist a lack expertise in the financial markets. This responsibility and accountability may be delegated to the treasurer who then has the authority to manage the risk. The situation to avoid is one where the treasurer has accountability without authority.

However, appointing one of the financial personnel as corporate treasurer/treasury risk manager with a broad band of terms of reference is not sufficient. That is akin to appointing the scapegoat for when all hell breaks loose, which is inevitably going to happen when actions are taken without understanding the issues and when responsibility is delegated without monitoring or feedback.

In conclusion, management must have specific objectives and clearly defined criteria within the policy statement so that it can develop the necessary strategy and structure. Inevitably, any restructuring will meet both support and resistance from all levels concerned, but this is a known fact where any change is involved, and, therefore, restructuring should be handled with care.

Budget and Costs

Any corporate program requires a budget. Appointing a treasurer with extensive terms of reference but with no budget for systems and staff is not a step in the right direction. It gives the impression of implementing a program, but the program is doomed. This is because the mere presence of a functional head does not ensure success, for without the resources and the tools to execute the mandate properly, a major problem is created.

However, giving an open mandate to the treasurer to spend what is required may also be inappropriate. The internal processes and checks of a corporation to approve capital expenditure should be strictly adhered to, with the necessary justification for the expense to be provided before proceeding.

The costs of not managing risk, in the event of market turmoil, can be very expensive. Hence, the corporation needs to purchase the necessary resources. However, management can argue that the exposure and cost to the corporation is not significant enough to warrant such major expenditures.

As a general rule, some form of resources must be invested depending on the scope of the implementation. To some extent, where new techniques and systems are being implemented, the use of expensive external consultants is unavoidable. The budget must be realistic and may have to allow for expenditure on new computer hardware to run the software acquired.

Management must therefore ensure that the budget given is sufficient to cover all aspects of the program.

The recruitment of experienced staff is another major issue. In emerging markets with expanding market penetration, the demand for risk personnel is high, and compensation packages increase quickly. This practice of high entry-level compensation may cut across long-held cultural beliefs concerning reward for long service. This practice may be an additional complexity for East Asian corporations, which Western corporations are unlikely to encounter.

The increasing demand for treasury staff and their services is also creating a niche sector of professional associations. Initially, the objective of the treasury bodies was to promote and develop professional practices, but this has evolved into education and training of treasury professionals. Corporations should consider active participation in such associations in order to promote their views on treasury-related issues, particularly on regulatory matters.

Systems and Systems Infrastructure

Systems are critical for the effective operation of a treasury function. With the development of the personal computer, the cost of purchasing hardware is falling rapidly. The software required to run the treasury operations and to manage risk, however, remains expensive given the development time and functionality required. However, increased competition is having a positive impact on pricing.

Any corporation venturing for the first time into the acquisition of a treasury risk-system or consolidating a variety of subsystems will deal with (1) a selection process that is fraught with functionality claims from competing vendors, (2) price ranges from the cheap to the ridiculous, and (3) the basic need to define what the corporation needs in order to fulfill its requirements.

With both the cash and time cost being high, the view of management on the importance of systems is critical to the implementation process. There are some issues for management to consider in the selection process, so that scarce resources are not wasted.

Systems requirements depend on the current level of sophistication of the corporation. There is little point in buying a state-of-the-art system for handling five spot-deals and three forward-deals a day in an environment where forecasting is nonexistent. In this situation, a simple spreadsheet will suffice with end-of-day rates keyed in for revaluation. The only justification for a high level of expenditure is that the whole corporate structure is being revamped and replaced with a new operating environment which focuses on effective risk management.

Systems vendors will also be encouraging corporations to purchase extra functionality to handle advanced instruments that the corporations are not currently using. Extra functionality translates into extra cost, so any additions must be carefully evaluated on a needs basis. A time-frame limitation may be appropriate (i.e., the instruments that the corporation is likely to use in the next two years should be included in the requirements). The other instruments may be placed on hold for the time being in order to minimize up-front cost.

An issue to be aware of is that most available risk management systems are designed for financial institutions and not for corporations. These existing systems are being modified to cater to corporations, and new custom-made corporate treasury systems are also being developed in order to cater to this new and expanding market.

The primary issue to bear in mind is that risk management objectives of financial institutions are different from those of corporations. Financial institutions' systems manage the risk of positions taken (i.e., a transaction is executed and creates an asset or liability which gives rise to exposure). The financial institution is focused on managing the risk of the asset's or liability's value, which changes in response to market pressures.

The corporation, however, is managing cash-flow risk, which for operating flows is a forecasted number. It is working on a cash-flow-at-risk concept, unlike the financial institution which focuses on asset/liability value. For this reason, care must be taken when considering software which was meant for financial institutions but rewritten for corporate use.

The issue of legacy systems is another major issue in systems selection. As noted in the section on organizational structure, the corporation, which has been managing risk in varying degrees of sophistication, may have a mix of systems and procedural solutions in place. These legacy systems will cause headaches in a consolidation process, and existing procedures will also be affected. This is a problem encountered by few emerging-markets corporations, because they are delving into this field for the first time and are not saddled by the legacies.

It is important to note that systems do not make decisions for the treasurer; it is the treasurer who makes the final judgment call. The system is a tool to measure exposure and to provide information for analysis, so that an informed decision can be made. The treasurer, therefore, cannot hide behind the system in the event of incorrect judgment calls.

A system is an important part of the risk management process, is used to improve efficiency, and to provide timely and quality analysis for decision making. Any management which does not recognize the importance of systems and which imposes limitations in functionality or budget may pay out more in losses over time.

Risk Measurement and Modeling

The identification of risk is pointless without measuring the exposure and the impact on the corporation when there is market volatility. In this respect, the corporate treasurer can adopt the measures developed by the financial services industry in order to measure the exposures.

The simplest measure of performance is in monetary terms, because this is understood by all parties. Therefore, risk measures which measure the impact on a corporation, in terms of profit and loss impact, would be very helpful in communicating messages to senior management.

The use of *value at risk* (VAR) methodology was developed by financial institutions in order to apply statistical techniques to risk measurement. While fairly widely used in the financial services industry, the concept is not popular yet among corporations in the West and is virtually nonexistent in the emerging markets.

Value-at-risk methodology is a step forward from the older measures, because it uses the language that the layperson understands (i.e., dollars and cents). The use of probability theory in its models may not allow for extreme volatility situations, although many financial institutions now run periodic stress tests on their portfolio.

It is important to keep in mind that most risk management models still exist within the realm of academic study and the application to real world business situations is still a little tenuous. Management must be prepared to accept that this practice is not an exact science and to view the situation in this context when considering the treasurer's report. The basic premise here is that, in this world of uncertainty, the availability of a measure which is 80 percent accurate is better than no measure at all.

Performance Measures

The performance measure given by management has a major influence on the actions of the treasurer. In this context, an unrealistic target can be dangerous. For example, giving a target of achieving funding at 25 basis points below LIBOR or of contributing five million to the profit figure is asking the treasurer to take risk, not to manage it. Such targets show management's lack of understanding of the function of the treasurer, and have caused corporations to enter into complex derivatives markets, where they have incurred substantial losses.

The foreign exchange world is full of hindsight experts. The hindsight expert works to the rule that in the solution of any problem, it always helps to know the answer first. The treasurer does not have the benefit of that assistance, and, hence, makes an educated guess about the future. In this line of business, if your call success rate is better than 50 percent, you have performed well. Unfortunately, management may not view it that way, which makes life very difficult for the treasurer.

To assist management and the treasurer in performance review, relevant performance measures must be drawn up. Performance measures should:

1. Be objective—the methodology and calculation must be acceptable to all parties and be based on verifiable benchmarks.

2. Have a finite timeframe—measuring performance over a long or infinite time-frame is meaningless and may result in cherry-picking rates for use.

3. Measure overall performance and not individual trades—the performance measure must be objective-driven and not trade-driven.

For example, if we take two major business divisions, one with sterling payables and another with yen receivables, and the treasurer hedges sterling correctly but yen incorrectly, the overall result is that the gain overshadows the loss. Hence, on a net basis, the corporation has benefited. The treasurer has accordingly discharged his or her responsibility and has performed satisfactorily.

However, the head of the division with yen payables will be very upset because, from this manager's perspective, the treasurer has not performed. Management must address such situations properly and protect the treasurer, who is accountable for the overall performance of the corporation and not of individual divisions.

A performance measure based on generating opportunity gains and on minimizing opportunity losses should be considered as a performance measure. While opportunity gains improve the bottom line, they are not easily identifiable. Management may want to adopt some form of opportunity-measure in order to monitor the performance of treasurers, particularly for cost-center-style treasury departments.

Profit or Cost Center

The treasury department may be set up operate as either a profit center or a cost center. This specification must be made clear at the outset, because the procedures and reporting will be different. Recent surveys have shown that corporate treasuries are usually set up as cost centers, because their primary focus is to manage risk. Profit-center treasuries tend to be set up in corporations with an aggressive risk-taking management style; corporations which may take a very different approach to their treasury setup.

A profit-center treasury must be able to distinguish its dealing trades from its hedging trades. In-house policy on how a profit-center treasury transacts with the operating subsidiaries must also be clearly defined. The dealing operation, costs, and results must be segregated from the treasury's hedging activities, and the control issues must be addressed. In such a setup, the complexity increases, and systems requirements will expand and require management to refocus on certain critical issues.

Other Issues

The hedging of competitive risk (i.e., where the corporation's competitors have a different cost base or run hedging programs of their own) is not normally addressed in most risk programs. It may be crucial in terms of competitiveness and market share. If it is significant enough, management may wish to consider hedging that exposure.

Regulatory constraints, especially in the emerging markets where central bank control is still fairly tight, will affect risk implementation and operations. For example, free flow of foreign currency may be restricted, thereby preventing international pooling of foreign currency or limiting the use of certain financial products such as swaps. The treasury department, therefore, needs to examine the individual regulatory environments in order to establish an avenue to exploit any opportunities available.

The removal of trade barriers, which is creating a global market, is also presenting challenges to management. Essentially, the issues can be viewed from two viewpoints: that of the Western corporation entering the fast-expanding East Asia region, and vice versa. The liberalization of trade via the Asian Free Trade Agreement (AFTA) and the opening up of the emerging markets will present many new and frustrating challenges to the treasurer in the realm of risk management and control. The challenges are inevitable, and the corporation that adapts the fastest will gain a competitive advantage.

Conclusion

Contrary to popular belief, risk management and control do not require the use of derivatives, although derivatives are one of the tools available to the treasurer. Risk control is a philosophy which must be adopted by any risk-averse corporation in order to manage operations, protect assets, and sustain profits. Risk control requires the discipline to enforce the concepts and to commit the resources necessary to meet the objective of a risk-control program.

The costs are high but the rewards may be higher, although the rewards may seem elusive at first. Therefore, objectives and easily interpreted performance measures are crucial to a corporation's operation. As with any pioneering program, the resistance will be there but the end result will be a corporation which has the ability to identify, quantify, and control its risk, and one that is ready to meet the global challenge of the future.

The management team that implements a risk program which has taken into consideration the issues described earlier will have adequately discharged its responsibility for controlling risk. This chapter is not exhaustive but covers the major issues that must be addressed for effective risk control. Most important, management must be able to accept the new ideas proposed in the program and to modify its perception, as necessary, in order to ensure its success.

CHAPTER 13

Risk Measurement

Thomas J. Linsmeier
Assistant Professor of Accounting
University of Illinois at Urbana-Champaign

Neil D. Pearson
Assistant Professor of Finance
University of Illinois at Urbana-Champaign

A Difficult Question

You are responsible for managing your company's foreign exchange positions. Your boss, or your boss's boss, has been reading about derivatives losses suffered by other companies, and wants to know if the same thing could happen to his or her company. That is, he or she wants to know just how much market risk the company is taking. What do you say?

You could start by listing and describing the company's positions, but this is not likely to be helpful unless there are only a handful. Even then, it helps only if your superiors understand all of the positions and instruments, and the risks inherent in each. Or you could talk about the portfolio's sensitivities (i.e., how much the value of the portfolio changes when various underlying market rates or prices change) and perhaps option deltas and gammas.[1] However, you are unlikely to win favor with your superiors by putting them to sleep. Even if you are confident in your ability to explain these in English, you still have no natural way to net the risk of your short position in Deutschemarks against the long position in Dutch guilders. (It makes sense to do this because gains or losses on the short position in marks will be almost perfectly offset by gains or losses on the long position in guilders.) You could simply assure your superiors that you never speculate but rather use derivatives only to hedge, but they understand that this statement is vacuous. They know that the word *hedge* is so ill-defined and flexible that virtually any transaction can be characterized as a hedge. So what do you say?

Perhaps the best answer starts: "The value at risk is . . . "[2]

How did you get into a position where the best answer involves a concept that your superiors might never have heard of, let alone understand? This doesn't seem like a good strategy for getting promoted.

The modern era of risk measurement for foreign exchange positions began in 1973. That year saw both the collapse of the Bretton Woods system of fixed exchange-rates and the publication of the Black-Scholes option-pricing formula. The collapse of the Bretton Woods system and the rapid transition to a system of, more or less, freely floating exchange rates among many of the major trading countries provided the impetus for the measurement and management of foreign exchange risk, while the ideas underlying the Black-Scholes formula provided the conceptual framework and basic tools for risk measurement and management.

The years since 1973 have witnessed both tremendous volatility in exchange rates and a proliferation of derivative instruments useful for managing the risks of changes in the prices of foreign currencies and interest rates. Modern derivative instruments such as forwards, futures, swaps, and options facilitate the management of exchange- and interest-rate volatility. They can be used to offset the risks in existing instruments, positions, and portfolios because their cash flows and values change with changes in interest rates and foreign currency prices. Among other things, they can be used to make offsetting bets to *cancel out* the risks in a portfolio. Derivative instruments are ideal for this purpose, because many of them can be traded quickly, easily, and with low transactions-costs, while others can be tailored to customers' needs. Unfortunately, instruments which are ideal for making offsetting bets also are ideal for making purely speculative bets: offsetting and purely speculative bets are distinguished only by the composition of the rest of the portfolio.

The proliferation of derivative instruments has been accompanied by increased trading of cash instruments and securities, and has been coincident with growth in foreign trade and increasing international financial linkages among companies. As a result of these trends, many companies have portfolios which include large numbers of cash and derivative instruments. Due to the sheer numbers and complexity (of some) of these cash and derivative instruments, the magnitudes of the risks in companies' portfolios often are not obvious. This has led to a demand for portfolio level quantitative measures of market risk such as *value at risk*. The flexibility of derivative instruments and the ease with which both cash and derivative instruments can be traded and retraded in order to alter companies' risks also has created a demand for a portfolio-level summary risk measure that can be reported to the senior managers charged with the oversight of risk management and trading operations.

The ideas underlying option pricing provide the foundation for the measurement and management of the volatility of market rates and prices.

The Black-Scholes model and its variants had the effect of disseminating probabilistic and statistical tools throughout financial institutions and companies' treasury groups. These tools permit quantification and measurement of the volatility in foreign currency prices and interest rates. They are the foundation of value at risk and risk measurement systems. Variants of the Black-Scholes model, known as the Black and Garman-Kohlhagen models, are widely used for pricing options on foreign currencies and foreign currency futures. Most other pricing models also are direct descendants of the Black–Scholes model. Even the pricing of simpler instruments such as currency and interest rate swaps is based on the *no-arbitrage* framework underlying the Black-Scholes model. Partial derivatives of various pricing formulas provide the basic risk measures. These basic risk measures are discussed in the first appendix to this chapter.

The concept and use of value at risk is recent. Value at risk was first used by major financial firms in the late 1980's to measure the risks of their trading portfolios. Since that time period, the use of value at risk has exploded. Currently, value at risk is used by most major derivatives dealers to measure and manage market risk. In the 1994 follow-up to the survey in the Group of Thirty's 1993 global derivatives project, 43 percent of dealers reported that they were using some form of value at risk and 37 percent indicated that they planned to use value at risk by the end of 1995. J.P. Morgan's attempt to establish a market standard through its release of its RiskMetrics^{TM} system in October 1994 provided a tremendous impetus to the growth in the use of value at risk. Value at risk is increasingly being used by smaller financial institutions, nonfinancial corporations, and institutional investors. The 1995 Wharton/CIBC Wood Gundy *Survey of Derivatives Usage among U.S. Nonfinancial Firms* reports that 29 percent of respondents use value at risk for evaluating the risks of derivatives transactions. A 1995 *Institutional Investor* survey found that 32 percent of firms use value at risk as a measure of market risk, and 60 percent of pension funds responding to a survey by the New York University Stern School of Business reported using value at risk.

Regulators also have become interested in value at risk. In April 1995, the Basle Committee on Banking Supervision proposed allowing banks to calculate their capital requirements for market risk with their own value-at-risk models, using certain parameters provided by the committee. In June 1995, the U.S. Federal Reserve proposed a *precommitment* approach which would allow banks to use their own internal value-at-risk models to calculate capital requirements for market risk, with penalties to be imposed in the event that losses exceed the capital requirement. In December 1995, the U.S. Securities and Exchange Commission released for comment a proposed rule for corporate risk disclosure which listed value at risk as one of three possible market-risk disclosure measures. The European Union's

Capital Adequacy Directive which came into effect in 1996 allows value-at-risk models to be used to calculate capital requirements for foreign exchange positions, and a decision has been made to move toward allowing value at risk to compute capital requirements for other market risks.

So What Is Value at Risk, Anyway?

Value at risk is a single, summary, statistical measure of possible portfolio losses. Specifically, value at risk is a measure of losses due to *normal* market movements. Losses greater than the value at risk are suffered only with a specified small probability. Subject to the simplifying assumptions used in its calculation, value at risk aggregates all of the risks in a portfolio into a single number suitable for use in the boardroom, reporting to regulators, or disclosure in an annual report. Once one crosses the hurdle of using a statistical measure, the concept of value at risk is straightforward to understand. It is simply a way to describe the magnitude of the likely losses on the portfolio.

To understand the concept of value at risk, consider a simple example involving a foreign exchange (FX) forward contract entered into by a U.S. company at some point in the past. Suppose that the current date is 20 May 1996, and the forward contract has 91 days remaining until the delivery date of 19 August. The three-month U.S. dollar (USD) and British pound (GBP) interest rates are $r_{USD} = 5.469$ percent and $r_{GBP} = 6.063$ percent, respectively, and the spot exchange rate is 1.5355 \$/£. On the delivery date the U.S. company will deliver \$15 million and receive £10 million. The U.S. dollar mark-to-market value of the forward contract can be computed using the interest and exchange rates prevailing on 20 May. Specifically,

USD mark-to-market value

$$= \left[(\text{exchange rate in USD/GBP}) \times \frac{\text{GBP 10 million}}{1 + r_{GBP}\,(91/360)} \right] - \frac{\text{USD 15 million}}{1 + r_{USD}\,(91/360)}$$

$$= \left[(1.5355 \text{ USD/GBP}) \times \frac{\text{GBP 10 million}}{1 + 0.06063(91/360)} \right] - \frac{\text{USD 15 million}}{1 + .05469(91/360)}$$

$$= \text{USD 327,771.}$$

In this calculation we use that fact that one leg of the forward contract is equivalent to a pound-denominated 91-day zero-coupon bond and the other leg is equivalent to a dollar-denominated 91-day zero-coupon bond.

On the next day, May 21, it is likely that interest rates, exchange rates, and thus the value of the forward contract have all changed. Suppose that the distribution of possible one day changes in the value of the forward contract is that shown in Figure 1. The figure indicates that the probability that the loss will exceed \$130,000 is two percent, the probability that the loss

Figure 1 Histogram of Hypothetical Daily Mark-to-Market Profits and Losses on a Forward Contract (in $thousands)

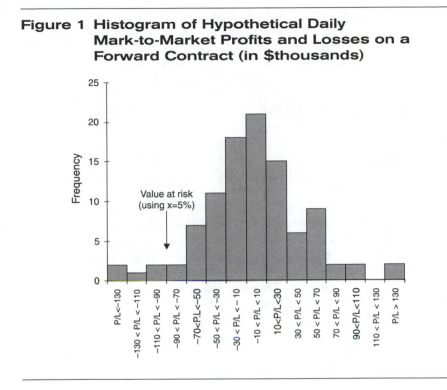

will be between $110,000 and $130,000 is 1 percent, and the probability that the loss will be between $90,000 and $110,000 is 2 percent. Summing these probabilities, there is a 5 percent probability that the loss will exceed approximately $90,000.[3] If we deem a loss that is suffered less than 5 percent of the time to be a loss due to unusual or "abnormal" market movements, then $90,000 divides the losses due to abnormal market movements from the "normal" ones. If we use this 5 percent probability as the cutoff to define a loss due to normal market movements, then $90,000 is the (approximate) value at risk.

The probability used as the cutoff need not be 5 percent, but rather is chosen by the either the user or the provider of the value-at-risk number: perhaps the risk manager, risk management committee, or designer of the system used to compute the value at risk. If instead the probability were chosen to be 2 percent, the value at risk would be $130,000, because the loss is predicted to exceed $130,000 only 2 percent of the time.

Also, implicit in this discussion has been a choice of holding period: Figure 1 displays the distribution of *daily* profits and losses. One also could construct a similar distribution of 5-day, or 10-day, profits and losses, or perhaps even use a longer time horizon. Since 5- or 10-day profits and losses typically are larger than 1-day profits and losses, the distributions would be more disperse or spread out, and the loss that is exceeded only 5 (or 2) percent of the time would be larger. Therefore the value at risk would be larger.

Now that we have seen an example of value at risk, we are ready for the definition. Using a probability of x percent and a holding period of t days, an entity's *value at risk* is the loss that is expected to be exceeded with a probability of only x percent during the next t-day holding period. Loosely, it is the loss that is expected to be exceeded during x percent of the t-day holding periods. Typical values for the probability x are 1, 2.5, and 5 percent, while common holding periods are 1, 2, and 10 (business) days, and 1 month. The theory provides little guidance about the choice of x. It is determined primarily by how the designer and/or user of the risk management system wants to interpret the value-at-risk number: Is an *abnormal* loss one that occurs with a probability of 1 percent or 5 percent? For example, J.P. Morgan's RiskMetrics system uses 5 percent, while Mobil Oil's 1994 annual report indicates that it uses 0.3 percent. The parameter t is determined by the entity's horizon. Those which actively trade their portfolios, such as financial firms, typically use one-day, while institutional investors and nonfinancial corporations may use longer holding periods. A value-at-risk number applies to the current portfolio, so a (sometimes implicit) assumption underlying the computation is that the current portfolio will remain unchanged throughout the holding period. This may not be reasonable, particularly for long holding-periods.

In interpreting value-at-risk numbers, it is crucial to keep in mind the probability x and holding period t. Without them, value-at-risk numbers are meaningless. For example, two companies holding identical portfolios will come up with different value-at-risk estimates if they make different choices of x and t. Obviously, the loss that is suffered with a probability of only 1 percent is larger than the loss that is suffered with a probability of 5 percent. Under the assumptions used in some value-at-risk systems, it is 1.41 times as large.[4] The choice of holding period can have an even larger impact, for the value at risk computed using a t-day holding period is approximately $\sqrt{t}$ times as large as the value at risk using a one-day holding period. Absent appropriate adjustments for these factors, value-at-risk numbers are not comparable across entities.

Despite its advantages, value at risk is not a panacea. It is a single, summary, statistical measure of normal market risk. At the level of the trading desk, it is just one more item in the risk manager's or trader's tool kit. The traders and front-line risk managers will look at the whole panoply of Greek letter risks (i.e., the deltas, gammas, and vegas), and may look at the portfolio's exposures to other factors such as changes in correlations. In many cases, they will go beyond value at risk and use simulation techniques to generate the entire distribution of possible outcomes, and will supplement this with detailed analyses of specific scenarios and *stress tests*. The only environment in which value-at-risk numbers will be used alone is at the level of oversight by senior management. Even at this level, the value-at-risks numbers often will be supplemented by the results of scenario analyses, stress tests, and other information about the positions.

In the balance of this chapter, we describe the three main methods for computing value-at-risk numbers: historical simulation, the variance/co-variance or analytic method, and Monte Carlo or stochastic simulation. We then consider the advantages and disadvantages of the three methods, how they can be supplemented with *stress testing*, and a brief discussion of some of the alternatives to value at risk. Appendices to the chapter review option deltas and gammas and explain the concept of *risk mapping*, which is used in the variance/covariance method. First, however, we need to discuss a fundamental idea which underlies value-at-risk computations.

Fundamentals: Identifying the Important Market Factors

In order to compute value at risk (or any other quantitative measure of market risk), we need to identify the basic market rates and prices that affect the value of the portfolio. These basic market rates and prices are the *market factors*. It is necessary to identify a limited number of basic market factors, simply because otherwise the complexity of trying to come up with a portfolio-level quantitative measure of market risk explodes. Even if we restrict our attention to simple instruments such as forward contracts, an almost countless number of different contracts can exist, because virtually any forward price and delivery date are possible. The market risk factors inherent in most other instruments such as swaps, loans (often with embedded options), options, and exotic options of course are ever more complicated. Thus, expressing the instruments' values in terms of a limited number of basic market factors is an essential first step in making the problem manageable.

Typically, market factors are identified by decomposing the instruments in the portfolio into simpler instruments more directly related to basic market-risk factors, and then interpreting the actual instruments as portfolios of the simpler instruments. We illustrate this using the foreign exchange (FX) forward contract we introduced above. The current date is 20 May 1996. The contract requires a U.S. company to deliver $15 million in 91 days. In exchange, it will receive £10 million. The current U.S.-dollar market value of this forward contract depends on three basic market factors: S, the spot exchange rate expressed in dollars per pound; r_{GBP}, the three-month pound interest rate; and r_{USD}, the three-month dollar interest rate. To see this, we decompose the cash flows of the forward contract into the following equivalent portfolio of zero-coupon bonds:

Position	Current $ Value of Position	Cash Flow on Delivery Date
Long position in 91-day £ denominated zero-coupon bond with face value of £10 million	$S \times \dfrac{GBP\ 10\ \text{million}}{1 + r_{GBP}\,(91/360)}$	Receive £ 10 million
Short position in 91-day $ denominated zero-coupon bond with face value of $15 million	$\dfrac{USD\ 15\ \text{million}}{1 + r_{USD}\,(91/360)}$	Pay $15 million

The decomposition yields the following formula, used above, for the current mark-to-market value (in dollars) of the position in terms of the basic market factors r_{USD}, r_{GBP}, and S:

$$\text{USD mark-to-market value} = \left[S \times \frac{GBP\,10\ \text{million}}{1 + r_{GBP}\,(91/360)} \right] - \frac{USD\,15\ \text{million}}{1 + r_{USD}\,(91/360)}.\}$$

Because this is an over-the-counter forward contract subject to some credit risk, the interest rates are those on three-month interbank deposits (LIBOR) rather than the rates on government securities. Similar formulas expressing the instruments' values in terms of the basic market factors must be obtained for all of the instruments in the portfolio.[5] Once such formulas have been obtained, a key part of the problem of quantifying market risk has been finished. The remaining steps involve determining or estimating the statistical distribution of the potential future values of the market factors, using these potential future values and the formulas to determine potential future changes in the values of the various positions that comprise the portfolio, and then aggregating across positions in order to determine the potential future changes in the value of the portfolio. Value at risk is a measure of these potential changes in the portfolio's value.

Of course, the values of most actual portfolios will depend upon more than three market factors. A typical set of market factors might include the spot exchange rates for all currencies in which the company has positions, together with, for each currency, the interest rates on zero-coupon bonds with a range of maturities. For example, the maturities used in the first version of J.P. Morgan's RiskMetrics[TM] system were 1 day, 1 week; 1, 3, 6, and 12 months; and 2, 3, 4, 5, 7, 9, 10, 15, 20, and 30 years.[6] A company with positions in most of the actively traded currencies, and a number of the minor ones, could easily have a portfolio exposed to several hundred market factors.

This dependence on only a limited number of basic market factors typically remains implicit in the historical and Monte Carlo simulation methodologies, but must be made explicit in the variance/covariance methodology. The process of making this dependence explicit is known as *risk mapping*. Specifically, risk mapping involves taking the actual instruments and *mapping* them into a set of simpler, standardized positions or instruments. We describe this process when we discuss the variance/covariance method below, and in Appendix B to this chapter.

Value-at-Risk Methodologies

Historical Simulation

Historical simulation is a simple, nontheoretical approach that requires relatively few assumptions about the statistical distributions of the underlying market factors. We illustrate the procedure with a simple portfolio consisting of a single instrument, the three-month FX forward for which the distribution of hypothetical mark-to-market profits and losses was previously shown in Figure 1. In essence, the approach involves using historical changes in market rates and prices to construct the distribution of potential future portfolio profits and losses in Figure 1, and then reading off the value at risk as the loss that is exceeded only 5 percent of the time.

The distribution of profits and losses is constructed by taking the *current* portfolio, and subjecting it to the *actual* changes in the market factors experienced during each of the last N periods, here days. That is, N sets of hypothetical market factors are constructed using their current values and the changes experienced during the last N periods. Using these hypothetical values of the market factors, N hypothetical mark-to-market portfolio values are computed. Doing this allows one to compute N hypothetical mark-to-market profits and losses on the portfolio, when compared to the current mark-to-market portfolio value. Even though the actual changes in rates and prices are used, the mark-to-market profits and losses are hypothetical because the current portfolio was not held on each of the last N periods. The use of the actual historical changes in rates and prices to compute the hypothetical profits and losses is the distinguishing feature of historical simulation, and the source of the name. Below we illustrate exactly how to do this. Once the hypothetical mark-to-market profit or loss for each of the last N periods have been calculated, the distribution of profits and losses and the value at risk, then can be determined.

Performing the Analysis for a Single Instrument Portfolio

We carry out the analysis as of the close of business on 20 May, 1996. Recall that the forward contract obligates a U.S. company to deliver $15 million on the delivery date 91 days hence, and in exchange receive £10 million. We perform the analysis from the perspective of the U.S. company. Even though our example is of a single instrument portfolio, it captures some of the features of multiple instrument portfolios because the forward contract is exposed to the risk of changes in several basic market factors. For simplicity, we assume that the holding period is one day ($t=1$), the value at risk will be computed using a 5 percent probability ($x=5$ percent), and that the most recent 100 business days ($N=100$) will be used to compute the changes in the values of the market factors, and the hypothetical profits and losses on the portfolio. Because 20 May is the hundreth business day of 1996, the most recent 100 business days start on 2 January 1996.

Historical Simulation

Historical simulation can be described in terms of five steps:

Step 1. The first step is to identify the basic market factors, and obtain a formula expressing the mark-to-market value of the forward contract in terms of the market factors. The market factors were identified in the previous section: they are the three-month pound interest rate, the three-month dollar interest rate, and the spot exchange rate. Also, we have already derived a formula for the U.S. dollar mark-to-market value of the forward by decomposing it into a long position in a pound denominated zero-coupon bond with face value of £10 million and short position in a dollar denominated zero-coupon bond with face value of $15 million.

Step 2. The next step is to obtain historical values of the market factors for the last N periods. For our portfolio, this means collect the three-month dollar and pound interbank interest rates and the spot dollar/pound exchange rate for the last 100 business days. Daily changes in these rates will be used to construct hypothetical values of the market factors used in the calculation of hypothetical profits and losses in step 3 because the daily value-at-risk number is a measure of the portfolio loss caused by such changes over a one-day holding period, 20 May 1996 to 21 May 1996..

Step 3. This is the key step. We subject the current portfolio to the changes in market rates and prices experienced on each of the most recent 100 business days, calculating the daily profits and losses that would occur if comparable daily changes in the market factors are experienced and the *current* portfolio is marked-to-market.

To calculate the 100 daily profits and losses, we first calculate 100 sets of hypothetical values of the market factors. The hypothetical market factors are based upon, but *not* equal to, the historical values of the market factors over the past 100 days. Rather, we calculate daily historical percentage changes in the market factors, and then combine the historical percentage changes with the current (20 May 1996) market factors to compute 100 sets of hypothetical market factors.[7] These hypothetical market factors are then used to calculate the 100 hypothetical mark-to-market portfolio values. For each of the hypothetical portfolio values we subtract the actual mark-to-market portfolio value on 20 May to obtain 100 hypothetical daily profits and losses.

Table 1 shows the calculation of the hypothetical profit/loss using the changes in the market factors from the first business day of 1996, which is day 1 of the 100 days preceding 20 May 1996. We start by using the 20 May 1996 values of the market factors to compute the mark-to-market value of the forward contract on 20 May, which is shown on line 1. Next, we determine what the value might be on the next day. To do this, we use the percentage changes in the market factors from 29 December 1995 to 2 January 1996. The actual values on 29 December 1995 and 2 January 1996, and the percentage changes, are shown in lines 2 through 4. Then, in lines 5 and 6, we use the values of the market factors on 20 May 1996, together with the percentage changes from 29 December 1995 to 2 January 1996, to compute hypothetical values of the market factors for 21 May 1996. These hypothetical values of the market factors on 21 May 1996 are then used to compute a mark-to-market value of the forward contract for 21 May 1996 using the formula

USD mark-to-market value =

$$\left[S \times \frac{GBP\,10\ \text{million}}{1 + r_{GBP}\,(90/360)} \right] - \frac{USD\,15\ \text{million}}{1 + r_{USD}\,(90/360)}$$

This value is also shown on line 6. Once the hypothetical 21 May 1996 mark-to-market value has been computed, the profit or loss on the forward contract is just the change in the mark-to-market value from 20 May 1996 to 21 May 1996, shown in line 7.

This calculation is repeated 99 more times, using the values of the market factors on 20 May 1996 and the percentage changes in the market factors for days 2 through 100 to compute 100 hypothetical *mark-to-market* values of the forward contract for 21 May 1996, and 100 hypothetical mark-to-market profits or losses. Table 2 shows these 100 daily mark-to-market profits and losses.

Step 4. The next step is to order the mark-to-market profits and losses from the largest profit to the largest loss. The ordered profits/losses are shown in Table 3, and range from a profit of $212,050 to a loss of $143,207.

Step 5. Finally, we select the loss which is equaled or exceeded 5 percent of the time. Since we have used 100 days, this is the fifth worst loss, or the

Table 1: Calculation of Hypothetical 5/21/96 Mark-to-Market Profit/Loss on a Forward Contract Using Market Factors from 5/20/96 and Changes in Market Factors from the First Business Day of 1996

	Market Factors			Mark-to-Market Value of Forward Contract ($)
	$ Interest Rate (% per year)	£ Interest Rate (% per year)	Exchange Rate ($/£)	
Start with actual values of market factors and forward contract as of close of business on 5/20/96:				
(1) Actual values on 5/20/96	5.469	6.063	1.536	327,771
Compute actual past changes in market factors:				
(2) Actual values on 12/29/95	5.688	6.500	1.553	
(3) Actual values on 1/2/96	5.688	6.563	1.557	
(4) Percentage change from 12/29/95 to 1/2/96	0.000	0.962	0.243	
Use these to compute hypothetical future values of the market factors and the mark-to-market value of the forward contract:				
(5) Actual values on 5/20/96	5.469	6.063	1.536	327,771
(6) Hypothetical future values calculated using rates from 5/20/96 and percentage changes from 12/29/95 to 1/2/96	5.469	6.121	1.539	362,713
(7) Hypothetical mark-to-market profit/loss on forward contract				34,942

Note: The hypothetical future value of the forward contract is computed using the formula

USD mark-to-market value =

$$\left[(\text{exchange rate in USD/GBP}) \times \frac{\text{GBP 10 million}}{1+r_{GBP}\,(90/360)}\right] - \frac{\text{USD 15 million}}{1 + r_{USD}\,(90/360)}$$

Table 2 Historical Simulation of 100 Hypothetical Daily Mark-to-Market Profits and Losses on a Forward Contract

	Market Factors			Hypothetical Mark-to-Market Value of	Change in Mark-to-Market Value of Forward
Number	$ Interest Rate (% per year)	£ Interest Rate (% per year)	Exchange Rate ($/£)	Forward Contract ($)	Contract ($)
1	5.469	6.121	1.539	362,713	34,942
2	5.379	6.063	1.531	278,216	−49,555
3	5.469	6.005	1.529	270,141	−57,630
4	5.469	6.063	1.542	392,571	64,800
5	5.469	6.063	1.534	312,796	−14,975
6	5.469	6.063	1.532	294,836	−32,935
7	5.469	6.063	1.534	309,795	−17,976
8	5.469	6.063	1.534	311,056	−16,715
9	5.469	6.063	1.541	379,357	51,586
10	5.438	6.063	1.533	297,755	−30,016
•					
•					
•					
91	5.469	6.063	1.541	378,442	50,671
92	5.469	6.063	1.545	425,982	98,211
93	5.469	6.063	1.535	327,439	−332
94	5.500	6.063	1.536	331,727	3,956
95	5.469	6.063	1.528	249,295	−78,476
96	5.438	6.063	1.536	332,140	4,369
97	5.438	6.063	1.534	310,766	−17,005
98	5.469	6.125	1.536	325,914	−1,857
99	5.469	6.001	1.536	338,368	10,597
100	5.469	6.063	1.557	539,821	212,050

loss of $97,230, which appears in Table 3 in the row numbered 96. Using a probability of 5 percent, this is the value at risk.

Figure 1 which was discussed previously shows the distribution of hypothetical profits and losses, with the value at risk indicated by an arrow. On the graph, the value at risk is the loss that leaves 5 percent of the probability in the left hand tail.

Table 3   Historical Simulation of 100 Hypothetical Daily Mark-to-Market Profits and Losses on a Forward Contract, Ordered From Largest Profit to Largest Loss

| Number | Market Factors | | | Hypothetical Mark-to-Market Value of Forward Contract ($) | Change in Mark-to-Market Value of Forward Contract ($) |
	$ Interest Rate (% per year)	Interest Rate (% per year)	Exchange Rate ($/£)		
1	5.469	6.063	1.557	539,821	212,050
2	5.469	6.063	1.551	480,897	153,126
3	5.469	6.063	1.546	434,228	106,457
4	5.469	6.063	1.545	425,982	98,211
5	5.532	6.063	1.544	413,263	85,492
6	5.532	6.126	1.543	398,996	71,225
7	5.469	6.063	1.542	396,685	68,914
8	5.469	6.063	1.542	392,978	65,207
9	5.469	6.063	1.542	392,571	64,800
10	5.469	6.063	1.541	385,563	57,792
•					
•					
•					
91	5.469	6.005	1.529	270,141	−57,630
92	5.500	6.063	1.529	269,264	−58,507
93	5.531	6.063	1.529	267,692	−60,079
94	5.469	6.004	1.528	255,632	−72,139
95	5.469	6.063	1.528	249,295	−78,476
96	5.469	6.063	1.526	230,541	−97,230
97	5.438	6.063	1.526	230,319	−97,452
98	5.438	6.063	1.523	203,798	−123,973
99	5.438	6.063	1.522	196,208	−131,563
100	5.407	6.063	1.521	184,564	−143,207

Multiple Instrument Portfolios

Extending the methodology to handle realistic, multiple instrument portfolios requires only that a bit of additional work be performed in three of the steps. First, in step 1 there are likely to be many more market factors, namely the interest rates for longer maturity bonds and the interest and exchange rates for many other currencies. These factors must be identified, and pricing formulas expressing the instruments' values in terms of the market factors must be obtained. Options may be handled either by treating the option volatilities as additional market factors that must be estimated and collected on each of the last N periods, or else by treating the volatilities as constants and disregarding the fact that they change randomly over time. This latter method has the potential of introducing significant errors for portfolios with significant options content. Second, in step 2 the historical values of all of the market factors must be collected. Third, it is crucial that the mark-to-market profits and losses on each instrument in the portfolio be computed and then summed for each day, before they are ordered from highest profit to lowest loss in step 4. The calculation of value at risk is intended to capture the fact that typically gains on some instruments offset losses on others. Netting the gains against the losses within each of the 100 days in step 3 reflects this relationship.[8]

What Determines the Value at Risk?

In order to understand the next methodology, it is useful to discuss the determinants of the value at risk in the simple example above. The value at risk of $97,230 was determined by using the magnitudes of past changes in the market factors or their variability, the number of contracts in the portfolio (which was simply one), the size of the forward contract (i.e., the quantities of dollars and pounds to be exchanged), and the sensitivity of its mark-to-market value to daily changes in the market factors. The number of forward contracts and its size translate into the face values of the zero-coupon bonds into which it was decomposed, while the sensitivity of its value to changes in the market factors is captured by the sensitivities of the zero-coupon bonds. The role of each of these is straightforward. More variable market factors, greater numbers of contracts, larger contracts, and contracts with greater sensitivities all result in a greater value at risk.

The value at risk is also determined by the comovement between the changes in the prices of the zero-coupon bonds into which it was decomposed, or the extent to which changes in the value of the long position in the pound denominated bond are offset by changes in the value of the short position in the dollar denominated bond. This is determined by the extent to which dollar and pound interest rates, and the dollar/pound exchange rate, move together.

Variance/Covariance Approach

The variance/covariance approach is based on the assumption that the underlying market factors have a multivariate normal distribution.[9] Using this assumption (and other assumptions detailed below), it is possible to determine the distribution of mark-to-market portfolio profits and losses,

Figure 2 Probability Density Function and Value at Risk Obtained Using Variance-Covariance Method

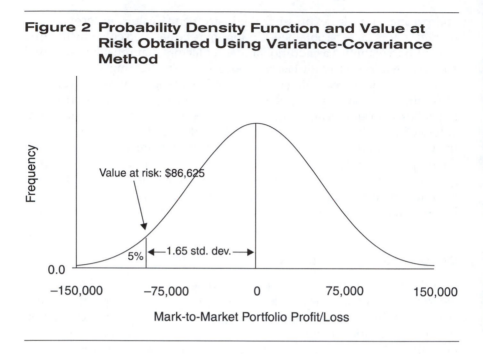

Mark-to-Market Portfolio Profit/Loss

which is also normal. Once the distribution of possible portfolio profits and losses has been obtained, standard mathematical properties of the normal distribution are used to determine the loss that will be equaled or exceeded x percent of the time, (i.e., the value at risk).

For example, suppose we continue with our example of a portfolio consisting of a single instrument, the three-month FX forward contract introduced above, and also continue to assume that the holding period is one day and the probability is 5 percent. The distribution of possible profits and losses on this simple portfolio can be represented by the probability density function shown in Figure 2. This distribution has a mean of zero, which is reasonable because the expected change in portfolio value over a short holding period is almost always close to zero. The standard deviation, which is a measure of the *spread* or dispersion of the distribution, is approximately \$52,500. A standard property of the normal distribution is that outcomes less than or equal to 1.65 standard deviations below the mean occur only 5 percent of the time. That is, if a probability of 5 percent is used in determining the value at risk, then the value at risk is equal to 1.65 times the standard deviation of changes in portfolio value. Using this fact,

$$\text{value at risk} = 1.65 \times \left(\begin{array}{c} \text{standard deviation of} \\ \text{change in portfolio value} \end{array} \right)$$

$$= 1.65 \times 52{,}500$$

$$= 86{,}625.$$

This value at risk is also shown in Figure 2. From this, it should be clear that the computation of the standard deviation of changes in portfolio value is the focus of the approach.

While the approach may seem rather like a *black box* because it is based on just a handful of formulas from statistics textbooks, it captures the determinants of value at risk mentioned above. It identifies the intuitive notions of variability and comovement with the statistical concepts of standard deviation (or variance) and correlation. These determine the variance/covariance matrix of the assumed normal distribution of changes in the market factors. The number and size of the forward contract are captured through the *risk mapping* procedure discussed below. Finally, the sensitivity of the values of the bonds which comprise the instruments to changes in the market factors is captured in step 4.

Risk Mapping

A key step in the variance/covariance approach is known as *risk mapping*. This involves taking the actual instruments and *mapping* them into a set of simpler, standardized positions or instruments. Each of these standardized positions is associated with a single market factor. For example, for the three-month forward contract the basic market factors are the three month dollar and pound interest rates, and the spot exchange rate. The associated standardized positions are a dollar denominated three-month zero-coupon bond, a three-month zero-coupon bond exposed only to changes in the pound interest rate (i.e., it as if the exchange rate were fixed), and spot pounds. The covariance matrix of changes in the values of the standardized positions can be computed from the covariance matrix of changes in the basic market factors.[10] This is illustrated in step 3 below. Once the covariance matrix of the standardized positions has been determined, the standard deviation of any portfolio of the standardized positions can be computed using a single formula for the standard deviation of a sum of normal random variables.[11]

The difficulty is that the formula applies only to portfolios of the standardized positions. This creates the need for risk mapping. In order to compute the standard deviation and value at risk of any other portfolio, it must first be *mapped* into a portfolio of standardized positions. In essence, for any actual portfolio one finds a portfolio of the standardized positions that is (approximately) equivalent to the original portfolio in the sense that it has the same sensitivities to changes in the values of the market factors. One then computes the value at risk of that equivalent portfolio. If the set of standardized positions is reasonably rich and the actual portfolio doesn't include too many options or option-like instruments then little is lost in the approximation.

Performing the Analysis for a Single Instrument Portfolio

We again illustrate the various steps involved using a portfolio consisting of a single instrument, the three-month FX forward contract to deliver $15 million on the delivery date 91 days hence, and in exchange receive £10 million. The method requires 4 steps.

Step 1. The first step is to identify the basic market factors and the standardized positions that are directly related to the market factors, and map the forward contract onto the standardized positions.

The designer of the risk measurement system has considerable flexibility in the choice of basic market factors and standardized positions, and therefore considerable flexibility in setting up the risk mapping. We use a simple set of standardized positions in order to illustrate the procedure. A natural choice corresponds to our previous decomposition of the forward contract into a long position in a three-month pound denominated zero-coupon bond with a face value of £10 million and short position in a three-month dollar denominated zero-coupon bond with a face value of $15 million. As indicated above, we take the standardized positions to be three-month dollar-denominated zero-coupon bonds, three-month pound denominated zero-coupon bonds that are exposed only to changes in the pound interest rate (i.e., as if the exchange rate were fixed), and a spot position in pounds. By decomposing the forward contract into a dollar leg and a pound leg, we have already completed a good bit of the work involved in mapping the contract. We need only to finish the process.

The dollar leg of the forward contract is easy. The value of a short position in a dollar denominated zero-coupon bond with a face value of $15 million can be obtained by discounting using the dollar interest rate. Letting X_1 denote the number of dollars invested in the first standardized position and using a negative sign to represent a short position, we have

$$X_1 = \frac{\text{USD 15 million}}{1 + r_{USD}\,(91/360)} = -\frac{\text{USD 15 million}}{1 + .05469\,(91/360)} = \text{USD} -14{,}795{,}471 \,.$$

The pound leg must be mapped into two standardized positions because its value depends on two market factors, the three-month pound interest rate and the spot dollar/pound exchange rate. The magnitudes of the standardized positions are determined by separately considering how changes in each of the market factors affects the value of the pound leg, holding the other factor constant. The dollar value of the pound leg is

$$\text{dollar value of pound leg} = (S \text{ USD/GBP}) \times \frac{\text{GBP 10 million}}{1+r_{GBP}(91/360)}$$

$$= (1.5355 \text{ USD/GBP}) \times \frac{\text{GBP 10 million}}{1+.06063(91/360)}$$

$$= \text{USD } 15{,}123{,}242.$$

Holding the spot exchange rate S constant, this has the risk of $X_2 = 15{,}123{,}242$ dollars invested in three-month pound bonds. Holding the pound interest rate constant, the bond with a face value of GBP 10 million has the exchange rate risk of a spot position of $\frac{\text{GBP 10 million}}{1+.06063(91/360)}$ pounds (its present value), or \$15,123,242. Hence the dollar value of the spot pound position is $X_3 = 15{,}123{,}242$. The equality of X_2 and X_3 is not a coincidence, because both represent the dollar value of the pound leg of the forward contract. The dollar value of the pound leg of the contract appears twice in the mapped position because, from the perspective of a U.S. company, a position in a pound denominated bond is exposed to changes in two market risk factors.

Having completed this mapping, the forward contract is now described by the magnitudes of the three standardized positions, X_1, X_2, and X_3. Appendix B to this chapter sketches a mathematical argument which justifies this mapping.

Step 2. The second step is to assume that percentage changes in the basic market factors have a multivariate normal distribution with means of zero, and estimate the parameters of that distribution. This is the point at which the variance/covariance procedure captures the variability and comovement of the market factors: variability is captured by the standard deviations (or variances) of the normal distribution, and the comovement by the correlation coefficients. The estimated standard deviations and correlation coefficients are shown in Table 4.

Step 3. The next step is to use the standard deviations and correlations of the market factors to determine the standard deviations and correlations of changes in the value of the standardized positions. The standard deviations of changes in the values of the standardized positions are determined by the products of the standard deviations of the market factors and the sensitivities of the standardized positions to changes in the market factors. For example, if the value of the first standardized position changes by 2 percent when the first market factor changes by 1 percent, then its standard deviation is twice as large as the standard deviation of the first market factor.

The correlations between changes in the values of standardized positions are equal to the correlations between the market factors, except that the

Table 4   Standard Deviations of and Correlations Between % Changes in Market Factors

Market Factor	Standard Deviations of % Changes	Correlations Between % Changes in Market Factors			
		Market Factor	3-month $ interest rate	3-month £ interest rate	$/ £ exchange rate
3-month $ interest rate	0.61	3-month $ interest rate	1.00		
3-month £ interest rate	0.58	3-month £ interest rate	0.11	1.00	
$/£ exchange rate	0.35	$/£ exchange rate	0.19	0.10	1.00

correlation coefficient changes sign if the value of one of the standardized positions changes inversely with changes in the market factor. For example, the correlation between the first and third market factors, the dollar interest rate and the dollar/pound exchange rate, is 0.19, while the correlation between the values of the first and third standardized positions is –0.19 because the value of the first standardized position moves inversely with changes in the dollar interest rate. The sidebar formalizes this discussion.

Step 4. Now that we have the standard deviations of and correlations between changes in the values of the standardized positions, we can calculate the portfolio variance and standard deviation using standard mathematical results about the distributions of sums of normal random variables and determine the distribution of portfolio profit or loss. The variance of changes in mark-to-market portfolio value depends upon the standard deviations of changes in the value of the standardized positions, the correlations, and the sizes of the positions, and is given by the standard formula

$$\sigma^2_{portfolio} = X_1{}^2\sigma_1{}^2 + X_2{}^2\sigma_2{}^2 + X_3{}^2\sigma_3{}^2 + 2X_1X_2\rho_{12}\sigma_1\sigma_2$$
$$+ 2X_1X_3\rho_{13}\sigma_1\sigma_3 + 2X_2X_3\rho_{23}\sigma_2\sigma_3 .$$

The standard deviation is of course simply the square root of the variance. For our example, the portfolio standard deviation is approximately $\sigma_{portfolio}$ = 52,500.

One property of the normal distribution is that outcomes less than or equal to 1.65 standard deviations below the mean occur only 5 percent of the time. That is, if a probability of 5 percent is used in determining the value at risk, then the value at risk is equal to 1.65 times the portfolio standard deviation. Using this, we can calculate the value at risk:

Calculation of Standard Deviations and Correlations of Percentage Changes in the Values of the Standardized Positions

In essence, if the value of the standardized position changes by x percent when the market factor changes by 1 percent, then the standard deviation of percentage changes in the standardized position is equal to x times the standard deviation of percentage changes in the market factor.

To see this more formally, let X_1 denote the value of the first standardized position, and use the fact that

$$\% \text{ change in } X_1 \approx \frac{\partial X_1}{\partial r_{USD}} \times \frac{1}{X_1} \times \text{change in } r_{USD}$$

$$\approx \frac{\partial X_1}{\partial r_{USD}} \times \frac{r_{USD}}{X_1} \times \% \text{ change in } r_{USD}$$

This implies that

$$\begin{array}{c} \text{std. deviation of} \\ \% \text{ change in } X_1 \end{array} \approx -\frac{\partial X_1}{\partial r_{USD}} \times \frac{r_{USD}}{X_1} \times \begin{array}{c} \text{std. deviation of } \% \text{ change} \\ \text{in } r_{USD} \end{array}$$

where the minus sign appears because $\dfrac{\partial X_1}{\partial r_{USD}}$ is negative (i.e., the value of the first standardized position moves inversely with USD interest rates). Letting σ_1 denote the standard deviation of percentage changes in X_1 and σ_{USD} denote the standard deviation of percentage changes in the dollar interest rate, this can be rewritten

$$\sigma_1 \approx -\frac{\partial X_1}{\partial r_{USD}} \times \frac{r_{USD}}{X_1} \times \sigma_{USD}.$$

Similarly, for the other two standardized positions:

$$\sigma_2 \approx -\frac{\partial X_2}{\partial r_{GBP}} \times \frac{r_{GBP}}{X_2} \times \sigma_{GBP},$$

$$\sigma_3 \approx \frac{\partial X_3}{\partial S} \times \frac{S}{X_3} \times \sigma_s.$$

In addition, the signs of two of the correlation coefficients must be changed because the values of the first and second standardized positions move inversely with the USD and GBP interest rates. Due to this, we have $\rho_{13} = -\rho_{USD,S}$, and $\rho_{23} = -\rho_{GBP,S}$. The correlation between the first two standardized positions is unaffected because both move inversely with interest rates, and $\rho_{12} = \rho_{USD,GBP}$.

$$\text{value at risk} = 1.65 \times \sigma_{\text{portfolio}}$$
$$= 1.65 \times 52{,}500$$
$$= 86{,}625.$$

As was discussed above, Figure 2 shows the probability density function for a normal distribution with a mean of zero and a standard deviation of 52,500, along with the value at risk.

Realistic Multiple Instrument Portfolios

Using a three-month forward contract in the example allowed us to sidestep one minor difficulty. If the market risk factors include the spot exchange rates and the interest rates at 1, 3, 6, and 12 months, what do we do with a four-month forward contract? It seems natural to write a formula for its value in terms of the four-month U.S. dollar and British pound interest rates, just as we did with the three-month forward. But doesn't this introduce two more market factors, the four-month dollar and pound interest rates?

The answer is no. The 1-, 3-, 6-, and 12-month interest rates are natural choices for market risk factors because there are active interbank deposit markets at these maturities, and rates for these maturities are widely quoted. In a number of currencies there are also liquid government bond markets at some of these maturities. There is not an active four-month interbank market in the U.S. dollar, the British pound, or any other currency. As a result, the four-month interest rates used in computing the model value of the four-month forward would typically be interpolated from the 3 and six-month interest rates. (The interpolated four-month rates might also depend on rates for the other actively quoted maturities, depending upon the interpolation scheme used.) Through this process, the current mark-to-market values of all dollar/pound forward contracts, regardless of delivery date, will depend on the spot exchange rate and the interest rates at only a limited number of maturities. As a result, value at risk measures computed using theoretical pricing models depend upon only a limited number of basic market factors.

The four-month forward just mentioned could be handled as follows. We suppose that the forward price is 1.5 $/£, and that the contract requires a U.S. company to deliver $15 million and receive £10 million in four months. The first step is to decompose the forward contract into pound and dollar denominated four-month zero-coupon bonds just as we did with the three-month forward. Next, the four-month zeros must be *mapped* onto the three- and six-month zeros. The idea is to replace each of the four-month zeros with a portfolio of the three- and six-month standardized positions that has the same market value and risk, where here *risk* means standard deviation of changes in mark-to-market value, which is proportional to value at risk. An instrument with multiple cash-flows at different dates, for example a 10-year gilt, would be handled by mapping the 20 semiannual cash flows onto the 6- and 12-month, and 2-, 3-, 4-, 5-, 7-, 9-, and 10-year pound denominated zero-coupon bonds, the standardized positions. Each cash flow would be mapped onto the two nearest standardized positions.

The second section of Appendix B to this chapter uses the four-month dollar denominated zero to illustrate one way to perform this mapping. Appendix B to this chapter also describes how options are mapped into their *delta-equivalent* standardized positions.

Relatively minor complications of realistic portfolios are that standard deviations and correlations must be estimated for all of the market factors, and the portfolio variance must be calculated using the appropriate generalization of the formula used above.

Monte Carlo Simulation

The Monte Carlo simulation methodology has a number of similarities to historical simulation. The main difference is that rather than carrying out the simulation using the observed changes in the market factors over the last N periods to generate N hypothetical portfolio profits or losses, one chooses a statistical distribution that is believed to adequately capture or approximate the possible changes in the market factors. Then, a psuedo-random number generator is used to generate thousands or perhaps tens of thousands of hypothetical changes in the market factors. These are then used to construct thousands of hypothetical portfolio profits and losses on the current portfolio, and the distribution of possible portfolio profit or loss. Finally, the value at risk is then determined from this distribution.

A Single Instrument Portfolio

Once again, we use the same portfolio of a single forward contract to illustrate the approach. The steps are as follows.

Step 1. The first step is to identify the basic market factors, and obtain a formula expressing the mark-to-market value of the forward contract in terms of the market factors. This has already been done: the market factors are the three-month pound interest rate, the three-month dollar interest rate, and the spot exchange rate, and we have already derived a formula for the mark-to-market value of the forward by decomposing it into a portfolio of dollar and pound denominated three-month zero-coupon bonds.

Step 2. The second step is to determine or assume a specific distribution for changes in the basic market factors, and to estimate the parameters of that distribution. The ability to pick the distribution is the feature that distinguishes Monte Carlo simulation from the other two approaches, for in the other two methods the distribution of changes in the market factors is specified as part of the method. For this example, we assume that that percentage changes in the basic market factors have a multivariate normal distribution, and use the estimates of the standard deviations and correlations in Table 4.

The assumed distribution need not be the multivariate normal, though the natural interpretations of its parameters (means, standard deviations, and correlations) and the ease with which these parameters can be estimated weigh in its favor. The designers of the risk management system are free to choose any distribution that they think reasonably describes possible future changes in the market factors. Beliefs about possible future changes in the market factors are typically based on observed past changes, so this amounts to saying that the designers of the risk management system are free to chose any distribution that they think approximates the distribution of past changes in the market factors.

Step 3. Once the distribution has been selected, the next step is to use a psuedo-random generator to generate N hypothetical values of changes in the market factors, where N is almost certainly greater than 1000 and perhaps greater than 10,000. These hypothetical market factors are then used to calculate N hypothetical mark-to-market portfolio values. Then from each of the hypothetical portfolio values we subtract the actual mark-to-market portfolio value on 20 May to obtain N hypothetical daily profits and losses.

Steps 4 and 5. The last two steps are the same as in historical simulation. The mark-to-market profits and losses are ordered from the largest profit to the largest loss, and the value at risk is the loss which is equaled or exceeded 5 percent of the time.

Multiple Instrument Portfolios

Just as with historical simulation, extending the methodology to handle realistic, multiple instrument portfolios requires only that a bit of additional work be performed in three of the steps. First, in step 1 there are likely to be many more market factors, namely the interest rates for longer maturity bonds and the interest and exchange rates for other currencies. These factors must be identified, and pricing formulas expressing the instruments' values in terms of the market factors must be obtained. Again, options may be handled either by treating the option volatilities as additional market factors that must be simulated, or else treating the volatilities as constants and disregarding the fact that they change randomly over time. Second, in step 2 the joint distribution of possible changes in the values of all of the market factors must be determined. This joint distribution must include the option volatilities, if they are to be allowed to change. Third, similar to historical simulation, to reflect accurately the correlations of market rates and prices it is necessary that the mark-to-market profits and losses on every instrument be computed and then summed for each day, before they are ordered from highest profit to lowest loss in step 4.

Which Method Is Best?

With three methods from which to choose, the obvious question is: which method of calculating value at risk is best? Unfortunately, there is no easy answer. The methods differ in their ability to capture the risks of options and option-like instruments, ease of implementation, ease of explanation to senior management, flexibility in analyzing the effect of changes in the assumptions, and reliability of the results. The best choice will be determined by which of these dimensions the risk manager finds most important. Below we discuss how the three methods differ on these dimensions, and Table 5 summarizes the differences. We also discuss a closely related issue, the choice of the holding period *t*.

It may be that the best choice is not to use value at risk at all. Nonfinancial corporations might find that value at risk's focus on mark-to-market profit or loss over a holding period of *t* days doesn't match their perspective. Rather, they may be more interested in the distributions of quarterly cash flow over the next 20 quarters, and how these distributions are affected by transactions in financial instruments. This suggests a *cash-flow-at-risk* measure, which we briefly discuss below when we describe alternatives to value at risk. Finally, as described below, companies with exposures to only a few different market factors may find simple sensitivity analyses to be adequate.

Ability to Capture the Risks of Options and Option-Like Instruments

The two simulation methods work well regardless of the presence of options and option-like instruments in the portfolio. In contrast, the variance/covariance method works well for instruments and portfolios with limited options content, but is less able to capture the risks of options and option-like instruments than are the two simulation methods. The limitation of the variance/covariance method is that it incorporates options by replacing them with, or mapping them to, their *delta-equivalent* spot positions (see Appendix B to this chapter). This amounts to linearizing the options positions, or replacing the nonlinear functions which give their values in terms of the underlying rates and prices with linear ap-

Table 5   Comparison of Value at Risk Methodologies

	Historical Simulation	Variance/ Covariance	Monte Carlo Simulation
Able to capture the risks of portfolios which include options?	Yes, regardless of the options content of the portfolio	No, except when computed using a short holding period for portfolios with limited or moderate options content	Yes, regardless of the options content of the portfolio
Easy to implement?	Yes, for portfolios for which data on the past values of the market factors are available.	Yes, for portfolios restricted to instruments and currencies covered by available off-the-shelf software. Otherwise reasonably easy to moderately difficult to implement, depending upon the complexity of the instruments and availability of data.	Yes, for portfolios restricted to instruments and currencies covered by available "off-the-shelf" software. Otherwise moderately to extremely difficult to implement.
Computations performed quickly?	Yes.	Yes.	No, except for relatively small portfolios.
Easy to explain to senior management?	Yes.	No.	No.
Produces misleading value at risk estimates when recent past is atypical?	Yes.	Yes, except that alternative correlations/standard deviations may be used.	Yes, except that alternative estimates of parameters may be used.
Easy to perform "what-if" analyses to examine effect of alternative assumptions?	No.	Easily able to examine alternative assumptions about correlations/standard deviations. Unable to examine alternative assumptions about the distribution of the market factors, i.e., distributions other than the Normal.	Yes.

proximations. For instruments or portfolios with a great deal of options content, the linear approximations may not adequately capture how the values of the options change with changes in the underlying rates and prices.

In the variance/covariance method, the problem of adequately capturing the risks of options and option-like instruments is least severe when the holding period is one day ($t=1$). Large changes in the underlying rates or prices are unlikely over such a short holding period, and the linear approximation in this method works well for small changes in the underlying rates and prices. As a result, the variance/covariance method works well even for positions with moderate options content, provided that the holding period is short. However, over longer holding-periods such as two weeks or one month, larger changes in underlying rates and prices are likely, and value-at-risk estimates produced using the variance/covariance method cannot be relied upon for positions with moderate or significant options content.

The simulation methods work well regardless of the presence of options in the portfolio because they recompute the value of the portfolio for each "draw" of the basic market factors. In doing this, they estimate the "correct" distribution of portfolio value, though this statement must be qualified. The distribution of portfolio value generated by Monte Carlo simulation depends upon the assumed statistical distribution of the basic market factors and on the estimates of its parameters, both of which can be "wrong" and can therefore lead to errors in the calculated value at risk. Similarly, the distribution of portfolio value generated by historical simulation will be misleading if the prior N days from which the historical sample was drawn were not representative.

A final risk measurement issue related to options and option-like instruments is the ability of the value-at-risk methodologies to incorporate the fact that option volatilities are random and option prices change with changes in volatilities. As indicated previously, the variance/covariance method also does not capture these features of options very well. In contrast, Monte Carlo simulation can incorporate, in principle, the facts that volatilities are random and option prices change with volatilities by extending the simulation to include a distribution of volatilities, though this typically is not done in actual implementation of this methodology. Historical simulation also can incorporate changes in option prices with changes in volatilities if option volatilities are included as additional factors and collected for the N day period used in the simulation.

Ease of Implementation

The historical simulation method is easy to implement for portfolios restricted to currencies for which data on the past values of the basic market factors are available. It is conceptually simple, and can be implemented in a spreadsheet because pricing models for financial products are now available as spreadsheet add-in functions. The principal difficulty in implementing historical simulation is that it requires that the user possess a time series of the relevant market factors covering the last N days or other periods. This can pose a problem for multinational companies with operations and local currency borrowing in many countries, or with receivables and other instruments in a wide range of currencies. While spot exchange rates are readily available for virtually all currencies, obtaining reliable daily market interest rates for a range of maturities in some currencies without well developed capital markets can be difficult.

A range of vendors offer software which computes value-at-risk estimates using the variance/covariance method, so this method is very easy to implement for portfolios restricted to currencies and types of instruments covered by the available systems. The variance/covariance method can be moderately difficult to implement for portfolios which include currencies and types of instruments not covered by the available systems. First, estimates of the standard deviations and correlations of the market factors are required. Computing these estimates is straightforward if data are available, but as indicated above reliable market interest rates may not be available for a range of maturities in all currencies.[12] Second, and more difficult, instruments must be mapped to the delta-equivalent positions as described in Appendix B to this chapter.

Off-the-shelf software is starting to become available for the Monte Carlo simulation method, making it as easy to implement as the variance/covariance method for portfolios covered by the available systems. One difference is that computation times will be longer with Monte Carlo simulation. For portfolios not covered by the existing software, Monte Carlo simulation is in some ways easier, and in some ways more difficult, than the variance/covariance method. It is easier because it is not necessary to map instruments onto the standard positions, and it is more difficult because the user must select the distribution from which the psuedo-random vectors are drawn, and select or estimate the parameters of that distribution. Actually carrying out the simulation is not difficult because psuedo-random number generators are available as spreadsheet add-ins. However, selecting the distribution and selecting or estimating the parameters require high degrees of expertise and judgment. Another disadvantage of Monte Carlo simulation is that for large portfolios the computations can be time consuming.

All three methods require that pricing models be available for all instruments in the portfolio.[13] While the variance/covariance method does not directly make use of instruments' prices, options are mapped to their delta-equivalent positions, and the computation of deltas requires pricing models. The need for pricing models can pose a problem for portfolios which include certain exotic options and currency swaps with complex embedded options.

Ease of Communication with Senior Management

The conceptual simplicity of historical simulation makes it easiest to explain to senior management. The variance/covariance method is difficult to explain to an audience without technical training because the key step, the reliance on the mathematics of the normal distribution to calculate the portfolio standard deviation and the value at risk, is simply a black box. Monte Carlo simulation is even more difficult to explain. The key steps of choosing a statistical distribution to represent changes in the market factors and engaging in psuedo-random sampling from that distribution are simply alien to most people.

Reliability of the Results

All methods rely on historical data. Historical simulation is unique, though, in that it relies so directly on historical data. A danger in this is that the price and rate changes over the last 100 (or 200) days is that the last 100 (or 200) days might not be typical. For example, if by chance the last 100 days were a period of low volatility in market rates and prices, the value at risk computed using historical simulation would understate the risk in the portfolio. Alternatively, if by chance the U.S. dollar price of the Mexican peso rose steadily over the last 100 days and there were relatively few days on which the dollar price of a peso fell, value at risk computed using historical simulation would indicate that long positions in the Mexican peso involved little risk of loss. Moreover, one cannot be confident that errors of this sort will "average out." Traders will know whether the actual price changes over the last 100 days were typical, and therefore will know for which positions the value at risk is underestimated, and for which it is overestimated. If value at risk is used to set risk or position limits, the traders can exploit their knowledge of the biases in the value-at-risk system and expose the company to more risk than the risk management committee intended.

Other methodologies use historical data to estimate the parameters of distributions (for example the variance/covariance methodology relies on historical data to estimate the standard deviations and correlations of a multivariate normal distribution of changes in market factors for which the means are assumed to be zero), and are also subject to the problem that the historical period used might be atypical. However, assuming a particular distribution inherently limits the possible shapes that the estimated distribution can have. For example, if one assumed that the changes in the U.S. dollar price of a Mexican peso followed a normal distribution with a mean of zero, one would predict that there was a 50 percent chance that the price of a peso would fall tomorrow even if the price had risen on each of the last 100 days. Since theoretical reasoning indicates that the probability that the price of the peso will fall tomorrow is about 50 percent, regardless of what it has done over the past 100 days, this is likely a better prediction than the prediction implicit in historical simulation.

The variance/covariance and Monte Carlo simulation methods share a different potential problem: the assumed distributions might not adequately describe the actual distributions of the market factors. Typically, actual distributions of changes in market rates and prices have fat tails relative to the normal distribution. That is, there are more occurrences away from the mean than predicted by a normal distribution. Nonetheless, the normal distribution assumed in the variance/covariance method appears to be a reasonable approximation for the purposes of computing value at risk.[14] An issue unique to the Monte Carlo simulation method stems from the fact that the designer of the system can choose the statistical distribution to use for the market factors. This flexibility allows the designer of the system to make a bad choice, in the sense that the chosen distribution might not adequately approximate the actual distribution of the market factors.

Concerns about the reliability of the methods can be partially addressed by comparing actual changes in value to the value-at-risk amounts. This sort of validation is feasible because the value-at-risk approach explicitly specifies the probability with which actual losses will exceed the value-at-risk amount. It is performed by collecting a sample of value-at-risk amounts and actual mark-to-market portfolio profits and losses, and answering two questions. First, does the distribution of actual mark-to-market profits and losses appear similar to the distribution used to determine the value-at-risk amount? And second, do the actual losses exceed the value-at-risk amount with the expected frequency? A limitation of this approach to validation is that chance occurrences will almost always cause the distribution of actual portfolio profits and losses to differ somewhat from the expected distribution. Because of this, reliable inferences about the quality of the value-at-risk estimates can only be made using by comparing relatively large samples of value-at-risk amounts and actual changes in portfolio value. If validation of this sort is considered essential, a short holding period must be used in computing the value-at-risk amounts, because it will take many years to collect a large sample of monthly or quarterly value-at-risk amounts and portfolio profits and losses.

Flexibility in Incorporating Alternative Assumptions

In some situations the risk manager will have reason to think that the historical standard deviations and/or correlations are not reasonable estimates of the future ones. For example, in the period immediately prior to the departure of the British pound from the European Monetary System (EMS) in September 1992, the historical correlation between changes in the dollar/pound and dollar/mark exchange rates was very high. Yet a risk manager might have suspected that the pound would leave the EMS, and therefore that the correlation would be much lower in the future. How easily could she have calculated the value at risk in this what-if scenario using each of the three methods?

Historical simulation is directly tied to the historical changes in the basic market factors. As a result, there is no natural way to perform this sort of what-if analysis.[15] In contrast, it is very easy to carry out this sort of what-if analysis in the variance/covariance and Monte Carlo simulation methods. In these, the historical data are used to estimate the parameters of the statistical distribution of changes in the market factors. The user may override the historical estimates, and use any consistent set of parameters she chooses. The only constraint is that the user-interfaces in some software implementations of the methods may make this cumbersome.

Supplementing Value at Risk: Stress Testing and Scenario Analysis

Value at risk is not a panacea. It is a single, summary, statistical measure of normal market risk. If a probability of 5 percent and a holding period of one day are used in computing the value at risk, you expect to suffer a loss exceeding the value at risk one (business) day out of 20, or about once per month. A level of loss that will be exceeded about once per month is reasonably termed a *normal* loss. But when the value at risk is exceeded, just how large can the losses be?

Stress testing attempts to answer this question (see Figure 3). It is a general rubric for performing a set of scenario analyses to investigate the effects of extreme market conditions. To the extent that the effects are unacceptable, the portfolio or risk management strategy needs to be revised. There is no standard way to carry out stress testing, and no standard set of scenarios to consider. Rather, the process depends crucially on the judgment and experience of the risk manager.

Stress testing often begins with a set of hypothetical extreme market scenarios. These scenarios might be created from stylized extreme scenarios, such as assumed 5 or 10 standard deviation moves in market rates or prices, or they might come from actual extreme events. For example, the sce-

Figure 3 Focus of "Stress Testing"

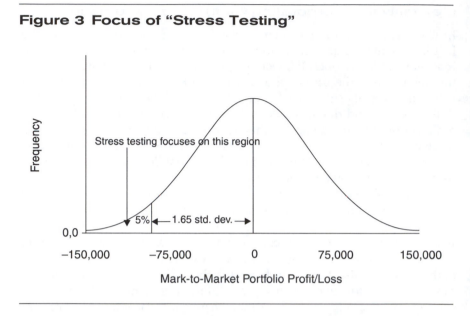

After developing a set of scenarios, the next step is to determine the
effect on the prices of all instruments in the portfolio, and the impact on

narios might be based upon the changes in U.S. dollar interest rates and
bond prices experienced during the winter and spring of 1994, or the dramatic changes in some of the European exchange rates that occurred in September 1992. Alternatively, the scenarios might be created by imagining a
few sudden surprises, and thinking through the implications for the markets. For example, how would the unanticipated failure of a major dealer
affect prices and liquidity in the currency swaps market? What would be the
effect on the Korean won and the Japanese yen if the North Koreans crossed
the 38th parallel? What would be the effect of such an incident on the U.S.
and Japanese equity markets? In developing these scenarios, it is important
to think through the implications for all markets. An event sufficiently significant to have a sudden, major impact on the dollar/yen exchange rate
would almost certainly affect other exchange rates, and would likely affect
interest rates in many currencies. A full description of a scenario will include the changes in all market rates and prices.

After developing a set of scenarios, the next step is to determine the
effect on the prices of all instruments in the portfolio, and the impact on
portfolio value. In addition, companies whose risk management strategies depend on *dynamic hedging,* or on the ability to frequently adjust or
rebalance their portfolios, need to consider the impact of major surprises
on market liquidity. It may be difficult or impossible to execute transactions at reasonable bid/ask spreads during periods of market stress.

Companies which use futures contracts to hedge relatively illiquid assets or financial contracts must consider the funding needs of the futures contracts. Gains or losses on futures contracts are received or paid immediately, while gains or losses on other instruments are often not received or paid until the positions are closed out. As a result, even a well-hedged position combining futures contracts with other instruments can lead to timing mismatches between when funds are required and when they are received.

Finally, contingency plans might be developed for certain of the scenarios. Declines in market value, once suffered, typically cannot be recovered, so contingency plans have little to offer in this dimension. However, potential funding mismatches created by the cash demands of futures positions can be managed by arranging backup lines of credit. The potential importance of this is illustrated by MG Refining and Marketing (MGRM), a classic example of a firm which was not prepared to meet the funding demands of its futures positions. MGRM is a U.S. subsidiary of Metallgesellschaft A.G., the fourteenth largest German industrial firm, and was engaged in the refining and marketing of petroleum products in the United States. Among its activities, MGRM used futures contracts and short-term commodity swaps on crude oil and various refined products to hedge long-term delivery obligations. In early 1994 it had to be rescued by a group of 150 German and international banks when it was unable to meet the funding needs created by staggering losses on its futures contracts and swaps. Regardless of one's view of the wisdom of using futures to hedge long-term delivery obligations and of MGRM's risk management strategy,[16] in retrospect it seems clear that MGRM's failures included the lack of a plan for meeting the funding demands of its futures contracts.

Scenario analyses also are used to examine the effects of violations of the assumptions underlying the value-at-risk calculations. For example, immediately prior to the British pound's departure from the EMS in September 1992, all three value-at-risk methodologies would have indicated that, from the perspective of a U.S. dollar investor, a long position in sterling combined with a short position in Deutschemarks had a very low value-at-risk. The low value-at-risk would have been a result of the historically high correlations between the dollar/pound and dollar/mark exchange rates, for all three value-at-risk methodologies rely upon historical data. Yet in September 1992, the position would have suffered a large loss, because the historical correlations could no longer be relied upon. This risk could be evaluated either by changing the correlation used as an input in calculating the value at risk, or by examining directly the impact on the portfolio if the pound fell relative to the mark. Regardless, the key input to this process is the risk manager's judgment that the scenario is worth considering.

Alternatives to Value at Risk

As indicated above, value at risk may not be appropriate for all entities. Two alternatives are sensitivity analysis and cash flow at risk. Sensitivity analysis is less sophisticated than value at risk. In contrast, cash flow at risk can be considered more sophisticated than value at risk.

Sensitivity Analysis

Companies with exposures to only a few market factors may find that the benefits of value at risk don't justify the difficulty of mastering the approach and implementing a system to compute the value-at-risk estimates. As discussed next, sensitivity analyses are a reasonable alternative for sufficiently simple portfolios.

The approach in sensitivity analysis is to imagine hypothetical changes in the value of each market factor, use pricing models to compute the value of the portfolio given the new value of the market factor, and then determine the change in portfolio value resulting from the change in the market factor. For example, if the dollar price of a pound increases by 1 percent, the value of the portfolio will decrease by $200,000; if the dollar price of a pound decreases by 1 percent, the value of the portfolio will increase by $240,000. There is nothing magical about 1 percent. Rather, the computations will typically be performed and reported for a range of increases and decreases that cover the range of likely exchange-rate changes. Similar computations would also be reported for other relevant market factors such as interest rates.

When combined with knowledge of the magnitudes of likely exchange rate or interest rate changes, these sorts of computations provide a very good picture of the risks of portfolios with exposures to only a few market factors. In fact, they comprise the most basic risk management information, and are very closely related to the delta risk measure discussed in Appendix A to this chapter. In one form or another, market risk sensitivities have been available to traders and risk managers since at least 1938.[17] Their principal limitation stems from the fact that a sensitivity analysis report for a portfolio with exposures to many different market factors can easily contain hundreds or thousands of numbers, each representing the change in portfolio value for a particular hypothetical change in market rates and prices. Absent some approach like value at risk, it is difficult or impossible for a risk manager or senior manager charged with oversight of trading and risk management activities to meaningfully read and review sensitivity analysis reports for portfolios with exposures to many different market factors and assimilate the information to get a sense of portfolio risk.[18]

Cash Flow at Risk

As stated previously, cash flow at risk is arguably more sophisticated than value at risk. As of this writing, it appears to have a limited, but growing, number of users. Cash flow at risk is a reasonable choice for nonfinancial corporations which are concerned with managing the risks inherent in operating cash flows and find that value at risk's focus on mark-to-market profit or loss over a holding period of t days doesn't match their perspective.

For example, Merck is a user of both derivatives and cash flow at risk. The motivation for derivatives usage appears to be the fact that changes in cash flows due to changes in interest rates and exchange rates were negatively affecting research and development (R&D) programs by causing shortfalls of funds.[19] Currency and interest rate swaps, appropriately used, are able to ameliorate this problem. But this motivation for derivatives usage suggests that the risk measurement system ought to focus on quarterly or annual cash flows over a horizon of at least several years. For example, a company in a similar situation might be interested in the distributions of quarterly cash flow over the next perhaps 20 quarters, and how these distributions are affected by transactions in financial instruments.[20]

Cash flow at risk measures are typically estimated using Monte Carlo simulation. However, there are important differences from the use of Monte Carlo simulation to estimate value at risk. First, the time horizon is much longer in cash-flow-at-risk simulations. For example, values of the underlying market factors might be simulated for the next 20 quarters. Second, the focus is on cash flows, not changes in mark-to-market values. This is the distinguishing feature, and in fact the whole point, of cash-flow-at-risk measures. Rather than using the hypothetical values of the market factors as inputs to pricing models to compute changes in mark-to-market portfolio value, the hypothetical market factors are combined with the terms of the cash and derivative instruments to compute hypothetical quarterly or annual cash flows, and their distributions. Third, *operating* cash flows are typically included in the calculation. This is of course essential if the goal of the risk measurement system is to assess the impact of derivatives and other financial transactions on companies' total cash flows. As a result, the *factors* included in the simulation are not just the basic financial market factors included in value-at-risk calculations, but any factors which affect operating cash flows. Changes in customer demand, the outcomes of R&D programs (including competitors' R&D programs), and competitors' pricing decisions are a few operating factors that come to mind. Finally, the emphasis is often on planning rather than control, oversight, and reporting.

A serious drawback is that successful design and implementation of a cash-flow-at-risk measurement system requires a high degree of knowledge and judgment.[21] First, the designer of the system must develop a model of the company's operating cash flows, determining the important operating factors and how they affect operating cash flows. This alone may be a major undertaking. Next, this model of the operating cash flows must be integrated with a model of the financial market factors. Then the user must select the statistical distribution from which the hypothetical values of the factors (both operating and financial) are drawn, and select or estimate the parameters of that distribution. This can be particularly difficult for the operating factors. In contrast with the financial market factors, data on actual past changes in operating risk factors may not be available to guide the choice of distribution. Finally, the user must carry out the computations. Somewhat offsetting the difficulty of the problem is that the model of the financial market factors can be relatively crude, as there is no point in refining it to be more precise than the model of the operating cash flows. Nonetheless, building a cash-flow-at-risk measurement system is likely to be a major undertaking.

Appendix A

Basic Risk Measures: Option Deltas and Gammas

Delta

The delta (or Δ) is perhaps the most basic risk management concept. Delta indicates how much the theoretical price of an instrument or portfolio changes when the price of the underlying asset, currency, or commodity changes by a small amount. Therefore it is very closely related to sensitivity analysis. While originally developed for options, the concept can be applied to other derivatives, and to cash positions as well.

We illustrate the concept of delta using a call option on British pounds with a strike price of 1.50 $/£ and three months to expiration. We suppose that the current dollar/pound exchange rate is also 1.50 $/£ and the current price of the call option is $0.0295 per pound. The price of this option will vary as the dollar/pound exchange rate varies. Figure 4 shows the theoretical price (computed using the Garman-Kohlhagen model) as a function of the dollar/pound exchange rate. The graph indicates that if the dollar/pound exchange rate changes slightly from the current value of 1.50 $/£, the change in the option price will be about one-half as large as the change in the exchange rate. For example, if the exchange rate changes to 1.51 $/£, the (theoretical) option price will change by $0.0051 to $0.0346.

Figure 4 Price of a Call Option on British Pounds

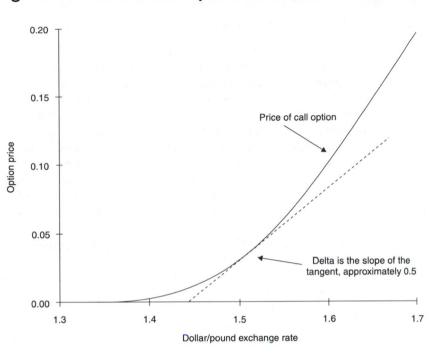

The ratio of the change in the option price to the change in the currency price, $\dfrac{\$0.0051}{\$0.01} = 0.51$, is the option delta. Graphically, the delta is the slope of the line which is tangent to the option price function at the current exchange rate. This tangent is shown in Figure 4.

Formally, delta is the partial derivative of the option price function with respect to the underlying currency price. Letting S denote the dollar price of a British pound and $C(S)$ denote the option price as a function of S, the option delta is

$$\Delta \equiv \frac{\partial C(S)}{\partial S}.$$

Since delta is given by the ratio of price changes, i.e.,

$$\Delta = \frac{\text{change in option price}}{\text{change in price of underlying instrument}}.$$

the change in the option price resulting from a change in the spot price can be calculated from the delta and the change in the price of the underlying instrument:

change in option price = $\Delta \times$ change in price of underlying instrument

For example, if $\Delta = 0.51$ and the price of a pound changes by $0.01, the predicted change in the option price is $0.0051 = 0.51 \times \$0.01$. One interpretation of this relationship is that an option on one pound is equivalent to a spot position of delta British pounds, because the change in value of a spot position of delta British pounds is also given by the product of delta and the change in the spot price of a pound. Loosely, for small changes in the exchange rate the option *acts like* delta British pounds. The significance of this for risk measurement is that one technique for measuring the risk of an option position is to use the option delta to compute the equivalent spot position, and then estimate the risk of the equivalent spot position. Most applications of the variance/covariance methodology for computing value at risk which we discuss below rely on this technique.

An important feature of options and option-like instruments is that delta changes as the price of the underlying asset, currency, or commodity changes. This is illustrated in Figure 5, which shows the theoretical price of a three-month call option on pounds with a strike price of 1.50 $/£, together with the option deltas. At the current spot price of 1.50 $/£ the delta is approximately one-half, while for high spot prices the delta approaches one and for low spot prices it approaches zero. The delta approaches one for high spot prices because if the spot price is well above the strike price the option is almost certain to be exercised. An option that is almost certain to be exercised behaves like a levered position in the underlying asset or currency. The delta approaches zero for low spot prices because if the spot price is well below the strike price the option is almost certain to expire unexercised. An option that is almost certain to expire unexercised is worth almost nothing now, and behaves like almost nothing.

The changing delta illustrated in Figure 5 doesn't appear to be a severe problem for risk measurement. However, for many options positions, reliance solely on delta can be misleading. Figure 6 shows the value of one such position as a function of the dollar/pound exchange. The portfolio shown in Figure 6 consists of a spot position in one pound along with two written three-month options. At the spot exchange rate 1.50 $/£, the delta of the spot pound is 1 and the delta of the call option is approximately 0.5, so the portfolio delta is approximately $1 - 2 \times .5 = 0$. Using a delta of zero to compute the equivalent spot position, we would conclude that this options position is equivalent to a spot position of zero British pounds, and therefore has no market risk. But clearly the position does have market risk, for if the exchange rate changes in either direction by more than a small amount the position will suffer a loss.

Figure 5 Delta Changes as the Exchange Rate Changes

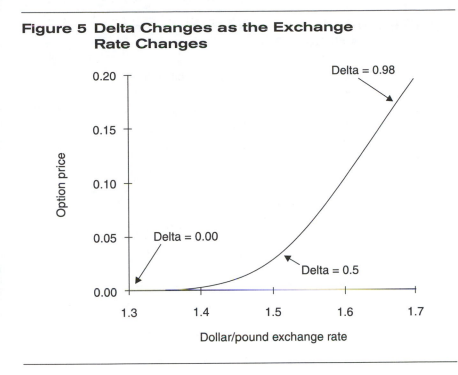

Delta = 0.98

Delta = 0.00

Delta = 0.5

Option price

Dollar/pound exchange rate

Gamma

Gamma (or Γ) supplements delta by measuring how delta changes as the price of the underlying asset, currency, or commodity changes. In Figure 6 delta decreases as the dollar price of a pound increases, so gamma is negative. (The slope is positive for $/£ exchange rates less than 1.50 $/£, and negative for exchange rates greater than 1.50 $/£.) If delta increases as the dollar price of a pound increases, then gamma is positive. Gamma is defined as the partial derivative of delta with respect to the price of the underlying asset, currency, or commodity, or equivalently as the second partial derivative of the option price with respect to the price of the underlying asset, currency, or commodity. Letting S denote the spot price of the underlying asset and $C(S)$ denote the option price as a function of S, the option gamma is

$$\Gamma \equiv \frac{\partial \Delta(S)}{\partial S}$$

$$= \frac{\partial^2 C(S)}{\partial S^2}.$$

Figure 6 Example of a Risky Portfolio That Has Delta = 0

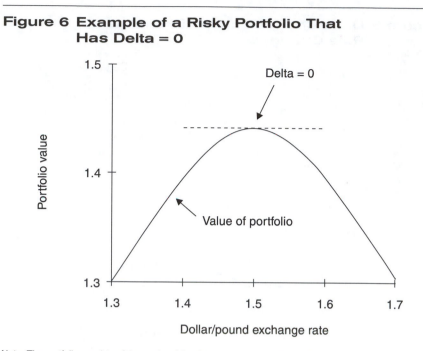

Note: The portfolio consists of 1 pound and 2 written call options, each on 1 pound.

Delta and gamma together can be used to predict the change in the option price resulting from a change in the spot price of one pound using the following formula:

$$\text{change in option price} = \Delta \times \left(\begin{array}{c} \text{change in price of} \\ \text{underlying instrument} \end{array} \right)$$
$$+ \frac{1}{2} \Gamma \times \left(\begin{array}{c} \text{change in price of} \\ \text{underlying instrument} \end{array} \right)^2.$$

Comparing this to the earlier equation which predicts the change in the option price using only delta, one can see that when gamma is negative the change in the option price is more adverse than that predicted using delta alone. Conversely, when gamma is positive the change in the option price is more favorable than that predicted using delta alone.

The significance of this for value-at-risk measures is that the variance/covariance method typically measures the risk of options by converting them to their equivalent spot positions using delta alone and thereby somewhat understates the risk of positions with negative gammas. The effect will be small for value-at-risk computations done using short holding periods, because for short holdings periods the change in the spot price of the underlying asset is typically small and the term

$$\frac{1}{2}\Gamma \times \left(\begin{array}{c}\text{change in price of}\\\text{underlying instrument}\end{array}\right)^2$$

is small. However, the understatement of the risk of negative gamma portfolios can be significant when value-at-risk measures are computed for long holding periods.

Appendix B

Risk Mapping

Theory Underlying Mapping the Forward Contract into the Three Standardized Positions

Here we show that the forward contract can be described as a portfolio of the three standardized positions with the same sensitivities to the market factors. In other words, they have the same risks. This is the key to risk mapping. We do this by using first order Taylor series approximations to represent the changes in the values of both the forward contract and the portfolio of the three standardized positions in terms of changes in the three market factors, and choose the standardized positions so that the coefficients of the two Taylor series approximations are the same. If the coefficients of the Taylor series approximations are the same, then (up to the approximation) the two portfolios respond identically to changes in the market factors.

First, we consider the forward contract. Let

$$V_F \equiv S \times \left[\frac{\text{GBP 10 million}}{1 + r_{\text{GBP}}(91/360)}\right] - \frac{\text{USD 15 million}}{1 + r_{\text{USD}}(91/360)}$$

denote the mark-to-market value of the forward contract. Using a Taylor series, the change in V_F can be approximated

$$\Delta V_F \approx \frac{\partial V_F}{\partial r_{\text{USD}}} \Delta r_{\text{USD}} + \frac{\partial V_F}{\partial r_{\text{GBP}}} \Delta r_{\text{GBP}} + \frac{\partial V_F}{\partial S} \Delta S.$$

Next, we will write down a similar Taylor series approximation of changes in the value of the portfolio of standardized positions, and show that if the standardized positions are chosen appropriately then the coefficients of the two approximations are identical. If this is true then $\Delta V \approx \Delta V_F$, implying that (up to the approximation) the portfolio of standardized positions has the same sensitivities to the market factors as the forward contract.

Let $V \equiv X_1 + X_2 + X_3$ represent the value of the portfolio of standardized positions. If each of the X's depends on only one market factor, then the change in V can be approximated

$$\Delta V \approx \frac{\partial X_1}{\partial r_{USD}} \Delta r_{USD} + \frac{\partial X_2}{\partial r_{GBP}} \Delta r_{GBP} + \frac{\partial X_3}{\partial S} \Delta S.$$

We need to choose X_1, X_2, and X_3 so that each depends on only one market factor, and the two Taylor series approximations are identical. This amounts to choosing them so that

$$\frac{\partial X_1}{\partial r_{USD}} = \frac{\partial V_F}{\partial r_{USD}}, \frac{\partial X_2}{\partial r_{GBP}} = \frac{\partial V_F}{\partial r_{GBP}}, \text{ and } \frac{\partial X_3}{\partial S} = \frac{\partial V_F}{\partial S}.$$

The choice that works is

$$X_1 = \frac{\text{USD 15 million}}{1 + r_{USD}(91/360)},$$

$$X_2 = \frac{(1.5355 \text{ USD/GBP}) \times \text{GBP 15 million}}{1 + r_{GBP}(91/360)},$$

$$X_3 = (S \text{ USD/GBP}) \frac{\text{GBP 15 million}}{1 + .06063(91/360)}.$$

These are the three standardized positions we used before to carry out the risk mapping of the forward contract. As indicated earlier, they are interpreted as follows. The first, X_1, is simply the value of a position in three-month dollar denominated bonds. The other two are more complicated. X_2 is the dollar value of the position in three-month pound denominated bonds, holding the exchange rate fixed, while X_3 is the dollar value of a spot position in pounds equal to the present value of the pound bonds, holding the pound interest rate fixed. Note that both X_2 and X_3 represent the value of the pound denominated bond, but each of them is exposed to only one of the two market factors that affect the value of the bond.

Mapping a Four-Month Dollar Denominated Cash Flow onto the Three- and Six-Month Standardized Positions

The idea is to replace the four-month cash flow with a portfolio of the three- and six-month standardized positions that has the same risk or distribution of changes in market value as the original cash flow. This requires that the portfolio has the same market value and standard deviation (or variance) of changes in market value.

To find the market value of the original four-month cash flow, we need an interest rate with which to discount it. One way to obtain a four-month U.S. dollar interest rate is simply to interpolate using the three- and six-month rates. This amounts to taking the four-month rate to be a weighted average of the three- and six-month rates, or

$$r_{4\text{-mo}} = (2/3)r_{3\text{-mo}} + (1/3)r_{6\text{-mo}}.$$

The present value of the dollar leg of the four-month forward is then

$$PV = \frac{\text{USD 15 million}}{1 + (1/3)r_{4\text{-mo}}},$$

where the $1/3$ appears in the denominator because the cash flow must be discounted for one-third of a year.

The standard deviation of changes in the value of the four-month cash flow depends upon the sensitivity of changes in its value to changes in the interest rate and the standard deviation of changes in the interest rate. In symbols,

$$\sigma_{PV} = \frac{\partial PV}{\partial r_{4\text{-mo}}} r_{r\text{-mo}} \sigma_{4\text{-mo}},$$

where $\dfrac{\partial PV}{\partial r_{4\text{-mo}}}$ is the sensitivity of changes in the value of the dollar leg to changes in the interest rate, $\sigma_{4\text{-mo}}$ is the standard deviation of percentage changes in the four-month rate, and $r_{4\text{-mo}}\sigma_{4\text{-mo}}$ is the standard deviation of *absolute* changes in the four-month rate. The parameter $\sigma_{4\text{-mo}}$ can be computed from the three- and six-month rates, the standard deviations of percentage changes in the three- and six-month rates, and the correlation between these changes using standard results for linear combinations of normal random variables.

Next, introduce a fourth standardized position consisting of six-month dollar denominated zero-coupon bonds, and let X_4 denote the value of the position. The mapping of the four-month cash flow onto the three- and six-month standardized positions is completed by finding a portfolio of X_1

dollars in three-month bonds and X_4 dollars in six-month bonds. This portfolio must have the same value and standard deviation of changes in value as the four-month cash flow. Also, the signs of X_1 and X_4 must be the same as the sign of the four-month cash flow. In symbols, we need to find a portfolio X_1 and X_4 such that:

$PV = X_{1} + X_{4}$,   (values match)

$\sigma_{PV} = $ standard deviation $(X_1 + X_4)$,   (standard deviations match)

$\text{sign}(X_1) = \text{sign}(X_4) = \text{sign}(-15 \text{ million})$,   (signs match)

The last equation is needed because the first two equations will typically have two different solutions for X_1 and X_4, one of which will involve a negative sign. The standard deviation of the portfolio with value $X_1 + X_4$ is computed using the technique discussed in step 3 of the section on the variance/covariance method. Finally, these equations are solved for X_1 and X_4.

Mapping Options

Options positions typically are mapped into delta-equivalent positions in spot foreign currency and in the standardized zero-coupon bonds. An option delta is the partial derivative of the option price with respect to the price of the underlying asset. Letting V denote the theoretical value of the option and S denote the price of the underlying asset, the delta is

$$\Delta = \frac{\partial V}{\partial S}.$$

As discussed more fully in Appendix A to this chapter, the change in the option price resulting from a change in the spot price can be calculated from the delta and the change in the price of the underlying asset:

$$\text{change in } V = \Delta \times \text{change in } S.$$

For example, if the option is on one million British pounds, $\Delta = 0.5$ million or 0.5 per pound, and the spot price of one pound changes by $0.01, the predicted change in the option price is $0.005 = 0.5 \times $0.01 million. One interpretation of the equation above is that for small changes in the exchange rate an option is equivalent to a spot position of Δ British pounds, because the change in value of a spot position of Δ British pounds is also given by the product of Δ and the change in the spot price of 1 pound. Loosely, the option *acts like* Δ British pounds.

Mapping of other options positions is conceptually the same, though sometimes more complicated. Consider an over-the-counter option on a 10-year British gilt. Usually, one would say that the underlying asset is a 10-year gilt. However, recall that we indicated that the 20 semi-annual cash flows of a 10-year gilt might be mapped onto the 6- and 12-month, and 2-, 3-, 4-, 5-, 7-, 9-, and 10-year pound-denominated zero-coupon bonds. If we took the perspective of a pound investor, we would interpret the option on the gilt as an option on a portfolio of these nine zero-coupon bonds, and think of the option as having nine underlying assets and nine deltas, one for each underlying asset. However, the dollar price of the gilt also depends on the dollar/pound exchange rate. From the perspective of a dollar investor, there are 10 underlying assets: the nine pound-denominated zero-coupon bonds, along with the dollar/pound exchange rate, and for each we can define a delta. Letting V denote the dollar value of the gilt and P_n denote the pound price of the nth pound-denominated zero, for the first nine deltas we have

$$\Delta_n = \frac{\partial V}{\partial P_n}.$$

The tenth delta, the partial derivative with respect to the spot exchange rate, is

$$\Delta_{10} = \frac{\partial V}{\partial S}.$$

The change in the option price resulting from changes in the prices of the underlying assets is given by

$$\text{change in } V = \sum_{n=1}^{9} (\Delta_n \times \text{change in } P_n) + \Delta_{10} \times \text{change in } S.$$

The change in V is identical to the change in the value of a portfolio of Δ_n units of each of the nine pound-zeros, along with Δ_{10} spot pounds. Exploiting this observation, the option is *mapped* into this portfolio.

To understand why this procedure can be useful, remember that value at risk is a portfolio level risk measure. It is computed by assigning a risk measure to each position, and then aggregating up to a portfolio-level measure. A difficulty is that there are an immense variety of different options. Even if we just consider ordinary options, wide ranges of both strike prices and expiration dates are possible, and of course there are both calls and puts. In addition, there are exotic options which can have virtually any terms. How can one reasonably assign a risk measure to every option? The approach in most variance/covariance value-at-risk systems is to measure the risk of a set of standardized positions, and then measure the risk of options in terms of the delta-equivalent positions.

Explicit risk mapping of this sort is only necessary in the *analytic* or *variance/covariance* methodology. However, in this framework it is the key issue in the design of a value-at-risk system. To hint at the complexities, consider a second option, but this time suppose it is a futures option on the

British-pound currency futures traded on the International Money Market (IMM) of the Chicago Mercantile Exchange. It seemed natural to map the first option on spot pounds into a Δ-equivalent spot position. Should the IMM futures option also be mapped into a Δ-equivalent spot position by using the theoretical relationship between currency spot and futures prices to reinterpret it as an option on spot pounds? Or should we introduce a second basic market risk factor, the futures price, and map the futures option into a Δ-equivalent futures position? What if we consider another futures option on a pound futures contract with a different delivery date? And what about the fact that option and futures prices change with changes in interest rates? The answers to these questions are not obvious. Nonetheless, the questions need to be answered by the designer of a value-at-risk system.

Endnotes

1. Option deltas and gammas are defined in Appendix A to this chapter.

2. Your answer doesn't start: "The most we can lose is . . . ," because the only honest way to finish this sentence is "everything." It is possible, though unlikely, that all or most relevant exchange rates could move against you by large amounts overnight, leading to losses in all or most currencies in which you have positions.

3. As we will see in the discussion of the historical simulation method, the daily value-at-risk using a 5 percent probability is actually $97,230.

4. The variance/covariance method assumes that the distributions of the underlying market risk factors and the portfolio value are normal. Under this assumption, the loss exceeds 1.645 times the standard deviation of portfolio value with a probability of 5 percent, and exceeds 2.326 times the standard deviation of portfolio value with a probability of 1 percent. The ratio of these is 1.414=2.326/1.645.

5. In some cases formulas are not available and instruments' values must be computed using numerical algorithms.

6. The maturities need not be the same for every currency. The interest rates for long maturities typically will not be relevant for currencies in which there are not active long-term debt markets.

7. This procedure of using the 20 May 1996 market factors together with the historical changes in order to generate hypothetical 21 May 1996 market factors makes sense because it guarantees that the hypothetical 21 May 1996 values will be more or less centered around the 20 May values, which is reasonable because the 20 May daily value-at-risk is a measure of the potential portfolio gain or loss that might occur during the next trading day. An alternative procedure of computing the hypothetical mark-to-market portfolio values using the actual levels of the market factors observed over the past 100 days will frequently

involve using levels of the market factors that are not close to the current values. This reasoning, however, doesn't imply that one must use percentage changes together with the 20 May values in order to compute the hypothetical values of the market factors. Alternatives are to use logarithmic changes or *absolute* changes. By using percentage changes, we are implicitly assuming that the statistical distribution of percentage changes in the market factors does not depend upon their levels.

8. The alternative procedure of ordering the profits and losses on the individual instruments before summing them to obtain the portfolio profits and losses implicitly assumes that the profits and losses on the individual instruments are perfectly positively correlated and usually results in a value-at-risk number that overstates the potential portfolio loss.

9. The name *variance/covariance* refers to the variance/covariance (or simply covariance) matrix of the distribution of changes in the values of the underlying market factors. An alternative name is the *analytic* method.

10. The designer of the risk measurement system may choose the standardized positions to be the basic market factors, in which case this step isn't necessary.

11. The change in the value of a portfolio is the sum of the changes in the values of the positions which comprise it, so the standard deviation of changes in the value of a portfolio is the standard deviation of a sum.

12. This problem is slightly less severe than with historical simulation, because the correlations and standard deviations may be estimated using any of a number of techniques.

13. However, the pricing models need not be perfect because value-at-risk focuses on changes in value. If the error in the pricing model is reasonably stable in the sense that the error in today's price is about the same as the error in tomorrow's, then changes in value computed using the pricing model will be correct even though the level of the prices is not.

14. A good discussion of this issue may be found in J.P. Morgan's *RiskMetrics–Technical Document*.

15. In this method, alternative assumptions about the standard deviations of a market factor can be incorporated by subtracting the mean change in the market factor from the vector of changes, and then multiplying the result by a constant to rescale the changes in the market factor. Handling alternative assumptions about the correlations between a market factor and each of the others is possible, but considerably more cumbersome.

16. The wisdom of MGRM's hedging strategy, and the parties primarily to blame for the losses have been the subject of considerable controversy. Views generally supportive of MGRM's risk management strategy and critical of the parent management's response to the difficulties are expressed by Christopher L. Culp and Merton H. Miller in a number of papers: "Metallgesellschaft and the Economics of Synthetic Storage," *Journal of Applied Corporate Finance* 7, No. 4

(Winter 1995), pp. 62-76; "Hedging a flow of Commodity Derivatives with Futures: Lessons from Metallgesellschaft," *Derivatives Quarterly* 1, No. 1 (Fall 1994), pp. 7-15; "Auditing the Auditors," Risk 8, No. 4 (April 1995); and "Hedging in the Theory of Corporate Finance: A Reply to Our Critics," *Journal of Applied Corporate Finance* 8, No. 1 (Spring 1995), pp. 121-8. Contrary views are expressed by Antonio Mello and John Parsons in "Maturity Structure of a Hedge Matters: Lessons from the Metallgesellschaft Debacle" *Journal of Applied Corporate Finance* 8, No. 1 (Spring 1995), pp. 106-20, and by Franklin R. Edwards and Michael S. Canter in "The Collapse of Metallgesellschaft: Unhedgeable Risks, Poor Hedging Strategy, or Just Bad Luck," *Journal of Applied Corporate Finance* 8, No. 1 (Spring 1995), pp. 86-105.

17. The concept of the duration of a bond was invented by Frederick Macaulay in 1938 (*Some Theoretical Problems Suggested by the Movements of Interest Rates, Bond Yields, and Stock Prices in the United States Since 1865*, National Bureau of Economic Research). Macaulay duration is closely related to modified duration, which is a sensitivity expressed in percentage terms.

18. Alternatively, a portfolio sensitivity analysis calculation could be performed assuming that all market risk factors change by given percentages simultaneously. However, this joint sensitivity to multiple changes in market factors also suffers in comparison to value at risk because it does not ensure that equally likely losses are aggregated across different classes of instruments. While of course one can add the profit or loss stemming from an x percent change in dollar interest rates to the profit or loss stemming from a y percent change in the dollar/yen exchange result, it isn't clear that the resulting sum has any meaningful interpretation.

19. See, for example, Gregory J. Millman, "The Risk Not Taken: American Corporations Hesitate at a Fork in the Financial Road," Barrons (May 1, 1995), p. 41.

20. In contrast, a company whose Treasury group actively manages a portfolio of borrowing, swaps, and other interest and exchange rate instruments, perhaps in order to exploit perceived profit opportunities or trends in market rates and prices, would be more likely to find value at risk useful. Some corporations might use both methods.

21. Off-the-shelf software is currently not available, and may never be available because cash-flow-at-risk systems typically include operating cash flows, the characteristics of which are company-specific and difficult to incorporate in an off-the-shelf system. However, at least one major derivatives dealer has been willing to provide some current and potential future customers with the framework of a cash-flow-at-risk system, the simulation engines, and assistance in implementing the system.

22. The delta of a cash position in the underlying asset, currency, or commodity is always 1, because when the *derivative* and the underlying instrument are identical the ratio of the change in the price of the derivative to the change in the price of the underlying instrument is simply 1.

CHAPTER 14

The Use of Analytics

Ezra Zask
President, Ezra Zask Associates, Inc.
Principal, Law & Economics Consulting Group

Introduction and Background

It is fair to state that the use of analytical methods by most corporations is, with some notable exceptions, relatively rudimentary compared to those used by banks and investment managers. While the latter are exploring the applications of chaos theory to markets and developing massive computer systems to analyze markets and instruments, corporations' use of analytical methods is still primarily spreadsheet-based analysis of financial exposures and hedging portfolios. Indeed, the majority of systems development in corporations is still tied to accounting and treasury MIS systems rather than to analytical programs.

The reasons for this are not difficult to find:

1. In contrast to financial institutions, each corporation faces a unique set of factors and forces which work against standardization and analytical techniques.

2. Corporate exposures are caused by assets and liabilities which are not traded and whose value is difficult to measure and analyze.

3. The relationship between gaining a competitive advantage and the use of advanced analytical techniques is less explicit in the corporate arena compared to the financial arena.

4. Until recently, corporations have not felt the pressure of regulation which has spurred on financial institutions in the development of their analytical methods.

The Use of Analytics: The Early Period

The use of analytic tools by corporations had a jump start in the late 1970s and early 1980s when a number of factors made it essential for the treasury area to computerize its information and analysis:

1. Interest rates, commodities, and foreign exchange markets became more volatile at the same time that corporations' exposures to these markets increased dramatically.

2. FAS 8 followed by FAS 52 caused enormous changes in the way companies managed their currency exposures, which increased the need to quantify and analyze these exposures.

3. The development of new instruments (i.e., swaps and currency options) made it necessary for companies to adopt pricing and analytical tools in order to use these new instruments.

4. The rapid development of microcomputer and software programs aided the adoption of new analytic systems.

The result was a proliferation of systems—both in-house and vendor-based—for the (1) measurement of currency and interest rate exposures; (2) pricing and analysis of portfolios of options, forwards, and swaps; (3) simulation programs to measure the impact of market changes on a company's exposures; and (4) portfolio management programs which looked at the overall exposures and hedges of a company. These systems attempted to find correlation between various currency positions and proxy hedges for these positions.

In addition, the quest for economic exposure and capital budgeting led to the development of some interesting quantitative and analytical techniques which included discounted cash flow (reducing anticipated cash flow by a factor that is proportional to risk), Monte Carlo simulation techniques, and quantitative country-risk analysis.

The Present Situation—Regulatory Initiative

While financial institutions have felt the full brunt of the worldwide effort to manage market and derivative risk, the corporate world has not been immune to the headlines, reports, and methods that have revolutionized the banking world. For example, the Securities and Exchange Commission (SEC) has issued a *Derivatives Disclosure Proposal* which is bound to increase the use of analytical techniques among corporations. The SEC has broadened its areas of concern beyond derivatives to include not only futures, forwards, swaps, and options, but also other nonderivative financial instruments such as investments, loans, structured notes, mortgage-backed securities, indexed debt instruments, and depositsin other words, all financial instruments that entail market risk.

Similarly, the Financial Accounting Standards Board has issued an Exposure Draft on accounting for derivative financial instruments and hedging activities, which, if adopted, will call for the recording of all derivatives at fair value (i.e., mark-to-market) and will place a premium on timely analytical systems.

At the same time, a number of government, regulatory, and industry groups have adopted a common analytical method for measuring and reporting financial risk for both corporations and financial institutions: value at risk (VAR). The list of these groups includes the Federal Reserve Bank, the Bank of England, the Group of 30, the Derivatives Policy Group, and the BIS/Basle Committee. The remainder of this chapter looks at the definition of value at risk, the difficulty of applying the approach to corporations, alternative analytical risk measurement methods, and the steps taken by companies to use VAR to measure and report on financial risk.

Value at Risk

Value at risk (VAR) is defined as the expected minimum loss (or worst loss) over a target time-horizon within a given confidence level.[1] Value at risk provides an estimate for risk by translating nominal exposures (face amounts) into market risk using volatility and (sometimes) correlation estimates. As in most cases in modern finance, VAR is able to produce results by making several assumptions:

1. VAR models assume linear-instrument payouts which make it difficult to measure the risk of nonlinear instruments or positions (i.e., options risk).

2. VAR assumes normally distributed market movements which are often a poor reflection of reality.

3. VAR assumes that historical volatility and past correlation between instruments and markets will continue into the future.

Value at risk attempts to measure the potential loss of value resulting from market movements over a period of time given a predefined probability. For example, a typical VAR statement for a portfolio of bonds may state that there is a 95 percent chance that the firm will lose no more than one million dollars in the next week, based on market movements. VAR examines potential loss based on statistical probability. Other methods

Figure 1 Normal Distribution

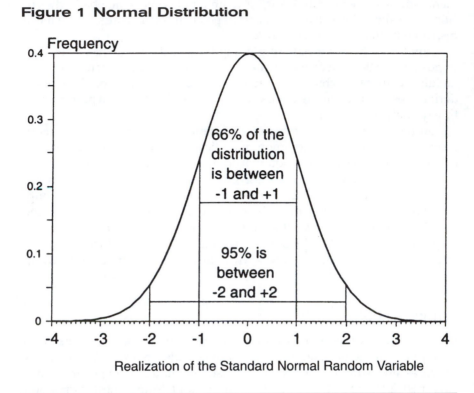

Realization of the Standard Normal Random Variable

evaluate risk by using discrete future scenarios (i.e., worst-case scenario and stress testing) or by using a large number of alternative future scenarios (i.e., Monte Carlo simulation methods).

Figure 1 shows the VAR of a currency position under the assumption of normal market.[2] It assumes a U.S. investor is long 140 million deutsche marks (DEM). The DEM/USD (U.S. dollar) foreign-exchange volatility is 0.932 percent, and the foreign exchange (FX) rate is 1.40 DEM/USD. Given a probability level of 95 percent (i.e., two standard deviations), the value at risk can be defined as

Value at risk = the forecast amount that may be lost given an adverse
                 market move
              = amount of position x volatility of instrument
              = DEM 140 million x 0.932%/1.40
              = USD 932,000.

Of course, as we reduce the probability level, say to one standard deviation (66 percent), the VAR decreases.

Figure 2 Distribution under Stress Testing

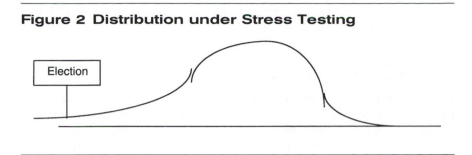

The contrast between using VAR and a stress test or worst-case scenario can be seen by comparing this example with that portrayed in Figure 2. Here, rather than assuming a normal distribution of returns for the dollar, we project several scenarios based on extreme past market movements or on political and economic events such as elections. In this case, the scenarios fall well-outside the confidence limit that we established in the VAR example, which leads to larger potential losses.

Problems in Corporate Applications of VAR

A number of problems make the application of VAR in a corporate setting extremely difficult. These can be broadly placed in the following five categories.[3]

Nature of Corporate Exposures

Unlike financial institutions, whose assets and liabilities—and therefore the institutions' risks—are largely comprised of financial instruments, corporations have a complex and diverse portfolio. This portfolio includes (1) forecast sales and dividends, (2) offshore royalty payments, (3) commodity purchases and sales, (4) short- and long-term borrowings, (5) balance-sheet and economic exposure, (6) speculative trades, and (7) hedges (in order to reduce the volatility of cash flow). This difficulty can be shown by attempting to incorporate a manufacturing plant in Mexico into a VAR analysis.

Interpreting VAR

A second element of difficulty is the interpretation of VAR in a corporate setting where the measure is less intuitive than in a financial institution. For example, a VAR of $50 million is difficult to interpret as a measure of the complex of exposures, assets, liabilities, and income streams that comprise a multinational corporation. Similarly, explaining the concept of VAR to a board of directors is a daunting task.

Time Frame for Analysis

Corporations are typically interested in a period of months and years when they evaluate their exposures, which is a major reason that scenario analysis rather than statistical probability is still the preferred method of analysis in corporate treasuries. Evaluating longer-term time horizons (say, 6 to 24 months) brings up three serious problems in VAR analysis:

1. Longer-term estimates of volatility tend to be unstable over time and to be difficult to estimate. J. P. Morgan, for example, only provides estimates of volatility for a one-day and a 28-day time horizon in its RiskMetrics program. Recently, a number of vendors (notably Bankers Trust and its RAROC program) have started providing standard deviations for up to one year.

2. Correlation between various markets and instruments, which is based on historical data, becomes less reliable the farther out that one goes in time.

3. Operating assumptions and forecasts regarding the relationship between operating variables (i.e., sales and imports) and financial flows become less reliable the farther out one goes, and this weakens the VAR approach.

Treatment of Hedges

Since a significant part of a corporation's financial instruments will consist of hedges (partial or complete) of underlying cash flows, it is important to capture both the hedge and the underlying exposure in the VAR analysis. A VAR which is performed only on the hedge instruments will tend to show a speculative or open position and will show a risk which does not exist.

Consolidation of Exposures

The VAR methodology is based on the assumption that vastly different exposures and risks can be made comparable by reducing them to three factors: nominal size, volatility, and correlation. Thus, a factory and an export can, in theory, be defined by their dollar amount, the volatility of their value, and the correlation between their volatility and those of other exposures.

This approach is antithetical to many corporations' risk management methodologies which focus on the *differences* between cash flows and exposures. This is shown in the treatment of currencies. While VAR reduces currencies to a common denominator, which can be aggregated and compared, many corporations tend to view currencies individually or in currency blocks.

New Approaches to Corporate Risk Management

The basic idea which allows VAR and similar approaches to be used to measure firmwide risk in corporations can be found in the area of finance known as valuation or shareholder value.[4] In this field, theorists and practitioners long ago gave up the notion of decomposing companies to all their component parts in order to place a value on a firm. Rather, theorists and practitioners now start with the assumption that the overwhelming proportion of a firm's value rests with its cash flows projected into the future, plus a residual (much smaller) value from the sale of the firm's assets in the far future.

This simplifying assumption, for example, makes possible the famous *dividend discount model* which reduces a firm's value to the following formula:

$$\text{Value per share of stock} = \sum_{t=1}^{t=\infty} \frac{DPS}{(1+r)^t}$$

where

DPS = expected dividend per share
r = required rate of return on stock.

If we follow the same logic in measuring risk that the valuation model uses to measure value, our task is to distill the complexity of a corporation to its essential cash flows, and then to measure the risk to those cash flows using VAR and related approaches. In turn, the value of the firm is driven by such "value drivers" as revenue, cost of goods sold, current assets and liabilities, and capital expenditures. Other relevant flows include changes in the value of interest expense, foreign-exchange-denominated cash flows, and commodity prices for buyers and sellers of commodities. See Figure 3.

A number of banks, software companies, and consulting firms have been using this cash-flow approach in order to allow corporations to use VAR. Chase Bank's Cash Flow at Risk (CFAR)[5] is one example of this approach to risk analysis. According to Chase, "[CFAR] may be thought of as a family of tools whose applications are differentiated by three factors: the composition of exposure; the definition of risk; and the cycle of measurement. By varying these factors, VAR can be applied to a wide variety of problems . . . CFAR's measure of financial price risk is complete because it

Figure 3 Corporate Value Drivers for Shareholders Value

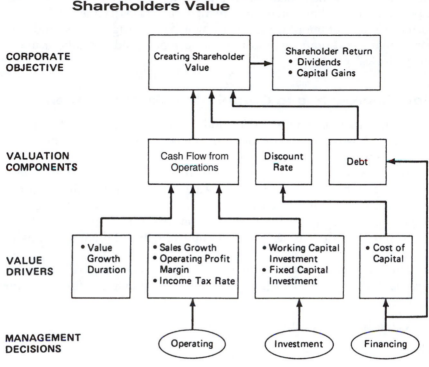

Source: Alfred Rappaport, "Creating Shareholder Value," *Free Press,* 1986, p. 76.

accounts fully for interactions among the firm's risksit treats the firm as a portfolio of exposures. Some firms might have additional exposures but all are likely to be exposed to financial price risk through the following items: *Sales revenues, Cost of goods sold and Interest expense."* See Figure 4.

In the case of valuing corporate risk, CFAR's dimensions are as broad as possible:

1. The definition of exposure encompasses all (or most) of the firm.

2. Risk is defined in terms of earnings, or some other measure of operating performance, rather than asset value.

3. CFAR employs the same measurement cycle as the definition of risk.

Figure 4 Risk Management Cash Flows

Risk Exposure Platform

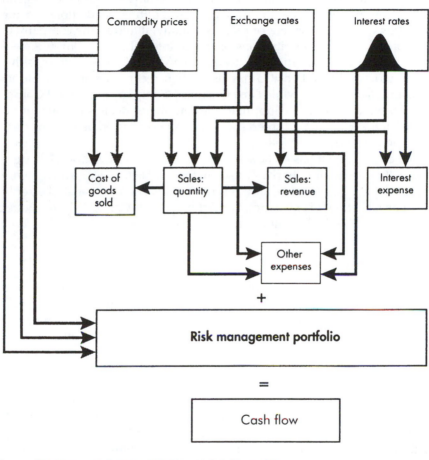

Source: Chris Turner, "VAR as an Industrial Tool," *Risk*, March 1996.

A number of related approaches to CFAR have been used by companies including stock price at risk (SPAR), of MEK Associates, which uses the ultimate value measure of a company, its stock price, as the measure at risk. Similarly, Genentech has developed a variant called earnings at risk (EAR), while Emcor has come out with a variant called corporate-value-at-risk.

Examples from the Corporate World

Some corporations are putting their own spin on these techniques,[6] which reflects their specific industry and company differences. Genentech, for example, has developed a model which is an Earnings-at-Risk variation on VAR. This model reflects the impact of accounting regulations on the definition and measurement of risk. Essentially, it allows the company to generate probability distributions of future interest rates along the yield curve and to then test the risks to the company's interest-rate-sensitive assets and liabilities. PepsiCo has used VAR techniques to evaluate its exposure to credit risk, while Dow Chemical Company and Mobil Corporation use the same type of approach as derivatives dealers do to monitor the foreign-exchange and interest-rate-risk exposures embedded in their debt and derivatives portfolios.

One firm which has eschewed VAR is Merck. Because Merck hedges over a three-year time horizon, uses natural offsets in exposures before using hedging instruments, and self-insures a portion of its risk (i.e., only does partial hedges of exposure), Merck finds Monte Carlo analysis a better way to model the dollar value of its foreign cash-flows.[7]

Conclusion

Given the focus on derivatives and risk management, it seems hard to believe that corporations will not greatly increase their use of analytical systems in order to manage currency and other risks. Already, companies and vendors are tackling the shortcomings of VAR and are refining some of the other risk management tools in order to take into account corporations' unique requirements.[8]

Ultimately, the method which corporations use for their risk management will be a hybrid which adopts parts of (1) the VAR approach, with its normal-distribution assumptions, and (2) the scenario-based approach (such as worst-case scenario or stress test) in order to combine the strong analytical powers of VAR and the real-world assumptions of scenario-based approaches.

Endnotes

1   Those who wishing to read an excellent treatment of the value-at-risk subject are referred to Philippe Jorion, *Value at Risk,* Chicago, IL: Irwin, 1996

2   This example is based on J. P. Morgan's, *Introduction to Riskmetrics_* , 4th ed., November 21, 1995.

3   Jacob Boudouch, Mathew Richardson, and Robert Whitelaw, "Expect the Worst," *Risk,* September 1995; and Jeffrey Wallace, "The Long-Term & Corporate VAR," *International Treasurer,* May 27, 1996.

4   See Alfred Rappaport, "Creating Shareholder Value," New York: Free Press, 1986.

5   Chris Turner, "VAR as an Industrial Tool," *Risk,* March 1966; and James MeVay and Christopher Turner, "Could Companies Use Value-at-Risk?" London: *Euromoney,* October 1955.

6   Karen Spinner, "Companies Put Their Own Spin on VAR," *Global Finance,* August 1996.

7   Karen Spinner, "Companies Put Their Own Spin on VAR," *Global Finance,* August 1996.

8   See Appendix for a partial listing of vendors.

Appendix: VAR Consultants and Software Vendors

Consultants
Advanced Risk Management Solutions
American Management Systems
Andersen Consulting
Coopers & Lybrand Consulting, L.L.P.
Deloitte Touche Tohmatsu International
Emcor Risk Management Consulting
Ernst and Young
KPMG
Logica
Price Waterhouse
Ezra Zask Associates, Inc.

Software Developers
Algorithmics Incorporated
BARRA International, Ltd.
Brady, Plc.
C*A*T*S Software, Inc.
Centre Financial Products Limited
Derivatives Strategy/Computer Masters
Dow Jones/Telerate
EDS Systems and Management SpA
Financial Engineering Associates, Inc.
Infinity Financial Technology, Inc.
INSSINC
Leading Market Technologies
Lombard Risk Systems Limited
Microcomp GmbH
Midas-Kapiti

Objective Edge, Inc.
Oy Trema Ab
Quantec, Ltd.
Renaissance Software, Inc.
PappersData
Sailfish Systems, Ltd.
Summit System, Inc.
TrueRisk, Inc.
Value & Risk GmbH
Wall Street Systems

CHAPTER 15

Passive versus Active Management

Leslie K. McNew
Director, Financial Risk Management
Reynolds Metals Company

It is the purpose of this chapter to show that the style of currency management is dependent on how the hedger views the foreign exchange market. A perfectly efficient market demands a style of passive currency management, because this style would lead to optimal results. However, if the market is not perfect, if in fact a market has some kind of relational dependence, then past prices could be used to predict future price movement—meaning that passive hedging could carry a high opportunity cost. It is the further purpose of this chapter to show that the foreign exchange market is not entirely efficient, and that a style of active foreign exchange management is more conducive to optimal results.

Before a discussion of the style of management is to be pursued, a corporation should discuss the underlying fundamentals of style, as a concept. At the board-of-directors level, a corporate policy should be determined on whether or not the company will hedge, and what exposures are deemed hedgeable. Pushing all other considerations aside, the decision to hedge depends on the corporation's concept (view) of time. The concept of time and its link to hedging can be broken down into two parts: long-run view of time and short-run view of time.

The Corporate Goals: Long Run or Short Run

Some have viewed currency movement as a zero-sum game in which, over the long run, the gains made at some point will equal the losses incurred at other points. Therefore, the net effect of currency investing in the long run is zero. If a corporation subscribes to this zero-sum-game view, then there is no need to hedge its foreign exchange portfolio, and the discussion on hedging and a particular management style of hedging is over. In addition, subscribers to the zero-sum-game theory of currency management also site two other points that lend credence to their desire not to hedge: First, zero-sum subscribers feel that the currency market is virtually impossible to forecast. Second, these same people also feel that currency management is so complex that corporations would need to hire qualified and expensive personnel to manage the foreign exchange book, and thus question whether the benefits from these personnel outweigh the expense of hiring them.

What is impossible to predict is exactly how long is the long run, and at what point does a corporation subscribing to the zero-sum-game theory of currency management break even. It is the view of this author that corporations cannot, and do not, have the liberty of a hypothetical long-run view of time of which to contend. Annual reports are published every year. Quarterly results are issued every three months. Positions are marked-to-market daily or monthly. Further, the usual corporate planning horizon is five years or less. A market-driven book is marked-to-market each month. The relative value of any currency exposure is usually reported to accounting. Extreme gains or extreme losses would certainly have to be recognized to senior management and perhaps reported to shareholders. Corporations are not judged in the long run, they are judged in the short run, and by short-run profitability. It is quite possible that a corporation could not outlast long-run foreign exchange volatility, as any abrupt losses could seriously jeopardize the cash flow of the company, which in the worst case could lead to a shut-down of operations affected by this volatility. In an extreme example, a corporation could be bankrupt by waiting for the foreign exchange gains and losses to balance out.

Management should also consider short-run benefits. One of these benefits is hedging. The *New World Dictionary* defines hedging: "to try to avoid or lessen loss."[1] The definition is extended to include activities intended to alter exposures to foreign exchange, in conjunction with protecting the company's earnings from adverse changes in foreign exchange prices. Second, a corporation must be very aware of exactly what hedging is not. Paraphrasing the 1994 *Harvard Business Review*, Kenneth Froot, David Scharfstein, and Jeremy Stein state that hedging (risk management) cannot improve the underlying economics of a corporation, but instead should help ensure that a company has the cash it needs to create value by making good investments. Hedging is a reduction in volatility. Volatility is a form of business risk. Excessive investment volatility can threaten a company's ability to meet its strategic objectives. Hedging as a tool to reduce volatility and protect cash flows is both a short-run and a long-run goal. However, this goal is more evident in the short run, as reporting and protecting shareholder value are extremely important to the corporation.

The Costs of Hedging Regardless of the Style of Management

In the real world, the economic short-run is where corporations live. Corporations are risk adverse. They need to protect cash flows to ultimately protect share holder value. Therefore, it will be assumed that hedging is necessary for the corporation. Before proceeding on to discuss the style of management, it must be noted that hedging is not free. Briefly, and this will be discussed in-depth further into this chapter, hedging has two costs: actual (accounting) and opportunity costs. It has been cited that there are four basic costs associated with hedging:[2]

1. Cash-flow related costs for contract settlement.

2. Contract trading costs.

3. Management fees.

4. Custodial costs.

Cash-Flow Related Costs for Contract Settlement

Not every hedge is a successful monetary hedge. For example, if the hedger locks cheap foreign currency with a hedge, and the currency market continues to cheapen, the corporation must settle the hedge contract at a loss to the company. This is an actual cash payment. Further, the loss may not be immaterial. The good illustration of the cash-flow related costs inherent in hedging is a graphical and hypothetical numerical hedge involving the negotiation of a U.S. sale of equipment.

An Example

Description of the Event Refer to Figure 1 for an illustration of the Italian lira for the past two years and for an illustration of how the market performed during the life of this hedge. Let us assume that our corporation is notified on September 7, 1995 (today), that we will be receiving the equivalent of U.S. $20 million on March 7, 1996 (182 days from now), in lira from an Italian company that wants to buy equipment from our corporation. Our problem is that we know that in the future we will be receiving some amount of lira equivalent to U.S. $20 million, but we do not know exactly how many lira we will receive. The corporation is facing a rate risk. The U.S. corporation is essentially long a lira exposure, and the exposure risk is that the lira weakens. We decide to protect our future cash-flow today with a hedge, in order to ensure a certain amount of lira. Refer to Figure 1 for a historical illustration.

Figure 1 Italian Lira

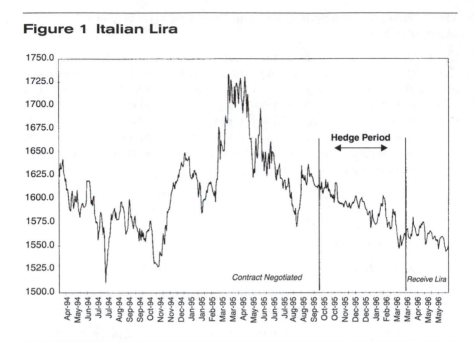

The following diagrams illustrate the cash flows.

Italian Company contracts to buy U.S. equipment on September 7, 1995.
Italian Company to pay U.S. $20 million equivalent on March 7, 1996.

Today (September 7, 1995)	Receive $20 million equivalent
Spot lira trading at 1623	for equipment (March 7, 1996)
Contract to Receive $20 million equivalent in lira.	

The foreign exchange exposure risk is that the lira weakens. To hedge this risk, the corporation sells forward lira at the current spot plus forward points. The accounting risk is that the dollar weakens substantially during the hedging time period. The corporation is receiving lira on an equivalent $20 million position.

The Hedge We want to hedge our lira exposure in the most conservative manner available, with no premium or execution costs to the corporation. We choose to use forward contracts.[3] Currently (on September 7, 1995) the market is trading at 1623 lira to the dollar, and 182-day forward points are 36.50. We lock in the risk for the next approximate six months at a all-in rate of 1659.50 lira to the dollar. We have sold a forward contract at an equivalent rate of 1659.50. We now know that we will receive 1659.50 lira to the dollar on March 7, 1996, regardless of where the lira is trading at that time. We will receive 33,190,000,000 lira on March 7, 1996 (U.S. $ 20 million × 1659.5 = 33,190,000,000) from the sale of the forward contract. The corporation will not receive any less than 33,190,000 lira on March 7, 1996. Let us roll forward in time to March 7, 1996. We can see from the graph that the lira strengthened dramatically against the dollar. The lira is now trading at 1549 on March 7, 1996. The Italian company is sending us the U.S. equivalent of $20 million now, as contracted on September 7, 1995, which at the delivery rate is only 30,980,000,000 lira.

Dollar-Weakening Environment

September 7, 1995   March 7, 1996

Sold forward lira at   Receive lira at 1549
  1659.50 (33,190,000,000)   (30,980,000,000)

The hedge resulted in a loss of 2,210,000,000 lira, converted to dollars at an exchange rate of 1549. Equivalent of a loss of $ 1,426,727 on the hedge using forwards. The loss on the hedge is equal to approximately 7.13 percent of the principal.

This example does not overstate the importance of realizing that there are real cash-flow related costs to hedging. The corporation protected its exposure, but the hedge generated an accounting loss. Some hedge costs may be more than others, depending on the hedging vehicle. There is some evidence to suggest that contract settlement cash can amount to almost 20 percent of an international portfolio for a fully hedged program.[4] An optimal cash reserve is a good byline for a corporation before it instigates a hedging program. The board of directors must be made aware by senior management that hedging, although reducing risk, especially in the area of forecasting cash flows, will not be free.

The above example illustrates an accounting cash-flow cost of hedging. This example was in a falling dollar environment. Hedges can also have cash-flow related gains. What would happen in a rising dollar environment, using a hedge instigated at the same point of time, the same hedging vehicle (a forward contract) and the same spot and forward points (the interest rate differential is constant). We have sold a forward at a hedging rate 1659.50 lira all-in per dollar. Instead of the dollar falling, let us assume that the dollar rises. At the end of six months, the lira is now trading at 1770 per dollar.

Dollar-Strengthening Environment

September 7, 1995   March 7, 1996

Sold forward lira at   Receive lira at 1770
1659.50 (33,190,000,000)   (35,400,000,000

The hedge resulted in a gain of 2,210,000,000 lira, converted to dollars at an exchange rate of 1770, equivalent of a gain of $ 1,248,588 on the hedge using forwards. The gain on the hedge is equal to approximately 6.24 percent of the principal.

Contract Trading Costs

When a hedger gets a quote in the market, it usually comes from the dealer in two parts. For example, a dealer quoting a dollar/German deutsche-mark hedge will tell the hedger that the market is trading 1.5240–1.5245. This quote means that the hedger can buy U.S. dollars at a ratio of 1.5245 deutsche marks per dollar, and the hedger can sell U.S. dollars at a ratio of 1.5240 deutsche marks per dollars. This is referred to as the bid/ask spread. In a normal liquid market, the bid/ask spread is roughly .0003 to .0005 for German deutsche marks.[5] For example, for a $1,000,000 transaction in German deutsche marks, the bid/ask spread is roughly $500. Other currencies have different spreads. Translating the bid/ask spread for deutsche marks to actual terms, the foreign exchange dealer (the market maker) buys $1,000,000 from one corporate customer and sells $1,000,000 to another corporate customer, the dealer will earn (will take out of the market) $500. The bid/ask spread is an indirect cost to the corporate client. Most important, regardless of the market, if the hedger buys currency with a dealer and then later sells it with the same dealer, the currency will cost the hedger a price greater than the change in the market.[6]

Management and Custodial Fees

Finally, there are management and custodial fees. Even if the corporation manages its hedging program internally, the management fee should be the cost (be that in wages, salary, and/or benefits) of the people doing the management. Some styles of management require very little knowledge for the person who is to manage the hedging program, and thus, these styles would be substantially cheaper than a program that requires a more sophisticated and educated manager. If the corporation chooses to turn the management of its portfolio over to an outside source, then the cost of this management should be incorporated into the cost of the hedging program.

Depending on whom it is that manages the portfolio, the costs can vary greatly. In addition, if an outside management source is chosen, the corporation may also have to pay custodial costs to a custodian bank. Even though the custodial costs are usually small (usually two basis points), they are still part of the cost of a hedging program.

Passive Hedging: A Management Style

After the corporation has decided that it is in its best interest to hedge, and all pertinent costs of hedging are known in advance, the next step is to decide on the style of management. There are basically *two styles of foreign exchange management: passive and active*. The simplest style of management is called *passive*.

The most traditional form of implementing a passive management strategy is to buy or sell a currency forward to hedge a predetermined percentage of the underlying exposure on a monthly/quarterly basis.[7] The most defined tool for a passive hedging strategy is the forward contract . In statistical terms, the forward rate is an unbiased predictor of the future spot exchange.[8] First, we define the instrument used in passive management, and then we lay out a typical passive management framework.

Forward Contracts

A forward contract is the simplest derivative security available. It is an agreement (an obligation) to buy or sell a foreign currency at a certain future time for a certain price today. The contract is usually between two financial institutions or between a financial institution and one of its corporate clients. This is not normally an exchange-traded instrument.[9] A forward contract is usually settled at maturity; however, the client can reverse the agreement earlier than maturity for a fair price, considering a new interest-rate differential and the then-current spot rate. However, a forward contract is still an obligation. It is a fairly flexible contract that can be tailor-made to fit the clients specifications. Usually forwards can be adjusted to fit size and maturity qualifications.

A forward contract assumes that all information is available in the market, and that the market is acting in perfect equilibrium. An efficient market is a market in which exchange rates fully and immediately reflect all available information. The use of a forward contract in a hedging strategy assumes that the hedger agrees that the currency market is efficient, all known information regarding currencies is embedded in the forward contract, and any future currency movement henceforth will be random.

A closer look at a forward contract is needed to fully understand the instrument. For the following example, it is assumed that the hedger is buying USD (U.S. dollars) and selling FRF (French francs). The first thing that a hedger wants to know is the spot rate at which the two currencies can be exchanged. The spot price is 5.15. Next the hedger looks at the length of the hedge. The exposure is three months (90 days) from now, and the hedger wants to hedge 100 percent of the exposure. The amount of the exposure is not important to this example. What is important to this example is the length of time of the exposure (three months) and the corresponding three month interest rates in each of the respective countries.

Exposure Due

January: Spot at 5.15   3 months: April

The market must make adjustments for the three month interest rates that occur in France and the United States. This adjustment is in the form of *forward points.* The interest rates paid on three-month money in France and the United States are usually different. If the interest rates were the same, the interest rate differential would be zero, and thus the forward points would be zero (i.e., the spot and the forward rate would be the same). Due to the fact that interest rates in different countries may not be the same, there is an adjustment to the spot price that takes into account the differential. In the case of this example, the interest rate differential is the spread between three month rates in the United States and in France. The adjustment that must be made to the spot price assumes that *interest rate parity* holds between these two countries (and other countries). The interest rate parity assumption implies that there are no risk-free arbitrage opportunities;[10] the market is pricing all known information into the forward rates. There is nothing magical about this adjustment to the spot rate or interest rate parity in general. The following equation can be used to determine the approximate forward rate.[11]

Interest-Rate-Parity Example: The Calculation of Forward Points

Relevant Data:

- The 3-month interest rate in France is 3.75 percent.

- The 3-month interest rate in the United States is 5.375 percent.

- The day count in both France and U.S. is 360. Some countries use more than 360 days in a year, this is referred to as the *day count.* Australia and the United Kingdom use 365 days per year.

- The spot price is 5.15 francs per dollar.

The equation

$$\text{Spot} \times \left[\frac{1 + rf\,[\text{\# of days for hedge}/360]}{1 + rd\,[\text{\# of days for hedge}/360]} \right] = \text{Forward Price}$$

where

rf = foreign interest rate
rd = domestic interest rate: U.S. dollar rate

therefore,

$$5.15 \times \left[\frac{1 + .03750\,[90/360]}{1 + .05375\,[90/360]} \right] = 5.129.$$

The calculated forward rate is 5.129, which is what the hedger would lock-in over the 90-day hedging period. The adjustment from 5.15 spot to 5.129 forward is worth (.0210) points. In this case, the points are negative. Note that the basic formula for calculating the forward rate is

Forward Rate = Spot Price + Forward Points.

The hedger has to know if the forward points are positive or negative. This depends on the relationship between the two countries' interest rates. Use the relationship below for an indirect quote[12] in order to determine if the forward points are positive; or negative, if the hedger is getting a forward quote from the dealer:

$rf > rd$ the forward points are > 0
$rf < rd$ the forward points are , 0.

Talking with the Dealer

If this transaction was conducted with the foreign exchange dealer, the corporate hedger would ask the dealer where the French franc is (assuming that it is against the dollar). Sometimes this relationship is referred to as *dollar/Paris*.

The dealer would reply, "Indications only at 5.1520–50." The dealer has quoted the bid/ask spread, which is the 20–50 portion of the quote—this gives the hedger the opportunity to deal on either side of the market. The dealer next asks the hedger, "Do you have any specific interest, buying or selling?"

The hedger says, "I want to sell 10 million francs for three months. What is your dealing rate?"

The dealer responds, "Checking .... ." The dealer checks with the foreign exchange trader, and then the dealer states, "I will buy French at

5.1550 minus three-month points. The points are 210 discount, the all-in rate is 5.1340. Anything done?"

The hedger can now decide if this rate is good for the hedge or not, and if so he or she will choose to deal.[13]

What Does a Forward Hedge Look Like

The hedger must know what a forward contract looks like graphically. Because it is a definite obligation, it carries with it some definite responsibilities. Recall earlier the discussion of cash-flow-related costs for contract settlement. A forward locks in a particular rate for the corporation. Refer to Figure 2, which illustrates how a forward contract will change the risk structure of a position. Let us assume that the corporation wants to hedge a CAD (Canadian dollar) exposure by buying CAD. The U.S. corporation is going to buy Canadian machinery and pay for it in Canadian dollars. Therefore, the cheaper the corporation can buy CAD, the better. The market is currently trading at C$ 1.36 to the $USD. Another way of looking at this is that the market is trading $00.7350 per C$.

The hedger thinks that 1.36 is a good rate to lock-in a hedge against the exposure. At this point, a forward is bought. If the currency then moves to a strengthening position against the U.S. dollar (toward 1.34), the hedge would result in a gain for the hedger. If the CAD moves toward a weaker position against the U.S. dollar (toward 1.38), the hedge results in a loss to the hedger. There is an accounting cost at the time of contract settlement, either a gain or a loss to the hedging book. There is

Figure 2 Looking at a Forward against a Currency Movement Scenario

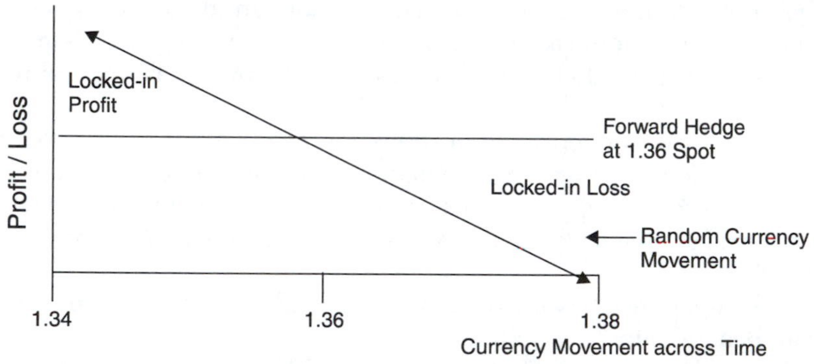

an opportunity cost if the market traded toward 1.38 (a cheaper CAD), as the hedger could not participate in buying cheaper CAD for the corporation. This example also illustrates that forwards work best in a U.S.-dollar-strengthening environment.

Why Use Forwards

In a passive currency-management-strategy environment, the use of forward contracts as a hedging vehicle is a logical choice. It is important to note that the forward market is very liquid, much more liquid than any other instrument. For example, at this point in time, there is a very active market for forwards in the Irish punt, but there is little or no market in the punt options. The same could be said for the Mexican peso or the Norwegian kroner. Further, according to Goldman Sachs estimates of daily market turnover, the spot foreign-exchange market is $1 trillion, the total forward market is $1 trillion, the forward market for hedging is $60 billion, and the option market is $45 billion.[14] Liquidity spells ease of entry and exit. It means that the hedger will never be caught in a trade and be unable to get out of it.

Not only is the forward market liquid, it is simple to use. Forwards are easy to understand, and one does not have to be a rocket scientist to use them. The math that is necessary to figure out the cost of the forward contract is straight forward. Most individuals can calculate a forward quote on their calculators, which aids in verifying dealer quotes, if these individuals are aware of the different interest-rate environments. Forwards are very flexible. The minimum and maximum size of the contract is virtually unlimited.

Unlike options, which carry an initial premium that must be paid if the user wishes to enter into a counter, forwards have no initial user fee. There is no upfront cost for entering into a forward contract. The hedger must be made aware of the bid/ask spread, as that is how the dealer is going to make money on the trade, but an aggressive hedger can *squeeze* the spread (tighter). It is up to the dealer to take as much money out of the market as is possible, and it is up to the hedger to avoid being taken, to whatever extent possible. However, unlike an option, a forward has no initial premium.

If the corporation is new to the concept of hedging or is under a cost constraint vis vis developing a hedging program (i.e., paying option premiums), forwards are an excellent hedging vehicle. They are particularly easy to track. Forwards easily lend themselves to a simple indexing strategy as will be described in the next section. Further, using forwards to hedge means that the corporation only has to track the following information: deal date, maturity date, currency, size of contract, spot, forward points, all-in forward rate, direction of the trade (buy/sell), and counterparty. This could be done in a simple spreadsheet or database program. There is no need to hire sophisticated personnel to program or model. This is a big cost savings. The same spreadsheet/database that holds the hedging positions can be used to confirm deals for legal settlement. Further, when it comes time to mark the hedging position to market, forwards require no sophisticated models to figure out their profit and loss. The accounting for forward transactions is simple, and the auditing of the same transactions should be equally simple.

Forwards can be an effective tool with which to implement a hedging strategy or to begin a risk management program. All initial programs have a learning curve. The new concept must be explained all the way up the ladder to the board of directors. Because forwards are easy to understand, both conceptually and mathematically, they are easy to explain to most senior management and ultimately to the board of directors. The hedger/treasurer has to realize that the board may not have any market background, so implementing a hedging program may be handing the board a steep learning curve. Using a hedging instrument that is easy to understand helps lessen the steepness of the curve. Further, it is well-known that people will tend to implement plans that they understand.

A Framework for Passive Management

Passive risk management involves following a set of rules for hedging an exposure, such as foreign currency receivables. These rules do not vary with market conditions or the current circumstances of the corporation. Passive strategies are reassessed infrequently.[15] The most traditional form of implementing a passive management strategy is to *sell a currency forward* to hedge a predetermined percentage of the currency on a monthly/quarterly basis,[16] assuming that the particular currency is being repatriated to U.S. domestic headquarters. Selling a predetermined amount of the currency forward is an attempt by the corporation to hedge out a certain percentage of the price risk from the exposure. For example, the corporation may decide that it will hedge all foreign exchange transactions (back to dollars) for a period of one year—a 100 percent index. A simple passive strategy would be to hedge on a quarterly basis out through the yeara quarterly index. The hedger would start hedging projected exposures one year from the date due, and continue augmenting the hedge by a set percentage on a quarterly basis until three months before the exposure is due. Roughly three months before the exposure is realized, the position is fully hedged. It works particularly well with transaction exposures. Transaction exposures have exposures that have a cash flow associated to them. By definition, they are *forward* looking.

The actual decision on the time horizon to be hedged can be dependent on two components: the comfort level of senior management, and the accounting treatment of the hedges. Regarding accounting treatment, most corporations are adverse to marking their hedge book to market. In order for foreign exchange exposures to receive hedge accounting treatment, they must be committed. A committed transaction exposure is an exposure with known third-party commitments. A third-party commitment is a party from outside the corporation and does not encompass commitments from subsidiaries.

A good example of transaction exposures are foreign currency receivables. Following is an illustration of a quarterly passive index for a one-year hedging time horizon. Review the hypothetical timeline.

Hypothetical Corporate Hedging Timeline:

Q195	Q295	Q395	Q495	Q196
Jan	Apr	Jul	Oct	Jan

Passive Quarterly Benchmark:

Q195	Q295	Q395	Q495
100%	75%	50%	25%

The Passive Quarterly Benchmark diagram illustrates the quarterly passive hedging strategy, starting in January of a year. Our hedging time horizon is one year. Let us assume that it is January 2, 1995. The hedger already will have hedged 100 percent of the exposure hedged for the first quarter, 75 percent of the exposures hedged for the second quarter, 50 percent of the exposures hedged for the third quarter, and 25 percent of the exposures hedged for the fourth quarter. Moving forward one month in time, the hedger will now have 100 percent of the exposures hedged for February, March, and April; 75 percent of the exposures hedged for June, July, and August; 50 percent of the exposures hedged for September, October, and November; and 25 percent of the exposures hedged for December, January (1996), and February (1996). On a quarterly basis, the hedger adds another 25 percent of a hedge to the position. In this way, by the time the receivable is actually due, the hedge is in place to transact it. At the end of one year, all of the price risk has been hedged out of the receivable. In fact, the index for the passive hedge rate is composed of four rates from the market, starting from one year before the exposure is due. This is a very typical and very acceptable passive hedging strategy.

Table 1. Example of a Passive Benchmark: German Deutsche-Mark Receivables (000s)

	June	July	Aug.	Sep.	Oct.	Nov.	Dec.	Jan.
Exposures	8,000	10,320	11,440	6,000	6,000	5,360	11,600	
Qtly. Index	1.4421	1.4348	1.4559	1.4526	1.4478	1.4488	1.4337	1.462
% Hedged	100%	100%	100%	75%	75%	75%	50%	50%

Table 1 is an example of how this strategy would look on a simple printout. These are all hypothetical numbers. Assume that the deutsche-mark receivables are in deutsche marks (the country of origin). The deutsche marks are to be repatriated back to headquarters in the United States. In the passive strategy, the first three months of an exposure are 100 percent hedged, the next three months are 75 percent hedged, six months out the exposures are 50 percent hedged, and so forth.

For example, the June benchmark rate is composed of four rates, gathered the previous four quarters. However, the September benchmark rate only has three rates to its average because it should be only 75 percent hedged. The quarterly index for June 1995 would have been composed of the following spot and forward points, collected in the following months:

Jun 94   Hedge 25 percent of June 95 Exposure at Jun 94 spot + 1 year forward points.

Sep 94   Continue hedging another 25 percent of June 95 Exposure at Sep 94 spot + 9 forward points.

Dec 94   Continue hedging another 25 percent of June 95 Exposure at Dec 94 spot + 6 months forward points.

Mar 95   Hedge final 25 percent of June 95 Exposure at Mar 95 spot + 3 months forward points.

As it can be seen, the passive hedging index for any particular month is composed of four rates, and the index is locked-in three months before the receivable is due. The passive index gives the hedger a cumulative rate at which the price risk of the exposure had been hedged.[17]

This type of passive-hedging-strategy benchmark is an appropriate start to managing foreign currency transaction exposures. Most importantly, it is very easy to maintain and not very time consuming. Every month, the person responsible for maintaining the benchmark enters four rates and their forward points: 3 months out, 6 months out, 9 months out, and 12 months out. Because the forward market is very liquid, much more liquid than any other instrument, it will be very easy to obtain the pricing data needed for input into the passive strategy. As a beginning risk control program for foreign exchange, a passive index strategy could be very useful.

Inherent Problems with Forwards

The hedger must understand that there are several embedded biases in the forward contract, and by using the forward contract to hedge, the hedger becomes party to these biases. The first bias has already been discussed. The hedger who uses forwards to implement a passive strategy should be aware that, by using this instrument, the hedger buys into the concept that the market is random. From the concept that the market is random flows the next idea that all available market information *(the known total information concept)* is embedded into the cost of the forward, and any foreign exchange price movement henceforth is strictly random. A passive hedger believes that the direction of each day's currency movement is strictly random, and independent of the previous day's movement. In other words: Past performance does not dictate future performance. A hedger using only forwards to hedge is basically acknowledging that exchange-rate movements cannot be predicted.

Another problem with using forwards is that the calculation of the forward rate is dependent on the interest rate differentials between the two countries. A pitfall of using forwards is that the forward may understate the relationship between intercountry interest rates. Purchasing a higher-yielding currency forward earns a forward discount that should illustrate the interest rate differential between the two countries over the term of the forward contract. Essentially, the use of a forward to hedge means that the hedger is also taking an interest rate view on the two countries' borrowing rates. The hedger is stating that over the life of the forward contract, the two countries' interest rates either will not change or will move in a parallel fashion (meaning that there is a simultaneous change which effectively negates any movement). Interest rates move all the time. Look at Figure 3 of six-month LIBOR (a six-month short-term interest rate). This rate has moved substantially over the last six months. The hedger must realize that the longer the forward contract is in place, the greater the risk that the intercountry interest-rate spread will move.

In addition, forward rates have an inherent bias. A long forward-position has an inherent bias toward a strengthening U.S. dollar. This was depicted in the previous CAD hedge illustration. Return also to the cash-flow related costs for contract settlement example using a sale of the Italian lira against the dollar. From Figure 1, it is shown that there was a historical

Figure 3 6-Month LIBOR

dollar decline against the lira. In a declining-dollar environment, forward contracts will underpredict the devaluation of the dollar, and that is why they settle at a loss. In the lira trade, the forward points that were calculated underpredicted the devaluation of the dollar against the lira, and this put the trade in the red. The hedger should have been prepared for this cash-flow related cost at the beginning of the hedge. Conversely, in a rising-dollar environment, the use of forwards can be beneficial to the hedger, because forward points (and thus the resulting forward rate) will overpredict the appreciation of the dollar, and the resulting trade should be profitable.

Dollar Environment	Forward Points Prediction
Strengthening	Under prediction of future value of U.S. dollar
Weakening	Over prediction of future value of U.S. dollar

Using forwards to hedge requires the hedger to have a sizable cash slush-fund for contract settlement. The hedger must be prepared to pay for the mistakes of the undervalued forward points in a dollar-depreciation environment when the hedges settle at a loss. From the example used, the loss on the lira hedge used at the start of this chapter was about 7 percent the size of the entire position. The hedger must be prepared to pay contract settlement for any hedges in the red, and the fund must be allowed to accumulate the settlements that are in the black in order to pay for any settlement losses. In addition, the hedger should not lose sight that the hedge, the delivery of foreign exchange, will be used to pay bills or sell unwanted receipts. Hedging against the exposure is a practical matter. Using forwards to hedge not only has an accounting cost, it has an accompanying opportunity gain or loss.

Finally, there is the concept of opportunity cost. Return to Figure 2 for the illustration of the forward contract against the movement of the Canadian dollar (CAD). From Figure 2, it can be seen that any currency movement stronger than 1.36 will result in the potential for accounting profit.. What is not illustrated is that, by locking in the hedge at 1.36, the hedger cannot take advantage of a cheaper CAD if it were to occur. The hedger has lost the opportunity to participate in a changing market. Essentially, if the currency were to weaken toward 1.38, both the accounting cost and the opportunity cost for the hedge would be negative.

Is There an Efficient Foreign Exchange Market?

What is important to remember about different styles of management is how the hedger views the market. For a hedger to assume a style of passive management, the hedger would have to take the view that the foreign exchange market is efficient and random and that the market in no way trends. If a market is efficient, the change in the price of a currency which is taking place today should be completely unrelated to the change in price that took place yesterday or any other day in the past. The crucial condition, which must hold, is that the expected change in the price on any given day must be unrelated to the past series of changes that have already taken place.[18]

An efficient market means that all the information available to date is reflected in the price of the currency. Available information means all information that has been announced and/or predicted from past announcements to date. Information must flow into the market in an unpredictable and random fashion. The market price responds accurately and instantly to the receipt of data, and the price of the currency will change in a random and unpredictable fashion. Therefore, all information is embedded into the forward rate, and the future is impossible to predict. However, if the market is not efficient, then using a forward rate to blindly hedge may be akin to shooting oneself in the foot. The hedger would be missing the potential to profit or to reduce the costs of the hedges. The next half of this chapter attempts to illustrate that the market is not efficient, and if the market is not efficient, then a more active style of currency management would be more appropriate. The following argument discusses both the theoretical and statistical reasons why the market is not efficient.

The Theoretical Conditions for an Efficient Market

There are five conditions that must be met for the market to be efficient:

1. Individual investor expectations are homogenous—all investors interpret the new information in the same manner.

2. There is no uncertainty among market participants regarding whether the new information reaching the market was of a transitory or of a permanent nature.

3. The market knows with certainty, given all the available information, what constitutes a currency's true long-run equilibrium value.

4. Investors are not risk adverse—they are willing to bring exchange rates instantly into line with the market's estimated long-run equilibrium value.

5. There are no private or official barriers that restrict investors from bringing exchange rates into line with their long-run equilibrium value.[19]

From these conditions, we can constitute a market which is in equilibrium. Exchange rates would adjust rapidly to new information. There would be no market trends of any kind. Let us consider each of these theoretical conditions one at a time.

Homogenous Investors: Not Available

First, it is ridiculous to assume that all investors' expectations are the same. Individuals are not robots, and investors do not all have the same I.Q. It stands to reason that individuals interpret information differently, sometime because of why they have to use it. A Wall Street arbitrage trader may have very short-run expectations of making a profit, whereas a pension fund, by default, may have very long-run expectations of paying out. Short-term information, such as information that has a tendency to create volatility in the market, will be of more use to the arbitrage trader. Further, in our electronic age, information reaches some people faster than others. Obviously, a person reading the newspaper and a person reading the electronic-news bulletin board will get information at different times, and each will react to the information faster or slower than the other.

Issue of Permanency of Information

Information is suspect in this age. Everyone aquainted with the U.S. market has heard the phrase that the Federal Reserve is jawboning the market.[20] In this day and age, the big question regarding information is: Is it real or is it transitory? For example, let us say that the president of the United States had one year left in his term of office. The president has issued a statement that he would like to see a stronger dollar now. The hedger must contend with several problems. First, the hedger must assess if this is actual information or simply the wish of one man. Second, the hedger must determine if the information is transitory in nature. The president has only one year in office left. If he gets re-elected, then the president has five years to implement a stronger dollar. The hedger must assess if the information is permanent.

Purchasing Power Parity: A Currency's Long-Run True Equilibrium Value

A perfectly efficient market assumes that all participants know what the long-run equilibrium value should be for the currency and that they are working toward this value. The closest thing that the market has as an indicator of the long-run equilibrium value of a currency is purchasing power parity analysis (PPP). PPP is one of the oldest methodologies that has been applied in forecasting the future movement of exchange rates.[21] Most of the modern research for PPP is attributed to Gustav Cassel (1920s), however there has been some indication that the theory stretches back as far as the 1500s in Spain. Basically, the theory states that the long-run equilibrium value of a currency is determined by the level of domestic prices relative to the level of prices in another country. A very simple example is the price of a loaf of bread in the United States compared to the price of the same loaf of bread in Germany. The equilibrium exchange rate is determined by the ratio of national price levels in the United States and in Germany, and the ratio can be described by the following equation:

$$\$/DM = Price \ (U.S.) \ / \ Price \ (Germany)$$

To make use of the theory, market participants would know that if a currency's exchange rate deviates away from its long-run PPP value, then the market should force the exchange rate back toward the calculated long-run PPP value. Unfortunately, there is a major problem in using PPP to determine a long-run equilibrium level of exchange rates: it concentrates solely on relative prices as the driving force for determining exchange rate movements. There are other real factors that may cause exchange rates to diverge permanently from their PPP long-run equilibrium levels. Some of the more obvious factors are supply shocks, political events (and political posturing), fiscal policies, shifts in money demand, natural resources discoveries, difference in productivity, and trade barriers.[22] The jury is still out on whether central bank intervention causes exchange rates to diverge permanently from their long-run PPP levels.

An Aside into Factors That Drive Long-Run Equilibrium Rates Away from Their PPP Levels

The evidence on central bank intervention is at best inconclusive. Theoretically, central banks are supposed to influence exchange rates by directly intervening in the foreign exchange markets. Intervention is encouraged by the IMF (International Monetary Fund) as long as it helps to stabilize the markets. The result of statistical studies to test the effectiveness of intervention has been found to be indeterminate. In those cases where a statistically significant relationship between intervention and exchange rates has been found, the impact of intervention has not been quantifiably important. The effect of intervention was predictable but not sizable or long-lasting.[23] This is not to say that no episodes of successful intervention have been documented, it is just that as of yet there has been no systematic relationship uncovered between intervention and exchange rates. It seems that the central banks are more easily able to influence an existing trend in exchange rates; such was the case with the Plaza Accord, in which the central banks looked to drive the dollar lower, which was an existing trend. The lack of statistical documented success has been contributed to by the fact that the volume of the intervention is often small compared to the size of the market, as composed of the daily market turnover of foreign exchange activity, the money stock held by the private sector, and the stock of domestic and foreign bonds held in private portfolios. However, what is important to this argument is that central bank intervention occurs and sometimes it is successful. The fact that there is intervention at all lends a wild card to the foreign exchange market and certainly does nothing to promote the efficient market, random-walk theory of the market.

A real factor that may cause exchange rates to diverge permanently from their PPP long-run equilibrium levels is political posturing. This chapter defines political posturing as to where the governing political body hopes the exchange rate will move. Political posturing is the stance in which the governing party takes on a matter such as the direction of the currency. Looking back over the past 20 years in the United States, different presidents (with different political affiliations) had different agendas for the U.S. dollar. In the period from 1969–1973, President Nixon ultimately ended up uncoupling the dollar from the gold standard and allowing the dollar to devalue. The next elected president was Carter, a Democrat. President Carter allowed the decline of the dollar to continue during 1977 through 1978, but then actively brought about intervention in the period of 1978–1980 in order to halt the dollar's decline. The following elected presidents were Republican: Reagan and Bush. From the period of 1981–1992, the dollar was alternately neglected, encouraged to decline (a trend in the market place reinforced by the Plaza Accord), and then encouraged to stabilize (in conjunction with the Louvre Accord). It could be noted that the political posturing of the U.S. dollar exchange rate is as changeable as the president.

Using PPP in the Real World

There is a further problem with using purchasing power parity to define the long-run equilibrium value of an exchange rate: market participants do not always calculate the same number. For example, many Wall Street firms have adjusted their PPP models to try to provide better predictions of a better long-run equilibrium level of exchange rates. From the following quotes, it can be seen that even the Wall Street specialists cannot decide on the long-run level of the $/DM:

Westdeutsche Landesbank Girozentrale	2.09
Goldman, Sachs and Company	1.6175
Royal Bank of Canada	1.8520[24]

Perhaps the following quote by Paul A. Samuelson[25] best sums up the problem with using PPP to determine a long-run equilibrium level of exchange rates: "Unless very sophisticated . . . PPP is a misleading pretentious doctrine, promising us what is rare in economics, detailed numerical predictions."

Investors and the Risk Curve

For a market to be efficient, the participants must be risk averse. It could be argued that not all investors are risk averse. Not all investors have the resources to hang on to a position that may eventually make them money in the long run. For example, the U.S. dollar/deutsche mark ($/DEM) is trading today at 1.5250. Goldman, Sachs and Company states that the long-run equilibrium value of the $/DEM (according to their PPP model) is 1.6175. This means that the U.S. dollar should appreciate over the long run against the deutsche mark from 1.5250 to 1.6175, earning the investor profits on a long-dollar/short-deutsche-mark position. However, it is illogical to expect the dollar to move on a straight path to 1.6175. It may meander and waffle its way to 1.6175, in which case the investor is left with the *deep pocket question:* Over what period of time will I need to have large financial resources in order to weather the ultimate appreciation of the dollar? Can the investor be risk-averse enough to hold out on a position over the long run (a period of time as yet unstated other than that it is not the short run), perhaps losing money in the interim, to maybe make money?

Further, what if the spot quote on the $/DEM moves from 1.5250 today to 1.48 tomorrow, taking prices further away from the fair value? Would a long-run investor be willing to risk his or her capital in the face of such uncertainty? In other words, a risk-averse participant in the market could also be termed a stabilizing speculator: a person willing to move the market toward the long-run equilibrium value, and one having deep enough pockets to do so. The question may boil down to the fact that although the investor may want to hold the position indefinitely in order to wait for the move toward 1.6175, there may not be enough capital available to allow it. The investor would have to be willing to invest capital (risk capital) for uncertain profits.

Other Restrictions to Equilibrium

Finally, there are private and official barriers that restrict investors from bringing exchange rates into line with their long-run equilibrium value. Even if a participant were willing to place a huge sum of money into the financial market in order to try to force the market toward equilibrium, it may not be possible to do so. Quoting Ronald I. McKinnon (*Money in International Exchange: The Convertible Currency System*, published by the Oxford University Press in 1979), there may be various legal and institutional constraints that prohibit a person from becoming a stabilizing speculator. An example of a legal constraint is that in some countries there are limits on bank positions, which are imposed by the monetary authorities. Corporations themselves limit the amount of money used for a stabilizing influence. Due to the introduction of risk management policies into large multinational corporations, there are clearly defined, board-dictated policies against speculating in foreign exchange. Corporations limit how much capital they intend to put at risk. In these corporations, the aim is to minimize the risk exposure to foreign currency, not maximize the profit potential. Even if the hedger truly believed that the Goldman Sachs PPP stated $/DEM rate of 1.6175 was probable, in corporate America such speculation may not be possible due to risk management policies. The hedger may reach the maximum level of capital permitted to be put at risk before the market ever approaches the long-run equilibrium value of 1.6175.

Statistical Evidence That the Market May Not Be Efficient

From the discussion above, it is apparent that, theoretically, the foreign exchange market may not be efficient. It may not be random. In fact, the slant of this chapter is that the foreign exchange market is not efficient. It is felt that past market data can be used to predict future market data. A trend does develop in the market and it lasts long enough to signal to investors that it is apparent and that these same investors, when recognizing the trend, profit from it. There is hard statistical evidence that the market is not efficient. To further test nonrandom hypothesis, filter rule trading, positive serial correlation, leptokurtic distributions, and nonlinear distributions are examined below.

Evidence of a Nonperfect Market as Illustrated by the Filter Rule

Filter rules were initially used by Sydney Alexander to test for trading profits in the American equity market in 1961.[26] A filter rule is a primary technique for testing spot market efficiency that uses a mechanical trading strategy. The following is a description of a simple filter rule, and Figure 4 illustrates the rule graphically.

The assumptions are as follows:

1. The trader has no initial positions, but the trader does have a stock of money (wealth).

2. The trader uses this money to establish a line of credit with a commercial bank such that the trader can trade in the spot currency market.

Figure 4 Example of Filter Rule Concept: $/DM, 3% Rule

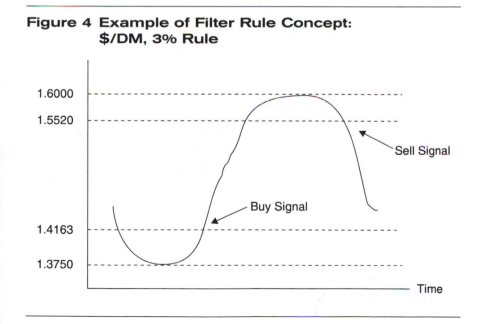

3. The trader, for the purposes of this example, is trading the $/DM (U.S. dollars against German deutsche-marks).

The filter (the trading strategy) is as follows:

- *The Buy Signal.* Whenever the deutsche mark rises by x percent above its most recent trough (a trading bottom), borrow U.S. dollars, convert them to deutsche marks at the spot exchange rate, and take a long position in deutsche marks.

- *The Sell Signal.* Whenever the deutsche mark falls by x percent below its most recent peak (a trading top), sell any long deutsche-mark position acquired and go short deutsche marks by borrowing deutsche marks and converting the proceeds to U.S. dollars at the spot exchange rate.

The filter is the x percent. This is the magic number that the trader is testing the market in which to find the highest degree of profit. If the market is perfectly efficient then no x percent would ever be available in which to earn a significant profit over a certain period.

A survey of several research papers has found profitable trading filters when none should logically exist in a perfect market. Several individuals have found an x percent in which they can earn profit over the period of study. Dooley and Shafer studied the period of 1973-1981, looking at daily spot rates for nine currencies.[27] Their results indicate that small filters, where $x = 1$ percent, 3 percent, or 5 percent, would have been profitable for all currencies over the entire sample period. Sweeney[28] had similar results with small trading filters for the period of April 1973 to December 1980 for 10 currencies. Profit was found in 80 percent of all cases. Sweeney also found profit with a filter of 10 percent, but found better results with smaller filers.

Levich and Thomas[29] backed into the filter rule test. They were testing to see if the sample itself was random. First, they took a series of futures prices (period of 1976–1990) for five currencies: sterling, deutsche marks, yen, Swiss francs, and Canadian dollars. These were their test data. Then they randomly shuffled the original time series of data, reordering the original data. The only constraint on the reshuffling was that the starting price and ending price were the same. Now they had two samples to compare and contrast. They applied various filter rules and moving-average crossover rules to the original data series. They found that the original series earned substantial risk-adjusted profits (profits generated by following a trend) under the filter-rule/moving-average scenarios. Then they applied the same tests to the randomly ordered series, and found that the profits on the trading strategies were near zero. One would expect that if the two series, composed of the same numbers, were both randomly distributed, then the profits generated by one set of trading rules on one of the series would equal the profits generated by the other. This was not the case. Obviously, the first series, the original, was not randomly ordered. It followed a trend that could be captured for profit. Levich and Thomas suggest that there exists in the foreign exchange market some form of serial dependency, although they could not pinpoint that source of dependency. The implication from this study is that the filter-rule-/moving-average trend following system was capturing nonlinear dependency in the data.

Positive Serial Correlation, Leptokurtic Distributions, and Nonlinear Distributions

Academics argue that for a market to be efficient, a currency's value today cannot be based on its value in a preceding period. In other words, the value of ΔS_t is not based on any value in any preceding period: ΔS_{t-1}. Serial-correlation tests seek to determine if there is a stable relationship between the two currency rates. Any evidence of a stable relationship between ΔS_t and ΔS_{t-1} would confirm the existence of trends. A stable relationship would confirm that one could predict the value of a currency today from its past history.

It is interesting to note two things. The first is that most researchers found no evidence of positive serial correlation on daily data, or the dependence was found to be unstable over time (Dooley and Shafer).[30] There is some evidence that monthly data show a greater serial dependence than daily data (Ito).[31]

The second item of note is the problem with the standard serial-correlation test itself. Serial-correlation tests rely on the data being normally distributed (showing a normal, bell-shaped curve). Evidence on the distribution of exchange-rate changes indicates that there are too many extreme observations relative to what one would find if exchange-rate changes were normally distributed.[32] These extreme observations (wild variances away from the mean) could be because of some type of risky event. An *event risk* is an unforeseeable unhedgable risk that suddenly appears, totally distorting the value of a currency (or some other tradable instrument). For example, let us say that a war broke out unexpectedly in the Middle East, and there was a flight-to-quality to the U.S. dollar. The value of the dollar would appreciate steeply, and be out of kilter with its preceding data. This flight-to-quality would produce an extreme observation in the data set. Due to these extreme observations, the data do not display a normal, bell-shaped curve. The data display a distribution that is *leptokurtic* (from the Greek, meaning thin). As compared to the bell-shaped curve of the normal distribution, a leptokurtic distribution has a higher peak, and flatter tails (supporting the large number of extreme positive and negative observations.)

Figure 5 Probability

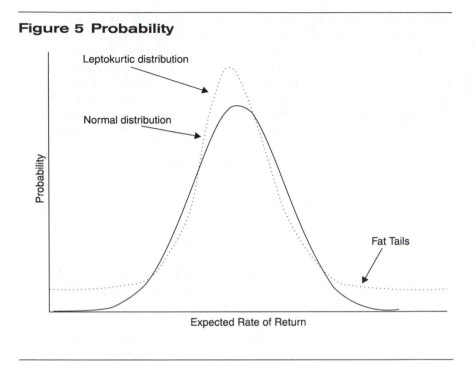

Figure 5 is an example of a leptokurtic distribution as compared to a normal distribution.

According to Hsieh,[33] tradition serial correlation tests will not be able to detect if nonlinear dependence exists. Using alternative approaches, it was demonstrated that exchange-rate changes do not exhibit linear dependence, but they do exhibit strong nonlinear dependence. Note that both the filter rule tests and the tests for positive linear correlation demonstrated that strong nonlinear dependence exists in the foreign currency market. This dependence could be the underlying reason for the existence of trends. It certainly could be the underlying reason for a nonefficient market.

The Market Is Not Efficient, It Trends: Use Technical Analysis to Spot Trends

All told, there is enough evidence illustrated above that the foreign exchange market is not efficient, that it exhibits strong nonlinear dependency, and that it moves in defined trends. In the most basic sense, the past can be used to read the future. If the foreign exchange market is not efficient, then a passive management approach toward currency management would be willfully ignoring profitable trends, and therefore trades, that exist in the market place. The hedger, within the concept of opportunity costs, would be costing the company the possibility of attaining higher profits or further reducing the cost of hedging. The responsibility is on the hedger to examine the tools available to help spot trends in the market place. Note that a trend-following system is not designed to catch the turning points (top or bottom), but rather to alert the hedger to the trend after it has been established, and allow the hedger to exploit it. Trend-following systems fall under the realm of something called *technical analysis.* Technical models are designed to help the trader identify the trend and to trade with it and not against it. Technical traders are less concerned with the theoretical fair value of a currency, and are more concerned with the market value of the currency. Technical traders acknowledge that there is a divergence between the theoretical fair value of a currency and the market value of a currency.

| Passive Management | → | Random Market | → | "Fair" Value of Currency |
| Active Management | → | Nonrandom Market | → | "Market" Value of Currency |

Figure 6 Italian Lira

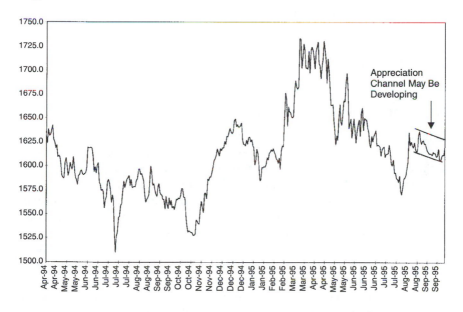

Opportunity Cost: An Example of Passive versus Active Management

An example of the opportunity cost of not actively managing the currency, even if the only management leeway is in the timing of the hedge, can be found at looking at the U.S. dollar/ Italian lira ($/ITL). See Figure 6. Let us assume that the hedger gets notice in October of 1995 of a receipt of Italian lira. The corporation is now long lira, and would want to set up a short position as a hedge. The hedger now has the flexibility to hedge the position up, or, at the outside, wait six months to hedge. The hedger looks at Figure 6 of the Italian lira and sees that a possible appreciation channel may be developing. In view of the this trend, the hedger decides to wait to put on the hedge. A passive hedger would have hedged blindly in October. On October, 3, 1995, the $/ITL was 1625.60. The trend-following hedger waits until April to hedge. On April 23, 1996, the $/ITL traded at 1547.25. This was a much better rate at which to sell the lira. Assuming the exposure amount was ITL 20,000,000,000, what was the *opportunity cost* of the passive hedge?

Active	20,000,000,000 / 1547.25 = $12,926,159.31
Passive	20,000,000,000 / 1625.60 = <u>$12,303,149.61</u>
Opportunity Cost	$ 633,009.70

A passive hedger would not have really lost the half a million plus dollars. This money was the opportunity cost of a passive decision versus an active decision. However, the active hedger really did save the corporation money by waiting for the trend. As the saying goes: The trend is your friend.

Types of Technical Analysis

Technical analysis is varied. One type of technical analysis deals with reading the chart. Chartism is a forecasting technique based on a visual nonlinear price pattern and thus refrains from hypothesizing any quantitative relationships between variables.[34] It is very popular, and very useful. A study by Allen and Taylor found that approximately 90 percent of chief foreign-exchange dealers surveyed in the London foreign-exchange market used some technical-model input to help forecast exchange rates over the short-run periods.[35] *Reading a chart* means that the user will identify standard patterns on a currency chart (whether the chart is daily, weekly, etc.), and these standard patterns allow the user to identify the existence of a trend. Chartism is part science and part art. Available texts on *chartism* are Pring[36] or Murphy.[37] Chartism is a topic which is far too complex to cover in this brief chapter. Without going into an in-depth discussion of charts, a chartist attempts to look at the past data of a currency's movement in order to determine whether the price action conforms to the behavior of an advancing or declining trend. There are certain rules that the chartist follows when identifying the trends, and when determining how long the trends will last. It does not take a rocket scientist to be a chartist, but it does take a good feel for patterns. Some imagination is helpful, and a good memory of the rules is key.

Perhaps the one major criticism against charting is that it is subjective (part science and part art). Reading a chart requires subjective interpretation, and thus it is obvious that not all people will see the same pattern. Obviously, if one's interpretation is incorrect, one cannot properly identify either the existence of a trend or its direction. Some investors have turned to computer-aided technical analysis. Two popular computer-driven models are the filter models, as described previously, and the moving-average models. A moving average smooths out the noise of daily price moves. Moving-average models look to isolate the primary trend hidden within the currency movement from the noise of the daily bump and grind. Usually two moving averages are used to give a signal to the trader: a short-run average and a slightly longer average. For example, a five-day moving average as compared to a 10-day moving average. If the five-day moving average moves above the 10-day moving average, the hedger will read this as a buy signal.

Other points are necessary to remember when using technical analysis. The market does not always have a direction. The market does not always trend. Sometimes it consolidates. Sometimes it trades in a very narrow range and appears directionless. The key to the hedger is to climb onboard after the trend has been established. Logically, it could be assumed that if there were no trend then the hedger would have no need to be in the market.

Technical Analysis: Used, Respected, and Profitable

Technical analysis is not voodoo. In 1985 the Group of Thirty[38] conducted a study which examined whether technical analysis had any impact on the foreign exchange market. In other words, the study asked, Does the method of following the market (technical analysis) have any impact on the market itself? Banks (97 percent) and securities dealers (87 percent) responded in the affirmative. In 1989, a study conducted by Allen and Taylor[39] found that approximately 90 percent of all chief foreign-exchange dealers surveyed in the London foreign exchange market used some form of technical analysis in order to help them trade in the short run. In the longer run, they have tended to rely more on fundamentals. This is not insignificant, because the London market is the world's largest foreign-exchange market. Research has proven the profitability of technical analysis, and studies have shown that large groups use technical analysis. One study, Goodman,[40] compared technical advice versus fundamental (economic) advice. The study concluded that the technical service outperformed the fundamental service.

Fundamentals are not tools that the hedger completely disregards. However, the hedger must realize that economic data have a lag time (the point from which the information is collected to the point at which it is distributed and absorbed), and sometimes this lag is significant. Gross national product (GNP) information is distributed quarterly, inflation data are distributed monthly. The data are suspect, and are often revised, sometimes more than once. Further, often economic data cannot be compared across national boundaries. The nuances of data collection in Germany and the United States, for example, must be accounted for when making any comparisons in fundamental indicators.

Technical analysis, even the most subjective charting, will give the user an indication of what value the market places on an exchange rate. According to economic theory, value is what the market will bear, not what the market thinks it will bear. The theoretical value of a currency can be a shot in the dark, especially if the currency is trading at a significant divergence from its fair market. At this point, the only information on which the hedger has to rely is the market value of the currency.

Conclusion

The foreign exchange market is not random, nor is it positively serially correlated. Exchange-rate changes exhibit strong nonlinear dependence and, because of this dependence, the market is not perfect, efficient, and random. Foreign exchange markets exhibit trends. The hedger must deal with the fact that there is a divergence from a currency's market value and theoretical fair value. The only outcome available from the preceding analysis is that the hedger must actively hedge, using some form of technical analysis as a guide, at least in the short run. To disregard the fact that the marketplace trends would be irresponsible, and ultimately costly. The foreign exchange market is not efficient, thus the style of active management based on technical indicators is the only logical management style.

Endnotes

1. David B. Guralnik, ed., *The New World Dictionary of the American Language*, 2nd. ed., Cleveland: William Collins + World Publishing Co., 1976, p. 648.

2. Andrew W. Gitlin, ed., *Strategic Currency Investing*, Chicago: Probus Publishing, 1993, p. 27.

3. A currency forward is an agreement to exchange a specified amount of one currency for another currency at a future date and at a certain rate. The exchange is priced such that there is no risk-free arbitrage: the pricing of the exchange is

not a market estimate of the spot at that date, but is made according to the two currencies' respective interest rates. The spot rate is adjusted by the forward points implied by the interest rate differentials. The concept of forwards is further explained later is this chapter.

4. Michael Rosenberg, "Hedging a Non-Dollar Fixed-Income Portfolio," in *Managing Currency Risk,* The Institute of Chartered Financial Analysts, 1989, pp. 3537.

5. Stephen M. Skillman, Vice President, Foreign Exchange Corporate Advisory, Westdeutsche Landesbank Girozentrale, New York branch, May, 1996.

6. A buy and a sell with the same dealer is called a *round-trip.*

7. Andrew W. Gitlin, ed., *Strategic Currency Investing,* Chicago: Probus Publishing Co., 1993, p. 31.

8. Modern Theory of Forward Exchange Rate Determination.

9. John C. Hull, *Options, Futures, and Other Derivative Securities,* 2nd ed., New Jersey: Prentice Hall, 1993, p. 2.

10. *The Chase/Risk Magazine Guide to Risk Management,* London: Peter Field, 1996, p. 25.

11. Merrill Lynch , Foreign Exchange Sales, World Financial Center, North Tower, New York Branch. This equation does not include the slightly more complicated discount-to-yield analysis.

12. An indirect quote is a currency that is quoted in units per U.S. dollar, such as the mark, the yen, or the Canadian dollar. A direct quote is a currency quoted in its own units, such as the pound sterling or the Australian dollar.

13. Elliott J. Passman, Assistant Vice President, First Chicago NBD, Detroit, Michigan Branch, May, 1996.

14. *Estimates of Daily Foreign Exchange Market Turnover,* as quoted by Robert G. Catalanello, Associate, Foreign Exchange, Goldman, Sachs & Co., New York branch, May, 1996.

15. Christopher M. Turner, Risk Management Advisories, *Policies and Procedures Source Book,* Chase Manhattan Bank, New York, 1996

16. Andrew W. Gitlin, ed., *Strategic Currency Investing,* Chicago: Probus Publishing Co., 1993, pg. 31.

17. If the corporation were using a more active foreign-exchange management strategy, the hedger would judge the active hedge performance of the exposure month against the cumulative rate of that same month locked in by the passive strategy. In essence, *two* foreign exchange books would have to be monitored: the first is composed of the passive index rates, the second is composed of the actual rates used in the risk manager's hedging strategy. If the active strategy achieved a better rate than that of the passive index, then the hedger would be outperforming the index. Note that the passive index is one developed to control

price (rate) risk. Therefore, if the risk manager is outperforming the passive index, then the risk manager is actually hedging at a lower opportunity cost than that of the passive index. It is misleading to refer to this lower opportunity cost as the hedger *earning money* or *profiting* over the benchmark. No money is actually earned. The benchmark is a type of least-cost method of controlling foreign-exchange-rate risk. Any strategy that deviates from it (for example, whatever hedging method that the risk manager actually used) would have to produce a less costly hedge in order to outperform the least-cost method of the passive benchmark. Theoretically, the only thing that has happened in out-performing the benchmark is that the cost of the hedge is reduced by a management method that has provided a better hedge rate. The hedger has reduced the *opportunity cost* of the hedge. The term *profiting over the benchmark* is incorrect and misleading.

18. Robert A. Haugen, *Modern Investment Theory*, 3rd ed., New Jersey: Prentice Hall Inc., 1993, pp. 643644

19. Michael R. Rosenberg, *Currency Forecasting Using Technical Analysis: Theory and Evidence*, Merrill Lynch and Co., Global Securities Research and Economic Group, Global Fixed-Income Research, September 30, 1994, p. 19.

20. *Jawboning* is a term used to describe a highly placed market participant trying to verbally move the market, to talk the market into a desired position.

21. Michael R. Rosenberg, *Purchasing Power Parity*, Merrill Lynch and Co., Global Securities Research and Economic Group, Global Fixed-Income Research, March 20, 1990, p. 1.

22. Michael R. Rosenberg, *Purchasing Power Parity*, Merrill Lynch and Co., Global Securities Research and Economic Group, Global Fixed Income Research, March 20, 1990, p. 7.

23. Michael R. Rosenberg, *Central-Bank Intervention and the Determination of Exchange Rates*, Merrill Lynch and Co., Global Securities Research and Economic Group, Global Fixed Income Research, October, 1992, p. 17.

24. Indication levels taken by telephone survey on May 9, 1996.

25. Paul A. Samuelson, "Theoretical Notes on Trade Problems," *Review of Economic and Statistics*, Vol. 46, May 1964, pp. 145–154.

26. Sydney S. Alexander, "Price Movements in Speculative Markets: Trends or Random Walks," *Industrial Management Review* 2, May 1961, pp. 7–26.

27. Michael P. Dooley and Jeffrey Shafer, "Analysis of Short-Run Exchange Rate Behavior: March 1973September 1975," International Finance Discussion Papers, No. 76. Washington, D.C., Federal Reserve System, 1976, as well as Michael P. Dooley and Jeffrey Shafer. "Analysis of Short-run Exchange Rate Behavior: March 1973November 1981," in D. Bigman and T Taya, eds., *Exchange Rate and Trade Instability* (Cambridge, Mass.: Ballinger Publishing), 1983.

28. Richard J. Sweeny, "Beating the Foreign Exchange Market," *Journal of Finance* 41, no. 1 (March 1986), pp. 163182.

29. Richard Levich and Lee Thomas , "The Significance of Technical Trading-Rule Profits in the Foreign Exchange Market: A Bootstrap Approach," NBER Working Paper, No. 3818, 1991.

30. Michael P. Dooley and Jeffrey Shafer. "Analysis of Short-Run Exchange Rate Behavior: March 1973September 1975," International Finance Discussion Papers, No. 76, Washington, D.C., Federal Reserve System, 1976.

31. Takatoshi Ito, "Short-Run and Long-Run Expectations of the Yen/Dollar Exchange Rate," NBER Working Paper, No. 4545, November, 1993.

32. Michael R. Rosenberg, *Currency Forecasting Using Technical Analysis: Theory and Evidence*, Merrill Lynch and Co., Global Securities Research and Economic Group, Global Fixed Income Research, September 30, 1994, p. 13.

33. David A. Hsieh, "Testing for Nonlinear Dependence in Daily Foreign Exchange Rates," *Journal of Business*, Vol. 62, No. 3, 1989, pp. 33968.

34. Laurent L. Jacque, *Management and Control of Foreign Exchange Risk*, Kluwer Academic Publishers, 1996, p. 119.

35. Helen Allen and Mark P. Taylor, "Charts, Noise, and Fundamentals: A Study of the London Foreign Exchange Market," *CEPR Discussion* Paper, No. 341, September 1989. Martin J. Pring, Technical Analysis Explained, 3rd ed., New York: McGraw Hill Inc., 1991.

36 Martin J. Pring, *Technical Analysis Explained*, 3rd ed., New York: McGraw Hill Inc., 1991.

37. John J. Murphy, *Technical Analysis of the Futures Markets*, New York: New York Institute of Finance, 1986.

38. Group of Thirty, *The Foreign Exchange Market in the 1980s*, New York, 1985.

39. Helen Allen and Mark P. Taylor, "Charts, Noise, and Fundamentals: A Study of the London Foreign Exchange Markets," CEPR Discussion Paper, No. 341, September 1989.

40. Stephen H. Goodman, "Technical Analysis Still Beats Econometrics," *Euromoney*, August 1981.

CHAPTER 16

Foreign-Exchange Risk Management at Tenneco

James O. West, Jr.
Director of Capital Budgeting
Tenneco

Under new leadership, Tenneco is changing its market perception from that of an unfocused conglomerate to one that concentrates on noncyclical, high-growth business opportunities in the packaging and automotive parts industries. The goal is to achieve average annual 15 percent earnings growth through the business cycle going forward. While short-term gains in earning could come from cost-cutting measures, long-term earnings growth requires new markets with higher margins. In addition, the mature domestic-packaging, automotive, and gas pipeline markets force Tenneco's divisions to focus internationally in order to find business opportunities. Like other international corporations, Tenneco has been faced with foreign-exchange risk management issues, ranging from daily operations to the purchase or divestiture of large segments. The following vignettes provide a sample of the activities producing foreign-exchange exposure issues and the approaches used to manage them.

Hedging a Divestiture—Sale of Albright & Wilson on the London Exchange

The sale of its chemicals subsidiary, Albright & Wilson, marked Tenneco's first attempt at accomplishing an initial public offering through a foreign stock-exchange. The arena for the offering was the London Stock Exchange with the resulting proceeds denominated in pounds sterling.

Year-end 1994, Tenneco's management began a detailed examination of the possibility of selling Albright & Wilson prior to the end of the first quarter 1995. A target date for the transaction of March 8 was established, with proceeds estimated at £600 million. Tenneco's Treasury Department was asked to provide a recommendation on the appropriate hedge mechanism and the amount of the exposure to hedge. Given that the objective was to hedge the exposure of a nonexistent transaction, the accounting treatment of any hedge became an important issue.

The accounting rules provided that hedges of identified foreign-currency commitments be marked to market at reporting dates and gains/losses offset on the related commitment. Hedges of foreign-currency net equity investments are revalued at reporting dates and the gain/loss reflected in the equity accounts with no income statement treatment. Speculative transactions, those not identified to foreign currency commitments or foreign net equity investments, are to be revalued at reporting dates with gains/losses taken to income.

One alternative explored was hedging the net equity balance of Tenneco's investment in Albright & Wilson. A major advantage to this approach was the absence of income statement impact if the intial public offering were not completed. Another factor facilitating the use of this approach was that Tenneco had already sold £75 million forward to May 1995. Albright & Wilson represented the majority of Tenneco's unhedged net equity investment at the time, with a current unhedged equity investment of £130 million (total equity investment in Albright & Wilson was £205 million).

Coverage could be provided by entering into a forward sale of £'s, or by buying a put option on £'s (obtaining the right, but not the obligation, to sell £'s at a known price on a date or dates in the future). Coupled with a hedge of the net equity investment, the option premium would be charged to discontinued operations and deducted from the gain or loss on the sale. The advantages of utilizing an option included flexibility in timing, the ability to put a floor on the exchange rate, and the certainty of the premium. The principal disadvantage was the expense. At a strike price of $1.56/£, the then current exchange rate, an option expiring March 8, 1995, for £525 million (the £600 million expected proceeds less the £75 million already hedged) would cost approximately $13 million.

Several banks were surveyed with no consensus on either the direction or the magnitude of the exchange rate movement by March, but there was broad agreement on the lack of volatility. However, the majority of the currency traders were forecasting a slight weakening of the sterling. It was determined that the income statement exposure of hedging the uncertain transaction was unacceptable given the expected volatility. The inclination among the traders of the weakening of the sterling made it prudent to hedge at least a portion of the expected proceeds. Accordingly, the decision was made to hedge the existing unhedged equity-investment balance of £130 million.

The resulting forwards resulted in the hedging of the full net equity investment (this did not create income statement exposure), hedged approximately one-third of the expected proceeds, and timed the exposures to coincide with the expected intial public offering. By not hedging the entire expected proceeds, the cost of the contracts were also substantially reduced.

Hedging an Acquisition—Tenneco Energy's Purchase of the Pipeline Authority of South Australia

In 1995, the assets of the Pipeline Authority of South Australia (PASA) were privatized by the government of the State of South Australia. The pipeline included a 488-mile, 22-inch line delivering gas from Moomba to the city of Adelaide, and a 44-mile, 6-inch line serving the southeast corner of the state. Tenneco Energy reviewed this opportunity and determined that a purchase of these assets was consistent with its broader Australian strategy. Tenneco board of directors' approval was obtained at a special meeting on April 25, 1995. Tenneco decided to originally finance the acquisition with existing financial resources at the corporate level that were converted to Australian dollars (AUS$) and loaned to Tenneco Energy's Australian subsidiary.

The government's offering memorandum provided that unconditional final bids be submitted by May 1, 1995. The preferred purchaser would be notified on May 9, with the sale of the PASA assets completed by June 30. Tenneco was faced with two foreign-exchange risk management opportunities. The first was that an adverse movement in the US$/AUS$ exchange rate before closing could result in a higher purchase price. The second was that an exchange rate fluctuation on the intercompany loan could result in foreign exchange gains or losses on the settlement of the original loan. Figure 1 illustrates the two forward contracts used to manage the exposure. For the purposes of this discussion, 100 percent debt financing is assumed.

As board authorization was obtained based on a U.S. dollar (US$) price and since the bid was made in AUS$, the project was exposed to a possible US$ overrun situation at closing should the AUS$ appreciate. While currency movements prior to the original booking of the asset would not have a currency translation adjustment (CTA) or an income impact, and since the purchase would be accomplished by an Australian subsidiary using AUS$ as its functional currency, this meant that there would be no cash impact. With the recent history of the peso, both the management and the board were sensitive to overruns due to currency fluctuations, and they sought a level of comfort.

Upon signing agreements as the preferred purchaser on May 11, board-approval exposure was managed by purchasing AUS$ forward to the anticipated transaction date of June 30. Since there was no asset related to this transaction, it was deemed a speculative hedge that required being marked to market each month with the resulting revaluation flowing through the income statement.

Figure 1

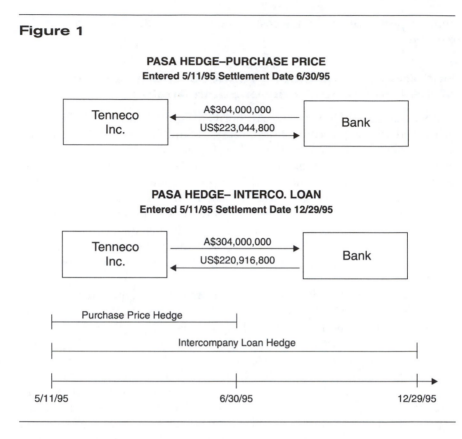

PASA HEDGE–PURCHASE PRICE
Entered 5/11/95 Settlement Date 6/30/95

Tenneco Inc. | A$304,000,000 / US$223,044,800 | Bank

PASA HEDGE– INTERCO. LOAN
Entered 5/11/95 Settlement Date 12/29/95

Tenneco Inc. | A$304,000,000 / US$220,916,800 | Bank

Purchase Price Hedge

Intercompany Loan Hedge

5/11/95   6/30/95   12/29/95

On the transaction date, Tenneco US$-denominated funds were used to purchase AUS$ under the forward contract. The AUS$ were then loaned to Tenneco Energy's Australian subsidiary for the purchase, creating an AUS$ asset. To hedge to the exchange rate exposure of the loan, Tenneco entered into a forward contract to sell AUS$ on December 29, 1995 (the loan's initial settlement date).

It is here that the transactions took an interesting twist. To manage any income-statement impact of the "speculative" forward to buy AUS$ on June 30, the second forward, to sell AUS$, was entered into on May 11 as well. This structure created a counter "speculative" hedge from May 11 to June 30 whose income statement impact was in an equal amount, yet opposite direction from, the original forward. With the asset purchase on June 30, the second forward began to hedge the loan and ceased to receive speculative hedge-accounting treatment.

On December 29, the forward contract was settled at the contracted exchange rates and the US$ loan was refinanced.

Hedging a Greenfield Project—Tenneco Energy's Construction of the Southwest Queensland Pipeline

Another venture in Australia illustrates the use of foreign-exchange risk management in the development of an overseas greenfield project. This project is interesting in that the foreign exchange exposure was to a subsidiary with a foreign functional currency, and its resolution involved the use of Tenneco's internal bank.

In 1994, Tenneco Energy was selected by the Queensland Government Gas Task Force as one of the potential developers of natural gas pipelines in Queensland. After a subsequent bidding and negotiation process, the State of Queensland government and Tenneco Energy reached agreement on December 23, 1994, for Tenneco to construct a 800 kilometer, 16-inch pipeline from the Cooper/Eromonga basins of Southwest Queensland to an existing pipeline serving Brisbane.

As with the privatization project discussed earlier, this new construction project would be performed by a subsidiary of Tenneco Energy Australia, with supply and delivery contracts and functional currency in AUS$. The foreign exchange exposure arose when U.S. firms were selected as the suppliers for much of the material used to construct the line. To provide a sense of the exposure, nearly US$100 million of the approximately US$170 million project was let in purchase orders to U.S. firms.

Pipe was ordered on May 1, 1995, with payment due on October 1, 1995 (actually there were numerous contracts and payment dates, but only one of each will be used in order to simplify this example). The funding to Tenneco Energy Australia for the purchase would be provided on the payment date via an AUS$ loan from the Tenneco parent company, a U.S. company. While corporate's functional currency and the payable to the suppliers would both be US$ denominated, Tenneco Energy Australia was exposed to the AUS$ impact, its functional currency, and its exchange rate movement. Accordingly, Tenneco elected to fix the AUS$ cost of the materials through forwards in order to eliminate income statement exposure. Figure 2 provides an illustration of the forwards and cash flows for this project.

The situation developed where at a future date Tenneco would need AUS$ for its loan to the subsidiary, and the subsidiary require US$ for its payment to its suppliers. Two forwards were contracted in order to manage this exposure. On May 1, Tenneco Energy Australia entered into a forward contract with TIFL, Tenneco's London-based finance subsidiary, wherein the subsidiary agreed to buy US$100 million on October 1. Simultaneously,

Figure 2

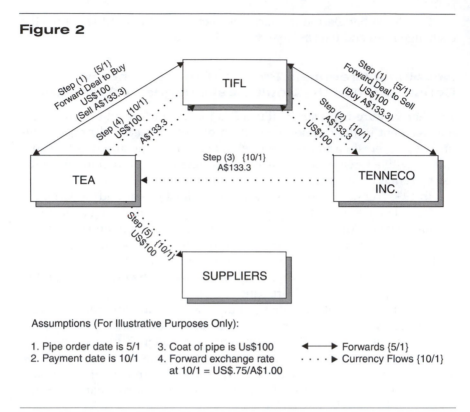

Assumptions (For Illustrative Purposes Only):

1. Pipe order date is 5/1   3. Coat of pipe is Us$100   ◄──► Forwards {5/1}
2. Payment date is 10/1   4. Forward exchange rate   · · · ·► Currency Flows {10/1}
                                at 10/1 = US$.75/A$1.00

Tenneco entered into a forward contract with TIFL to sell US$100 million on the same date. The second contract had the serendipitous effect of hedging TIFL's exposure from its contract with the Australian subsidiary.

On October 1, Tenneco sold $US100 million to TIFL in exchange for AUS$133.3 million. Tenneco immediately provided Tenneco Energy Australia with a loan of AUS$133.3 million. Tenneco Energy then consummated its forward with TIFL in exchange for US$100 million, the U.S. dollars needed to pay its suppliers. This illustrates the use of a captive in order to avoid going outside of the group to hedge exposures, a benefit to Tenneco of having a financial subsidiary.

Throughout the process, Tenneco Energy Australia was able to define both the US$ liability that it would owe to its suppliers and the AUS$ equity injection that would be required to satisfy it. Additionally, the foreign exchange exposure of Tenneco's loan to Tenneco Energy was hedged.

Operational Hedges—Tenneco Automotive's Operations within Mexico

Mexico has provided a unique opportunity for foreign-exchange risk management, as much for the publicity as the actual exposure. Tenneco Automotive is our most heavily invested business unit in Mexico, and it is to their activities that we will turn for our next examples.

The automotive components segment has two broad customer-bases, vehicle manufacturers and sales/installation of replacement or upgrade components sold through distributors for use in shops or by retailers. Tenneco Automotive, through its Monroe and Walker subsidiaries, is the world's largest manufacturer and marketer of ride control and exhaust systems, respectively, for the original equipment and replacement markets. As global suppliers, Walker and Monroe have a manufacturing presence in Mexico to supply both domestic and U.S. markets. The market difference in the two customer sets has dictated distinct approaches to the foreign-exchange risk management issue.

Sales to original equipment manufacturers involve relatively large monthly volumes shipped to a small number of customers. Such is the case with Walker's Mexican exhaust facility. From a risk management perspective, this provides a predictable risk profile with a few defined counterparties. Thus, Walker has been able to negotiate mitigation procedures with its customers in lieu of using financial markets.

Prices between Walker and the original equipment manufacturers are negotiated in US$, while payments are denominated in Mexican pesos at the then-current exchange rate. Invoices are payable 30 days from the date of issuance. Two exposures exist. The obvious is the movement in the exchange rate between issuing the invoice and the customer's payment. The second exposure is a derivative of the banking practices within Mexico. Unlike the United States, a depositor's account is not credited until the bank receives actual cash from the payer's bank. This clearing process is typically three days, during which time additional exchange rate movements are possible. Of course, the customers are exposed to the same movements.

Tenneco Automotive and its customers have established a billing and payment practice to manage these exposures. While invoices are prepared in U.S. dollars, payment is made in pesos based on the exchange rate at the time that the check is cut, maintaining the U.S. dollar value of the transaction. The check is then deposited and clears the banking system, at which point Tenneco Automotive repatriates its net available cash to the United States, or lends it to its sister company, Monroe. To maintain the U.S. dollar value of the transaction during the clearing process, Walker's depository is geographically located near the customers' remittance institutions in order to ensure timely clearance.

The relationship with the aftermarket customers is not so tidy. The larger number of customers, number of orders, and relatively small order size make it unfeasible for Tenneco Automotive to duplicate its arrangements from the original equipment manufacturer's side. Since aftermarket customers are invoiced in pesos, Tenneco is faced with a revolving peso 30-day receivable in excess of US$1 million equivalent. The more traditional approach of purchasing 30-day forwards is therefore used to manage the foreign exchange risk, with approximately 75 percent of the exposed currency hedged.

Regulatory Issues: Accounting and Financial Reporting for Instruments Subject to Global Currency Risk

Robert H. Herz
National Director of Accounting and SEC Services
Coopers & Lybrand L.L.P.

Thomas J. Linsmeier
Assistant Professor of Accountancy
University of Illinois

Bhaskar H. Bhave
Senior Manager
Coopers & Lybrand L.L.P.

Introduction

The accounting and financial reporting environment plays a critical role in designing new instruments to manage global currency risk, in implementing new strategies with regard to these products, and in monitoring, controlling, and evaluating the results of using these products. While accounting rule makers have been hard pressed to keep pace with the rapid development of new products, a number of pronouncements covering accounting for forwards, futures, and options exist. However, the authoritative literature represents a somewhat piecemeal, and often internally inconsistent, set of rules on the subject. Accordingly, the Financial Accounting Standards Board (FASB) continues to work on a major project on derivatives, similar financial instruments, and hedging activities, the goal of which is to develop a more comprehensive and consistent framework for accounting for all financial instruments, including derivatives. The first section of this chapter summarizes current and potential future authoritative guidance for accounting for instruments used to manage global currency risk.

Because of the complexity of the accounting issues involved, specifically with regard to the recognition and measurement issues, the FASB decided that an interim step, improved disclosure about financial instruments, was necessary. In this regard, three Statements of Financial Accounting Standards (SFAS)—Nos. 105, 107, and 119—have been issued. While these statements did not alter the existing accounting practices, they did mandate much more extensive disclosure about fair values of, and market and credit risk inherent in, financial instruments in general, and derivatives in particular. Further, in January 1996, the Securities and Exchange Commission (SEC) proposed new rules that will require companies to significantly expand and enhance these risk management disclosures. The second section of this chapter describes current and potential future disclosure rules for instruments exposed to global currency risk.

Finally, companies transacting business in multiple currencies and/or having business operations in numerous countries face additional accounting challenges in reporting those activities in a single currency (e.g., U.S. dollars). The last section of this chapter describes current accounting guidance, which is designed to facilitate the accounting for companies with multiple foreign-currency activities.

Accounting for Hedging Transactions

Accounting Considerations

An important element in evaluating and implementing hedging strategies, in addition to determining their economic impact, is the implications of these transactions on a company's financial position and results of operations.

At present, no one comprehensive authoritative pronouncement exists that addresses accounting for hedging transactions. Accordingly, current practice for a number of financial instruments is quite diverse. In an attempt to establish uniform accounting practices, the Financial Accounting Standards Board (FASB) has initiated a major project on financial instrument and "off-balance-sheet financing" issues, including hedging transactions. At the end of this section, we summarize the latest proposal from the FASB issued in June 1996.

Current Authoritative Pronouncements

Table 1 provides relevant authoritative literature relating to accounting and disclosure for specific transactions that may involve hedging and derivatives.

Table 1   What's the Word on Hedging and Derivatives So Far?

Document	Title	Application
SFAS No. 52	Foreign-Currency Translation	Establishes hedge accounting standards for foreign currency transactions, including forwards and currency swaps.
SFAS No. 80	Accounting for Futures	Establishes accounting and reporting standards for futures contracts.
SFAS No. 104	Statement of Cash Flows—Net Reporting of Certain Cash Receipts and Cash Payments and Classification of Cash Flows from Hedging Transactions	As described in title.
SFAS No. 105	Disclosure of Information About Financial Instruments with Off-Balance-Sheet Risk and Financial Instruments with Concentrations of Credit Risk	Establishes disclosure standards for information on financial instruments with off-balance-sheet exposure and credit risk concentrations.
SFAS No. 107	Disclosures About Fair Value of Financial Instruments	Requires disclosure of fair value of financial instruments.
SFAS No. 115	Accounting for Certain Investments in Debt and Equity Securities	Definition of equity securities includes purchased options.
SFAS No. 119	Disclosure about Derivative Financial Instruments and Fair Value of Financial Instruments	Requires specific disclosures on derivatives, distinguishing between derivatives held for trading purposes and those held for other than trading. Encourages other disclosures on derivatives. Amends certain aspects of SFAS Nos.105 and 107.
FASB Interpretation No. 39	Offsetting of Amounts Related to Certain Contracts	Discusses right of offset for derivative transactions executed with the same counterparty.

Table continues

Table 1   concluded

AICPA Issues Paper No. 86-2	Accounting for Options	Gives nonauthoritative guidance on accounting for options and hedging with options.
EITF Issue No. 84-36	Interest-Rate Swap Transactions	Gives guidance that reflects general practice rather than authoritative rules.
EITF Issue No. 90-17	Hedging Foreign Currency Risk with Purchased Options	As described in title.
EITF Issue No. 91-1	Hedging Intercompany Foreign Currency Risks	As described in title.
EITF Issue No. 91-4 and SEC Comments Thereon	Hedging Foreign Currency Risks with Complex Options and Similar Transactions	As described in title.
EITF Issue No. 95-2	Determination of What Constitutes a Firm Commitment for Foreign Currency Transactions Not Involving a Third Party	As described in title.

Accounting guidance for hedging transactions in specialized industries is also provided by the American Institute of Certified Public Accountants (AICPA) in its Industry Audit Guides.

Because of the evolving nature of generally accepted accounting principles (GAAP) for hedging transactions, and the judgment required to arrive at the appropriate accounting for these transactions, companies may be well served to consult with their accounting advisers on significant hedging transactions.

Hedge Accounting

Although no comprehensive authoritative pronouncement exists that addresses accounting for transactions involving hedges, there is general agreement that hedging transactions are accounted for differently from transactions for other purposes, and that certain criteria must be met to account for a transaction as a hedge.

In practice, whether a transaction qualifies for hedge accounting should be determined on a case-by-case basis. Before the appropriate accounting can be determined, however, the economics and purpose of the transaction must be fully understood.

Accounting for a transaction as a hedge generally means that the gains or losses from the hedge position are recognized in the same period as losses or gains on the hedged item. For example, if unrealized changes in the hedged item are included in income, the changes in the hedge will also be recognized in income as they occur. Alternatively, when the hedged item is an asset carried at lower of cost or market, changes in the hedge should be recorded as an adjustment of the carrying amount of the hedged item. However, the hedge-accounting adjustment cannot result in the asset being carried at an amount in excess of market value.

A deferred gain or loss on the hedge becomes part of the carrying amount of the hedged item that will be recognized when the item being hedged is disposed of or amortized. Similarly, when a transaction is a hedge of a net foreign investment, exchange gains and losses related to the hedging instrument are accumulated in the separate component of equity, thus offsetting the translation loss or gain. Finally, gains and losses on hedges of firm commitments and anticipated transactions are deferred and later included in the measurement of the related transaction. Losses should not be deferred, however, if it is estimated that deferral would lead to recognizing losses in future periods.

Exchange gains and losses on a forward-exchange contract or other foreign-currency transaction should be recorded in income if the transaction does not serve as an effective hedge. Also, income statement recognition rather than deferral of exchange gains and losses would be required on transactions that have been designated as a hedge when

- The hedging transaction remains outstanding beyond the date the foreign-currency commitment is recorded. Any exchange gain or loss that occurs after the date that the transaction is recorded should be recognized in the income statement.

- The amount of the hedging transaction exceeds the amount necessary to hedge the commitment on an after-tax basis. Any gain or loss attributable to the portion of the hedging transaction over the amount that provides a hedge on an after-tax basis should be recognized in the income statement.

- Deferral of losses on the hedging transaction would lead to recognizing losses in a later period (e.g., when deferral of losses may result in carrying inventory or purchase commitments at amounts higher than their net realizable value).

Table 2 summarizes these principles.

The appropriate accounting guidance for hedges of foreign-currency risks depends on the nature of the instruments used. See Figure 1 for an example. Hedges involving forward-exchange contracts or similar instru-

Table 2   Hedge Accounting

Hedged Item	Gains or Losses on Hedging Contract
Monetary asset and monetary liability which are marked to market	Included in income.
Monetary asset carried at lower of cost or market	Deferred and included in income on disposal of the asset.
Net investment	Recorded in the separate component of stockholders' equity.
Firm commitment	Deferred and included in the measurement of the subsequent transaction.
Anticipated transaction	Deferred and included in the measurement of the subsequent transaction.

ments, futures contracts, and swaps for foreign currencies must be accounted for in accordance with SFAS No. 52. Hedges involving purchased options, complex options, or similar instruments must be accounted for in accordance with EITF Issues No. 90-17, 91-1, and 91-4.

Differences between SFAS No. 52 and SFAS No. 80

Much of the complexity regarding the proper accounting for hedging transactions relates to the fact that there are some inconsistencies between SFAS No. 52 and SFAS No. 80. SFAS No. 80 provides hedging criteria for transactions involving nonforeign-currency-futures contracts. The FASB plans to address those differences as part of its financial instruments project. Revised accounting standards are expected for hedges involving foreign-currency transactions, and since these revised standards may integrate some aspects of SFAS No. 80 and its relationship to EITF Issue No. 90-17, we have included a discussion of SFAS No. 80.

Table 3 outlines the important differences between SFAS No. 52 and SFAS No. 80 with regard to hedge accounting.

A major difference between SFAS Nos. 52 and 80 relates to hedge accounting for anticipated transactions. SFAS No. 80 permits hedging of firm commitments as well as anticipated transactions if the significant characteristics and expected terms of the anticipated transaction are identified and it is probable that the anticipated transaction will occur. SFAS No. 52 permits hedging of firm commitments but not anticipated transactions.

An example of an anticipatory hedge is a financial institution that purchases Treasury-note futures contracts to lock in the yield on a Treasury note it expects to purchase in three months when cash becomes available. The institution may be able to designate the futures contracts as a hedge

Figure 1 Hedge-Accounting Criteria

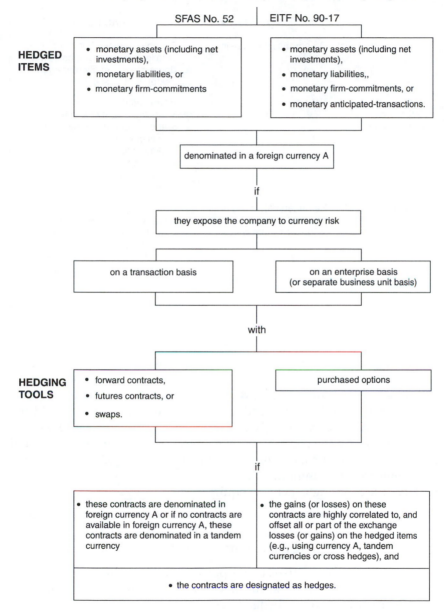

A company whose functional currency is the U.S. dollar may hedge its:

SFAS No. 52 | EITF No. 90-17

HEDGED ITEMS

- monetary assets (including net investments),
- monetary liabilities, or
- monetary firm-commitments

- monetary assets (including net investments),
- monetary liabilities,,
- monetary firm-commitments, or
- monetary anticipated-transactions.

denominated in a foreign currency A

if

they expose the company to currency risk

on a transaction basis | on an enterprise basis (or separate business unit basis)

with

HEDGING TOOLS

- forward contracts,
- futures contracts, or
- swaps.

purchased options

if

- these contracts are denominated in foreign currency A or if no contracts are available in foreign currency A, these contracts are denominated in a tandem currency

- the gains (or losses) on these contracts are highly correlated to, and offset all or part of the exchange losses (or gains) on the hedged items (e.g., using currency A, tandem currencies or cross hedges), and

- the contracts are designated as hedges.

Table 3   Important Differences between SFAS No. 52 and SFAS No. 80

	SFAS No. 52	SFAS No. 80
Assessment of Risk	On a transaction basis.	On an enterprise basis (or on a smaller business unit basis if a decentralized entity manages risk on that basis).
Hedging of Anticipated Transactions	Not permitted.	Permitted if • the significant characteristics and expected terms of the anticipated transactions are identified, and • it is probable that the anticipated transaction will occur.
Cross Hedging	Permitted only if it is not practical or feasible to hedge in the same currency.	Permitted if • there is a clear economic relationship between the future's underlying item and the item being hedged, and • high correlation is probable.

and defer the gains and losses of the future until the Treasury note is purchased (at which time the deferred gain or loss will become part of the carrying value of the Treasury note). However, if that same financial institution entered into a forward-exchange contract to hedge an anticipated borrowing it had arranged in the European market, it would not qualify for hedge accounting (i.e., it could not defer the gains or losses on the forward-exchange contract) because the anticipated borrowing would not be viewed as a firm commitment under SFAS No. 52 (e.g., usually a legally enforceable commitment).

Hedge accounting generally requires

- Risk—Item to be hedged exposes the entity (or for anticipated transactions, the enterprise as a whole or a decentralized operating unit for managing risk) to currency risk.

- Reduced Exposure—Hedge position reduces the exposure (e.g., there is high correlation between the hedge position and changes in market value of the hedged item).

- Designation as a Hedge—Hedge position is designated as a hedge.

Presence of risk. The first requirement concerning exposure to risk means that hedge accounting cannot be applied to situations where there is deemed to be no risk. The purpose of hedging is to reduce risk, so, without risk, hedge accounting is inappropriate. In situations without risk, gains or losses from positions in hedge-type instruments cannot be deferred.

In this regard, SFAS No. 80 describes risk as "the sensitivity of an enterprise's income for one or more future periods to changes in market prices or yields of existing assets, liabilities, firm commitments, or anticipated transactions." SFAS No. 80 recognizes that the specific circumstances that create risk can and do vary significantly from company to company. The hedge-recognition criteria for accounting purposes depend on whether the risk ultimately affects the enterprise's income.

As previously mentioned, SFAS No. 52 defines foreign-currency transactions as transactions whose terms are denominated in a currency other than the entity's functional currency. Typically, foreign-currency transactions result in receivable or payable balances, and expose companies to foreign-currency risk because, until settlement, the ultimate amount of functional currency the company will receive or pay remains uncertain.

However, from an economic point of view, not all foreign-currency transactions will expose an enterprise to exchange-rate risk. For instance, purchases (payables) denominated in a foreign currency will expose a U.S. enterprise to foreign-currency risk. However, assume that the enterprise has sales (receivables) of approximately the same amount and denominated in the same foreign currency. If the cash flows from the receivables and payables occur at approximately the same time, the receivables will act as a natural hedge against the foreign-currency risk from the payables.

Nonmonetary assets (e.g., fixed assets, inventories, nonmarketable equity securities) and nonmonetary liabilities (e.g., deferred income) do not directly expose companies to currency risk and may be hedged only as part of a net investment.

For instance, assume a foreign subsidiary purchases equipment in a transaction denominated in a currency other than its functional currency. If the subsidiary's functional currency weakens versus the foreign currency, the company will record a transaction loss on the foreign-currency-denominated payable. This loss will then be translated into the reporting currency (e.g., U.S. dollar) in the U.S. parent company's consolidated financial statements. Therefore, the subsidiary may hedge the currency risk associated with the foreign-currency-denominated payable. However, the equipment does not per se expose the subsidiary to currency risk, because its functional currency equivalent value is definitely established and recorded at the date of purchase.

On the other hand, exchange-rate changes between the subsidiary's functional currency and the U.S. dollar have an indirect effect on the net investment that may be realized by the U.S. parent company upon sale or liquidation of the subsidiary. If the U.S. dollar strengthens versus the subsidiary's functional currency, the dollar equivalent of the net investment decreases. As long as the parent company does not sell or liquidate the subsidiary, the potential exchange loss remains uncertain. For that reason, translation losses are reported separately in equity rather than net income. However, this does not mean that the U.S. parent company cannot hedge that risk. Indeed, SFAS No. 52 acknowledges that companies are exposed to exchange risk to the extent of their net investments in foreign operations, and specifically allows them to hedge this risk.

SFAS No. 80, dealing with nonforeign-currency-futures contracts, and the consensus of the EITF Issue No. 90-17, dealing with purchased currency options used to hedge anticipated transactions, differ from SFAS No. 52 as to how risk should be assessed. SFAS No. 80 and the EITF Issue No. 90-17 generally require that for a hedging instrument to be accounted for as a hedge, a risk condition must be present on an enterprise perspective. Determining whether an enterprise's income is at risk requires evaluating whether a potential risk condition at one location or operating center is mitigated by conditions at another location or operating center (i.e., natural hedges). For example, a parent company with several subsidiaries should apply SFAS No. 80, using a total enterprise perspective if relevant information to assess risk on that basis is available.

In contrast, SFAS No. 52 permits hedge accounting based on assessing risk on a specific-transaction basis. Therefore, a U.S. parent may hedge a foreign-currency commitment with a forward-exchange contract even though a foreign subsidiary whose functional currency is the U.S. dollar may have a foreign-currency balance equal and opposite to the commitment exposure of the parent.

Reduced exposure. The second criterion for hedge accounting concerns the correlation between the hedge position and changes in market value of the hedged item. The probability of high correlation is to be evaluated both at the inception of the hedge and throughout the hedge period. This means that changes in the market value of the hedging instrument must track the changes in the market value of the hedged item. Demonstrating the effectiveness of a hedge is essential because it is the basis for entering into the hedge transaction in the first place (i.e., that the gain or loss on the hedged item will be offset by the loss or gain on the hedging instrument). When determining whether high correlation is likely, an enterprise is required to consider such factors as actual correlation during relevant past periods and variations in correlation that could be expected.

While companies may use a variety of approaches to evaluate expected future correlation, regression analysis is the statistical method most commonly used to measure this relationship. Regression analysis techniques examine historical data relevant to each variable and calculate the expected value of one variable based on the value of the other. The result is a measurement of the expected sensitivity of the movement in one variable to movement in another variable (referred to as the correlation coefficient). Once the correlation coefficient has been calculated, statistical analysis must be used to verify its strength, since knowing the strength of this coefficient is critical to a successful hedging program.

The strength of the correlation coefficient is indicated by the R-square statistic. An R-square statistic of 1 (its maximum value) means that 100 percent of a change in one variable can be explained by a change in the other variable. For example, if a 1 percent change in the value of item A triggers a 0.5 percent change in the value of item B, and there is an R-square statistic of 0.90, then there is a 90 percent assurance that if the value of item A moves 1 percent, the value of item B will move 0.5 percent. The price movements would then be said to be highly correlated. In this situation, selling futures contracts on item B equal to two times the value of hedged item A will be highly effective in offsetting the effects of price changes on item A.

The assessment of correlation requires judgments that must be made on a case-by-case basis. Although measurement and analysis of correlation is an evolving process, and it is difficult to establish precise guidelines, a hedging instrument that is 80 percent or more correlated with the hedged item (i.e., that has an R-square statistic of 0.80) is generally considered to meet the test of "high correlation."

Indirectly related to the criterion regarding correlation is another difference between SFAS No. 80 and SFAS No. 52. Cross-hedging is a strategy where the hedging instrument's underlying item is different from the item being hedged.

- SFAS No. 80 permits cross-hedging as long as the high correlation requirement is met and a clear economic relationship exists between the item underlying the futures contract and the item being hedged.

- SFAS No. 52 permits cross-hedging only when it is not "practical or feasible" to hedge in the same currency. For example, even if a company could demonstrate that it was economically hedged by entering into a forward-exchange contract for Australian dollars to hedge its British-pound-denominated debt, SFAS No. 52 does not permit hedge accounting for the forward-exchange contract because British-pound forward-exchange contracts are available. The phrase "practical or feasible" refers to the availability of a hedging instrument in the exposed currency, not whether it is less expensive to hedge in a tandem currency.

As a result, hedge accounting for tandem currency hedges is generally permitted when they involve purchased options but not when the hedging instrument is a forward or a futures contract or a currency swap.

Designation as hedge. The third criterion for hedge accounting is the designation of the position by the entity entering into the transaction as a hedge. The designation of a transaction as a hedge must occur before the accounting begins. In other words, it is not appropriate to wait until it is determined that a loss has occurred in a position and then at that time decide to defer the loss.

It is the responsibility of management to document the designation of a transaction as a hedge. Typically, this consists of formal minutes of the board of directors or a special committee responsible for such matters. However, where a company regularly enters into numerous hedging transactions, clear identification in the accounting records of transactions as hedges or as speculative may suffice.

As a result of the above criteria, current accounting standards do not permit hedge accounting for hedging strategic risk and for hedging on a portfolio basis. Also, as discussed below in EITF Issue No. 90-17, hedge accounting is not permitted for hedging future net income of a foreign subsidiary.

The lack of authoritative literature and the differences between SFAS No. 52 and SFAS No. 80 make it difficult to apply specific criteria to many hedging transactions. Companies entering into foreign-currency transactions involving hedging instruments, particularly those not specifically covered by SFAS No. 52 or EITF Issue No. 90-17 (discussed below), should consult with their accounting advisers to determine the appropriate accounting.

Purchased Foreign-Currency Options

EITF Issue No. 90-17 permits hedge accounting for purchased foreign-currency options with little or no intrinsic value used to hedge anticipated transactions, provided that the conditions in SFAS No. 80 are met.

In evaluating these conditions, SFAS No. 52 establishes the nature of foreign-currency risk that may be hedged for accounting purposes—that is, risk associated with transactions and commitments in currencies other than the transacting entity's functional currency. Therefore, exposure to foreign-currency risk from existing assets or liabilities, net investments, and firm commitments should be evaluated on a transaction basis. In contrast, EITF Issue No. 90-17 requires that the exposure to foreign-currency risk from anticipated transactions be evaluated on an "enterprise basis," as defined in paragraph 4(a) of SFAS No. 80.

For a purchased option to qualify for hedge accounting, it must be probable that a high correlation will exist between the currency underlying the option contract and the currency in which the anticipated transaction is denominated. This correlation must exist at the time that the option is designated as a hedge and throughout the hedge period or the life of the option contract, if shorter. EITF Issue 90-17 also permits hedge accounting using purchased options in highly correlated tandem currencies.

Further, for a purchased option to qualify for hedge accounting, the significant characteristics and expected terms of the anticipated transaction must be identified, and it must be probable that the anticipated transaction will occur. Judgment will be required to determine whether these conditions are met and whether the likelihood of meeting the criteria diminishes the further into the future the anticipated transaction is expected to occur.

The EITF discussed the propriety of hedge accounting in specific situations using purchased foreign-currency options with little or no intrinsic value. One situation addresses an enterprise that estimated its minimum probable foreign sales for the next several years and wanted to reduce its exposure to the related foreign-exchange risk. In this case, the propriety of hedge accounting depends on whether the transactions meets the SFAS No. 80 anticipated transaction criteria. The EITF observed that the likelihood of meeting the criteria diminishes the further into the future the anticipated transaction is expected to occur.

Another situation addressed by the EITF is hedging by a U.S. parent of the net income of its foreign subsidiary. The foreign subsidiary generates revenues and incurs costs denominated in its functional currency. In this case, hedge accounting would not be appropriate because

- the parent would not have foreign-currency risk, as defined in SFAS No. 52, for its subsidiary's transactions are denominated in the subsidiary's functional currency, and

- future net income does not qualify as an anticipated transaction because it is the net result of many transactions and accounting allocations.

Hedge accounting would also not be appropriate when foreign-currency options are purchased as a "strategic" or "competitive" hedge, where the gains on the options are intended to offset lost operating profits from increased competitive pressure associated with exchange-rate changes that benefit competitors. To qualify for hedge accounting, EITF Issue 90-17 requires the options to be designated as a hedge of an existing asset (including a net investment in a foreign entity), an existing liability, a firm foreign-currency commitment, or an anticipated foreign-currency transaction.

Complex and Combination Options

EITF Issue No. 91-4, *Hedging Foreign Currency Risks with Complex Options and Similar Transactions,* addresses the use of hedge accounting for those option transactions that were specifically excluded from EITF Issue No. 90-17, such as deep-in-the-money purchased options, written options, options purchased and written as a unit (combination options), and similar transactions, including synthetic forwards, range forwards, and participating forwards. EITF Issue No. 90-17 addressed only foreign-currency options with little or no intrinsic value. EITF Issue No. 91-4 is limited to combinations that are established as contemplated integral transactions in which the components are entered into at or about the same time, are designated as a unit, and have the same expiration date.

At the March 19, 1992 EITF meeting, the chief accountant of the SEC indicated that the SEC will object to the deferral of gains and losses arising from complex options and other similar transactions with respect to anticipated transactions. In addition, the chief accountant noted that the SEC's staff will object to deferral of losses with respect to written options because they believe that written options increase, rather than reduce, risk. The SEC's staff will not, however, object to deferral of gains on purchased options having little or no intrinsic value, as addressed in EITF Issue No. 90-17.

Intercompany Foreign-Currency Risk

Economically, intercompany transactions denominated in foreign currencies do not expose an enterprise to currency risk. This is because the related cash flows remain within the enterprise. For instance, assume a U.S. enterprise has two subsidiaries: A and B. A's functional currency is the U.S. dollar and B's functional currency is a foreign currency (FC). A purchases goods from B for FC100 when the exchange rate is FC1.00 = U.S.$1.00. If, at settlement date, the exchange rate is FC1.00 = U.S.$2.00, A needs to disburse U.S.$200 to buy FC100 on the spot market. A incurs a loss of U.S.$100. On the other hand, the value of the U.S. parent's net investment in B increases by U.S.$100 because the cash B received is now worth U.S.$200 (rather than U.S.$100). Therefore, on an enterprise basis, there is no economic gain or loss.

However, EITF Issue No. 91-1 provides that transactions or commitments among members of a consolidated group with different functional currencies can present foreign-currency risk that may be hedged for accounting purposes. This is consistent with the functional-currency approach in SFAS No. 52.

The appropriate accounting guidance depends on the type of hedging instrument used. The provisions of SFAS No. 52 must be applied to forward-exchange contracts, foreign-currency futures, and agreements that are essentially the same as forward-exchange contracts. When hedging foreign-currency commitments, SFAS No. 52 requires that both of the following conditions exist:

- The foreign-currency transaction must be designated as, and effective as, a hedge of a foreign-currency commitment.

- The foreign-currency commitment must be firm.

In connection with the second condition, an intercompany foreign-currency commitment may be considered firm if there is a firm commitment to a third party obligating the affiliates to comply with the terms of the intercompany agreement.

In the event that a third-party commitment is not present, a firm commitment exists only if the agreement is legally enforceable and performance is probable because of sufficiently large disincentives for nonperformance. Examples of disincentives for nonperformance include minority interests, existing laws or regulations, and fiduciary responsibilities that result in significant economic penalties to the consolidated entity for nonperformance. To determine whether disincentives for nonperformance are sufficiently large, the specific facts and circumstances surrounding each transaction must be assessed. The EITF reached a consensus in Issue 95-2 that a significant economic penalty to the consolidated entity exists only when a penalty imposed by an unrelated party provides a sufficiently large disincentive for nonperformance such that performance under the intercompany foreign-currency commitment is probable, even if corresponding anticipated transactions do not occur.

When hedging intercompany transactions with purchased options, the provisions set forth in EITF Issue No. 90-17 must be applied.

Balance Sheet Presentation
SFAS No. 52 does not allow companies to net receivables or payables related to hedging tools against the liabilities or assets being hedged, unless there is a legal right of set-off.

Classification of Cash Flows from Hedging Transactions
In general, each cash receipt or payment is to be classified in the statement of cash flows according to its nature, without regard to whether it stems from an item intended as a hedge of another item. For example, the proceeds of a borrowing are a financing cash inflow even though the debt is intended as a hedge of an investment. Similarly, the purchase or sale of a futures contract is an investing activity even though the contract is intended to hedge a firm commitment to purchase inventory.

Cash flows from futures contracts, forward contracts, option contracts, or swap contracts that are accounted for as hedges of identifiable transactions or events including anticipatory hedges, may be classified in the same category as the cash flows from the items being hedged, provided that the accounting policy is disclosed. If, for any reason, hedge accounting for an instrument that hedges an identifiable transaction or event is discontinued, then any cash flows subsequent to the date of discontinuance shall be classified consistent with the nature of the hedging instrument.

Application of Hedge Accounting to Basic Hedging Tools
The following discusses how hedge-accounting concepts apply to the basic hedging tools: forwards, futures, swaps, and options.

Forward-Exchange Contracts A forward-exchange contract is an agreement to exchange currencies at a specified future date and rate, and is a foreign-currency transaction.

Gains and Losses on Forward-Exchange Contracts. Gains and losses on a forward-exchange contract are included in the determination of net income unless it is designated and effective as an economic hedge of net investment or of an identifiable foreign-currency commitment.

If gains and losses on forward contracts are deferred, they are reported as (1) separate component of equity if it hedges a net investment or a long-term intercompany transaction, or (2) as part of the transaction if it relates to a foreign-currency commitment. Losses are not deferred if it is estimated that deferral would lead to recording losses in future periods.

Premium or discount. SFAS No. 52 requires the premium or discount on a forward contract (i.e., the difference between the contract rate of the forward contract and the exchange rate at inception of the forward contract, multiplied by the FC face amount of the forward contract) to be amortized over the life of the forward contract. Since the amortization method is not specified in SFAS No. 52, the straight-line or the effective-interest method, in general, is used. However, in our example, the preferable method is the effective-interest method, because it is used to amortize the discount on the note.

If the forward contract was designated as a hedge of a net investment, the premium or discount may be included in the separate component of equity, rather than be amortized to income over the life of the forward contract.

Further, SFAS No. 52 is silent as to the specific expense or income item in which the premium or discount should be included. Given the financing nature of the hypothetical transaction, we believe that it is appropriate to reflect it as an adjustment to interest expense.

Foreign-Currency-Futures Contracts and Currency Swaps As discussed earlier, SFAS No. 52 establishes GAAP for foreign-currency-futures contracts and currency swaps. Accounting for such instruments would be similar to that previously discussed for forward-exchange contracts.

Foreign-Currency Options As described earlier, nonauthoritative guidance on accounting for options is provided by AICPA Issues Paper No. 86-2, dated March 6, 1986. Also, EITF Issues No. 90-17 and 91-4 address the

Table 4   Foreign-Currency Options

Hedged Item	Accounting for Intrinsic and Time Value
Monetary Position	Joint Accounting
Firm Foreign-Currency Commitment (or an anticipated transaction)	Separate Accounting Allowed
Net Foreign Investment	Separate Accounting Allowed

accounting for purchased options that are intended to hedge foreign-currency risk.

In applying hedge accounting to foreign-currency options, it may be necessary to separately account for the time value and intrinsic value components of option premiums paid by the holder. Table 4 indicates that separate or joint accounting of these two items depends on whether a foreign-currency option hedges a monetary position, a firm foreign-currency commitment, or a net foreign investment.

Time- and intrinsic-value components are accounted for jointly for foreign-currency options that hedge foreign-currency monetary positions. Changes in the option's market value are recognized as a gain or loss in the period of the change.

Separate accounting is allowed, but not required, for the time-value component of a purchased foreign-currency option that hedges a firm foreign-currency commitment (or an anticipated transaction). If the time value is accounted for separately, the amortization of time value is included in the determination of net income in the period of change, and changes in intrinsic value are deferred until the commitment is recorded. If the time value is accounted for jointly with the intrinsic value, market-value gains or losses are deferred and included in the measurement of the transaction resulting from the commitment.

Foreign-currency options hedging a net foreign investment are accounted for in the same manner as foreign-currency options that hedge a firm foreign-currency commitment, except that deferred gains or losses are included in the separate component of stockholders' equity.

FASB's Proposal on Accounting for Derivatives and Hedging Transactions

In June 1996, the FASB issued its long-awaited proposal on accounting for derivatives and hedging transactions. Comments are due by October 15,

1996, and a final standard is expected in April 1997 to be effective for calendar year 1998. The following is a summary of the proposal.

The proposed Statement would standardize the accounting for derivative financial instruments and certain other financial instruments that have similar characteristics by requiring that an entity measure those instruments at fair value and recognize them as assets or liabilities in the statement of financial position. If certain conditions are met, an entity may elect to designate a derivative financial instrument or other similar financial instrument as (1) a hedge of the fair value exposure of an asset or liability, including a firm commitment (referred to as a fair value hedge), (2) a hedge of the cash flow exposure of a forecasted transaction (referred to as a cash flow hedge), or (3) a hedge of the foreign-currency exposure of a net investment in a foreign operation.

In accordance with the proposed Statement, changes in fair value of the derivative financial instruments would be recognized in earnings in the period of change unless a derivative is designated as a hedge of

- A forecasted transaction (changes in fair value would be recorded in comprehensive income outside of earnings), or

- A net investment in a foreign entity (the foreign-currency transaction gain or loss component of the change in fair value would be recorded in comprehensive income outside of earnings as part of the cumulative translation adjustment).

An entity must specifically identify the asset, liability, or firm commitment being hedged or the proportion thereof. The "proportion" of the hedged item refers to its percentage, not the period of time (e.g., 40 percent of a five-year loan, not 100 percent of the loan to be hedged for the first two years). The change in the fair value of the hedged item would be recognized in earnings in the period of change (with a corresponding adjustment of the carrying amount or "basis" of the hedged item) *only to the extent* that cumulative changes in the fair value of the hedging instrument from the inception of the hedge offset the cumulative changes in the fair value of the hedged item from the inception of the hedge. The effect of that accounting is to adjust the basis of the hedged item by the amount of the gain or loss on the hedging derivative to the extent that those gains or losses offset losses or gains experienced on the hedged item. In all cases, an asset that has been designated as being hedged remains subject to any impairment-assessment provisions applicable to that type of asset.

In accordance with the proposed Statement, changes in the fair value of the derivative designated as a hedge of a forecasted transaction would be reported as a component of comprehensive income outside of earnings and would be recognized in earnings on the date initially identified as that on which the forecasted transaction was expected to occur.

The exposure draft specifies criteria to qualify for hedge accounting. The impact of the proposal on foreign-currency issues is summarized below.

Firm commitments with a financial and a nonfinancial component. An entity may have a firm commitment to purchase a nonfinancial asset (e.g., inventory or equipment) from a foreign manufacturer. Such a firm commitment involves two components: (1) a nonfinancial component (i.e., the right to receive a nonfinancial asset), and (2) a financial component (i.e., the obligation to pay foreign currency). Consistent with current practice, under the proposal, a derivative such as a forward-exchange contract can be designated as a hedge of the financial component of the firm commitment without affecting the accounting for the nonfinancial component. Therefore, only the change in the fair value of the financial component would be reported in earnings to the extent of offsetting changes in fair value of the hedging instrument. *The proposal essentially retains the current practice in this area, although some entities do not currently record the forward-exchange contract on the balance sheet.* The following example from the FASB exposure draft illustrates the proposed accounting.

On January 1, 19X6, U.S. Company enters into a firm commitment to buy a German machine on May 31, 19X6, for DM200 when the exchange rate is $1 = DM1. Also on January 1, 19X6, U.S. Company enters into a forward contract to purchase deutsche mark (DM)200 on May 31, 19X6, at the January 1, 19X6, exchange rate in order to "lock-in" the U.S. dollar amount that U.S. Company will pay on May 31, 19X6. On April 30, 19X6, the exchange rate changes to $1 = DM1.5 and remains at that rate until the maturity of the forward contract. On May 31, 19X6, U.S. Company pays for the machine and settles the forward contract for the stated amount of DM.

If this transaction is not designated as a hedge, U.S. Company would recognize changes in the fair value of the forward contract in earnings as they occur and would not recognize the firm commitment. However, in this example, on January 1, 19X6, U.S. Company separates the firm commitment into its financial instrument and nonfinancial asset components, that is, an obligation to pay DM and a right to receive a machine. It then designates the forward contract as a hedge of the obligation to pay DM (foreign-currency payable).

On January 1, 19X6, the entity determines the values for the foreign-currency payable and the right to receive the machine. At the inception of the firm commitment, the right and the payable are equivalent and net to zero. The separate amounts are not reported in the financial statements, but are maintained in a memorandum account. The amount reported in the statement of financial position is the net amount, or zero at January 1, 19X6.

On April 30, 19X6, exchange rates move to $1 = DM1.5, so that the fair value of the payable for the machine in U.S. dollars is only $133. This movement in rates also causes U.S. Company to have a $67 dollar decline in the fair value of the forward contract. The following entries would be recorded:

Firm commitment	67	
Gain on foreign-currency payable		67[1]

(To adjust value of financial instrument component of firm commitment)

Loss on forward contract	67	
Forward contract (settlement payable)		67

(To mark to market the forward contract)

For display purposes, the financial component ($133 foreign-currency payable) and the nonfinancial component ($200 right to receive the machine) of the hedged firm commitment are reported net in the statement of financial position. At April 30, 19X6, the statement of financial position and income statement would be as follows:

STATEMENT OF FINANCIAL POSITION:

Assets	Liabilities
Firm commitment $ 67	Forward contract payable $ 67

INCOME STATEMENT:

Gain on foreign-currency payable	($67)
Loss on forward contract	67
Net income effect	$ 0

On May 31, 19X6, the machine is delivered with rates still at $1 = DM1.5. The following entries would be recorded:

Fixed assets	200	
Forward contract (settlement payable)	67	
Cash		200
Firm commitment		67

Firm commitments without a nonfinancial component. An asset acquired under a hedged foreign-currency commitment that does not involve both a financial instrument and a nonfinancial asset or liability would be recorded at its fair value at the date of acquisition. An example would be a commitment to buy a foreign-currency-denominated debt or equity security. The firm commitment would be carried at fair value with changes recognized currently in earnings. The gains or losses on the hedging instrument for such firm commitments also would be recorded currently in earnings.

Hedges of a net investment. FASB Statement 52 would continue to allow entities to hedge their net investment in foreign enterprises. Under FASB Statement 52, foreign-currency transaction gain or loss on the instrument that hedges a net investment is reported in the same manner as translation adjustments.

Intercompany transactions. FASB Statement 52's provisions with respect to long-term and short-term intercompany transactions would continue to apply. Firm commitments and forecasted transactions between members of the consolidated group would not qualify for hedge accounting, except for certain foreign-currency exposures in intercompany transactions between subsidiaries that use different functional currencies. The Board agreed that hedge accounting would be permitted for situations similar to that described in the following example. A German entity incurs costs in deutsche marks (DM) to develop a product. The German entity sells this product to its French marketing affiliate, which has the French franc as its functional currency. The French marketing affiliate then sells the product denominated in French francs to other French companies. In this example, the consolidated entity would be exposed to foreign-currency risk (costs incurred in German DM and sales denominated in French francs) and, as such, would be permitted to apply hedge accounting for derivatives acquired for these exposures.

Cross-hedging. Use of a derivative with a different underlying basis from the hedged item (cross-hedging) as a hedging instrument would be permitted if the use of that instrument is justified. Under the proposal, cost efficiency is a sufficient justification. Currently, SFAS 52 permits tandem currency hedging *only* if it is not practical or feasible to hedge in the same currency; it does not permit cross-hedging for cost-efficiency reasons. SFAS 80 permits cross-hedging only if high correlation exists. The proposal, therefore, appears to be more flexible than current literature.

Cash instruments as hedging instruments. Cash instruments cannot be designated as hedging instruments *except* that entities would be permitted (as under current rules) to designate cash instruments denominated in a foreign currency as hedges of foreign-currency exposures of their firm commitments and as hedges of net investments in foreign enterprises. Consistent with current practice, however, cash instruments would *not* be permitted as hedges of forecasted foreign-currency transactions.

Disclosure Requirements Related to Hedging Activities and Market and Credit Risk

Table 1 provides a summary of relevant authoritative literature addressing disclosures related to hedging activities and reporting of the market risk and credit risk inherent in instruments subject to global currency risk. These current disclosure requirements are covered by a number of pronouncements including FASB Statements Nos. 52, 105, 107, and 119. The SEC recently has proposed potential future disclosure requirements relating to

market-risk-sensitive instruments. These current and potential future disclosure requirements are described in this section.

SFAS-No.-52-Related Disclosure Requirements

SFAS No. 52 requires disclosure of aggregate gains and losses from foreign-
currency transactions, including forwards and swaps. The EITF reached a
consensus in Issue No. 91-4 that, when using currency options, option
combinations, and similar instruments to hedge, the following should be
disclosed in the notes to the financial statements:

- The method of accounting for those instruments, including a description of the events or transactions that result in recognition in
  income of changes in value.

- The nature of the anticipated transactions for which there is no firm
  commitment that are hedged by those instruments.

- The maximum number of years over which anticipated, but not
  firmly committed, foreign currency transactions are hedged by
  those instruments.

- The combined realized and unrealized net gain or loss deferred as
  of each balance-sheet date on those instruments that are designated
  as hedges of anticipated transactions for which there is no firm
  commitment.

Judgment is required to determine the nature and extent of these
disclosures. Companies should review their hedging transactions and
discuss with their accounting advisers the effect, if any, the specific hedging activities may have on their present and future financial-statement
disclosures.

SFAS No. 105 Disclosure Requirements

SFAS No. 105, *Disclosure of Information about Financial Instruments with
Off-Balance-Sheet Risk and Financial Instruments with Concentrations of Credit
Risk,* applies to the four basic hedging tools discussed in the chapter. It
indicates that, while only the issuers (or writers) of options have off-balance-sheet risk, both parties to futures, forwards, or swaps have off-balance-sheet risk. A financial instrument has off-balance-sheet risk if it has
risk of accounting loss to the entity that may exceed the amount recognized
as an asset, if any, or if the ultimate obligation may exceed the amount that
is recognized as a liability on the balance sheet.

SFAS No. 105 requires the following disclosures for each class of
financial instruments with off-balance-sheet credit or market risk:

- The face or contract amount (or notional principle amount for swaps).

- The nature and terms of the instruments, including a discussion of the (1) credit and market risks, (2) cash requirements, and (3) accounting policies relating to those instruments.

- The amount of potential accounting loss (i.e., credit risk) if any other party to a financial instrument failed completely to perform according to the terms of the contract, and the collateral or other security, if any, proved to be of no value.

- The entity's policy of requiring collateral or other security to support financial instruments, a brief description of the collateral of other security supporting those financial instruments, access to such collateral, and related information.

"Credit risk" is defined as the possibility that a loss may occur from the failure of another party to perform according to the terms of a contract. "Market risk" is defined as the possibility that future changes in market prices may make a financial instrument less valuable or more onerous. SFAS No. 105 indicates that currency swaps, financial futures and forward contracts, and put (call) options on foreign currency (where premium is paid up front) *do not* have off-balance-sheet *credit risk* but *do* have off-balance-sheet *market risk*.

In addition, SFAS No. 105 contains requirements directed specifically to (1) financial instruments with off-balance-sheet credit risk and (2) significant concentrations of credit risk for financial instruments that are on or off the balance sheet. Companies that enter into significant hedging transactions need to review the disclosure requirements of SFAS No. 105, since most of the basic hedging tools are financial instruments with off-balance-sheet risks.

SFAS No. 107 Disclosure Requirements

SFAS No. 107, *Disclosures about Fair Value of Financial Instruments,* applies to *all* financial instruments, both on and off the balance sheet.[2] Therefore, all currency swaps, options, and foreign-exchange contracts, and similar hedging instruments are included in the scope of this Statement.

SFAS No. 107 requires all entities to disclose the fair value of all financial instruments for which it is practicable to estimate the fair value. It also requires disclosure of the methods and significant assumptions used to estimate the fair values. "Practicable" means the ability to estimate fair value without incurring excessive costs. However, the exercise of judgment is required in determining whether costs are excessive.

If it is not practicable to estimate fair value of a financial instrument or a class of financial instruments, SFAS No. 107 requires the following disclosures:

- Information pertinent to estimating the fair value, such as the carrying amount, the effective interest rate, and maturity.

- The reasons why it is not practicable to estimate fair values, or, in other words, why the estimation of values would result in excessive costs.

SFAS No. 107 requires that quoted market prices, if available, should be used for disclosures of fair values. If quoted market prices are not available, management's best estimate of fair value should be used. Therefore, fair values of financial instruments are determined by using either external sources or internal estimates. The former generally provides more objective and reliable fair values than the latter. However, when prices from external sources are not readily available or may be too costly to obtain, fair values can be estimated internally.

External Sources

There are five major categories of external sources.

Public exchange markets. Many foreign-currency futures and options trade in public exchange markets such as the Chicago Board of Trade or the London Stock Exchange. For those instruments, fair value is determined by reference to the last trade price (i.e., the closing price). For purposes of complying with SFAS No. 107, when quoted prices are used to compute fair values there should be no adjustment for thin markets.

Dealer market. In a dealer market, dealers stand ready to trade—either buy or sell—for their own account. Options and forward-exchange contract are examples of financial instruments traded in dealer markets. The bid and asked prices in these markets are used to estimate fair values. The last bid price (i.e., an offer to buy) is used to estimate fair value of an asset, while the last asking price (i.e., an offer to sell) is used to estimate fair value of a liability.

Quotation services. Quotation services, which gather quotes from dealers and report them to other dealers and investors, also can be used. Unlike dealers, quotation services do not hold themselves out as ready to trade at a given price. Nowadays, publishing prices electronically is very common. Some of the prominent electronic quotation services include Reuters, Telerate, and Bloomberg.

Pricing services. A fourth source for quotes is the pricing services such as Standard & Poor's, TREPPS, J. J. Kenny, and Interactive Data Services. Like quotation services, these services do not hold themselves out as ready to trade at a given price. Rather, they report their assessment of the price at which a given instrument is likely to trade. They generally price instruments that are widely held but not otherwise reported in the external sources described above. Their computations are not performed for specific investors but are generally available to any subscriber. Typically, pricing services will provide a brief description of the nature of their model and how they price the securities.

Valuation specialists/appraisers. These specialists, such as Coopers & Lybrand, provide customized valuation services that cover the entire spectrum of financial instruments. They use a variety of sources, apply different techniques, and exercise professional judgment in reaching a valuation conclusion.

Often, a specialist may be the only external source available for valuing certain currency swaps, options, and forward-exchange contracts where there is no active market. Their services are directed to specific investors and may include models or techniques developed for specific instruments.

Internal Estimates

Some instruments may be bought and sold only in principal-to-principal or brokered markets. In these situations, external sources for fair value may not be readily available or may be too costly, so companies may have to estimate fair value. Under such circumstances, it may still be prudent to retain a valuation specialist to act as an advisor as a means of ensuring that appropriate internal estimation techniques are being applied.

Three techniques for internally estimating fair values are common.

Market comparables (matrix pricing). This technique uses quoted prices of similar instruments to estimate the fair value of a nonquoted instrument.

Another market-comparable technique to estimating the fair of financial instruments is obtaining information about recent sales of similar instruments in either brokered or principal-to-principal markets.

Present value of expected cash flows. For some forward-exchange contracts, fair value may have to be estimated by determining the present value of expected cash flows. Judgment is required in determining both the expected cash flows and the discount rate to be used to compute their present value. The impact of the current creditworthiness of the counterparty should be considered by revising either the estimated future cash flows or the discount rate. This technique is inherently subjective and may be costly to apply. However, its use may be necessary if no external sources or other less expensive and reliable internal estimation techniques are available.

Option-pricing models. An option-pricing model uses mathematical formulas (and sometimes complex computer programs) to estimate option value. The factors affecting option value include the price of the underlying item, the strike price, the expiration date, the risk-free interest rate for the option period, and the underlying-currency price volatility. Options can be a stand-along type of financial instrument or can be embedded into another financial instrument, for example, a callable debt security.

External price quotes may be available for some currency options in exchange or OTC markets. If not, an option-pricing model can be used to estimate fair value. Some of these models can be complex in nature and, as a result, companies may not have the necessary resources or capabilities in-house. In such cases, they may need to consult with valuation specialists/appraisers to assist in the estimation process.

Two well-known valuation models are Black and Scholes; and Cox, Ross, and Rubinstein. These theoretical models, which derive a price based on the various factors enumerated above, including the price volatility of the underlying currency, were developed to value options on equity securities and need to be modified when applied to currency options.

SFAS No. 119 Disclosure Requirements

The continued tremendous growth in the use of derivatives by entities of all types led during 1993 and 1994 to widespread calls to further improve financial statement disclosures. In July 1993, the Group of Thirty, an international association of bankers and former government officials chaired by Paul Volcker, published a study entitled *Derivatives: Practices and Principles,* containing recommendations for the management of derivatives activity, including the need for improved and broader disclosures. Furthermore, in the wake of numerous highly publicized cases of significant losses reported by users of derivatives, the business press, financial analysts, members of Congress, and various regulators—such as the Federal Reserve, the Comptroller of the Currency, the GAO, and the SEC—all expressed concerns regarding the risks associated with derivatives and with the perceived lack of adequate disclosures by companies on their use. Essentially, there was a consensus that the disclosures under Statements 105 and 107 often are ambiguous and did not clearly present the extent of an entity's involvement with derivatives, its sensitivity to market risks (including global currency risk), and the extent and effect of its hedging policies.

Against this backdrop, the FASB in December 1993 undertook a "rapid response" project to improve derivatives disclosures. This project resulted in the issuance, in October 1994, of a new standard, Statement No. 119, *Disclosures about Derivative Financial Instruments and Fair Value of Financial Instruments.*

Statement 119 requires

- All entities to disclose amounts, nature, and terms of derivative financial instruments not subject to Statement 105 (that is, without off-balance-sheet risk of accounting loss).

- All entities to distinguish between financial instruments held or issued for the purpose of trading (including dealing and other trading activities measured at fair value with gains and losses recognized in earnings) and financial instruments held or issued for other purposes in certain disclosures required by Statements 105, 107, and 119.

- Entities that hold or issue derivative financial instruments for trading purposes to disclose the average fair values and net trading gains or losses during the period.

- Entities that hold or issue derivative financial instruments for purposes other than trading to disclose information about those purposes, about how the instruments are reported in financial statements, and, if the purpose is hedging anticipated transactions, about the anticipated transactions, the classes of derivative financial instruments used to hedge those transactions, the amounts of hedging gains or losses deferred, and the recognition of the deferred gains or losses in earnings.

Statement 119 also encourages, but does not require, all entities to disclose quantitative information about market risks of derivative financial instruments and to disclose such information in a manner that is consistent with the way the entity manages or adjusts risks. Examples of these encouraged disclosures include the value-at-risk and sensitivity-analysis measures, discussed previously in this book.

Statement 119 also amends

- Statement 105 to permit the disclosure to be disaggregated by class of financial instrument, business activity, risk, or other category that is consistent with the management of those instruments.

- Statement 107 to require, together with the related carrying amounts in the body of the financial statements, a single note, or a summary table in a form that makes it clear whether the amounts represent assets or liabilities.

SEC's Proposed Disclosures about Market-Risk-Sensitive Instruments

During 1994 and 1995, the SEC staff reviewed annual reports filed with the Commission by approximately 500 public companies. The primary purposes of these reviews were to (i) assess the quality of existing disclosures pertaining to market-risk-sensitive instruments and (ii) determine what, if any, additional information is needed to improve disclosures about these instruments. The SEC staff observed that while disclosures reviewed in

1995 were more informative than those reviewed in 1994, in part because of improved guidance in FASB Statement 119, three significant disclosure issues remained.

- Footnote disclosures of accounting policies for derivatives often were too general to convey adequately the diversity in accounting that exists for derivatives. Thus, it often was difficult to determine the impact of derivatives on the statements of financial position, cash flows, and results of operations.

- Disclosures often focused on derivatives and other financial instruments in isolation. Thus, it was difficult to assess whether these instruments increased or decreased the net market risk exposure of a company.

- Disclosure about items reported in the footnotes to the financial statements, Management's Discussion & Analyses (MD&A), schedules, and selected financial data did not reflect adequately the effect of derivatives on such reported items. Thus, without disclosure about the effects of derivatives, information about the reported items was incomplete, or perhaps misleading.

To address those disclosure issues, the SEC proposed in January of 1996:

- New disclosures requiring enhanced descriptions in the footnotes to the financial statements of accounting policies for derivative financial instruments and derivative commodity instruments.

- New disclosures outside the financial statements of qualitative and quantitative information about derivative financial instruments, other financial instruments, and derivative commodity instruments.

  The proposed quantitative information about market risk would be presented separately for instruments entered into for (1) trading purposes and other than trading purposes and (2) the different market risk exposure categories (e.g., interest rate risk, foreign-currency exchange-rate risk, commodity-price risk, other similar market risks, such as equity-price risk) within the trading and other than trading portfolios. In addition, this quantitative information could be presented using one or more of the following three disclosure alternatives: (1) Tabular presentation of fair value information and of contract terms sufficient to determine instruments' future cash flows categorized by expected maturity dates; (2) Sensitivity analysis expressing the possible loss in future earnings, fair values, or cash flows from selected hypothetical changes in market rates and prices (e.g., a 10 percent change in currency rates); or (3) Value-at-risk disclosures expressing the potential loss in future earnings, fair values, or cash flows from adverse market movements over a selected period of time and with a selected likelihood of occurrence.

The proposed disclosures of qualitative information about market risk would require a description of (1) a registrant's primary market risk exposures (e.g., foreign-currency risk, interest-rate risk, commodity-price risk) at the end of the current reporting period, (2) how the registrant manages those exposures (such as a description of the objectives, general strategies, and instruments, if any, used to manage those exposures), and (3) changes in the registrant's primary market risk exposures or how those exposures are managed when compared to the most recent reporting period and what is known or expected in future periods.

- The Commission also reminded public companies in this release that when they provide disclosure about financial instruments, commodity positions, firm commitments, and other anticipated transactions, such disclosure must include information about derivatives that affect directly or indirectly such reported items, to the extent that the effects of such information are material and are necessary to prevent the disclosure about the reported items from being misleading. For example, when information is required to be disclosed in the footnotes to the financial statements about interest rates and repricing characteristics of debt obligations, registrants should include, when material, disclosure of the effects of derivatives. Similarly, summary information and disclosures in MD&A about the cost of debt obligations should include, when material, disclosure of the effects of derivatives.

In preparing the qualitative and quantitative disclosures about market risk, public companies would be required to include derivative financial instruments, other financial instruments, and derivative commodity instruments. In addition, public companies would be encouraged to include in the scope of these disclosures other market-risk-sensitive instruments, positions, and transactions (such as commodity positions, derivative commodity instruments that are not permitted by contract or business custom to be settled in cash or with another financial instrument, and cash flows from anticipated transactions—such as foreign-currency operating cash-flows). To the extent these other market-risk-sensitive instruments, positions, and transactions are not included in the qualitative and quantitative disclosures about market risk, registrants must discuss this as a limitation of those disclosures.

The amendments pertaining to qualitative and quantitative information about market risk do not apply to registered investment companies and small-business issuers. However, to the extent that market risk represented a material known trend, event, or uncertainty, small-business issuers, like other registrants, would be required to discuss the impact of market risk on past and future financial condition and on results of operations, as required by SEC rules relating to MD&A.

The SEC believes that these proposed amendments would make disclosures about market-risk-sensitive instruments more useful to investors. The SEC and its staff currently are studying 100 or so comment letters that the Commission received from market participants, and expect to release final rulemaking amendments prior to December 31, 1996. When preparing financial reports, companies should consult their accounting advisers to determine which, if any, of these proposals are in effect.

Accounting Rules for Foreign-Currency Translation and Transactions

Authoritative guidance on foreign-currency translation and disclosure includes several Statements of Financial Accounting Standards (SFAS) and Emerging Issues Task Force (EITF) Issues. Appendix A provides a list of those pronouncements, which include SFAS No. 52, *Foreign Currency Translation*.

SFAS No. 52 provides accounting and reporting standards for

- The *translation* of foreign-currency financial statements that are incorporated in the financial statements of a reporting enterprise by consolidation, combination, or by the equity method of accounting under U.S. generally accepted accounting principles, and

- The foreign-currency *transactions* of a reporting enterprise.

For convenience, SFAS No. 52 (and this chapter) assumes that the reporting enterprise is a U.S. company that uses the U.S. dollar as its reporting currency. However, SFAS No. 52 also applies to financial statements prepared in conformity with U.S. generally accepted accounting principles where the reporting currency is not the U.S. dollar. For example, it would apply to the deutsche-mark financial statements of a German company that are prepared in accordance with U.S. generally accepted accounting principles.

The provisions of the standard apply to each stage in a multilevel consolidation. For example, if a U.S. parent has a British subsidiary that in turn has a French subsidiary, SFAS No. 52 rules would be applied first in consolidating the British and French operations, and then in consolidating these with the U.S. parent.

The objectives of Statement No. 52 are to:

- Provide information that is generally compatible with the expected economic effects of a foreign-currency rate change on an enterprise's cash flows and equity.

- Reflect in consolidated statements the financial results and relationships measured in the primary currency in which each entity conducts its business (its "functional currency"). The effect of translation should therefore be to preserve the financial-statement ratios (e.g., gross profit to sales) as measured in the functional-currency statements.

These objectives are accomplished by use of the functional-currency approach for foreign-currency translation.

Functional-Currency Approach

Before translation to U.S. dollars, the local-currency financial statements (prepared in accordance with U.S. generally accepted accounting principles) must be expressed in the entity's functional currency. The functional currency of an entity is the primary currency of the environment in which it operates. This is normally the environment in which an entity primarily generates and expends cash. Ordinarily, the functional currency is the currency of the country in which the entity is located. It may, however, be a different foreign currency. In addition, circumstances might indicate that the functional currency is the reporting currency of the parent (e.g., the U.S. dollar). The requirement to identify each entity's functional currency is the initial and key feature of SFAS No. 52 affecting the translation process, and thereby the reported results and the treatment of exchange gains and losses.

Determining the Entity's Functional Currency

In some cases, the identification of the functional currency is straightforward. For example, the functional currency of an entity with operations that are self-contained and integrated within a country would likely be the currency of that country. On the other hand, the U.S. dollar would likely be the functional currency of an operation that is a direct and integral component or extension of a parent's operations, such as a sales branch of the U.S. parent.

In many cases, however, determining the functional currency of a foreign affiliate requires considerable management judgment. The operations may be diverse, with cash flows, financing, and transactions occurring in more than a single foreign currency. The appropriate functional currency might be any one of the foreign currencies in which it transacts business (not necessarily the currency of the entity's books and records), or it might be the U.S. dollar.

In determining the functional currency of a foreign affiliate, a company should consider all relevant economic facts and circumstances affecting its operations. Management-operating policies may indicate the appropriate functional currency. For example, currency-hedging practices may reflect management's intent that a foreign operation conduct its business and be exposed in a particular currency. Dividend-remittance policies and financing may provide other economic indications of the entity's functional currency. Management must exercise judgment to determine the functional currency which best reflects its financial results and business relationships.

Appendix A of SFAS No. 52 describes various indicators that should be considered in identifying the functional currency. The FASB's Research Report, *Determining the Functional Currency Under Statement No. 52*, provides additional guidance. Refer to Table 5 for a summary of the key functional currency indicators.

Table 5 Functional-Currency Indicators

Indicator	Conditions Pointing to the *Local Currency* as the Functional Currency	Conditions Pointing to the *U.S. Dollar* as the Functional Currency
Cash flows	Mainly in the local currency and do not affect parent's cash flows	Directly impact the parent's current cash flows and are readily available for remittance to the parent
Sales prices	Mainly determined by local conditions; not primarily responsive on a short-term basis to exchange-rate changes	Responsive on a short-term basis to worldwide competition and changes in exchange rates
Sales market	Active local sales market for the entity's products	Most sales are in the U.S. or are denominated in dollars
Expenses	Mainly determined by local conditions	Production and materials are mainly obtained through U.S. sources
Financing	Primarily in the local currency and serviced by funds generated by the entity's operations	Significant dollar financing or reliance on the U.S. parent to service debt obligations
Intercompany transactions and arrangements	Few intercompany transactions with the parent	Frequent and extensive intercompany transactions with the parent, or the entity is an investment or financing device for the parent

Reporting a Change in the Functional Currency

SFAS No. 52 requires that, once the functional currency of a foreign operation is determined, that determination shall be used consistently, unless significant changes in economic facts and circumstances clearly indicate that the functional currency has changed. A change in the functional currency should be *reported prospectively* from the date of change. Because this date may be difficult to determine precisely, the change may be accounted for generally as of the beginning of the period that approximates the date of the change.

Local Currency to U.S. Dollar

If the functional currency changes from the local currency to the U.S. dollar, translation adjustments for prior periods should not be removed from equity. The translated amounts for nonmonetary assets at the end of the prior period become the accounting basis for those assets in the period of the change and in subsequent periods.

U.S. Dollar to Local Currency

However, if the functional currency changes from the U.S. dollar to the local currency, the cumulative adjustment attributable to translating nonmonetary assets at the current rate rather than the historical rate should be included in the separate component of equity in the period of the change. For example, assume a foreign subsidiary of a U.S. company purchased equipment with a 10-year useful life for 100,000 foreign currency (FC) on January 1, 19X0. The subsidiary's functional currency was the U.S. dollar, and the exchange rate was FC10.00 = U.S.$1.00. Therefore, the U.S.-dollar-equivalent cost of the equipment was U.S.$10,000. On December 31, 19X4, the equipment has a net book value of FC50,000 in the subsidiary's local books, and of U.S.$5,000 (i.e., foreign-currency basis measured at the historical exchange-rate) in the parent's financial statements.

As a result of the acquisition of a significant local business, the company changes its functional currency to FC as of January 1, 19X5. The functional-currency carrying amount of the equipment remains FC50,000. However, for U.S. reporting purposes, the foreign-currency basis is translated at the current exchange-rate of FC20.00 = U.S.$1.00. The new U.S.-dollar-equivalent cost of the equipment is U.S.$2,500. The difference from its carrying value using the historical exchange-rate in the U.S. parent's financial statements as of December 31, 19X4 (i.e., U.S.$5,000 less U.S.$2,500 using the current exchange-rate, or U.S.$2,500)) is reported as a debit in the cumulative translation adjustment component of equity.

Highly Inflationary Economies

SFAS No. 52 contains specific provisions for designating the functional currency of operations located in highly inflationary economies. SFAS

No. 52 requires use of the reporting currency (normally the U.S. dollar) as if it were the functional currency for all operations in countries where cumulative inflation approximates or exceeds 100 percent over a three-year period. In these situations, the monetary/nonmonetary method rather than the current-rate method would be used.

Under the monetary/nonmonetary method, nonmonetary accounts such as inventories and property, plant, and equipment are translated at historical exchange-rates. Monetary items such as cash, receivables, and payables are translated at the current exchange-rate. All translation gains and losses are included in determining net income.

In recent years, inflation rates in some countries previously considered to be highly inflationary have significantly decreased compared to those experienced in the 1970s and 1980s. The accounting for a change in functional currency from U.S. dollar to the local currency because of a change in status from a highly to a nonhighly inflationary economy was addressed by the EITF (Issue 92-4). The EITF concluded that, in this situation, the entity should restate the functional-currency accounting bases of nonmonetary assets and liabilities at the date of change in status to a nonhighly inflationary economy as follows:

- The reporting currency amounts at the date of change should be translated into the local currency at current exchange-rates, and

- those local currency amounts should become the new functional currency accounting bases for the nonmonetary assets and liabilities.

This treatment is different from that previously described for a change in functional currency from U.S. dollar to the local currency for reasons other than the change in the inflation rate. The equipment's functional-currency carrying amount would be FC100,000 (U.S.$5,000 x 20) instead of FC50,000 (as described earlier).

Companies may need to reassess their hedging strategies and business practices for a subsidiary that is no longer considered highly inflationary. For instance, if the local currency becomes the functional currency, U.S.-dollar transactions would be considered foreign-denominated transactions. Since the U.S.-dollar is no longer their functional currency, exchange gains and losses on U.S. dollar transactions would be included in income.

In addition, when analyzing the impact of a change in a subsidiary's status from a highly to nonhighly inflationary economy, companies must keep in mind that these subsidiaries may still be significantly affected by inflation. For instance, even though the economy is no longer considered highly inflationary, the annual local inflation rate may still adversely impact exchange rates and thus significantly reduce the value of a foreign subsidiary's nonmonetary assets when translated into U.S. dollars.

Translation of Foreign-Currency Financial Statements

The purpose of translation is to state foreign-currency financial statements in terms of a single reporting currency (e.g., the U.S. dollar). The requirements for translation apply to foreign-currency financial statements that are to be consolidated, combined, or accounted for on the equity method.

The procedures for translating a foreign entity's financial statements depend on two factors:

- The functional currency designation for that entity, and

- Whether its books and records are maintained in its functional currency.

Table 6 summarizes these procedures.

Table 6   Summary of Translation Procedures

Currency in Which the Books and Records Are Maintained	Functional Currency	Translation Method
Local currency (i.e., currency of the country in which the entity is located)	Local currency	Current-rate method of translation of functional currency to U.S. dollars
Local currency	Third currency (i.e., a foreign currency other than the local currency)	Remeasurement* from local currency to functional currency (monetary/nonmonetary method) and Current-rate method of translation of functional currency to U.S. dollars
Local currency	U.S. dollar	Remeasurement* to U.S. dollars (monetary/nonmonetary method)
U.S. dollar	U.S. dollar	No translation required

* The term "remeasurement" is the process of translating the accounts of a foreign entity into its functional currency when the books and records are maintained in another foreign currency. It uses the monetary/nonmonetary method, under which historical exchange rates are used for nonmonetary items and current exchange-rates are used for monetary items.

Translation When Local Currency Is the Functional Currency

The current-rate method of translation must be used if the local currency is the functional currency and the books and records are maintained in that currency:

- All the foreign entity's *assets* and *liabilities* are translated using the current exchange-rate at the balance sheet date (the current-rate method). Capital accounts (e.g., common and preferred shares issued) are translated at historical exchange-rates (i.e., the exchange rates in effect when the transactions occurred). Retained earnings are translated at the weighted average of the historical rates in effect when the income was earned.

- All of the foreign entity's *revenues* and *expenses* are translated using the exchange rate at the transaction date. For practical purposes an appropriate *weighted-average exchange rate* for the period can be used (e.g., the weighted-average rate for the month).

- Adjustments from translation of the foreign entity's financial statements are reported in a separate component of *equity*, (captioned translation-adjustment account) not in income.

- Exchange gains and losses from transactions and balances that are receivable or payable in a currency other than the functional currency are included in income.

These procedures are explained below using a Swiss subsidiary that maintains its books and records in Swiss francs. The Swiss-franc financial statements of the subsidiary (prepared in accordance with U.S. generally accepted accounting principles) are shown in Table 7.

The current-rate method of translation must be used if the local currency is the functional currency and the books and records are maintained in that currency. The current-rate method of translation for the Swiss subsidiary is illustrated in Table 8. The following exchange rates are assumed:

- Historical and average rate (for all prior years' transactions) is Swiss franc (SFr) 1 = $0.30.

- Year-end rate for current year is SFr 1 = $0.50, with a weighted average rate for the year of SFr 1 = $0.40.

Translation When a Foreign Currency Is the Functional Currency

There may be instances when an entity does not maintain its books and records in its functional currency. For instance, if the Swiss subsidiary of a

Table 7   Swiss-Franc Financial Statements

	Jan. 1, 19X1	Dec. 31, 19X1
Cash	SFr 10,000	SFr 13,000
Net plant	10,000	9,000
	20,000	22,000
Common stock	10,000	10,000
Retained earnings	10,000	12,000
	20,000	22,000
Gross profit		3,000
Depreciation		(1,000)
Net income		2,000
Retained earnings, beginning of year		10,000
Retained earnings, end of year		12,000

U.S. company conducts most of its business activities in deutsche marks, management may conclude that the deutsche mark is the functional currency of that entity, despite the fact that its records are maintained in Swiss francs.

SFAS No. 52 provides that, when an entity's records are not expressed in its functional currency, its financial statements must be *remeasured* into that currency before they are translated into the reporting currency or combined with reporting currency data. Remeasurement should provide results comparable to those that would have occurred had the entity used its functional currency to maintain its records. *Historical exchange-rates* between the currency in which the books and records are maintained and the functional currency would be used to remeasure *nonmonetary items*. Monetary accounts would be remeasured at the current rate at the balance-sheet date.

In our example, the records of the Swiss subsidiary would first be remeasured into deutsche marks and then translated into U.S. dollars using the current-rate method. These procedures are illustrated in Table 9. Appendix B to SFAS No. 52 provides further insight into the remeasurement process.

The following exchange rates are assumed:

- Historical and average rate (for all prior years' transactions) is Swiss franc (SFr) 1 = deutsche mark (DM) 1.2 and DM 1 = $0.25.

Table 8   Current-Rate Method of Translation
(Local Currency Is Functional Currency)

	End of Year (Francs)	Rate	End of Year (Dollars)
Cash	13,000	.50	6,500
Net plant	9.000	.50	4,500
	22,000		11,000
Common stock	10,000	.30	3,000
Retained earnings	12,000		3,800
Translation adjustments	—		4,200
	22,000		11,000
Gross profit	3,000	.40	1,200
Depreciation	(1,000)	.40	(400)
Net income	2,000		800
Retained earnings, beginning of year	10,000		3,000
Retained earnings, end of year	12,000		3,800

Analysis of Cumulative Translation-Adjustment during the Year

	Swiss-Franc Functional Currency	Exchange Rate	U.S. (Dollars)
Net assets, beginning of year	20,000	E—B.20	$4,000
Net income for the year	2,000	E—A.10	200
			$4,200

B—Beginning exchange-rate (0.30)
A—Average exchange-rate for the year (0.40)
E—Ending exchange-rate (0.50)

Since this example assumes that the historical and average rate for all prior years' transactions did not fluctuate, there is no opening balance in the translation-adjustments account.

Table 9 Remeasurement and Current-Rate Method of Translation (Third Currency Is Functional Currency)

	Remeasurement		Current-Rate Translation		
	Franc	Rate	Deutsche Mark	Rate	Dollars
Cash	13,000	1.25	16,250	.40	6,500
Net plant	9,000	1.20	10,800	.40	4,320
	22,000		27,050		10,820
Common stock	10,000	1.20	12,000	.25	3,000
Retained earnings	12,000		15,050		3,976
Translation adjustments*	—		—		3,844
	22,000		27,050		10,820
Gross profit	3,000	1.22	3,660	.32	1,171
Depreciation	(1,000)	1.20	(1,200)	.32	(384)
Foreign-exchange gain**	—		590	.32	189
Net income (loss)	2,000		3,050		976
Retained earnings, beginning of year	10,000		12,000		3,000
Retained earnings, end of year	12,000		15,050		3,976

* The translation adjustment of $3,844 results from applying the current-rate method in translating from deutsche marks to U.S. dollars. Stockholders' equity is summarized as follows:

- Stockholders' equity, beginning   DM   24,000
- Income for year   3,050
- Stockholders' equity, ending   DM   27,050
  The translation adjustment is calculated as follows:
- Opening equity   DM   24,000
- Change in exchange rate during the year (.40–.25)   x.   15
    $3,600
- The effect of translating net income for the year at average rate and balance sheet at year-end rate:

		DM	3,050
Income			x0.08
Change in exchange rate (.40–.32)			$ 244
• Total translation adjustment			$3,844

** The foreign-exchange gain of DM 590 results from remeasurement from Swiss francs to deutsche marks, and must be included in income. It is calculated as follows:

• Opening net monetary assets (cash)	SFr	10,000
Change in exchange rates during the year (1.25–1.20)		x .05
	DM	500

- The effect of translating gross profit at average rates and increase in net monetary assets at year-end rate:

Gross profit (increase in cash)	SFr	3,000
Change in exchange rates (1.25–1.22)		x .03
		90
• Total foreign-exchange gain	DM	590

- Year-end rates for current year are SFr 1 = DM 1.25 and DM 1 = $0.40.

- Weighted-average rates for the year are SFr 1 = DM 1.22 and DM 1 = $0.32.

Translation When the U.S. Dollar Is the Functional Currency

The remeasurement provisions described above also apply in translating the local currency financial statements into U.S. dollars, when the U.S. dollar is designated as the functional currency of a foreign entity. This means that when the U.S. dollar is the functional currency, the remeasurement process is as follows:

- *Monetary* assets and liabilities, such as cash, receivables, and payables, are translated using the current exchange-rate.

- *Nonmonetary* assets and liabilities, such as inventory, fixed assets, intangible assets and deferred income, are translated using historical exchange-rates. Capital accounts are also translated using historical exchange-rates.

- Revenues and expenses are translated using average exchange-rates for the period, except for items related to nonmonetary assets and liabilities (e.g., cost of sales, depreciation, and amortization of intangibles), which are translated using historical exchange-rates.

- All translation gains and losses are included in determining income for the period in which exchange rates change.

Translation under the monetary-nonmonetary method for our Swiss subsidiary is shown in Table 10. These exchange rates apply:

- Historical and average rate (for all prior-years' transactions) is Swiss franc (SFr) 1 = $0.30.

- Year-end rate for current year is SFr 1 = $0.50, with a weighted-average rate for the year of SFr 1 = $0.40.

Application of SFAS No. 52 to Equity Investments and Purchased Subsidiaries

SFAS No. 52 also applies to foreign operations included in the financial statements of a U.S. investor using the equity method. SFAS No. 52 requires that the investor's income for the period and stockholders' equity at the end of the period be the same whether an affiliate is consolidated or is accounted for under the equity method. Therefore, when the equity method is used, the investor's financial statements should include directly in equity a proportionate share of the investee's translation adjustments. The propor-

Table 10 Remeasurement (Functional Currency Is U.S. Dollar)

	Francs	Rate	Dollars
Cash	13,000	.50	6,500
Net plant	9,000	.30	2,700
	22,000		9,200
Common stock	10,000	.30	3,000
Retained earnings	12,000		6,200
	22,000		9,200
Gross profit	3,000	.40	1,200
Depreciation	(1,000)	.30	(300)
Foreign-exchange gain*	–		2,300
Net income	2,000		3,200
Retained earnings, beginning of year	10,000		3,000
Retained earnings, end of year	12,000		6,200

*The foreign-exchange gain of $2,300 on remeasurement is equal to:
- The effect of the change in the exchange rate during the year ($0.50 - $0.30) on net monetary assets (SFr 10,000) at the beginning of the year (SFr 10,000 x .20 = $2,000), plus
- The effect of translating the change in net monetary assets (cash income of 2,000 SFr plus depreciation of 1,000 SFr) at the weighted-average exchange rate for the year, instead of at the year-end rate (SFr 3,000 x .10 = $300).

tionate share of the translation adjustment should also be reflected in the carrying value of the investment.

SFAS No. 52 also applies to translation after a business combination. After a business combination accounted for by the purchase method, the amount allocated at the date of purchase to the assets acquired (including goodwill) and liabilities assumed should be translated in accordance with the standard.

Goodwill arising from the acquisition of a foreign affiliate whose functional currency is the local currency should be presumed to have a functional-currency value based on exchange rates at the date of acquisition. Goodwill should be subsequently translated at the current rate, whether the amount arises in consolidation or has been recorded ("pushed down") on the acquired company's books. Any resulting gain or loss would be included in the separate component of stockholders' equity.

For instance, assume that on January 1, 19X1, a U.S. company acquires a 70 percent interest in a French company for a purchase price of U.S.$100 million. The allocation of the purchase price results in a goodwill of U.S.$10 million being recorded in the U.S. company's books. As of January 1, 19X1, the exchange rate is U.S.$1.00 = FRF5.50. Therefore, goodwill is presumed to have a French-franc value of FRF55 million. If, on December 31, 19X1, the exchange rate is U.S.$1.00 = FRF5.00, the U.S.-dollar equivalent value of goodwill becomes U.S.$11 million. The U.S. $1 million translation gain is included in the translation-adjustment component of equity.

Accumulated translation adjustments attributable to minority interests should be allocated to and reported as part of minority interests in the consolidated financial statements.

Foreign-Currency Transactions and Balances

SFAS No. 52 defines foreign-currency transactions as "transactions denominated in a currency other than the entity's functional currency." These activities include but are not restricted to

- Purchasing or selling goods or services whose prices are stated in a foreign currency (i.e., a currency other than the entity's functional currency),

- Borrowing or lending funds that will be repaid in a foreign currency, and

- Entering into a forward-exchange contract.

Foreign-currency transactions result in receivable balances or payable balances that are fixed in terms of the amount of foreign currency that will be received or paid. They include, but are not restricted to:

- Trade receivables or payables denominated in a foreign currency,

- A loan or debt denominated in a foreign currency, and

- An unperformed forward-exchange contract.

The accounting for foreign-currency transactions and balances is as follows:

- Foreign-currency transactions should be recorded using the exchange rate at the date of the transaction. The use of weighted-average exchange rates as a reasonable approximation of actual rates is acceptable.

- Foreign-currency receivables and payables should be translated at the current rate at the balance-sheet date.

- Exchange gains and losses on foreign-currency transactions and balances may result from a change in exchange rates between the transaction date and the settlement date (or intervening balance-sheet date). These exchange gains and losses generally should be included in income. Three exceptions to this rule occur if the transaction or balance either (1) hedges a foreign-currency commitment, (2) effectively hedges a net investment in a foreign entity, or (3) is an intercompany transaction of a long-term investment nature.

In applying these rules, an interesting result occurs. Assume that on October 31, 19X2, a German subsidiary whose functional currency is the deutsche mark, sells goods to a U.S. company for U.S.$1,600, payable on January 1, 19X3. If the exchange rate on October 31, 19X2 is DM1 = U.S.$0.40, the German subsidiary will record a receivable and a sale of DM4,000 (U.S.$1,600 : 0.40).

If on December 31, 19X2, the exchange rate is DM1 = $0.50, the receivable will be translated as DM3,200 (U.S.$1,600 : 0.50). The unrealized loss of DM800 will be included in the German subsidiary's functional currency income statement. This loss will then carry over into the consolidated income statement after translation into U.S. dollars, even though it relates to a balance denominated in U.S. dollars.

To summarize:

	Financial Statements	
	Local Currency	Consolidated
DM1 = U.S.$0.40 at October 31, 19X2:	**Deutsche Marks**	**U.S. Dollars**
Receivable (dollar-denominated)	4,000	1,600
Retained earnings	4,000	1,600
Effect of Rate Change to DM1 = U.S.$0.50 at December 31, 19X2:	**Deutsche Marks**	**U.S. Dollars**
Receivable	3,200	1,600
Retained earnings	4,000	1,600
(Loss) on dollar receivable* (Income Statement)	(800)	(320)
Separate equity component (Balance Sheet)		320
	3,200	1,600

* Translated at assumed average for the period (DM1 = $0.40).

In comparing the U.S.-dollar results before and after the rate change, note that equity has not changed. However, the exchange loss in deutsche marks carries through to the U.S.-dollar consolidated income statement. An offsetting amount (the translation gain) is credited directly to the separate equity component.

Under these circumstances (i.e., when the local currency is the functional currency), companies may consider it desirable to hedge the U.S. dollar positions of foreign subsidiaries.

Intercompany Transactions

Distinguishing between Long- and Short-Term Transactions

SFAS No. 52 requires companies to differentiate between intercompany transactions of a long-term investment nature and all others. Gains and losses relating to intercompany transactions are generally included in income for the year, except that gains and losses relating to long-term investment transactions are recorded in the separate component of equity (whether the investment was denominated in U.S. dollars or in the local currency). SFAS No. 52 describes long-term transactions as those where settlement is not planned or anticipated in the foreseeable future. Application of these provisions require the use of judgment based on existing facts and circumstances, as well as on management's plans and intentions.

Intercompany Profit in Inventories

SFAS No. 52 requires the elimination of intercompany profits in inventory based on exchange rates at the date of sale or transfer (i.e., based on historical exchange-rates). The use of reasonable approximations or average rates is permitted. The following example of a sale from a parent to its foreign subsidiary illustrates this requirement:

Intercompany Profit Elimination

	Transfer Date (FC1 = U.S.$1)		Balance-Sheet Date (FC1 = U.S.$1.25)	
	Local Currency	U.S. Dollars	Local Currency	U.S. Dollars
Inventory transfer price	120	120	120	150
Parent cost		100		100
Parent profit component		20		20
Inventory after profit elimination		100		130

The consolidated balance sheet will include inventories carried at U.S.$130 (U.S.$150 less intercompany profit elimination of U.S.$20). The U.S.$30 increase in the inventory carrying value will be included in the separate component of equity.

Note that the U.S.$30 increase includes U.S.$5 related to the exchange-rate movement on the intercompany profit component (i.e., 25% x U.S.$20). The accounting treatment that in our example results in inventory being carried at U.S.$130 is based on the conclusion that the U.S.$5 increase results from a change in exchange rates, and is not attributable to intercompany profits.

If U.S. dollars were the functional currency in the above example, historical exchange-rates would be used to translate this nonmonetary item. As such, the consolidated balance sheet would include inventory carried at U.S. $100 (U.S. $120 less intercompany profit elimination of $20).

Other Provisions

Liquidation of a Foreign Investment

SFAS No. 52 provides for the transfer to income of all or part of the relevant portion of the separate component of equity attributable to an entity on complete or substantially complete liquidation of an investment in the foreign entity. If an entity is sold, all the amounts related to that entity in the separate component of equity should be included in the determination of the gain or loss on disposition of the foreign investment.

The effect of previous years' unrealized gains or losses arising from changes in the exchange rate are not included in income of a particular year, except on total or virtually total disposition of the investment, which is the event that causes realization.

Income Taxes

SFAS No. 109 requires that deferred tax assets and/or liabilities be recognized for the difference between assets and liabilities for financial-reporting and income-tax purposes. These "temporary differences" include differences in book and tax bases of foreign-currency assets and liabilities resulting from an entity's foreign-currency *transactions* that are included in income in a different period for financial-reporting and income-tax purposes (e.g., the divergent treatment of exchange gains and losses for book and tax purposes). When exchange gains and losses are included in the separate component of equity, the related deferred income taxes are also generally recorded in the separate component of equity.

Recording deferred tax assets and/or liabilities attributable to *translation-related* temporary differences (i.e., gains and losses) may also be required. To determine whether translation-related temporary differences should be tax effected, companies need to review the specific circumstances of each situation. Deferred taxes are not recognized for translation-related temporary differences of *foreign* subsidiaries and *foreign* corporate joint ventures whose undistributed earnings are essentially permanent in duration.

While *translation-related* temporary differences usually are not tax effected unless the unremitted earnings of that subsidiary are tax effected, situations may arise where tax-effecting is appropriate. For example, translation gains may be sufficiently material so that there is no longer any basis for believing that the *excess* of the amount for financial reporting over the tax basis of the investment in a foreign subsidiary or a foreign corporate joint venture is "essentially permanent in duration." It may also be appropriate to tax effect foreign-translation losses up to the amount of unremitted earnings for which taxes have been provided. Translation losses in excess of unremitted earnings on which taxes have been provided ordinarily should not be tax effected.

Whether a subsidiary or a corporate joint venture is foreign should be evaluated separately for consolidated and separate company financial statements. For instance, assume that a U.S. enterprise has a foreign subsidiary (FS1) which also has a subsidiary (FS2) in the same foreign country (i.e., second-tier sub). The unremitted earnings of FS2 are essentially permanent in duration. In the consolidated financial statements, the tiers are ignored. Therefore, in the U.S. parent company's consolidated financial statements, the unremitted earnings would be exempt, since FS2 is considered a foreign subsidiary of the U.S. parent company. If, however, FS1 prepared separate financial statements in accordance with U.S. GAAP, the unremitted earnings of FS2 would *not* be considered exempt from deferred tax accounting, since FS2 is not a foreign subsidiary of FS1.

In addition, if the U.S. parent had a domestic subsidiary with a second-tier foreign subsidiary, the unremitted earnings of the second-tier foreign subsidiary would be exempt from deferred tax accounting for the financial statements of both the U.S. parent and its first-tier domestic subsidiary, assuming that the unremitted earnings are essentially permanent in duration. Similarly, if the U.S. parent company had a foreign subsidiary with a second-tier U.S. subsidiary, the unremitted earnings of the second-tier subsidiary would be exempt from deferred tax accounting for the financial statement of the first-tier foreign subsidiary. However, the unremitted earnings would *not* be exempt in the U.S. parent company's consolidated financial statement unless they can be recovered tax-free under the tax laws.

SFAS No. 109 prohibits recognition of a deferred tax liability or asset for differences related to assets and liabilities that are remeasured from the local currency into the functional currency using historical exchange-rates and result from (1) changes in exchange rates, or (2) indexing for tax purposes.

Statement of Cash Flows

SFAS No. 95, *Statement of Cash Flows*, requires companies with foreign operations or foreign-currency transactions to report in the consolidated statement of cash flows the reporting-currency equivalent of foreign-currency cash flows

- Using exchange rates in effect at the time of the cash flows; or

- an appropriately weighted-average exchange rate for the reporting period, provided that the results are substantially the same as if actual rates were used.

These rules apply whether the functional currency is the local foreign currency or the reporting currency. In either case, the local foreign-currency cash flows are translated to U.S. dollars using the exchange rate in effect at the time of the cash flows, or using appropriate weighted-average exchange rates.

Exchange-rate changes, whether recognized in the income statement or in the separate component of stockholders' equity, do not give rise to cash flows. Therefore, exchange gains and losses included in net income that do not have any cash flow impact in the reporting period (e.g., from translation of an outstanding receivable denominated in a foreign currency) are excluded from net cash flow from operating activities. Companies using the indirect method of reporting net cash flow from operating activities should present those exchange gains and losses as a reconciling item between net income and net cash flow from operating activities.

In addition, the effects of exchange-rate changes on cash balances held in foreign currencies must be reported as a separate item of the reconciliation of the change in cash and cash equivalents during the period.

Under these rules, companies with foreign operations will generally have to follow a three-step process:

- Prepare a separate statement of cash flows in the foreign currency for each foreign operation (or group using the same foreign currency),

- Translate these statements to the reporting currency, and

- Consolidate the translated statements along with the statement of cash flows for domestic operations.

Cash flows from futures, forward, option, and swap contracts that are accounted for as hedges of identifiable transactions or events may be accounted for in the same category as the item being hedged. Companies electing to classify cash flows from hedging instruments consistent with the item being hedged must disclose their accounting policy.

When companies treat hedged forward contracts (SFAS No. 52) and hedged futures contracts (SFAS No. 80) as investing activities, net reporting is acceptable if:

- Turnover of the transaction is quick (three months or less),

- The amounts are large, and

- The maturities are short.

We believe that the three-month period should be measured based on actual cash flows.

Illustrative examples for the preparation of a statement of cash flows for a multinational company can be found in Appendix C of SFAS No. 95.

Exchange Rates

SFAS No. 52 contains these provisions for using exchange rates in translating foreign-currency financial statements or foreign-currency transactions:

- The rate to be used in translating a particular *foreign-currency transaction* should be the rate at which that transaction could be settled at the transaction date. At a subsequent balance-sheet date, the related receivable or payable should be translated at the current rate at that date.

- Where multiple exchange-rates exist, the rate to be used in translating *foreign-currency financial statements* should be, in the absence of unusual circumstances, the rate applicable to dividend remittances. The rate applicable to dividend remittances is considered more meaningful than any other rate, because that is the rate indicative of ultimate cash flows from the foreign entity to the U.S. investor.

- If an unsettled intercompany transaction is subject to, and translated using, a preference or penalty rate, using the dividend remittance rate may result in a difference between intercompany receivables and payables. Under these circumstances, the difference is treated as part of the intercompany receivable or payable until it is eliminated by settlement of the related intercompany transaction.

- When translating a foreign entity's income statement, an appropriate weighted-average exchange rate for the period can be used. However, using an average rate may result in a difference between intercompany expenses and revenues.

- Where the balance-sheet date of a foreign entity differs from that of the reporting enterprise, the current rate at the balance-sheet date of the foreign entity should be used in translating its financial statements for inclusion in the consolidated financial statements.

- If exchangeability between two currencies is temporarily lacking at the transaction date or balance-sheet date, the first subsequent rate at which exchanges could be made should be used. Where the lack of exchangeability does not appear to be temporary, companies should consider whether consolidation, combination, or equity accounting for that foreign operation is appropriate. The financial statements should not otherwise be adjusted for post-balance-sheet rate changes.

Conclusion

This chapter provided an overview of the current accounting and financial reporting rules and practices for derivatives and other instruments and transactions subject to global currency risk. As explained, these rules often are incomplete and often inconsistent, particularly for derivatives and hedging activities. However, the FASB is now focusing on this area in earnest and has arrived at proposed guidance that would significantly change the current rules. Further, the SEC has proposed expanded disclosure requirements relating to derivatives and other market-risk-sensitive instruments, which focus on, among other things, how a company utilizes, manages, and controls global currency risk as part of its financial-risk-management programs. Clearly, those involved in global-currency-risk management should be conversant with the current rules and should exercise care before initiating new transactions involving derivative instruments to ensure that the intended accounting, financial reporting, and disclosure ramifications are understood, and should consult with their accounting professionals on both the current rules and the FASB's and SEC's progress on developing new rules.

Appendix A

In addition to SFAS 52, the references listed below should be considered when addressing foreign-currency translation, foreign-currency transactions, and related disclosure issues:

- SFAS 95, *Statement of Cash Flows*
- SFAS 109, *Accounting for Income Taxes*
- SFAS 115, *Accounting for Certain Investments in Debt and Equity Securities*
- FIN 37, *Accounting for Translation Adjustments upon Sale of Part of an Investment in a Foreign Entity*
- EITF Issue 86-25, "Offsetting Currency Swaps"
- EITF Issue 87-2, "Net Present Value Method of Valuing Foreign Exchange Contracts"
- EITF Issue 88-18, "Sales of Future Revenues"
- EITF Issue 92-4, "Accounting for a Change in Functional Currency When an Economy Ceases To Be Considered Highly Inflationary"

- EITF Issue 92-8, "Accounting for Income Tax Effects Under FASB Statement No. 109 of a Change in Functional Currency When an Economy Ceases To Be Considered Highly Inflationary"

- EITF Issue 93-9, "Application of FASB Statement No. 109 to Price-Level-Adjusted Financial Statements"

- EITF Issue 93-10, "Accounting for Dual Currency Bonds"

- EITF Issue 95-2, "Determination of What Constitutes a Firm Commitment for Foreign Currency Transactions Not Involving a Third Party"

- EITF Abstracts, Appendix D, Topic D-12, "Foreign Currency Translation–Selection of Exchange Rate When Trading Is Temporarily Suspended"

- FRR 6, *Disclosure Considerations Related to Foreign Operations and Foreign Currency Translation Effects*

- AICPA Technical Practice Aids, Sections 2210.27 and 4200.01

Endnotes

1   Note that the gain or loss on the foreign-currency payable would not be limited to the lesser of the gain on the hedged item or the loss on the hedging instrument.

2   Financial instruments have been defined by the FASB in various pronouncements as follows: A financial instrument is cash, evidence of an ownership interest in an entity, or a contract that both

- Imposes on one entity a contractual obligation (1) to deliver cash or another financial instrument to a second entity, or (2) to exchange other financial instruments on potentially unfavorable terms with the second entity.

- Conveys to that second entity a contractual right (1) to receive cash or another financial instrument from the first entity, or (2) to exchange other financial instruments on potentially unfavorable terms with the first entity.

Index